Translation of
The Memorial Book of Buczacz

Memorial (Yizkor) Book of the
Jewish Community of
Buczacz, Galicia
(Buchach, Ukraine)

Sefer Buczacz: Matsevet Zikaron Le-kehila Kedosha

Originally in Hebrew
Edited by Yisrael Cohen
Published in Tel Aviv, 1956

Published by JewishGen

An Affiliate of the Museum of Jewish Heritage
A Living Memorial to the Holocaust
New York

Translation of Sefer Buczacz: Matsevet Zikaron Le-kehila Kedosha
Memorial Book of the Jewish Community of Buczacz, Galicia

Copyright © 2013 by JewishGen, Inc.
All rights reserved.
First Printing: August 2013, Adar 5773

Translation Project Coordinator: Norbert Porile
Editor of the Translation: Thomas F. Weiss
Cover Design: Jan R. Fine
Publicity: Sandra Hirschhorn

This book may not be reproduced, in whole or in part, including illustrations in any form (beyond that copying permitted by Sections 107 and 108 of the U.S. Copyright Law and except by reviewers for public press), without written permission from the publisher.

Published by JewishGen, Inc.
An Affiliate of the Museum of Jewish Heritage
A Living Memorial to the Holocaust
36 Battery Place, New York, NY 10280

"JewishGen, Inc. is not responsible for inaccuracies or omissions in the original work and makes no representations regarding the accuracy of this translation. Digital images of the original book's contents can be seen online at the New York Public Library Web site with spelling"

The mission of the JewishGen organization is to produce a translation of the original work and we cannot verify the accuracy of statements or alter facts cited.

Printed in the United States of America by Lightning Source, Inc.

Library of Congress Control Number (LCCN): 2013945310
ISBN: 978-1-939561-01-5 (hard cover: 360 pages, alk. paper)

The **Cover Photograph** shows an election rally in Buczacz (1907) in support of the candidate of the Jewish National Party for a seat in the Austro-Hungarian parliament. The candidate, Dr. Nathan Birnbaum, is shown in the centre of the photograph, wearing a formal grey suit and holding a cane. He solicited help of local Ukrainians many of whom can be seen in the crowd. Dr. Birnbaum was defeated for this seat by the corrupt practices of the Poles who were a distinct minority in Buczacz. The crowd contains many prominent Buczacz Jews including future Nobel Prize winner Shmuel Yosef Agnon. The cover photograph was obtained courtesy of Dr. Birnbaum's grandson, David Birnbaum, from the Nathan & Solomon Birnbaum Archives, Toronto. A similar though not an identical crowd scene is shown on Page 154, which also lists some of the people in the crowd.

JewishGen and the Yizkor Books In Print Project

This book has been published by the **Yizkor Books in Print Project**, as part of the **Yizkor Book Project** of **JewishGen, Inc.**

JewishGen, Inc. is a non-profit organization founded in 1987 as a resource for Jewish genealogy. Its website [www.jewishgen.org] serves as an international clearinghouse and resource center to assist individuals who are researching the history of their Jewish families and the places where they lived. JewishGen provides databases, facilitates discussion groups, and coordinates projects relating to Jewish genealogy and the history of the Jewish people. In 2003, JewishGen became an affiliate of the **Museum of Jewish Heritage - A Living Memorial to the Holocaust** in New York.

The **JewishGen Yizkor Book Project** was organized to make more widely known the existence of Yizkor (Memorial) Books written by survivors and former residents of various Jewish communities throughout the world. Later, volunteers connected to the different destroyed communities began cooperating to have these books translated from the original language—usually Hebrew or Yiddish—into English, thus enabling a wider audience to have access to the valuable information contained within them. As each chapter of these books was translated, it was posted on the JewishGen website and made available to the general public.

The **Yizkor Books in Print Project** began in 2011 as an initiative to print and publish Yizkor Books that had been fully translated, so that hard copies would be available for purchase by the descendants of these communities and also by scholars, universities, synagogues, libraries, and museums.

These Yizkor books have been produced almost entirely through the volunteer effort of researchers from around the world, assisted by donations from private individuals. The books are printed and sold at near cost, so as to make them as affordable as possible. Our goal is to make this important genre of Jewish literature and history available in English in book form, so that people can have the personal histories of their ancestral towns on their bookshelves for themselves and for their children and grandchildren.

Lance Ackerfeld, Yizkor Book Project Manager

Joel Alpert, Yizkor Book in Print Project Coordinator

This book is presented by the
Yizkor Books in Print Project
Project Coordinator: Joel Alpert

Part of the
Yizkor Books Project of JewishGen, Inc.
Project Manager: Lance Ackerfeld

These books have been produced solely through volunteer effort of individuals from around the world. The books are printed and sold at near cost, so as to make them as affordable as possible.

Our goal is to make this history and important genre of Jewish literature available in English in book form so that people can have the near-personal histories of their ancestral towns on their bookshelves for themselves and for their children and grandchildren.

Any donations to the Yizkor Books Project are appreciated.

Please send donations to:
Yizkor Book Project
JewishGen
36 Battery Place
New York, NY 10280

JewishGen, Inc. is an affiliate of the
Museum of Jewish Heritage
A Living Memorial to the Holocaust

Memorial Book of Buczacz, Galicia

ספר בוטשאטש

מצבת זכרון לקהילה קדושה

בעריכת ישראל כהן

תל־אביב   תשט"ו
על־ידי הוצאה לועצה יד לבוצ'אץ'
בהוצאת "עם עובד"

Translation of the Title Page of Original Hebrew Edition

Book of Buczacz

In Memory of a Martyred Community

Edited by: Yisrael Cohen

Tel Aviv   5716 [1956]
By the Buczacz Memorial Committee
Published by "Am Oved"

Title Page of the Translation of the original Hebrew Edition

Book of Buczacz; in Memory of a Martyred Community (Ukraine)

49°05'/ 25°24'

Sefer Buczacz: Matsevet Zikaron Le-kehila Kedosha

Edited by: Yisrael Cohen

Published in Tel Aviv, 1956

Acknowledgments

Project Coordinator

Norbert Porile

Our sincere appreciation to Ze'ev Anderman and Moshe Shpritzer, for the Buczacz Landsmanschaft in Israel, for permission to put this material on the JewishGen web site.

This is a translation of: *Sefer Buczacz; matsevet zikaron le- kehila kedosha* (Book of Buczacz; in memory of a martyred community), Editors: I. Kahan, Tel Aviv, Am Oved, 1956 (H, 302 pages)

Preface for the Buczacz Yizkor Book In Print Project

As a child growing up in New York City, I often heard my parents laughing after my step-father said to my mother in mock derision, "What can you expect from a Galitzianer?" I failed to see the humor. I knew that my mother was born in Vienna, where her parents lived and both my father and I were born in Prague. My step-father was born in Mattersdorf on the Austrian-Hungarian border. What was so funny and what was a Galitzianer? I never knew.

In 1998 at age 64, I visited Vienna for the first time in 60 years; I had also acquired "roots disease" (an unrelenting search for ancestors). In the Israelitische Kultusgemeinde Wien (Jewish Community Center in Vienna), I found my mother's birth record, her marriage record, and the marriage record of her parents. I learned that my grandfather was born in Buczacz, Galicia and my grandmother in Rozniatow, Galicia. The mystery was partially resolved. My maternal grandparents were Galitizianers and, therefore, I was a ½ Galitzianer! I still failed to see the humor in that. It took a few more years of learning about Jewish culture before I began to see the humor in the geographically-based rivalries of Eastern European Jews.

But new questions arose. Where were these towns that would hold the birth records of my maternal ancestors? The towns were found relatively easily (both were in Eastern Galicia, now in Western Ukraine). Historical accounts indicated that changing political boundaries placed both towns successively in Poland, Austria, Austria-Hungary, Poland, USSR, Germany, USSR, and currently in Ukraine.

After a great deal of searching, I unfortunately discovered that the vital records of these two towns were not to be found. They may have been lost during the Holocaust or may still reside undiscovered in some Eastern European archive. What to do? I decided to travel to Ukraine and visit these sites, which I had learned contained Jewish cemeteries with some erect gravestones. Naively, I thought to find my relatives' gravestones and learn something from the inscriptions.

In 2000 and 2001,

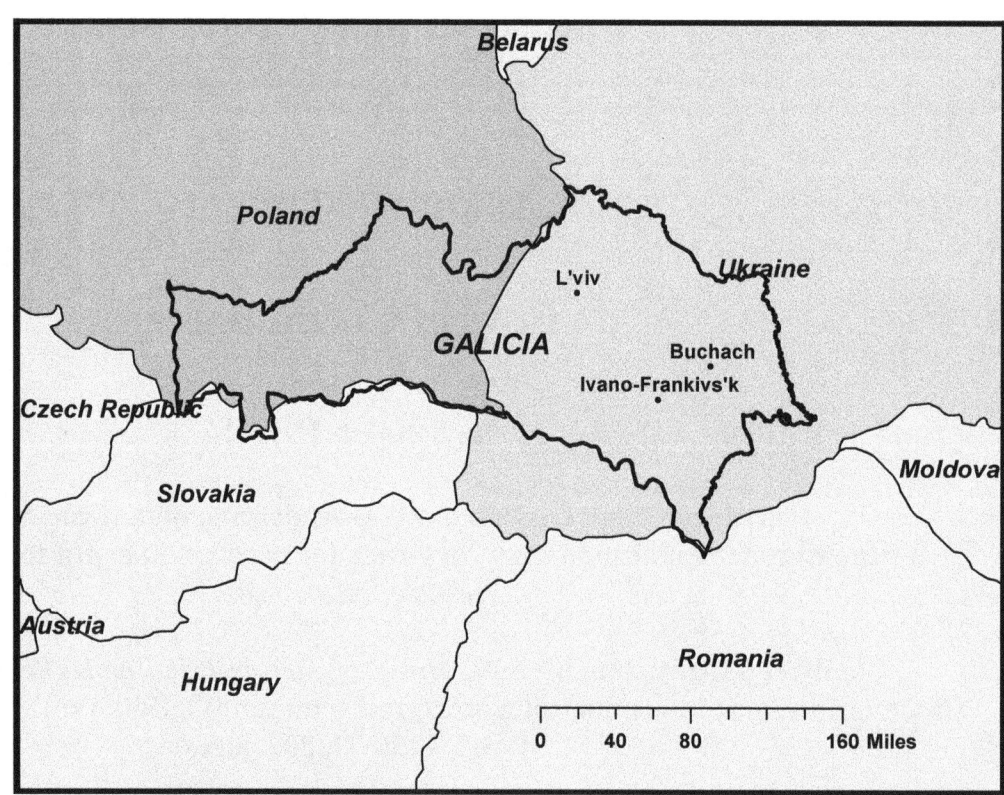

Contemporary map of central Europe on which an outline of the Province of Galicia of the Austrian Empire (thick line) is superimposed. Buczacz (now called Buchach) is in Ukraine located just north east of Stanislau (now called Ivano-Frankivsk) and south east of Lemberg (now called L'viv).

I traveled to Ukraine — together with family members and a guide/translator extraordinaire (Alex Dunai) — and eventually photographed every legible gravestone in the Buczacz and Rozniatow cemeteries. Many of these photographs are available on the Internet. Unfortunately, I discovered that in both cemeteries many gravestones are missing and I was unable to find any gravestones of close family members.

What else could I do to learn about my Galician family? I learned that there were Yizkor Books for both towns and that these were filled with information about the towns and the fate of the Jewish communities during the Holocaust. Using the Internet, I purchased a copy of the Yizkor Book for Buczacz from a used-book dealer. It is in Hebrew, which I do not read. However, I also discovered that this book was already being translated as a part of the Yizkor Book Translation Project of JewishGen with Norbert Porile as the coordinator of the translation. Translators included Rose Shoshana Ages (Kleiner/Neufeld), Jessica Cohen, Betsy Halpern-Amaru, Alejandro Landman, Israel Pickholtz, Norbert Porile, Adam Prager, and Melanie Rosenberg. With the translation of the Buczacz Yizkor Book well underway, I volunteered to coordinate the translation of the Rozniatow Yizkor Book.

When the translations of both the Buczacz and Rozniatow Yizkor Books were completed, I put all the text and graphics into desktop publishing software (Adobe InDesign) and produced bound copies of the translation of both books for my own use. When I learned about the Yizkor Books in Print Project, I contacted Joel Alpert and made both books available.

As I became more knowledgeable about Buczacz, I began to realize that its history is a microcosm of the history of Galician shtetls and yet Buczacz was a more prominent shtetl than many in Galicia. Beginning in the 13th century, Buczacz was on the Silk Road to China and was an important market town linking the Polish and Ottoman Empires. In 1340 Galicia was conquered by Casimir the Great of Poland to begin four centuries of Polish rule. By the end of the 14th century, the region surrounding Buczacz, which was inhabited largely by Ukrainian peasants, was taken over by Polish landowners. As in the rest of Galicia, the Polish landowners controlled the cultural, economic, judicial, and political life of their lands. Early in the 16th century, the Polish landowners brought in Jewish settlers, who were townspeople and craftsmen, some experienced in trade and finance. Polish kings and princes welcomed the contribution of Jews to the colonization of their eastern realms, encouraged them to settle, and offered them protection. The Polish landowners wanted to enrich themselves through the resources of their vast land holdings but they did not want to manage these properties. Jews were brought in to manage the properties as lease holders, under the so called *arenda* system. The Jews were an economic, social, and religious buffer between the Catholic Polish nobility and what the Poles regarded as the unruly and uneducated Eastern Orthodox Ukrainian peasants, most of them serfs. Jews were entrusted to collect taxes from the peasants, manage properties, hire and fire workers, and were often entrusted with the keys to local churches. The Ukrainian peasants were eking out a subsistence living and viewed the Jews as their oppressors. From the beginning of the 16th century there was enmity among Poles, Jews, and Ukrainians which persisted for the next 500 years with tragic consequences for all three groups.

The second half of the 17th century began with the Cossack uprisings, led by Hetman Bohdan Khmelnytsky (*Bogdan Chmielnicki* in Polish), against the landowners and nobility. Although the uprising was focused on the Polish landlords, the Jews were regarded as the henchmen of the landlords and were slaughtered in large numbers. Bohdan Khmelnytsky, a national hero to Ukrainians because he led an uprising against the hated Polish nobles, was despised by the Poles and is regarded by Eastern European Jews as second only to Hitler in the slaughter of Jews. With the Partition of Poland in 1772-1795, Galicia became a province of Austria. Thus, Austrian law replaced Polish law for governing the province although Polish nobility maintained a great deal of political power. The Austrian Empire granted Jews a measure of civil rights in the late 18th century and full citizenship in 1867. Emancipation opened new secular educational as well as economic opportunities, of which many Jews took great advantage. As a spiritual center for Galician Jews, Buczacz produced a number of prominent rabbis, many of whom are named in the Yizkor Book. Buczacz was a center for scholarship as can be seen in the long list of books by Buczacz authors (pages 15-30). Buczacz also produced prominent internationally known scholars including: Shmuel Yosef Agnon (winner of the Nobel Prize in Literature in 1966); Schlomo Freud (grandfather of Sigmund Freud) and several generations of the Freud ancestors; Emanuel Ringelblum (historian, politician, and Holocaust chronicler); Simon Wiesenthal (post-World War II Nazi hunter). The Jewish community of Buczacz was organized to produce a wide variety of social and religious services including, a hospital, an old-age home, an orphanage, as well as a synagogue, and a prayer house. The community contained a heterogeneous mix of orthodox, secular, and Zionist Jews.

Despite its history of episodic ethnic and class violence, Buczacz remained a multi-cultural community in which the various ethnic groups lived in mostly harmonious interdependence until the ethnic cleansings of World War II and its aftermath. Today, Buchach (as it is now called) is inhabited largely by Ukrainians; there are no Jews left and few Poles.

Thomas F. Weiss Buczacz Yizkor Book in Print Editor, July 12, 2013

Memorial Book of Buczacz, Galicia

Table of Contents

Section	Author	[Page] in original book	Page in this book
People of the Book	Israel Cohen	7	1
In My Town	S.Y. Agnon	9	7
Stories about Buczacz	S.Y. Agnon	14	12
Books by Buczacz Townsmen	S.Y. Agnon	17	15
Buczacz in Old Books	S.Y. Agnon	32	31
A Letter to S. Y. Agnon	Asher Barash	33	33
Buczacz (Geographical Sketch)	M.Y. Braver	39	41
History of the Jews in Buczacz	Dr. N. M. Gelber	44	45
Rabbi Abraham David	Yekutiel Kamelbar	74	76
Z. Meshulam Igra	Rabbi Y. L. Maimon	81	82
Rabbi Abraham	David M. Buber	87	88
Rabbi Shalom Mordechai HaCohen	Schwadron Moshe Zinovitz	87	88
Synagogues in the Town	David Neuman	89	95
The Buczacz Community	Israel Cohen	92	98
Buczacz Hasidim	Shimon Horovits	97	103
"Der jüdische Wecker" ['The Jewish Awakener']		100	106
Professor David Tsvi (Heinrich) Mueller	G. Kresl	109	118
Letter from Professor Mueller	David Tsvi Mueller	118	127
Sigmund Freud's Family Tree		119	129
Encounters with Sigmund Freud	Dr. M. Grinwald	119	131
Yitskhak Fernhof	Israel Cohen	122	133
Family Memories	William Fernhof	127	139
How Buczacz Jews Voted in Austrian Parliamentary Elections	Dr. Koppel Blum	131	144
From My Memories	Dr. Tsvi Heller	142	156
From the Days of My Youth	Dr. Naftali Menatseyakh	166	190
The First Hebrew School in Buczacz	Baruch Y. Berkowitz	174	199
Histadrut Hechalutz in Buczacz	Moshe Held	179	205
Hospital and Old Age Home in Buczacz	Khaye Roll	180	207
The Orphanage	Peppa Anderman-Neuberger	184	211
More about the Orphanage	Dr. David Pohorila	185	217
WIZO	Khaye Roll	186	217
The Jewish Health Organization	Aryeh Roll	187	218
Buczacz Jews in Vienna	Ezekiel (Yekhezkl) Aderer	188	219
Activity of the New York Buczacz Jewish Welfare Society	Abraham Zommer	191	223
From the Town's Life	Dr. David Pohorila	194	226
Fragments	Khaye Roll	202	234

Gleanings	Joseph Urbach	204	236
Town Worthies			
Rabbi Haim Weinraub	Sh. M.		241
Rabbi Yakov Leib Alfenbein	Efraim Alfenbein	211	241
About Several Figures in Our Town	David Neuman [Neiman]	212	242
Two Figures	David Neuman [Neiman]	214	244
Shlomo (Solomon) Dik	G. Gafner	216	245
Dr. Baruch (Bernard) Farnhof	Dr. Y. Fernhof	219	254
Dr. M. Hirschhorn	R. [p. 220 has Y. P.]	220	254
Outstanding Women in Our Town	D. N.	220	255
Memorable Women	Dr. D[avid] Pohorila	222	256
My Brother Shmuel (Samuel)	Dr. M. Karniel [Hirshhorn]	223	257
Meir Fried	Moshe Held	224	258
Emanuel Ringelblum in the Warsaw Ghetto	Nathan Eck	225	259
Emanuel Ringelblum	Meylekh Ravitsh	227	261
Dr. Avraham Khalfan	N[aftali] M[enatseyakh]	228	263
The Shoa in Buczacz			
Letter from Dr. Abraham Halfan		233	265
Letter from Dr. Regina Zohker		235	267
Letter from Dr. Max Enderman		236	268
How It Happened:			
First Witness	Isaac (Yitskhak) Shikhor	237	268
Second Witness	Samuel (Shmuel) Rosenthal	258	297
Third Witness	Elyash Khalfan	264	303
Fourth Witness	Israel Gilbert	272	311
The Resistance Movement in Buczacz	E. Bazan	284	319
Birthday in a Concentration Camp	Simon (Shimon) Wiesenthal	295	334
Shoa Echoes in Buczacz		297	336
The Buczacz Memorial Committee		304	343

[Page 7]

People of the Book
Translated by Adam Prager

Eight years ago a group of people from Buczacz came up with the idea of commemorating our venerable community, whose history and influence go far beyond its narrow borders. During these eight years – with some interruptions – this book was prepared.

The editor of this volume understands that much remains to be done and that our work will probably never be complete. With the destruction of the magnificent community of Buczacz and the death of its inhabitants, information and memories were lost together with those pure souls, making it impossible to gather all the historical facts needed to portray the town in full detail. It was necessary to collect material from remote places, to order the most varied bits and pieces and to encourage individuals from near and far to contribute to the preparation of this book. The editor and other members of the Book Committee spared no labors in trying to find both public and private sources for the completion of the book plan. Nevertheless, many gaps in both the near and distant past could not be bridged with the material that accumulated by chance.

We were aware, however, that this would be the last opportunity to erect a sacred memorial for Buczacz, to collect what we could from the mouths of the townspeople and to recover documents that were left scattered about. For with each passing year fewer remain who remember and who are of connecting strand to strand, fragment to fragment, story to story, description to description, picture to picture and memory to memory so as to revive the image of the community of Buczacz, to leave a record and give it a name.

The literary criterion was not the only one for determining what to include in the book; value and usefulness also played a role in its arrangement. For the book's sole purpose is to collect material from wherever and whomever possible in order to reconstruct Jewish Buczacz. Therefore, certain repetitions dealing with the city's cultural and civic life were not omitted, even if they failed to introduce any novelties or add a personal touch. The editor especially followed this principle in the section describing the ruin of the town and the acts of destruction by the soldiers of Hitler (may his name be blotted out!). The editor had no intention of editing the style of sections dealing with bloodshed and heroism, but simply allowed the speakers to tell in their own words what they saw and what they experienced. For all the descriptions were written close to the time of the events, shortly after their writers succeeded in saving themselves and finding asylum in Israel, the United States, or Europe.

Although responsibility for the book lies with the editor alone, he has the great pleasure to add that he consulted S.Y. Agnon at various stages in the book's preparation. Not only did Agnon write a unique bibliographical study especially for this volume, as well as several stories of Buczacz; he also gave learned and fascinating advice to the editor; his remarks are diffused throughout the book and for this the editor is grateful. It is only natural that the name Agnon is mentioned so often in the book. Agnon has contributed to Hebrew literature a kind of celestial Buczacz, having for decades nurtured and been nurtured by this source. Agnon as a writer is no longer associated with and of interest to the people of Buczacz alone; he plays a major role within the Jewish people and its literature. However, if the special pride the Buczacz survivors take in Agnon is too apparent, may they be forgiven – it is only human to take pride in one's townsman.

* The reader will probably notice the various spellings of the town's name. This cannot be avoided. Due to the form of the name and its different pronunciations, especially by Jews and Christians, different spellings have been used since the time the town was mentioned both in old and new Hebrew and Yiddish books. Therefore the editor has decided to follow the rule: the standard spelling is Buczacz, although in cases where the name is mentioned from different sources, it will be given as in those sources.

** Prior to the publishing of the book Mrs. Chaya Roll (may she rest in peace), passed away. Chaya was the moving spirit of the Book Committee. Out of her love for this town and its Jewish life, she worked with great enthusiasm for the writing of this book, encouraging others to do the same. Much of the credit for the publishing of the book is due to her. Blessed be her memory...

Israel Cohen

General view of the town, the Stripa River encircles the town

General view from the West

The famous Lipa known by the name Soveyski Lipa,
near the estate of Count Potocki

The fortress (The Empty Castle)

Historic building in the town center (Ratusz)

[Page 9]

In My Town
Translated by Adam Prager
One Chapter of One Story

In memory of my teacher and friend, the Gaon Rabbi Shmuel Bialovlotski. hy"v
[May the Lord watch over him and restore him to life]

a) At the entrance of my town

There is a best place and a best time to tell a story, and so I will talk elsewhere of the day I left my hometown, why I did so, and what I discovered in all those places for which I left my town. Here I will describe what I encountered on my return, as well as relating to what happened in Buczacz during my absence. I will begin with my town, then talk about my townspeople, and along the way I will say a little about myself as a townsman would speak of a fellow townsman.

Mine is the town of towns. As to its age, it is most venerable, being one of the oldest communities of the Jewish Diaspora in Poland. As to customs, it is blessed with fine customs received from its forefathers, exiles from Ashkenaz, who received them from the scholars of Rome, who received them from the Gaonim of Erets-Yisrael, who received them from the great Talmudists, all the way to Moses who received them on Mt. Sinai. Concerning wisdom, there is no department of knowledge without its base here, especially the study of the Torah – the highest wisdom of all. Alongside wisdom, allow me to mention humility. In all of its history, Buczacz never chose a rabbi from among its own townsmen even if he were expert in all matters of Judaism.

While I was away from my town, it lived through stormy days, breaking a calm that lasted through most of the period from after the atrocities of 1648-1649 until my emigration to Israel. I don't know whether the gentiles were the cause of the eruption or whether the Jews were to blame, or whether these two explanations are actually one. For as long as we follow God's will, all gentiles in their lands see that we are the people of God and fear us. Once we cease to follow God's will, God ignores us, leaving us subject to persecution and humiliation by the gentiles. This has been so through the ages, from the days of Egypt till now, when our estrangement from God has grown.

From the pure joy of thinking of my town, I ignored the grave rumors that reached my ears on the way to Buczacz. These rumors described gangs of idlers returning from the war who were about to enter our town. Was it possible that something had changed in our town? This is what I asked myself. I sat up in my bed after a short summer-night's sleep and was ready to go further, feeling confident as in the days of my youth when our town was safe and tranquil and all the gentiles saw the Jews as the source of all livelihoods and no one would even think of the possibility that anything could change there till the coming of the Messiah.

Before the pillow under my head could wrinkle, I was out of bed, dressed and off to see the town. I had not seen it for quite a few years, except in my dreams.

b) The picture of the town

Since my town is not well known to you, I will try to draw it for you, at least insofar as one can describe a place inspired by the heavenly spheres themselves.

My town lies on hills surrounded by and intertwined with rivers and lakes. Pleasant springs flow down to forests thick with trees and full of singing birds. Some of the birds are natives of the land; others are foreign and have chosen to stay, for only a fool would give up so blissful a paradise. Whoever can distinguish between the different bird songs can tell the native from the foreign birds.

The streets and avenues in the town lie in contrast to the hills. They are the work of both man and nature, each complimenting the other. This is one example where the makings of God and those of man join together peacefully in a complementary manner. One can imagine that those same streets and avenues go back to times when peoples' hearts were pure and uncorrupted.

Along the main thoroughfares, houses of worship were established. Actually, they established themselves. After 1649 when the riots ceased, things began to return to normal; survivors of the Khmelnitski horrors trickled home. The town was mostly in ruins. Gentiles had occupied those houses that had remained intact; synagogues and study halls were devastated; the Great Synagogue was turned into a church. While Jews were searching for a place to build a house of worship, a fragment of a scroll from one of the ruined Torah scrolls started to flutter in the wind. Some say it fell from the heavens, for all knew that the spot on which it had finally fallen was sacred. A house of study for prayer and learning was built on it. This is the old Bet Hamidrash. When they prospered, the Jews built the Great Synagogue, a great monument, stronghold of the Jews, for in times of trouble – May we not see such again – Jews would come there to pray to our merciful Lord, guardian from all evil.

When the town had grown and developed, and the house of study proved too small for everyone, a second one was built, financed by a few homeowners. It consisted of one room for prayer and study, with books, a table, benches and a sink. People called this the New Bet Midrash as opposed to the already existing old Bet Midrash.

Past glory was restored to that generation. They were honored with a permanent rabbi, the true gaon, Rabbi Tsvi Kara, who left behind him as a blessing his book of responsa Neta Shaashuim, and was buried in the town cemetery. All the gaonim who preceded him were recruited to serve in other towns. But not R' Tsvi Kara. He resided in Buczacz till the day he was called to his residence above.

In order to make him feel as comfortable as possible, a spacious house with two rooms, plus a kitchen for his wife, was built for him. One room was called "the summer house" while the other, in which an oven was installed, was known as "the winter house." R' Kara was also given a spacious area for his sukkah, on which very spot, years later, a large bet midrash was built. I shall speak of it later on. After it was observed that R' Kara walked daily from his house to the Great Synagogue, the townspeople lay square stones along his route. Square stones were also laid around the synagogue, creating a floor of sorts around its walls. I knew an old man who knew an even older one who recalled that as a child his father pointed out to him the Gaon, with pipe in mouth on his daily walk. While walking, R' Kara would reflect upon the many questions he received concerning the halakha. Our teacher, the Gaon, was an affable person, always ready to respond to scholars, except those who turned to him in order to brag of their own knowledge. These he would send on their way in a jesting manner, his eyes smiling, constantly puffing on his pipe. Scholars would come to visit him to discuss problems of halakha and if they remained until the time for afternoon prayers [minkha]), they prayed there in the study house, except in the month of Elul and on the High Holidays. In line with the practice of our forefathers, from the first day of Elul to the night of Simkhat Torah, R' Kara conducted all prayers at the Great Synagogue.

Following the death of our rabbi, the Gaon, head of our rabbinical court, his position was inherited by his son-in-law, the Gaon, the pious R' Avraham David, a holy man of God, a gaon in revealed as in secret matters, venerated throughout the land, who illuminated the way for many through his books of sacred knowledge. I have already hinted in one of my books at how he came to be our rabbi, how he was commandeered in the middle of the night at his home in the town of Yazlovits where he served as rabbi, and how he was literally carried from his bed all the way to his house in our town. I will not repeat what I have written, even though it is only hinted at. I will, however, add this: it is to his credit (may it protect us) that he built a small temple and instituted the Sefardic rite in his prayer service. This rite was already in use by the Bet Khasidim [House of Hasidim] that was built a generation earlier. Most of the people called this hasidic center "the clowns' chapel" ["leytsim shilikhl" – Yiddish shilikhl 'little shul']. The new hasidim, the disciples of the Baal Shem Tov of blessed memory were looked upon in our town as a bunch of clowns due to their strange movements and dances during prayer and due to their dress. Townspeople felt no compunction about speaking of their house of prayer scornfully.

After the death of this tsadik there was disagreement as to who would inherit his place. Some wanted his son to replace him, while others opposed this. The deceased himself had stated before his death that he did not want his son to inherit his position, though he held him worthy of it. Our tsadik was said to fear it would become a custom for sons to inherit the positions of their fathers. A situation could arise whereby the rabbinical chair would not always pass to the most worthy candidate, which in turn could lead to the position being desecrated.

The son did not inherit the position; however, he and his family lived in the chosen rabbi's house. The rabbi chosen was our teacher, the true Gaon, R' Avraham Teumim, author of Khesed leAvraham. The tsadik's son lived in the rabbi's home and expanded his righteous father's study house, which was called the Rabbi's Study House. In recent generations people have been calling it "America," since most of those who come there to pray stem from different places, just as in America the inhabitants originate from many different countries. Before the Rabbi's Study House was built, there existed the Tailors' Synagogue. If you want to know why the tailors had their own synagogue, read my book Oreakh Nata Lalun [A Guest for the Night]. Once the town was larger and its inhabitants more numerous, other houses of study and prayer were built. If you wish to know more about them, this too you may find in Oreakh Nata Lalun. However, there I altered my town's name. But now, after those profane madmen have annihilated its Jewish inhabitants and the town is no more, I call it by its name Biczacz, as our forefathers of blessed memory did, or Buczacz as it is written in the history books.

Now I return to the Great Synagogue.

c) The Great Synagogue of our town

From my love for the sacred, I will spare no effort in describing our Great Synagogue. Our Great Synagogue is shaped like an erect ark and has a stone floor on all sides. It is narrow on three sides and wide at its front, its walls are smooth and look like old parchment, When I was a small child, I thought the Great Synagogue was a hand phylactery. But because it was larger than a man's phylactery and even of a giant's, I wondered whose it was. That was the first wonderment of my childhood. One day a relative took me to the old study house where I saw old men sitting with books before them, and one man among them was teaching them as a tutor teaches little children. I heard him say, "How is it that the Almighty [hakadosh barukh hu] puts on phylacteries [tefilin]? And what is written in those phylacteries? And who are like the people of Israel, one people in all the land?" And I knew what I knew.

Now that I have discussed the building's shape, I shall go into further detail. Part of it is sunk into the ground, for "from the depths I cried out to God" [Psalms 130: 1]. It has twelve windows for the twelve tribes, one of which lies above the Holy Ark on the eastern side. It is made of various pieces of glass through which a spectrum of light passes. Because those lights are constantly in motion, I believed as a child that one gleam of the sunlight of the Land of Israel glowed within them. And even today, after reading science books and studying about the sun, I find it most difficult to set aside this notion, even though it does not go hand in hand with the laws of nature.

Four quill pens on each and every finger are not sufficient to describe the splendor of the Great Synagogue and also that of the old study house and of all the other study houses in our town. As to height, there were taller buildings among both the gentiles and the Jews. As to illumination, lights from other buildings shined more brightly. However, past midnight, when all the lights in town were extinguished, the lights of our study houses shined with the light of the Torah. As regards height, tall and solid buildings collapse, but he who raises the Torah raises himself and continues to grow. This was said of previous generations that loved the Torah.

d) From Torah to Tefilah

When the sun has begun to shine and it is time for prayer, all arise from their places. The aged gird their loins and wrap themselves in prayer shawls and adorn themselves with their phylacteries. The young men gird their loins and adorn themselves with their phylacteries. Small boys, below the age when it is obligatory to put on phylacteries, gird their loins and recite blessings and prayers and say "amen" and "vayehe shemaya raba." No one stops praying to hold a friendly chat or for conversation of any kind. If you witnessed a man distracted from his prayer, you could be sure he was not from our town. It is not an accident that after the congregation's "mi shebeyrakh," the sheliakh tsibur [cantor] blessed the congregation. And how did he bless them? That God Almighty hear their prayers and make all their wishes come true. These are the words of the prayer: "He who blessed our forefathers, Avraham, Yitskhak and Yaakov, will bless all those who abstain from speaking during prayer in the synagogue from the moment the cantor commences with the words 'baruch sheamar' until the end of the prayers." This blessing was brought from the first exiles of Ashkenaz. And why does it not mention the reading from the Torah? There is no need, for never has any man thought of interrupting at such a moment, not even a whisper to his neighbor. Why do I mention all this? For if one will say that it is impossible for people to assemble together and abstain from conversation, I will say that in our town that was the custom.

e) Messiah

A tale of Elijah the prophet, of blessed memory, that happened to visit our town during a circumcision [brit mila]. In those days a baby was circumcised at the Great Synagogue immediately after the morning service [tefilat shakharit], before reciting the "Aleynu" prayer. A large chair beneath a canopy of red silk cloth was situated at the western side of the synagogue, below the women's gallery. This was the chair of Elijah the prophet, the angel of the circumcision. On the day of a circumcision, the chair would be carried down by ladder and placed beside the ark. Everyone would then wait until the infant was brought and it would be circumcised.

One day the son of a pious and modest scholar, a splendid man of good deeds, was to be circumcised. Father Elijah who loves the people of Israel, especially the humble, arrived an hour before the ceremony in order to stand among the Jews while they prayed to their Father in heaven.

On his arrival, Elijah found that the Jews had finished their prayers, for they would pray from the first signs of dawn. However, they were still standing, and were reciting the Thirteen Principles, as is the custom before a circumcision when the baby's arrival is delayed, a custom intended to prevent prayer from turning into conversation.

Elijah saw them standing together in one group reciting in unison: "I believe in the coming of the Messiah and will wait for him no matter how long he tarries." Elijah reflected on this and decided it would be a good idea to tell the Messiah about it.

After the circumcision, Elijah flew off and went straight to the Messiah. On his arrival, he turned to him and said: "Our righteous Messiah, if you were only to see how the townsmen of Biczacz await your arrival, you would immediately rid yourself of your shackles and hasten to redeem them." The Messiah heard these words and said to Elijah, "I shall go and see." He covered his wounds with shackles and his shackles with rags and set off for our town.

On his way he came across a place where it was time for the afternoon prayer. He entered the synagogue to pray and found it full of congregants, with a cantor standing before the ark and repeating the prayer. But most of the Jews were talking, their voices drowning out the prayer. The Messiah shook his shackles out of pure misery, but they could not be heard since the conversation was louder. He turned away from them and returned to the gates of Rome.

He still sits at the same spot while we await his arrival each day.

S. Y. Agnon

[Page 14]

Stories about Buczacz
Translated by Adam Prager
Concerning one mitsvah

The Gaon R' Israel, blessed be his memory, head of the rabbinical court of Swierz and of half the Lvov District, lived in the days of the Gaon, author of Turey Zahav [Pillars of Gold], who also began there as a rabbi. In Swierz there is a fair which is held right after Passover. The tavern keepers would brew a large quantity of beer for Passover. They would sell the beer on the eve of Passover to a gentile by means of a bill of sale in order to have enough good beer for the fair after Passover.

The Gaon R' Israel heard of this and said: "Why this is sheer trickery – preparing unleavened beverages [khamets] for themselves and cunningly selling it to the gentiles." He then declared at the synagogue that no one was permitted to brew beer shortly before Passover. Any man who defied his words would be ostracized. The tavern keepers heard him and all obeyed, except for one man who did not take the threat of ostracism seriously, since the great gaonim, the author of Bayit Khadash and R' Aryeh Leyb, the rabbi of Krakow and the author of Turey Zahav, who reigned in Swierz, did not declare such a punishment for this crime. So the taverner went and secretly prepared his ale.

That same tavern keeper was a moneylender to the villagers. On the first intermediate day of Passover [khol hamoed], he took his debtors' records, some provisions and rode towards the villages on his horse. On the way he was attacked by peasants and felt that they intended to kill him. He had a good horse and urged it forward, and was able to escape from them.

At mealtime he felt hungry. He had no water with which to wash his hands and did not wish to eat before doing so. He kept on riding till he was too tired to continue. Recalling that there was a spring that ran out of the mountain, he thought to himself that if he reached it he would be caught by the murderers and killed; if he did not get to the spring he would die of starvation. For he had no water with which to wash his hands, and he could not defy the Jewish custom of washing hands before eating. "Whatever will be will be," he said to himself, "for I must eat." He went down to the spring and washed his hands. Peasants came and murdered him.

The Gaon R' Israel used to have his prize student stay at his house. He would awaken two or three times a night, each time washing his hands; he directed the student to do likewise, and on each occasion they discussed the halakha. On the night of the murder there stayed with him his student, the great rabbi R' Natan, who later became famous among the Jews. A great preacher, he settled in the sacred community of Buczacz and was known there as R' Natan Melamed.

Past midnight a knocking was heard at the door. The Gaon called out, "Who is there?" A voice behind the door answered, "I am a tavern keeper." The Gaon thought it odd to be visited at such an hour. He ordered his student, our teacher R' Natan, to open the door. The tavern keeper stood at the entrance, but they did not notice that he was dead. "Why do you stand there," asked the Gaon, "come inside." "You think I'm alive, but I am dead," said the tavern keeper and he told them of all that had happened to him.

The Gaon turned to him and asked: "What is it that you want?" The dead man replied that it had been announced in the upper world that he was not to undergo a trial. God Almighty had already forgiven him for all his sins, for he had sanctified the name of God at the cost of his life while obeying one of the secondary commandments [mitsvot] ordained by oral tradition [divrey sofrim]. His soul was allowed to return to its place of origin, undetained by adversary or angel. When he arrived at the gates of heaven, an angel said: "Halt until I have inquired, for you have been ostracized by R' Israel." The angel was informed that the dead man could enter on condition that he obtain a writ from the rabbi canceling his punishment. "I am here," said the tavern keeper to the rabbi, " to request a writ of confirmation to win release of my soul from ostracism."

The rabbi asked: "Am I so important in that world? I am neither rich nor rabbi of a large town. The dead man replied: "Not every man merits two tables." [Berakhot 8: figurative expression of dual success, in Torah and in fame]. The Gaon asked: "How do you know how to speak in this manner?" For the tavern keeper was uneducated. He answered: "Now ask me about any Torah passage and I shall interpret it." And he added that when he was told to bring a writ from the rabbi, they spoke of the latter with two R's, respectfully saying R' R' Israel. The rabbi revoked the ostracism.

The rabbi asked the dead man who had killed him. He told him it was three peasants from a certain village and named their names. He added that his debtors' records were hidden in a barn of one the murderers. The rabbi said, "Rest in peace" and bade him farewell.

The following morning the rabbi asked to see the dead man's wife and told her that her husband had been hurt near a spring by the mountain, He instructed her to send a wagon with two men to bring him home. The wife wept and hurriedly rented a wagon and sent two or three men to fetch him. On their arrival they found the man dead. They laid him in the wagon and brought him to town.

His wife cried out in anguish and came weeping before the rabbi exclaiming, "My rabbi said he hurt his thigh, but he is dead." The rabbi replied: "I knew it was so, but I wanted to spare you the bad news. That is why I told you to send a wagon with men to bring him home." He added that the killers were three men from a certain village and his debtors' records were hidden in one of the men's barns and his name was such and such.

When the news reached the castle, the governor ordered that the dead man's body be displayed in the market square. According to custom, anyone knowing the identity of the killer(s) was asked to come forward. Such a man was not found and so they proceeded to bury the murdered taverner.

The dead man's wife then visited the governor and told him she knew the names of the killers and that her husband's debtors' records were hidden in one of the men's barns and that his name was such and such. The governor immediately dispatched horsemen to arrest the murderers and to find the debtors' records. The killers, knowing they had no other choice but to confess, did so. The governor wrought vengeance upon them and executed them. May the Lord take vengeance for the blood we have lost. Everywhere he went and preached, our teacher, the great rabbi and preacher R' Natan of Buczacz, the student of the Gaon R' Israel, would reprove all those who took lightly the matter of washing hands. At the close of each sermon, he would tell the same tale. At the end he added: "If a man's soul is pardoned and given entrance to heaven for only one secondary commandment based on oral tradition, how much more so will he who keeps all the commandments of the Torah gain a place in the next world." (I give the origin of the story in Betoch Ha'Ir).

"And he will judge the poor righteously"

On the first day of the holiday, the day that our patriarch, Abraham, visits the sukkah, or perhaps it was on Hoshana Raba [the seventh day of the Feast of Tabernacles], the day the Messiah, King David, visits [these are folk beliefs], there gathered in the sukkah [booth] of Rabbi Meir of Przemyslany about thirty hasidim from various places. Rabbi Meir of Przemyslany asked," Is there anyone here who knew Rabbi Avraham David of Biczacz.

Rabbi Alter, son of the Biczacz dayan [religious court judge] (who rests in honor on the Mount of Olives in Jerusalem) replied and said: "I was born thanks to the prayers of that tsadik [Hasidic rabbi] and I was brought up in his house. For my father, may he rest in peace, at sixty years of age still had no son, and therefore he would ask the tsadik to pray for him. Once, on the night of the Day of Atonement, when father went to the tsadik to receive his blessing, the Rabbi of Biczacz congratulated him, saying, "Mazal tov, this year your wife will give you a son." And I was born. And when father went to his eternal rest, the Rabbi of Biczacz took me into his home and raised me, and I knew him very well.

Rabbi Meir of Przemyslany said: "You say you knew the Rabbi of Biczacz, and Meir says there is no one who knew the Rabbi of Biczacz – except Meir. You will not see such a rabbi until the coming of the Messiah. Meir once talked with the Rabbi of Biczacz for eight continuous hours. You don't have to know what we talked about, but there is one part of that discussion that I will relate.

Meir asked the Rabbi of Biczacz why it is said of the Messiah, "And he will judge the poor righteously." And what is remarkable about the Messiah, our salvation, judging righteously? Moreover, it is said that he will judge only the poor and will not judge the rich. For it is said of Moses that he would discern from among all the people the valiant who are god-fearing and truthful, haters of corruption, etc.; all large matters will be brought before him, whereas they will judge the small ones. This means that great matters are brought before the great and little matters before the little. And why in the passage is the Messiah burdened with matters of the poor, since most matters of the poor are menial? And the Rabbi of Biczacz made no reply to Meir. And Meir said, "I will answer."

When Messiah the King arrives – may he soon come – when God appoints him for our time, immediately the seven shepherds arrive, and the presidents, and the high priests and the kings and the prophets, and also the Tannaim [talmudic teachers] and the Amoraim [talmudic interpreters], and all the talmudic sages ["khokhmey shas"], and also the Saboraim. and the Gaonim and the great First Poskim [religious arbiters], and all the rest of the righteous tsadikim, until the temple is filled by them and there is no room for the rabbis.

But the righteous rabbis are allowed to sit outside in front of the temple. And to sit near to and next to the temple of the Messiah is a great privilege. At that time, everyone that wants to have a dispute judged upon, wants it brought before the Messiah, the King. The rich come first, it being their nature to lead. When they arrive at the threshold, they behold the rabbi of their city sitting there. "Rabbi, are you here? We have a dispute to settle. Perhaps you can be of use to us." Immediately, the rabbi hears their case and renders judgement. Poor people whose disputes involve pennies see the cases of the great and rich being settled, cases involving thousands. They become ashamed to put forward their disputes. The Messiah, the King calls to them and says: "My beloved brothers, who feel with me in all my suffering, come closer to me." They come near to the Messiah, the King. The Messiah, the King says to them, "My brothers, what do you want?" They reply to the Messiah, the King: "We have such and such disputes and wish to have judgements." The Messiah, the King replies: "You have disputes, and if you wish I will render judgements on them." They reply: "Messiah, the King, our cases involve pennies. The Messiah, the King answers: "My brothers, you have no need to feel ashamed. Your pennies are kosher; you toiled greatly to earn them and they are more significant than all the gold and silver in the world. Put forth your arguments. And immediately the Messiah, our salvation, heard their disputes and rendered judgements righteously. And thus it is said: "And he will judge the poor righteously" [Isaiah, 11:4].

S. Y. Agnon

[Page 17]

Books by Buczacz Townsmen
Translated by Adam Prager

At the request of my townsmen and in memory of lovers of Torah, I have listed the titles of books written in Hebrew letters by Buczacz scholars. The books I know but which are not to be found I have listed in detail. Those I recall but which I do not have before me I have listed as they appear in other books and put a star by their names. As the list was prepared during different periods and for various purposes I did not follow any one particular format. In any case, this is a memorial to learning in Buczacz, a town full of scholars and writers until the enemy arrived and destroyed it and its inhabitants. I hope this list, the first of its kind, will encourage knowledgeable persons to correct and complete it.

Unfortunately, I was not able to set eyes on a few books I know from childhood, like the Pentateuchs printed by Ze'ev Wolf Pohorile with the "Remnant of Judah" commentary (Lwow, 1881), and likewise the Yiddish weekly Yidishe veker which was edited in Buczacz by Dr. Eliezer Rokeakh of Safed and printed in Buczacz in the printing house of Ze'ev Dratler and in which I myself published poems and stories.

I also want to mention the books of my learned relative, R. David Tsvi Miller (of blessed memory), and also the Sarajevo Haggada (Vienna 1898), the Laws of Hammurabi (Vienna 1903) and other works which, however, I have not recorded in this list since their title pages and bindings are not in Hebrew letters.

I would like to thank the meticulous bibliographer Mr. Shlomo Shunami for helping me to arrange this

Some of the books published in Buczacz

material.

1. Sefer Evel Gadol. ('Great Mourning') by R. Abraham Teumim, former president, rabbinical court of the holy congregation of Zabriz in the region of Galicia, the light of whose teaching now shines upon the upright in the study house of Buczacz – a eulogy – on the death of the righteous rabbi, my teacher and rabbi, Rabbi Israel of Ruzhin of blessed and saintly memory, Lemberg, "yra"t lp"k" [= 1851], 1, 30 leaves.

[This book Sefer Evel Gadol and also Sefer Evel Kaved by Rabbi Abraham Teumim, president of the rabbinical court of Zalishtshik, were mistakenly attributed to his learned uncle, Rabbi Abraham Teumim, author of Khesed LeAvraham, president of the rabbinical court of the holy congregation of Buczacz. And see Sefer Nakhal Dim'ea by Rabbi Abraham Teumim, president of the rabbinical court of Zalishtsik, and the words of his son there. Zalishtshik, n.d.]

2. Kuntres Evel Kaved. ('Deep Mourning') eulogizes the righteous rabbi, prince of peace, [son of] the holy rabbi... ornament of Israel, of blessed and saintly memory, of Ruzhin. Lemberg, Mikhal [!] F. Poremba Printers, "yra"t lp"k" [= 1851], 20 leaves., octavo. [at the end of the book: "I am but dust and ashes {Gen. 18, 17} Abraham Teumim, president of the rabbinical court of Zbariz – it should be Zbariz and not Zabriz, etc."] And attached to this is one pamphlet from his great composition Bet Avraham ('House of Abraham') on the Shulkhan Arukh, a section of his Bet Evel, his responsa on the laws of mourning. He responded to his friend Rabbi Ze'ev Wolf Pohorile of Tusit (presently a wise counselor in the holy congregation of Buczacz), on the law regarding finding dry bones. He brings new interpretations on biblical legends [unpublished] and his New Year addresses during his Zbariz period. At the end of the book he signs his name "I am but dust and ashes Abraham Teumim, president of the rabbinical court of Zbariz."

3. Kuntres Ohev Mishpat. ('Lover of Justice') (Part One) In a legal dispute in Siget which divided the community in half... and became a public issue... against the Sefardic community whose enemies known as the Orthodox rose up against them and accused them of breaking the law. As a compromise it was decided to resolve the issue before a jury of five rabbis. But the fifth rabbi took matters into his own hands and issued a halachic judgement without discussing the matter face to face with the other deliberating rabbis. He indicted the Sefardic community who were held to be guilty; however, there stood up against him the most learned scholar, my teacher and rabbi, Rabbi Feivel Halevi, president of the rabbinical court of Bradshin... Lemberg, ohev tsedaka umishpat lp"k ('lover of justice and law') [=1897], 104 leaves, octavo.
[Regarding the division, separation and differences among the communities in Hungary and containing the opinion of the majority of halachic authorities in Galicia, Bukovina and Hungary and finally the form of the first statutes that was received by the general meeting with the agreement of all the townspeople and in the presence and with the agreement of the rabbi, Rabbi Yekutiel Judah Teitelbaum.]

4. Ahab by R. Elkhanan Shitzer. A tragedy in four acts. Radom, 1934, 65, 1 pp. octavo.

5.* Emuna veHaskala ('Faith and Enlightenment') by R. David Meyer Anderman. A vision in five acts. Drohobycz, 1882, 72, 1 pp., duodecimo.

6. Kuntres Amarot Tehorot ('Purification Writings') by the learned sage, my teacher and rabbi, Rabbi Abraham David, president of the rabbinical court of Buczacz [immersion for purification, immersion of utensils and the laws of the Sabbath] published by the efforts of my two brothers-in-law, the distinguished rabbis Tsvi Hirsh and my teacher and rabbi, Rabbi Simon, son of Rabbi Isaac (may he live long) of Buczacz, grandson of the rabbi, the author [in Hebrew and Tevilat Tahara also in Ivre-Taytsh]

7. Kuntres Amarot Tehorot ('Purification Writings'), As above. Lemberg, "birkat tov lp"k" ('good blessing') [1879]. [different from the above, containing rare letters, including a copy of a letter to the holy congregation of Batishan a) about a breach of using pig fat in soap and candles... b) about the transport of wine c) about work on the intermediate days of festivals d) about porging] Copy of a well-written tale for eliciting donations, "God Overturned the City," about a fire that left many householders without possessions... and unfortunately completely burned down the synagogue" and a letter concerning the father-in-law of Rabbi Naftali Hertsil, son-in-law of Rabbi Tsvi Hirsh of Ziditshov. Lemberg, at the press of Isaac Meshulam Nik. [in Latin letters: AMUROZ THORES, Verl. S, Wurman, Druck des U.W. Salat et I.M. Nik Lemberg 1879], 16 leaves., octavo.

8. Kuntres Amarot Tehorot ('Purification Writings'). As above... brought to press by Samuel Mordecai Drezdner from the city of Satmar. Satu-Mare, 1930, 28 leaves., 16mo.

8a.* Orkhot Khayim ('Way of Life') on "Orkhot Khayim" in the Shulkhan Arukh...by me... Nakhman Kahana... corrected by Shalom Mordecai Hacohen. M. Siget, Moshe Blumenfeld, 1898, [3], 178, [2], 203 leaves., folio.

9. Eshel Avraham ('Abraham's Grove'). New notes on the laws of "Orkhot Khayim" in the Shulkhan Arukh by Rabbi Abraham David, president of the rabbinical court of the congregation of Buczacz, which I, Israel Aryeh Leib Wurmann collected, Parts I-2, Lemberg, P. Balaban Press, 1886, 1, 32, 12 leaves., folio.

10. Eshel Avraham ('Abraham's Grove'). New notes and opinions on the laws of the Shulkhan Arukh, "Orkhot Khayim," Part One, by Rabbi Abraham David of blessed memory, president of the rabbinical court of the congregation of Buczacz, which I collected and copied from among his many writings, I Israel Leib Aryeh Wurmann, son of the rabbi, my teacher, Rabbi Isaac, son of the son of the rabbi, the author... Lemberg (Pesil Balaban), 1893, 22, 8 leaves., folio, two parts bound in one.

11. Sefer Eshel Avraham ('Abraham's Grove'), second edition, on chapters of "Orkhot Khayim" of the Shulkhan Arukh... fruit of the thoughts of the learned sage, my teacher and rabbi, Rabbi Abraham David, president of the rabbinical court of the congregation of Buczacz... I have brought this work to press, I the little grandson Israel Arye Leib Wurmann, son of my teacher the rabbi, Rabbi Isaac of blessed memory, son of the son of the righteous rabbi... Buczacz, at the press of the eminent scholar, my teacher the rabbi, Rabbi Ze'ev Dratler, 1906, 192 pp., quarto [in Latin letters: Verlag des Herrn Israel Leib Wurmann Buczacz (Galizien) Volksdrukerei W. Dratler Buczacz]. At the beginning of the book courageous letters by Rabbi Shalom Mordecai Hacohen, president of the rabbinical court

of Brezan and formerly senior president of the rabbinical court of Buczacz and by Rabbi Meir Arak, president of the rabbinical court of Yazlavits and afterwards president of the rabbinical court of the holy congregation of Buczacz. On pages 3-4 an apology by the typesetter and, from page 183 forward, notes by the learned sage Rabbi Meir [Arik], president of the rabbinical court of Yazlavits.

12. Sefer Beer Mayim Khayim ('Well of Living Waters'). A composition on the Torah by the wise, learned, holy, pious and humble sage, my teacher and rabbi, Rabbi Khayim of blessed memory, author of Sefer Siduro Shel Shabat and Sefer Sha'ar Hatefila and who served as rabbi in several holy congregations and at the end of his life in the Holy Land (may it soon be rebuilt) and from there was brought this composition with its wonders. Zhitomir, 1861, Part 1, 1, 147 leaves.; Part 2, 1, 161 leaves., quarto. [Sefer Beer Mayim Khayim was first printed in Czernowicz and afterwards in Zhitomir and has since been reprinted often and also appended to Pentateuch commentaries.]

13. Sefer Birkat Avraham ('Abraham's Blessing'). These were the words uttered by the mouth of my teacher Rabbi Abraham David, president of the rabbinical court of the congregation of Buczacz, which were written down by one of his exceptional students Moshe David, son of my rabbi Rabbi Tsvi, of blessed memory, of the holy congregation of Kolomea and which include several items of Moshe's own, and the son should honor his father, which is what our teacher Rabbi Tsvi Veizelberg tried to do in printing this precious book. Kolomea, at the press of my teacher and rabbi, Rabbi Alter Teicher, 1887, 23 leaves., octavo.

14. Sefer Birkat David ('David's Blessing') on the Pentateuch by Rabbi Abraham David, president of the rabbinical court of the holy congregation of Buczacz, 1800, 184 leaves., quarto. [in Latin letters: Lemberg, Gedrukt bei Iihdas Rosanis, 1800.]

[On Genesis alone. At the end a commentary on the tractate Pesakhim. The name of the printer and the year are falsified. It seems to have been printed in 1705.]

15. Bat Yiftakh ('Yiftakh's Daughter') by Elkhanan Shitzer. A biblical play in four scenes. Radom, 1933, 1 p., octavo.

15a.* Gilui Da'at Al "Yoreh Deya". ('Opinion on "Yoreh Deya"') (from paragraph 61 to paragraph 69) by our teacher Rabbi Shalom Mordecai, president of the rabbinical court of Brezan. Satmar, at the press of V. Shvarts, 1820, [3], 2-11, [1] pp., quarto. Sefer Davar Be'ito ('A Word In Time') Second part of Sefer Divrey Khakhamim [the third book of the great composition Agadat Azav] on the Talmud [order Moed] from the distinguished rabbi, author of She'eyrit Yehuda, Lemberg, at the press of Ze'ev Wolf Salat and Jacob Meshulam Nik, 1887.

[in Latin letters: Verlag des Verfassers Wolf Pohorille Buczacz Lemberg 1887]. folio.

17. Sefer Divrey Avot ('Words of the Fathers') by Rabbi Abraham David, president of the rabbinical court of the congregation of Buczacz. An exegesis of the tractate Avot published by the effort of my two brothers-in-law, the eminent rabbis Rabbi Tsvi Hirsh and my teacher, Rabbi Simon, son of Rabbi Isaac (may he live long and happily) of Buczacz, grandson of the author. Lemberg, at the press of

Jacob Meshulam Nik, 1879, 40 pp,, octavo. [in Latin letters: DIWREI ABOT Verl. S, Wurman, druck des U.W. Salat et D.M. Nik Lemberg 1879].

18. Sefer Divrey Avot ('Words of the Fathers') As above. Lemberg, 1879, 48 pp, octavo. [at the end omissions in the Passover Haggada to fill the margins and a letter that the author sent in his youth to the learned Rabbi Zalman Margoliuth of Brody]

19. Sefer Divrey Avraham ('Words of Abraham') A commentary on Sefer Daat Kedoshim (from paragraph 40 to paragraph 60) by Rabbi Abraham David and appended at the end Kuntres Hasagot on the rules in writing names in divorce writs... by me Yekhezkl Frenkel of the saintly congregation of Husyatin. Przemeshl, at the press of R. Aaron Zupnik and R. Khayim Knaller and Hamershmit, 1886, 2, 42 leaves., folio. The name of the book, etc., is also given in Cyrillic letters.

20. Sefer Divrey Avraham ('Words of Abraham'). Part One, Section One, commentary on Sefer Da'at Kedoshim... on all the rules of ritual slaughtering and of the laws of tr"l by me Yekhezkl Frenkel Husyatin. Kolomea, at the press of Alter Teicher, 1894, 60, 1 leaves., quarto. [in Latin letters: DIWRE ABRAHAM Druck von M. Bilous in Kolomea].

21. Sefer Divrey David ('Words of David')... These are words on the order of prayer in Sefer Tefila by Rabbi Abraham David, president of the rabbinical court of Buczacz, the publisher Simon son of R. Isaac, grandson of the author. Kolomea, 1892, 40 leaves., octavo.

22. Sefer Divrey Khayim ('Words of Life') Part One by R. Khayim Yerukham, veteran student of the learned sage of Buczacz, son of Simon Meshulam Feivush of the holy congregation of Buczacz and of high lineage in the order of piety. Munkacs, at the press of Kohn and Fried, 1906, [36 leaves.], quarto. [At the end of the pamphlet new interpretations and selections which he heard from renown personages and first among them the learned holy rabbi of Buczacz, material not published earlier]

23.* Divrey Khakhamim ('Words of Wise Men') collected, assembled and composed by my teacher and rabbi, Rabbi Judah Leib, son of Rabbi Yekutiel Melamed and reader of the holy congregation of Buczacz...who arranged them according to the order of the Torah portions and the festivals and seasons [at the beginning Divrey Khakhamim and at the end corrections of traditions according to Sefer Or Torah]. Zolkiew, at the press of the Lawgivers, grandsons of Rabbi Uri Feivush, 1757, [36 leaves.], quarto.

23a.* Divrey Yitskhak ('Words of Isaac') [by R. Yitskhak Isaac Weiss. With notes by Rabbi Shalom Mordicai Hacohen], Munkacs, Aaron Dov Maizels, 1906, 36 leaves. octavo.

24. Sefer Da'at Kedoshim ('Wisdom of the Saints') the first part of the sacred volumes which Rabbi Abraham David, president of the rabbinical court of Buczacz (may his memory be blessed) left after him... to clarify all the laws of ritual slaughter and of tearing (by wild beast or bird of prey), besides all the rules necessary for teaching. I have arranged and corrected it, and have added the corrections of Giduley Hakodesh and Mikdash Me'at ('Crops of the Holy Temple' and 'The Synagogue')... Feivel Halevi, president of the rabbinical court of Bradshin and now senior president of the rabbinical court

of the holy congregation of Kolomea. Published by Abraham Weidenfeld of Stanislaw. Lwow, at the press of Abraham Nissan Zis, 1871. [in Latin letters: DAAS KEDAUSCHIM Lemberg 1871], 146, 2, 31 leaves., folio.

25. Da'at Kedoshim ('Wisdom of the Saints') by Rabbi Abraham David Wurmann on the laws of ritual slaughter and tearing, with the corrections Giduley Hakodesh and Mikdash Me'at ('Crops of the Holy Temple' and 'The Synagogue' by Rabbi Feivel Halevi, president of the rabbinical court of Bradshin... and on the laws of the Scroll of the Law, Lwow, 1880, 199 leaves., folio.

26. Da'at Kedoshim ('Wisdom of the Saints') on the laws of the Scroll of the Law which contain four works, the inner columns are taken from Sefer Bney Yona and surrounding them are the Da'at Kedoshim and the corrections Giduley Hakodesh and Mikdash Me'at composed by Uri Feivel Halevi, president of the rabbinical court of Bradshin, Lwow, 1896, 2, 58 leaves., folio.

[26] Da'at Kedoshim on the laws of phylacteries and containing three books:

Da'at Kedoshim and additions to it by Rabbi Abraham David, president of the rabbinical court of Buczacz,... Mikdash Me'at and Giduley Kodesh and after them Mikdash Me'at ('The Synagogue') to clarify differences in the laws... composed by Uri Feivel Halevi, president of the rabbinical court of the congregation of Bradshin, Lwow, 1897, 1, 42 leaves., folio.

[26] Da'at Kedoshim on the laws of the mezuzah. As above. Lwow, 1896, 1, 16 leaves., folio.

27. Da'at Kedoshim ('Wisdom of the Saints') On the salting of meat in fat and the laws of small things, the holy works Rabbi Abraham David (may his memory be blessed), president of the rabbinical court of the congregation of Buczacz, left behind him and added to necessary rules for teaching which Rabbi Feivel Halevi, president of the rabbinical court of Bradshin ordered, corrected and added corrections to Giduley Hakodesh and Mikdash Me'at. Lemberg (A. Salat), 1911. 4, 4 leaves., folio.

27a. Seder Da'at Kedoshim ('Wisdom of the Saints') Includes all the prayers of the year according to the Sefardic and Ashkenazic rites with the commentary Tehila leDavid by the kabbalist... Rabbi Abraham David (may his memory be eternally blessed), president of the rabbinical court of Buczacz and attached to it the book Noam Megadim ('The Loveliness of Blessings') on the laws of prayer by the learned pillar of teaching with several additions missing from the first editions, with keys by the learned M. Jacob, president of the rabbinical court of Lisa... and in order that nothing should be missing I added Sefer Iyun Tefila by the learned Rabbi M. Shamri, president of the rabbinical court of Harimlab (may his memory be blessed), with many additions which were erased from the first editions. Peyrush Maspik ('Ample Interpretation') on liturgical hymns for selikhot and hosannahs and to complete the work I printed Rashi's commentary on the tractate Avot corrected from the Mishna Ets haKhayim by Rabbi Khagiz. Also included here are "Tikun khatsot," "Hagada," Tefila zaka," "Perek shira," "Tikuney shabat," Shir haYakhid." All of these were collected by Rabbi Khayim Knaller of Przemeshl and published by M. Abraham Isaac Amkroyt, Przesheml 1892 at the press of Zupnik, Knaller and Hammershmit, 16, 236 leaves., quarto. [Derekh khayim hashalem in 1891 with a special title page 1, 51 leaves.]

27b.* Da'at Torah al Halakhot Shekhita ('Torah Views on the Laws of Ritual Slaughter') by Rabbi Shalom Mordecai Hacohen, Lemberg, Feliks Bendarski, 1891, 6-109 leaves., folio.

28. Sefer Drishat HaZe'ev (The Wolf's Enquiry') by R. Ze'ev Wolf Pohorile of the holy community of Buczacz... and this book includes the first edition of his Khomat Anokh... and the second edition of Khomat Anokh on the Prophets and Writings and Sefer Divrey Khakhamim on the Talmud and Sefer Erekh haShulkhan on the Shulkhan Arukh brought to press by Jacob Meshulam Nik, Lemberg, 1895, 24, 122 leaves., quarto. [in Latin letters: DRISCHAS HAZEW. Verlag des Verfassers Herrn Wolf Pohrile (sic – A.P.) in Buczacz Buchdrukerei des Ch. Rohatyn, Lemberg 1895].
[24 pages includes the title page and the approvals of the learned of the age, heading the list the learned Rabbi Tsvi Hirsh Orenstein of Lwow, followed by the learned sage Rabbi Yekutiel Judah Teitelbaum of Siget (uncle of the author's wife), the sage Rabbi Simon Sofer of Krakow, and the learned Rabbi Meshulam Issachar Halevi Ish Hurevits of Stanislaw, and also approvals from the learned elders of Tshortkov and Matanya, from the righteous Rabbi Joshua Hurvitz of Dzikow, and Rabbi Yekhiel Brumir, senior president of the rabbinical court of Buczacz and Rabbi Shmuel Issachar Shtark of Buczacz, a judge and righteous teacher, and from Rabbi Dembitser of Krakow and from other rabbis who later became famous rabbis, and also from figures in the Land of Israel.]

29.* Sefer Derekh Emuna ('Way of Faith') by Rabbi Ze'ev Wolf Pohorile. A section on the Talmudic tractate "Berakhot" ('Blessings') and the Mishna order "Zeraim" ('Seeds'), the first section of Sefer Divrey Khakhamim which is the third section of the great composition Agadat Azav She'eyrit Yehuda, Lemberg, 1887, 70 leaves., folio.

30. Sefer Darkhey Shalom ('Ways of Peace') Rules of the Talmud and of the rabbinical arbiters including several hundred rules on new matters which are not mentioned in books of rules and an appendix by the publisher, his history and behavior entitled Ohel Shem. R. Shalom Mordecai Hacohen composed all this. Published by Rabbi Tsvi Hacohen Shvedron, son of the author, Bilgoray, at the press of the Weinberg Brothers, 1929, 74, 2 leaves., octavo.

31. Hagada shel Pesakh ('Passover Haggada') with the commentary "Yad Rama" by Rabbi Abraham David, president of the rabbinical court of Buczacz, Kolomea, 1897, 31 leaves., octavo.

31a.* Hagahot Maharsham al HaShas ('Talmudic Corrections of the Maharsham' [= Shalom Mordecai Shvedron]), Satu-Mare, M.L. Hirsh Printers, 1932, [4], 86 leaves, quarto.

32. Sefer Zekharye Hameyvin ('The Understanding Zacharia') Foundations of the wisdom of theology and the wisdom of the true kabbala for beginners divided into several chapters which retain the order of that which comes earlier and that which follows and contain many passages from our sages... the words of Rabbi Eliezer Hakalir... compiled by Rabbi Zekharye Mendel, son of the illustrious rabbi Leib of Buczacz and known in our region as Rabbi Mendel Podeyts, author of Sefer Menorat Zekharye and Sefer Zekharye Meshulam. Frankfurt-on-the-Oder, Printing House of the Widow of Prof. Dr. Grila, 1, 33 leaves., octavo.

33. Sefer Zekharye Meshulam ('Genuine Zacharia') A wonderful composition with halakhic depth and

with passages composed by Rabbi Zekharye Mendel of the holy congregation of Buczacz. Frankfurt-on-the-Oder, 1779, 72 leaves., folio.
[see the entry Menorat Zekharye] And because this book is a completion of the book Menorat Zekharye it is called Zekharye Meshulam because it is a "hashlama" ('completion') and because Zekharye is Meshulam... "and I will make my appeal to all who show interest in my book and listen to my words that they remember my name and everyone in Israel is obliged, as I write in my pleasant book Menorat Zekharye, to reform the soul of his fellow."

34. Khomat An"kh, Part Two ('Wall of the Law') [An"kh=Oraysa neviey kesuvey], Part Two. Commentaries on Prophets and Writings... according to grammar and rhetoric. Investigation of places in the Holy Land mentioned in Prophets and Writings. The time the prophets in Judah and Israel prophesied and the kings of Judah and Israel ruled and the history of the other peoples about whom the prophets prophesied... and exegesis of Rashi's commentary... by the illustrious [Rabbi Ze'ev Wolf Pohorile] in his books Sefer She'eyrit Yehuda on the Pentateuch and Sefer Divrey Khakhamim on the Talmud. Brought to press by Jacob Meshulam Nik. Lemberg 1889, 2, 198 leaves. [in Latin letters: CHOMATH ANOCH. Eigentum un Verlag vom Verfasser Wolf Pohorile in Buczacz Druck des Jacob Ehrenpreis Lemberg 1889]. [In the "Song of Deborah" the author copies from his book Tomar Dvora a song which he sang for rhetorical effect (as in a play), and he recalls his unpublished grammatical work Sefat Emet.]

35. Sefer Khosen Rav ('Great Riches') The third part of Sefer Divrey Khakhamim [the third part of the great composition Igeret Azav] on the Talmud... innovations on "Yebamot," "Ketubot," "Nedarim," "Nazir," "Soteh," "Gittin," "Kedushin" [by Rabbi Ze'ev Wolf Pohorile]. Lemberg, 1889, 30 leaves., folio.

36. Sefer Tal Orot ('Fresh Light') Corrections, notes and explanations on the Babylonian and Jerusalem Talmud by Rabbi Meir Arik, president of the rabbinical court of the congregation of Buczacz, son of Rabbi Aaron Judah, published by his pupil R. Yekhiel Mikhal Preminger, Vienna, "Union" Press of the Apel Brothers, 1921, 60, 48 leaves., folio.

36a.* Sefer Yagdil Tora ('Make Teaching Great') A memorial to Judah. New interpretations of Talmudic questions and certain responsa by Rabbi Judah Leibush Monk and accompanied at the end by responsa from Rabbi Maharsham [= Shalom Mordecai Shvedron], president of the rabbinical court of Berzan. Warsaw, Y. M. Alter Printers, 1929. [3], [5]-195 leaves., folio. On the second title page: Bilgoray, Weinberg Brothers Press, 1929, 78 leaves., octavo.

37. Sefer Yalkut David ('David's Notebook') A commentary on a number of Torah essays by Rabbi David Khalfan Halevi of the city of Buczacz. Przemeshl, 1927, 78 leaves., octavo. [At the beginning of the book the author's introduction on his experiences during the war and at the end two pages of rhymes which carry the meaning that at the time of the weekly Torah portion "Jethro," people donated to the poor of the Talmud Torah, and likewise at the weekly Torah portion "ve'etkhanen." ('and I shall entreat')]

38. Yikarey Deoraysa ('Read from the Biblical Source') Aggadic innovations and words of self-mas-

tery given publicly on the occasion of presenting a Scroll of the Law to a synagogue... also words of aggada and accompanying them new readings on "Orekh Khayim," "Mekor Khayim," the laws of Passover. Sketch and ornament on inside cover. [Shmuel Issachar Shtark teacher and dayan ('religious judge') here in the holy congregation of Buczacz.] Lemberg, Printed by Samuel David Roth, 1897, 1, 31 leaves., quarto. [in Latin letters: JIKUREI DEORAJSE, Verlag von Rabbiner Samuel Stark in Buczacz, Druck von Ch. Rohatyn in Lemberg 1897]

39. HaYarden. Literary and Scientific Monthly. ed, Dr. Eliezer Rokeach. vol. 1, no. 4 (Ab). Buczacz. Printed by V. Dratler, 1906. 72 pp., octavo. [No more were issued. The first three numbers were published by Eliezer Rokeach, Isaac Fernhof, Abraham Lebenshart, Stanislav Shevet – Ayar 1906. Printed by A. Salat]

40. Sefer Kesef Mezukak ('Refined Silver') which I refined... the Ramban [= Rabbi Moses ben Nakhman] on the Pentateuch... Abraham Liblein. Lemberg, Printed by Samuel David Roth, 1898, 4, 36 leaves. [in Latin letters: KESEF MESYKOK, Verlag von Abraham Lieblein in Buczacz, Buchdruckerei Chaim Rohatyn Lemberg 1897]
[Approvals of the rabbis Rabbi Feivel Halevi, president of the rabbinical court of Bradshin, author of Sefer Giduley Hakodesh and Rabbi Meir Arik, president of the rabbinical court of Yazlavits, and Rabbi Samuel Issachar Shtark, a righteous teacher of Buczacz. There is also an introduction by the author and notes by the illustrious Rabbi Meir, president of the rabbinical court of Yazlavits,] The aim of the book is to correct several errors in the commentary of the Ramban due to copyist or printer, the interpretation of two passages appearing as though of one, the reader failing to understand.

41.* Likutey Tora ('Torah Extracts') from Sefer Tekhelet Mordecai... by our teacher Rabbi Shalom Mordecai Hacohen. Satu-Mare, Meyer Leib Hirsh Printers, 1933, 16 [should be 24] leaves., octavo.

41a.* Magen Avot ('Shield of the Fathers') [by Rabbi Mordecai Banet and at the front a signature and notes by Shalom Mordecai Hacohen...] Piatrkov, A. Reisengarten, 1903, 6, 103 pp., folio. At the beginning of the book an introduction by the translator and at the end notes on terminology.

42. [3 books] Makhaze Avraham ('The Vision of Abraham') on the Pentateuch, Khoze David ('David the Seer') on the Prophets and Writings, and Khazon leMoed ('Vision of the Festivals') pleasant sayings on the festivals of God published by my two sons-in-law, Rabbi Tsvi Hirsh and my teacher Rabbi Simon, son of Rabbi Isaac of Buczacz. [Lemberg] birkat ledavid lepak [= 1876] 44, 2 leaves., quarto. [in Latin letters: MACHZE ABRAHAM Eigentum u. verl. des Simon Wahrmann, Druck von A, Waydomicz vormals M.F. Poremba in Lemberg 1876.]
[The introduction by the author's grandson has a little on the history of the senior president of the rabbinical court, may his memory be blessed.]

43. Miley deKhasiduta ('Hasidic Words') by Rabbi Abraham David Wurmann. Corrections of Sefer Khasidim. Published by Simon, son of Rabbi Isaac, grandson of the author. Kolomea, 1890, 40 leaves., octavo.

44. Sefer Miley deKhasiduta ('Hasidic Words') from our Rabbi Judah the Hasid (of blessed memory)

with commentary by the learned, holy teacher Rabbi Abraham David, president of the rabbinical court of Buczacz, reprinted with many additions from the author's manuscript and accompanying it corrections by the Maharsham [Rabbi Shalom Mordecai Shvedron], president of the rabbinical court of Brezan and brought to press by Menakhem Mani Kroper of the congregation of Khust. M. Siget, at the press of R. Abraham Kaufman and Sons, 1910, 22, 2 leaves., octavo.

45. Sefer Milkhamot Blokh ('The Blokh Wars') which I fought with utterances from my mouth in the house of the "Blokh Committee" and in assemblies of the communities of Israel, in the great synagogue of our city Buczacz, I the young Judah Halevi Leisner, preacher, native of Buznob and now living in Buczacz, in the year "kavod yosef shmuel blokh yikhye" [1891], Lemberg, 1891, 48 pp., 16mo.

46. Sefer Menorat Zekharye (Zacharia's Candelabrum') A marvelous composition of halakhic depth and with new readings which Rabbi Zacharia Mendel of the holy congregation of Buczacz composed. He was known in this country as Mendel Podheyts. He was the son of the famous learned sage Rabbi Aryeh Leib of Buczacz who was leader of the country in and around the region of Lwow and who was popularly known as Rabbi Leybush, leader of the country. Frankfurt-on-the-Oder, 1776, 3, 84 leaves., folio. [The author was the father-in-law of the brilliant author of Peney Yehoshua and in the beginning of his book he talks about his relationship to the Maharshal {=Rabbi Solomon Luria}, the Rama {=Rabbi Moshe Isserlish}, the Maharam {=Rabbi Meir} of Padua, and other great sages of Israel.]

47. Sefer Minkhat Oni ('Gift of Affliction') Innovations on Khoshen Mishpat [= fourth part of the Shulkhan Arukh] by Rabbi Shmuel Issachar Shtark, teacher and dayan ['religious judge'] in the city of Buczacz. Brought to press by Jacob Meshulam Nik. Lemberg, Lemberg, 1897, 2, 90 leaves., octavo.

48. Sefer Minkhat Kanaut ('Gift of Zeal') New interpretations on the tractate Soteh and corrections on "Orekh Khayim" of the Shulkhan Arukh which will be called Minkhat Pitim ('Gift of Morsels'), which I the young Meir Arik, president of the rabbinical court of Yazlavits, son of our teacher Rabbi Aaron Judah, composed with God's help. Lemberg, Khayim Rohatin Printer, 1894, 2, 70 leaves., octavo.

49.* Mekor Khesed ('Source of Grace') The testament of Rabbi Judah the Hasid; hasidic words, the testament of Rabbi Abraham David Wurmann with corrections by Rabbi Shalom Mordecai of Brezan and notes by Rabbi Margoliuth. Lwow, 1923, 43 pp., octavo.

50 Sefer Mekor Khesed ('Source of Grace') Testament of Rabbi Judah the Hasid with hasidic words by the learned holy Rabbi Abraham David of Buczacz, corrections from the learned Rabbi Shalom Mordecai Hacohen of Brezan and corrections and notes appended to these by me, Reuben Margoliuth. Second edition with additions, Lwow, 1928, 21, 2 leaves., octavo.

Sefer Mishmeret haKodesh ('Sacred Watch') Written with truth and honesty to protect the way by our teacher and rabbi, Rabbi Abraham David... In the respected book Da'at kedoshim published in the year 1871, there were many misprints both in the work proper and in the surrounding texts Giduley Hakodesh and Mikdash Me'at. Our teacher Rabbi Feivel Halevi, president of the rabbinical court of Bradshin, has now come to correct the printing errors and to fill in shortcomings and also to add writings from his learned rabbi who has corrected Giduley Hakodesh, the omissions in Da'at Kedoshim and has added Kuntres teshuvot...Lemberg, 1879, 1, 49 leaves, folio.

51a.* Mishpat Shalom ('Shalom's Judgement') on "Khosen Mishpat" in the Shulkhan Arukh... by our teacher Rabbi Shalom Mordecai Hacohen.Lemberg, Y. M. Shtand, 1871, 119 + 8, 1 leaves., folio.

51b. – Warsaw: P. Rozen; Piatrkov, Sh. Belkhatovski Printers, 1902, [1], 100, 7-23 leaves., folio.

Sefer Hamitnagdim ('The Misnagdim') by Isaac Fernhof. Stories. "Sifrey Nefesh" ('Spiritual Books') Israel Cohen brought this book to press and wrote the introduction. Tel Aviv, Hebrew Writers' Association and "Dvir" Publishers, 1952, 216 leaves., octavo. [a picture of the author, his signature and his gravestone]

[Table of contents, Israel Cohen, Isaac Fernhof, William Fernhof, memories of my father's house. Stories of misnagdim, 10. Other stories, 6. Lines and drawings 3. Essays 3. Appendices, two letters. Greetings.]

52a.* Nakhlat Yaakov ('Jacob's Legacy') The first part contains commentaries on the Pentateuch and many legends and also eulogies which our teacher Rabbi Jacob of Lisa gave. The second part contains halakhic interpretations on various questions and some responsa, and also replies from his grandson, Rabbi Abraham Teumim. Breslau, 1849, 6+ 40 + 58 leaves., folio.

52b* Nakhlat Yaakov ('Jacob's Legacy') Commentaries on the Pentateuch by our teacher Rabbi Jacob of Lisa. Lemberg, Uri Ze'ev Wolf Salat Printers, 1887, 10 + 78 leaves., octavo. With a long introduction by his grandson Rabbi Abraham Teumim. This book was printed for the first time in Breslau in 1849 and now for the second time without the responsa and interpretations of his grandson.

53. Nishmat Khayim ('Breath of Life') Eulogy and condolences on the death of the learned and pious Rabbi Abraham David, containing many words of the deceased rabbi. [The author did not seek permission from the great hasidic rabbis and tsadikim or from the relatives of the deceased, for he did not wish it to be known who the author was. He did not write the book for his own honor but to publish the words which he had heard from the deceased president of the rabbinical court.] [Zolkiew, 1841], 25 leaves., octavo.

54. Sefer Siduro shel Shabat ('Sabbath Prayer Book') composed by the great and learned Rabbi Khayim, who was president of the rabbinical court of the holy congregation of Mohilev and president of rabbinical courts in important congregations in the regions of Volkhay, Batshan, Kishenev, Czernowicz and Bukovina, and at the end of his life he traveled to the Holy Land. Brought to press by our wise and learned teacher Rabbi Mikhal Wolf. Lemberg, 1860, Part One 3, 50 leaves., Part Two 32 leaves., octavo.

55. Sefer Siduro shel Shabat ('Sabbath Prayer Book'). As above. Part One 4, 60 leaves., Part Two 40 leaves., [n.p.], [n.d.].

56.Sefer Shaashuim ('Book of Delights') Scenes, pictures, stories, poems, notes and exegeses by various writers, edited by Itsi Fernhof. Numbers 1-6, Krakow-Drohobycz, 1896-1898, 5 issues, 16mo.

[56] Sefer Shaashuim ('Book of Delights') Second group. scenes, pictures, stories, poems, and essays by various writers, edited by Isaac Fernhof. 1-2 Drohobycz, 1899, 1 issue, (56 pp.), octavo.

57. Sefer Ezer Mekudash ('Sanctified Help') On the laws of tractate "Gittin" ('Divorce') and the names of men and women... with Giduley Hakodesh and Mikdash Me'at... with commentary from Da'at Kedoshim to understand halakhic decisions. The learned Rabbi Shraga Feivel Halevi, president of the rabbinical court of Bradshin, pupil of our great and learned rabbi, occasionally adds some judgement of his own.
Bilgoray, at the press of Neta Kronenberg, 1923, 58 leaves., folio. The dust jacket was drawn by the painter Shtsherbetka. [in Latin letters: SEFER EZER MEKUDOSZ. St. Chowanies Drukarnia I Litogr. Stanislawow.]

58.* Hapalit miYerusholaim ('The Fugitive from Jerusalem') A story of the destruction of Jerusalem by Rabbi L. Philipsohn, translated from German by A. Ben-Rashal [R. Aryeh Leib Pohorile's son R. Samuel]. Przemyshl, 1888, 11 leaves., octavo.

58a.* Sefer Paaman [sic -- A.P.] Zahav ('Golden Bell') Interpretation and correction of Sefer Simla Khadasha ('New Garment'), rules regarding torn flesh (of beasts and birds) by our teacher Rabbi Eliezer Dikhter and several responsa by our teacher Rabbi Shalom Mordecai [Shvedron]. Bilgoray, Y. Kh. Weinberg Press, 1933, [2], 6, 327 pp., quarto.

59.* Tsiyun leNefesh haR. Shmuel Pohoriles ('Monument to Samuel Pohorile'). Poem and Lamentation by Itsi Fernhof. Drohobycz, 1884, 54 pp., octavo.

60. Kuntres Tr"l with rules by our teacher Rabbi Abraham David, president of the rabbinical court of Buczacz, which were already published in Sefer Da'at Kedoshim and have now been published with the commentaries of Divrey Avraham by me, the humble Yekhezkl Frenkel... Husyatin. Kolomea, in the press of Alter Teicher, 1883, 4, 48 leaves., quarto.

60.a* Sefer Kitsur Shulkhan Arukh ('Concise Shulkhan Arukh'), On the laws of the Sabbath (by Solomon Gantsfried) and to this composition is attached a pamphlet with the name Ahavat Shalom... many new interpretations of the Sabbath... interpreted by Rabbi Shalom Mordecai... Warsaw, Y.Ts. Lev, 1900, [1], 312 pp., octavo.

61. Sefer She'eylot uTeshuvot Imrey Yosher ('Responsa Imrey Yosher'], Part One by Rabbi Meir Arik, president of the rabbinical court of Yazlavits. Munkacs, press of Samuel Zanvil Kahana and his son-in-law Ozer Hacohen Fried, 1913, 4, 106 leaves, folio.

[61] Sefer She'eylot uTeshuvot Imrey Yosher ('Responsa Imrey Yosher')
Part Two by Rabbi Meir Arik, formerly president of the rabbinical courts of Yazlevits and Buczacz and now president of the rabbinical court of Tarnow, published by his pupil, his grandson Rabbi Kalonymus Kelman Arak and our teacher Rabbi Yekhiel Mikhal Preminger. Krakow, press of M. Lenkovitsh,

1925, 4, 124 pp.

62. She'eylot uTeshuvot Zikhron Moyshe (Responsa Zikhron Moshe ['In Memory of Moses']) On "Orekh Khayim" and "Yoreh Deya" by Rabbi Moshe Brumer (of blessed memory), former president of the rabbinical court of Buznob, with corrections by the author's son, our teacher Rabbi Yekhiel Mikhal Brumer, president of the rabbinical court of Buczacz. And at the end of the book some of the interpretations of the author's son, Rabbi Nahum Brumer, of blessed memory, who was gathered to his rest in his youth and who left behind him acute Torah interpretations named by name. Corrections Bney Moshe on the "Orekh Khayim." Published by the elder son, Rabbi Jacob Brumer. Husiatyn, in the press of P. Kvalek, 1906, 6, 104 leaves., folio.

63. Sefer Khesed LeAvraham ('Abraham's Goodness') Responsa on four parts of the Shulkhan Arukh by Rabbi Abraham Teumim, former president of the rabbinical court of Buczacz. Lemberg, press of Uri Ze'ev Wolf Salat, 1898, 1, 131, 73 leaves. folio.

64. Sefer Khesed Avraham ('Abraham's Goodness') Second edition of responsa on four parts of the Shulkhan Arukh and wonderful interpretations of Maimonides on the laws of the paschal sacrifice and the laws of worship on the Day of Atonement, the first part of "Orekh Khayim" and "Yore Deya" by Rabbi Abraham Teumim, president of the rabbinical courts of the congregations of Buczacz and Kamenets-Podolsk. When he was sixteen years old, he already won the crown of Torah in the holy congregation of Zbarov, from where his name spread through the world for his responsa attached to the Sefer Nakhlat Yaakov by his mother's father, the learned Rabbi Jacob of Lisa...Lemberg, 1898, 1, 42, 2 leaves., folio.

[64] Sefer Khesed Avraham ('Abraham's Goodness') second edition as above. Part Two, "Even Haezer" and "Khoshen Mishpat" and interpretations of Maimonides on the laws of paschal sacrifice and worship on the Day of Atonement. Lemberg, 1898, 1, 62 pp,, folio.

65. She'eylot uTeshuvot Maharsham ('Responsa of Maharsham') by Rabbi Shalom Mordecai Hacohen, formerly president of the rabbinical courts of Potk, Yazlavits and Buczacz and now president of the rabbinical court of Brezan in Galicia. One part of nine editions... Published by Feivel Rozin. Warsaw, at the press of Shuldberg and Partners, "ki eyn makhsor leyirav" ('there is no lack of his faithful') [= 1893], 40, 218 pp., folio. Following the Introduction there is an apology by the editor for not citing the names of the authors of the responsa according to their stature and reputation.

[65] [She'eylot uTeshuvot Maharsham ('Responsa of Maharsham') by Rabbi Shalom Mordecai Hacohen, Part Two – Piotrkow, at the press of R. Abraham Roysengarten, 1904, 242 pp., folio. [at the end keys and notes and corrections to his composition Gilui Da'at]

66. Sefer Neta Shaashuim ('Plantation of Pleasures'). Responsa on the four parts of the Shulkan Arukh by Rabbi Tsvi Hirsh, president of the rabbinical court of Buczacz.
Brought to press by the author's son, Rabbi Yekhiel Ikhl. Zolkiew, press of Meyer Ze'ev Meyer Hofer, 1829, 84 leaves., folio. [an introduction by the author's son, strictures by the prize student of Rabbi Abraham David, president of the rabbinical court of the holy congregation of Buczacz, 96 chapters in

the book including responsa to most of the sages of the age] "I named this book Neta Shaashuim for there arises from this book the name and life of Tsvi Hirsh son of Jacob ...." : Introduction to the book by his son Rabbi Yekhiel Ikhl, 1829.

67. Sefer She'eylot uTeshuvot Rabeynu Meshulam Igra by Rabbi Meshulam Igra, president of the rabbinical courts of the congregation of Tismenits and of the holy congregation of Pressburg, responsa on "Orekh Khayim" and "Even Haezer." Warsaw, 1885, 6, 132 pp., folio.

[67]. Sefer She'eylot uTeshuvot Rabeynu Meshulam Igra by Rabbi Meshulam Igra. Responsa on "Yoreh Deya" and "Khoshen Mishpat." Warsaw, 1885, 72, 38 pp., folio.

68. Sefer Sha'ar HaTefila ('Gateway of Prayer') by Rabbi Khayim, president of the rabbinical court of the holy congregation of Mohilev and of several congregations in the regions of Volkhay, Batshan, Kishenev, Czernowicz and Bukovina, and at the end of his life he traveled to the Holy Land, and from there sent this composition to be printed and circulated. Author of Sefer Siduro Shel Shabat and Sefer Beer Mayim Khayim on the Pentateuch. Mohilev "lehitpallel beasara lep"k [= 1817], 2, 115 leaves., octavo. [appended is a responsum by the author of Noda BeYehuda who challenged reciting the declaration of unity of God] 10 leaves.

69. Sefer Sha'ar HaTefila ('Gateway of Prayer') by Rabbi Khayim who was president of the rabbinical courts of Mohilev and Czernowitz and at the end of his life went to the Holy Land from where he sent this composition. 1, 77 leaves. [year of printing lacking], octavo. [appended at the beginning of the book a responsum on the matter of declaring the unity of God].

70. Sefer Sha'ar HaTefila ('Gateway of Prayer'). As above. Lemberg, 1858, 60 leaves. [appended at the beginning of the book a responsum on the matter of declaring the unity of God].

71.* Tehila leDavid ('Psalm to David') An interpretation of Psalms by Rabbi Abraham David Wurmann. Lwow, 1872, 200 leaves., octavo.

72. Sefer Toldot haRab"d in which will be told the history of the great man among giants, a holy man of God, sage of sages and among the first of the pious, Rabbi Abraham David, president of the rabbinical court of Buczacz, famous in Judah and Israel. Composed by me, Eliyahu Tsvi Shmerlir of Bradtshin. Lemberg, 1890, 72 pp., 16mo. [The author is the son of the daughter of Rabbi Feivel Halevi Shrayer, president of the rabbinical court of the holy congregation of Bradtshin] who studied for three years under our teacher Rabbi Abraham David and learned his whole life history from him. And as regards matters in question, I received letters from his grandsons, such as our teacher, Rabbi Isaac Wurmann, and his outstanding son, Rabbi Israel Leib Wurmann. From the outset I made all this known so that no one could criticize me for any untruth in my composition.

73. Sefer Teyvat Gam"a. Abbreviation for Gemara, Midrash, Agada. A composition on ethical matters. Exegeses, research and judgements written by our teacher Rabbi Joseph Teumim, famous for his writings. I have clarified his sayings, I, Shayish [Samuel Issachar Shtark, teacher and dayan here in the holy congregation of Buczacz.

Drohobycz, 1899, 2, 60 leaves, quarto.

73a.* Tikhlat Mordekhai ('Mordecai's Purpose') on the Pentateuch by our teacher Rabbi Shalom Mordecai Hacohen of Brezan. M. Siget, press of Y. Royzenthal, 1913, [7], 53, 152, 2, [1] leaves, quarto.

74.* Tefila leDavid ('David's Prayer') On prayers and kinds of prayer .. which our teacher Rabbi Abraham David, president of the rabbinical court of Buczacz left after him. This book is published now for its importance. I the young Simon, son of Rabbi Isaac, grandson of the author, printed it. Kolomea, in the press of Alter Teicher, "tfl"h ldv"d gdo"l ma"d lp"k" [= 1887].

75.* Tefila leDavid ('David's Prayer') by Rabbi Abraham David Wurmann. On prayers and kinds of prayer. Lwow, 1876; second printing, Lwow, 1886, quarto.

Finally I mention a book whose author was not a son of Buczacz, but the book was printed in Buczacz and I am the one who proofread it. The book is one of the three Hebrew books printed in Buczacz. Here briefly is the book's title page:

Pardes haMelekh ('The King's Orchard') the ruler of the world who planted a pine tree... in Eden, Pentateuch, Prophets, Writings, and the legends of the Talmud, midrashim read literally, metaphorically, exegetically and esoterically. This dear man, one of the righteous of old, a wondrous man, an expert in Torah and its mysteries, his honor, the eminent Rabbi Pinkhas B"kher David, who is popularly known as Rabbi Pinkhasl Sosish, after his mother. He studied under the man of spirit, our teacher, our rabbi, the sage of Nadburna, author of Tsemakh Daled leTsvi.
From the inhabitants of the illustrious city of Stanislaw.

Arranged, edited and annotated by young Benjamin ben-Israel who is known as Shmerler among the residents of Stanislaw.

May its light shine over the world through his valiant granddaughter of blessed memory, Yota, wife of Rabbi Moshe Kazvin (May his light shine), of Stanislaw.

The heavens have given me the opportunity to bring these new interpretations to print, to present his writings. These are some of the works of the great man who achieved much. Regard these writings and you will have pleasure. From the Hagir family known as the Berger family, the righteous sage, our teacher and rabbi, Rabbi Israel (May he live long), president of rabbinical courts in many holy congregations, 1907.
[in Latin letters: PARDAS HAMELECH Volksdrukerei W. Dratler Buczacz 1907.]
[on the back of the title page: At the press of Ze'ev Dratler, Buczacz, 1907/8, 6, 187 leaves, octavo.]

S. Y. Agnon

[Page 32]

Buczacz In Old Books
Translated by Adam Prager

We held a session as a rabbinical court with three judges and we were as one. We declared a ban in the synagogue, proclaiming that whosoever knew or heard of an engagement [kidushin] of the aforesaid Rakhel Bat Khayim should come and inform us and if he did not he would bear the sin for not doing so. And we sent the sexton from house to house to inquire if anyone had heard of such an engagement, since a ban had been proclaimed in the synagogue. But no one came forward to make a declaration, neither man nor woman, married or unmarried, came to give evidence. And we wrote and signed that here in the holy congregation of Biczacz, this day Wednesday the second day of Sivan 1572, we are witnesses that what was done was done. Yitskhak, son of Aharon David (of blessed memory); and head of the congregation [? ve-rak], the cantor of Biczacz Avraham son of Barukh (of blessed memory); Perets, the son of the reverend [khaver] Shlomo HaLevi (of blessed memory) Luri"a. The witnesses signed the aforementioned document before me with their own hand and I supervised the signing in the proper manner. Yuda [either Yehuda spelled to avoid tetragrammaton or influence of Yiddish Yude] Bar Binyamin z"l. Copied letter for letter in the body of the document.

(*Responsa* of Rash"l R' Shlomo Luria, Responsum 101. S. Y. Agnon told me that Avraham Khayim Freiman (May God avenge his blood) brought this source to his attention. Ed.)

*

"The holy Gaon R' Avraham David, head of the rabbinical court of the sacred congregation of Buczacz wanted badly to see a copy of *Sefer Khemdat Yamim* [authorship unknown; see Yaari]. He heard that a householder in the town owned one. He sent someone to ask to borrow it. When the book was brought to him, he was engrossed in study and his table was full of books so that there was no clear space on which to set it down. He would not place the book on the books he was studying from and stood up in order to lay it on his bench; however, he remained standing by the bench and did not sit down until he finished looking through *Sefer Khemdat Yamim*.

(from *Book, Author and Story*, 2nd ed., section 14, cited in Avraham Yaari, *Taalumat Sefer*, Jerusalem, 1954.

*

Your name will be remembered with love, my dear and exalted Gedalia, son of the holy Rabbi Avraham (May the Lord watch over him and restore him). Behold, most esteemed one, in the matter of the engagement [kidushin] report concerning the young woman Blume, your daughter (may she live). I looked into the matter in the rabbinical court of the sacred congregation of Buczacz and found that the report was baseless, since both the young man and the young woman deny there was an engagement [kidushin]. In every such situation everyone agrees that the report is meaningless. Nothing is clear except a vague report which is insignificant and we have no anxieties about an engagement.
(From the appeal of Binyomin to R' Binyomin Aharon (Solnik), head of the rabbinical court of the sacred congregation of

Podheyts, Mits, 1779, Responsum 88) [Forwarded from A. Y. Agnon]

*

To Our Master, Rabbi of all Israel, Delight of Our Era, Joy of Our Strength, Glory of Our Generation, Holy Seed Whom the House of Israel Glories In and Depends Upon, Servant of God, Holy Oracle, Most Holy Teacher, May his light shine. We needed an additional ritual slaughterer [shokhet] here in our congregation and there was a candidate for the post, A., in our area. The distinguished late head of the rabbinical court of Buczacz certified his qualifications. Our own illustrious rabbi thought to appoint him, for he had seen him use his knife and saw how swift he was both in slaughtering and in inspecting. But since the veteran learned Shimshon (May his light shine), son of the righteous rabbi of blessed memory of the holy congregation of Zabriz, intervened, his position was weakened. He then appealed to the local holy rabbi even though the presumption of his qualifications had not been invalidated according to our religion.

(Yosef Perl, *Megale Tmirin*, chapter 105. [This is an anti-hasidic satire.]

*

"This is the letter regarding his views about the Baal Shem Tov that Rabbi Rapoport wrote to his relatives in Buczacz. The letter lacks a date and at the head appears this addition by the misnaged Yisrael Leybl:

A letter from the honorable rabbi, gaon, illustrious paragon of his generation, and from his son, the great R' Shmuel Katz.

I hear that you intend to turn to the idolatrous physician that calls himself the Baal Shem. Never, never! He is awful and there is nothing to him. You would be throwing your money into the trash can. It is impossible to put on paper the extent of his deceits, for he does no good, but only evil. Thus I advise you to turn from this path and God will be with you and will send you a complete cure if you will be innocent and do not turn to this idolatrous physician. Enough said, and may they not multiply in Israel.

Khayim Kohen Rapoport

Leybl was probably worried that people might question the authenticity of the letter and so added this remark:

We felt it necessary to state that the above letter was copied from the original, which is in the possession of one of our relatives in Buczacz. We still have relatives there from this important family. And we are completely confident of this great man, and if any evildoer so much as questions the authenticity of this letter and its writer, then he would show them the original letter and they would be convinced. "When I first started writing this book in the sacred community of Buczacz situated in the district of Galicia, I was filled with great passion and enthusiasm and thus wrote quickly and intensively day and night. I would stay awake into the night until my eyes were too week to continue and could not see anymore. Eventually I became ill and my eyes ailed me greatly forcing me to spend all winter with treatments as all the citizens of Buczacz know."

(*Sefer HaBrit* by R' Pinkhas Eliyahu of Vilna. Brin 1797. With a forward of one page.)

(cited in Prof. M. Balaban's *History of the Frankist Movement*, p. 308)

[Page 33]

A Letter to Agnon
Translated by Adam Prager
Written by Asher Barash, of blessed memory, and published in HaAretz, celebrating Agnon's 50th birthday

You have, thank God, reached your jubilee year [age 50] sound in both mind and body, and fortunate in having so many admirers who are celebrating this day in honor of you and of all the spiritual wealth you have bestowed upon them. I would like to speak briefly of the bounty I have witnessed from the day I first heard of you until this time. I offer you these words as a portrait of sorts, given to you on your birthday by the painter himself. Please do not pay too much attention to superficial facial defects, for painters delve into the soul of their subject.

I first heard of you about 32 years ago as S. Y. Czaczkes, a young man of Buczacz, a writer and poet in two tongues who published frequently in *HaMitspe* of Krakow, in the *Togblat* of Lvov, and in various other Galician periodicals. The poems were written in a popular Hebrew in the Ashkenazic poetical style of Hebrew poems in the Letteris Galician tradition. This verse was not particularly exact as regards meter and rhyme, yet it sounded pleasant and the content was moving. The poems dealt with Jewish traditions, reminding one of folk ballads. The stories were for the most part written in Yiddish. These were short tales in the style of Perets, abounding with tenderness and humor, with limited dialog, the author's voice dominating the story, and tending to a story-within-a-story structure (which you developed later on a wider scale in *The Bridal Canopy*).

We were young readers and writers who wrote in secret in the Jewish towns; we saw you as a small rising star in the skies of our land. We were sheltered in the country of the Emperor [Austria-Hungary], warm and comfortable in our respectable poverty. And if our fellow Jews in Galicia complained of hardships and deprivation, this was minor compared to what resounded from the lands of malicious rule (Russia and Romania). And Zionist aspirations in Galicia were nothing but a means of pleasing the great leaders, the famous heroes whose love for Israel burned in their hearts and mouths, especially after the death of the truly admired leader, Dr. Herzl of blessed memory. We did not expect truly great literary figures to emerge in Galicia, for in years past Galicia had none. The opposite was true of our brothers beyond the border, the forceful Jews of Russia, whose misfortunes were as great as their formidable achievements.

The arrival of a few refugees from Russia who knew Hebrew was like a rude awakening for us. Shaken out of our stupor, we realized how narrow-minded we were and decided that something had to be done concerning our spiritual and intellectual enrichment. You were among the first to decide to turn the dream of the Return to Zion into reality. After the death of the Lion, we observed the foxes, his heirs, and we somewhat scorned them. We found it difficult to live among them, and wanted to flee from them and their followers. Then, on your way to Erets-Yisrael, you came to Lvov, where I first met you.

Surely you still remember that singular evening at the home of our friend, A. M. Lipshits, who spoke Hebrew in a heavy manner with a Sefardic pronunciation and was a source of encouragement to Hebrew speakers in our town. We were a small group, six or seven Hebraists, writers or teachers, and you were the young man from Buczacz on his way to the literary rostrum, the guest who was truly emigrating to Erets-Yisrael. Why? One did not need to ask. Each one of us was ready to emigrate to Erets-Yisrael and to subsist there on a pitta and two or three olives a day. We were prepared for a life of poverty, but a pure life, based on the principles of true nationalism and practical morality, engaging in agriculture, guard duty, or any task we knew of from the Mishna or from *Hapoel Hatsair* [The Young Worker]. However, there were still some delays. A. M. Lipshits, who was always eager to meet stimulating people, spoke that evening. As always, he ranged widely on a variety of subjects in an eloquent and humorous manner. At one point he turned to you and asked you read from your writings, and while doing so he discussed your work as well as that of great Jewish and gentile writers. You started to blush and your lips expressed both willingness and resistance; your dense hair pressed upon your worried-looking brow; your head was heavy and your back was slightly hunched over like that of a man who spends many hours reading. But, nonetheless, you walked over to your coat, a coat of a young man from a small town, searched through the pockets and also through a briefcase. You held a handful of small and large sheets, some in order and others turned upside down. You started leafing through them in a somewhat embarrassed manner, sifting and selecting until finally reading to us one story or poem after another, mainly in Yiddish, which lends itself to oral delivery. You read with a melodious voice with subtle emphasis and intonation. At one point you did not want to read anymore and intended to stop, but Lipshits urged you on. The rest of us were laughing and enjoying ourselves immensely, but your face constantly changed colors as you blushed. During an interval, things quieted down and refreshments were served. Our host once again spoke, comparing Jewish and gentile writers. He ventured to advise you somewhat obliquely and the rest of us added encouraging remarks. Once again our host urged you on, "I know you have written more. Let us hear." You blushed yet again and insisted it was not a good idea and that really you had no more suitable items for reading aloud. Nonetheless, you once again went over to your coat and briefcase, pulled out a smaller packet than the previous one, and read us several short pieces of criticism. Written in an unconventional way, these were bold and sarcastic observations on several Jewish writers. I still recall that phrase of yours: "fingers inspecting a decomposed lung," which you used in discussing Brenner's writings with mingled praise and censure.

You suddenly stopped in mid-sentence and refused to read further. All our pleadings were to no avail. It was as if you had locked your mouth and thrown away the key. We sat and spoke while you gazed at us as if a bit frightened and a bit curious, your eyes filled with a faraway sorrow or a dream of a foreign land with different skies. When it came close to midnight, we accompanied you to the Vienna Station. Outside there was a scent of cool spring, almost like a drizzling autumn. We stood there, five or six people with raised coat collars, while you bade us farewell. With a youthful Galician voice, you promised to write us from the Holy Land. We saw you set out into a night which would lead to a dawn of sun, mountains and fields. We returned somewhat sorrowfully to our dormant town and parted in a warmer fashion than usual.

For several months I heard no word of you. Then one day there arrived from Jaffa an issue of *HaOmer* in which I found your first outstanding story "*Agunot* " [Abandoned Wives]. At first I didn't know whether you, Czaczkes, were the author, because to "S.Y." was added the unknown and somewhat strange name "*Agnon*." I suspected it was you, but did not know for sure until I heard from A.M. Lipshits. He spoke of you proudly and lovingly, as if it were his own son who had become famous in that far-off land (later he proved his love in an elegant pamphlet). My heart instantly succumbed to that scented blossom of a tale evolving around a wondrous Jewish theme. I was deeply moved by the succinct but multi-layered description of the Holy Ark falling backwards out of the window into the garden. All eyes focused on your work and many congratulated you, saying "Yishar koakh" [Well done!] as they would to a young man who had read the Haftarah [Torah reading from Neviim (Prophets)] nicely. We were proud of our successful friend, a rising star who might very well become a great one.

Then came "*Tishri*", "*Be'era Shel Mayim*, "and "*Akhot*" [Sister], as well as other marvelous poetic and reflective Hebrew-Scandinavian-Agnonian stories. We have since come to see you as one clothed in rich silk garb, turning secular into sacred, reality into fantasy. You have joined our literary hall of fame beside such figures as Perets, Berditshevski and other masters. The last story, at the time, "*VeHaya he-Akov le-Mishor*" [And the Crooked Shall Be Made Straight] was to us an ancient talisman you had polished and made to shine anew. It was a perfectly constructed epic tale in which the hidden-that-is-revealed more than balanced its emotional and rhetorical qualities. Even though we knew the story plot, your adaptation was woven anew with divine craftsmanship. We greatly supported Brenner's decision to become your publisher.

When, in Nissan 1914, I was fortunate enough to reach Erets-Yisrael, you were in Germany, I found several "fans" of yours who would speak of the young romantic lover of eccentricities and indulgences, loved by all and well acknowledged by writers. Shazar saw him as a friend, Sh. Ben-Tsion as a student and Brenner as a doer of wonders. Stories were told of you as if they had been taken out of a book of legends – all out of affection and faith in your future.

And you did not disappoint your followers: after the war appeared in succession *Agadat HaSofer*, *HaNidakh* [The Solitary], *Maalot uMoradot* [Ups and Downs] and the list goes on. Also given to us was *HaOr Haneerav* [The Evening Light] and, indeed, your light shines before you everywhere you go. And we also received *Bi-Ne'areynu u-vi-Zekeneynu*, a satire whose thin needles are buried in a wool fluff of humor and beautiful lyricism. For us, your fellow countrymen who were acquainted with the plot background, the enjoyment was twofold: that of art lovers and that of "accomplices." Later appeared *Bi-Demi Yameha* [In the Prime of Life] in which western winds already blow, German culture leaving its mark. Yet your own wondrous weaving is present in every line. We were happy that you returned once again to the essence of literature: to life and reality. You were like the doe whose horns fan out as they grow. We understood your path in literature: you sought to reveal the light within the Jewish soul, heroism and spiritual devotion, love of the Torah and the yearning for Zion. Many of your stories praise Jerusalem, hasidim, people of action, and refined persons, and they denounce the ignorant, the assimilationists, the hypocrites and the misanthropes who help neither individuals nor community. In the new Yishuv [pre-state Jewish community in Erets-Yisrael], you loved the sons who were pleasing to God and nation, those who toiled to build the land while their souls aspired to the hidden light [haOr haGanuz 'saved seven days' light' for future tsadikim (Khagiga 12). Like a loving father who is engrossed in studying the Torah and communicates with his sons by signs, you tried to sing their song by allegory, exegesis, exposition and suggestion. And we witnessed how your language has been hewn from the marble quarry of our ancient and later literature, how you prefer the simple to the high-flown, how you revive words out of long-forgotten books. And we saw how you restore to public use words that people formerly would not dare to utter. You phrase your words clearly and rhythmically; you present ideas in a beautifully picturesque way that is always true to the sources. (We knew that you could not keep away from old books and parchment scrolls, and that you had become a great expert in finding all you needed.) We saw you, and I am not exaggerating, as a polisher of precious stones who chooses, polishes, and places his gems. We admired your work, although we knew of those who said that you over-embellished and sought to grow rich from mining old sources. These critics demanded that you speak like an ordinary human being so that they could plainly fathom who you were (M.Y. Berditshevski and others). For a time I too leaned towards this view and made a similar demand while referring to *bi-Demi Yameha* in an issue of *Hedim*. However, once I came to know your work as a whole and understood your style of writing (which has become second nature to you), I realized that no one may criticize you for what you lack. On the contrary, one should rejoice in the gifts that God has given you, gifts that enrich the human soul. Your oeuvre is plentiful; anyone may come and indulge in this literary plenitude. I also knew that no one should judge you for the few stories you wrote without divine inspiration (for who has not done so?) and for those which, though well-spiced, lacked the primary ingredients. But these are few compared to the many others that represent the essence of your work and that constantly reveal the vitality of your creative soul.

After perceiving the nature of your stories and how much you invested in them, I realized that all the praise you have won is well deserved. You, however, tended to underestimate your own work. I noted the exceptional way in which you compose your stories, for you do not aim to develop interest by plot alone. Rather, you try to reach the imaginative reader through serious substance that provokes thought. You use beautiful descriptions in epic style, portraying not by colors but by colorful dialogue. Your pen creates wonders as you concisely introduce traditional and sacred symbols in the language of scholars and believers [leshon khakhamim vekhasidim veyereim]. This vivid style is also seen in the Scandinavian Hamsun, the Frenchman Anatol France, the Jewish Yosef Perl and Glikl Hamlen, and in the works of the Bratslaver, Franz Kafka and other masters of mystery in the realm of literature. Your way of borrowing from old texts is as important as creating anew, for you take a bronze coin and return a gold one. I recall a passage in one of your short stories "*Al Even Akhat*" [Of One Stone]:"If we have entered this world in order to set right what previous generations have left undone, I can say that in certain respects I have succeeded in doing so." I believe this passage describes an essential element of your work and its value. In this matter I refer especially to your book *Polin* [Poland], first published by *Hedim*. Its beginnings go back to the book you edited in German during the war that beautifully portrayed the Jewish people in our native Poland. You found such a lovely motto for it in the Slikhot [supplicatory prayers recited before Rosh HaShana]: "Gentle Poland was destined to be kind to Torah and its practice from before the time the Jewish Commonwealth split into two (since

Ephraim left Judah)." [see Isaiah 7:17]. The most beautiful sections are: "*Maase HaEz*" [Story of the Goat], and "*Maase HaMeshulakh MeErets HaKodesh*" [Story of the Emissary from the Holy Land," in which Poland and the Land of Israel are intertwined and where you reveal the way that leads from the one to the other.

We could not imagine greater courage and determination when we saw you working on an epic tale of the Jewish people. We were glad that the short version of *The Bridal Canopy* turned into a two-volume epic. Even though the seams are obvious in some places, we saw that you wonderfully combined all the materials into a homogeneous whole. You raised R' Yudl the Idler to new heights, turning him into a symbolic figure. You created a brother for Binyamin the 3rd and the rest of the idlers in the world who in their time were a gold mine for their owners. Even though the symbolic element in your idler is somewhat narrow, it is still richer and more complex than one sees at first glance. Due to his flimsy, weak, and almost wraithlike existence, you sentence him to bear many experiences, characters, fairy tales, words of wisdom, Torah and anecdotes. Laden to the breaking point, he even carries the central character, R' Israel Shlomo Parnas, on his back without faltering. I only regret that you repeated a large part of the plot in a somewhat long and dry chorus.

Later on you added two more volumes to the four: one of them, *A Simple Story*, was completely new. However, title notwithstanding, the story is not simple, though it portrays simple Jews in everyday circumstances. Here you return to your wondrous weaving of human material, as can be seen in *Be-Demi Yameha*. Your fine filigree writing here shows acute perception of human nature. A single phrase brings the world to a standstill, a by-the-way remark illuminates a dark soul. One can find many fine picturesque and humorous passages. At one point, in the insanity episode, the story runs off track somewhat. Your cart wobbles for a while but finally arrives home safe and sound.

Your sixth volume (the last to date), *Be-Shuva va-Nakhat*, [In Return and in Rest – (see Isaiah 30:15)] – lives up to its name: legendary tales leisurely and tastefully told. It opens with *Bilvav Yamim* [In the Midst of the Seas – (see Jonah 2:4)] a tale on whose beauty many have commented. It is truly a fine hasidic story, a subtle work of art in praise of the first hasidim who emigrated to the Holy Land. It overflows with love for the Land of Israel; however, your magical pen does not transform all the miracles in the story into moving experiences – which miracles must be. This volume contains a number of legends of the greatest charm.

I have here surveyed almost your entire harvest, quickly examined your tools and implements at close hand, and I can say: May you be blessed for these bounteous gifts that so richly fill your granary: six handsome volumes, excellently edited and proofread, and bound in the best taste.

Whenever I take a volume of yours in hand and read any of its stories I immediately imagine you as I saw you that evening in Lvov. I see your blushing face and know what lies at the base of your work: your poetry originates from a youthful innocence of the soul. What blessing shall I wish you? I wish that that same gentle and sensitive soul who bursts forth from your writings will continue to do so in future volumes. You have been privileged to become a teller of tales in Israel; you have perfected your art uncompromisingly; your seal of originality is immediately detected. All those who try to imitate you are epigones. May you be blessed for many years to come.

I shall continue with my blessings and pray you find peace and solace with the Jewish people and in Erets-Yisrael. May our literature flourish like a fruitful garden. You will be placed among our greatest authors enjoying your art which in turn will bring joy to others. May our people be safe and sound and may they enjoy the teachings of their teachers. Amen.

My letter has become far too long and I have not even told you half of what is in my heart, but there will be time for that in future jubilees.

Yours truly, with love,

Asher Barash Ab, 1938

Shmuel Yosef Agnon

Yehuda Farb Hacohen,
Agnon's grandfather

Gitel Reisa,
Agnon's grandmother

[Page 39]

Buczacz - A Geographical Account
Translated by Adam Prager

1. The Name

Buchach in Ukrainian, Buczacz in Polish, according to which it was named in Western European languages, and the Jews called it B'tshuetsh (bet with *shva na* and the *mlupim* long [/u/], followed by a short *segol* [/e/] as in *Buenos* in the name *Buenos-Aires*). In Hebrew imprints, as in the names of subscribers or patrons (in Yiddish called *prenumerantn* [those who subscribe to a book prior to its publication – see the classic work, *Sefer HaPrenumeranten*, by Berl Kagan] – A.P.), the name in most cases is pronounced Buczacz. The origin of this name may be in the name of the forest buk (the beech tree.) If you look at a map of the distribution of this tree, you will find its eastern border near the town. Likewise, Bukovina was named after this tree. However, there is no sufficient explanation as to why the town was not named Bukacz. It is possible that the name originates from a non-Slavic ancient tongue. We know that in this area there existed a settlement dating back to the Neolithic period, long before the arrival of the Slavs. Perhaps the Slavs incorporated the name into their own language. The name of the Dnestr River, which is situated 21 km from Buczacz, is without doubt of Celtic origin. (This view is supported by the fact that on the Siret River of Moldavia, about 169 km southeast of Buczacz, there is a town named Bucecea. In Poland and Russia no similar name is to be found. In the Czech Republic there is a Bucica).

2. The Geographic Situation

Buczacz is situated above the western bank of the Strypa River, 49 degrees 6' latitude north of the equator and 25 degrees 25' longitude east of Greenwich. It is 55 km as the bird flies from Tarnopol (today Ternopil) the district capital today, and about 130 km from Lvov, which was Galicia's capital in the time of the Austrians, and the capital of Red Russia in the Polish period prior to the first partition (1772). During the restored Austrian and Polish period, Buczacz was 62 km from the Russian border, which for the Galician Jews was like an iron curtain. Buczacz is a typical bridge town, i.e. a settlement that developed into a town because it was on a river at a convenient point for crossing over on a bridge. It is one of twelve towns built in this fashion in the area north of the Dnestr.

There are several strategic advantages to Buczacz's geographical structure that helped in defending the town against the Tatars and the Turks, as well as during World War One. The Strypa River defends the town's eastern and southern borders. A forward line of defense is created by small lakes, pools and swamps through which the Olchowiec River streams. This river runs parallel to the Strypa 6 km to the East. There was a fortress (Zamek) in the town and a small one (Podzameczek) in the north. To understand the town and its origins, one must study the structure of the southwestern area of the Podolian plateau on which Buczacz is situated.

3. The Geology of the Town and Vicinity

Podolia lies on a high plateau ranging from 350 to 400 meters in height. It slopes slightly towards the Dnestr River Valley situated approximately 200 meters below the plateau. Next to the plateau's northern border runs the watershed of the river networks descending southward to the Dnestr, the network of the Wisla tributaries heading northwest and the rivers of the Dnepr heading northeast. The road leading from Lvov to Brody is near that watershed. Due to the fact that the plateau slopes southward in a uniform manner, all its rivers and streams flow south. They are almost parallel to each other, creating a striped landscape between the streams and river valleys of western Podolia. Since the Dnestr, the largest and chief river, receives water in plenitude from the eastern Carpathian Mountains, it has created a deep valley at the southern edge of the plateau. Also, its rivulets have deepened the valleys beneath the plateau. The deepening of the rivulets grew as they neared the Dnestr, the main river's estuary. The plateau above Buczacz is approximately 375 meters above sea level on both sides, whereas the town's Strypa River channel is no more than 260 meters above sea level. One must therefore descend 115 meters in which not only the railroad track but also the road lengthens its route in order to lessen the incline. From the south of Buczacz all the way to the Dnestr the slope is steeper and the channel is not suitable for a bridge. The Strypa River starts out southeast of Zolochev, about 78 km straight from northern Buczacz. Its estuary is about 21 km south of the town. The river winds the most at its lower end. Due to narrowness of the valley, there is no connecting road with the other settlements. The connection is at the plateau above and not in the valley. Between Buczacz and the town of Zborov (birthplace of R' Benyamin), situated at the beginning of the Strypa, there is but an indirect connection. Traffic in Bucacz is principally east to west and vice versa, and not north to south.

The top layers of the Podolian plateau consist of rock sediment of the Triassic Period. Beneath them are Mesozoic layers (intermediate geological age) and Paleozoic layers (ancient). All the layers are almost evenly balanced and parallel to one another. In the river valleys the layers that are beneath the Triassic are revealed and as one gets closer to the Dnestr one finds earlier layers. In the Strypa Valley where Buczacz lies, Devonian layers (a period in the Paleozoic Age) were discovered which consist of hard chalk and hard sandstone. According to one tradition, sand with gold deposits was found in the Strypa Valley. Gold veins dating back to the Devonian Period were found in other places in the world, and it is plausible that gold was found here as well. Above the Triassic layers lies a thick layer of black earth, the Podolian and Ukrainian chernozem, known for its fertility throughout the world by its Russian name.

4. Climate, Flora and Agriculture

Buczacz's annual average temperature is close to 9 degrees Celsius. In January it averages 4-5 degrees below zero; in July, 20-21 degrees above zero. The frost lasts 3 to 4 months. An average temperature of over 20 degrees lasts a little over a month. Rainfall reaches an annual 450 millimeters, most of it in the summer. However, there are no rainless seasons. The amount of rain is less than in Tel-Aviv, but due to the low temperature the evaporation rate is lower than the rain quantity. Thus, in the Buczacz district, forests of deciduous tress extend over several km on both sides of the Strypa all the way to the Dnestr. On the plateau above are left only small stands of trees. Wide fields of grain replaced the forests. Buczacz belongs to a region where the trees suffice for its own use, with some left for export.

Nearby to the south lies a large district with a shortage of trees. The agricultural land makes up almost three-quarters of its area. Wheat, barley, oats, potatoes and all kinds of pulses are the major produce and much is for export. Fruit trees are of poor quality, therefore apples, pears, plums and cherries are grown for local consumption only. Cattle raising came to the fore prior to World War Two, with almost one head of cattle for every two people; horses, pigs and sheep followed in importance. Poultry-raising was common, but the chickens were inferior, as were the geese and turkeys. However, Buczacz horses were famous for their excellence.

5. Industry, Crafts and Trade

As in all of eastern Galicia, Buczacz and vicinity did not have a developed industry except for the manufacture of liquor from potatoes on the large estates. This industry requires the rotation of sown land (one must not grow grain for three consecutive years in one specific field) and the by-products from potatoes that are used to make alcohol (which serve as feed both for dairy and meat herds). Scarcity of good roads made it easier to bring cattle and liquor, rather than grains, pulses and potatoes, to market. In town there were small food-processing and beverage plants, as well as workshops for clothing, footwear and furniture. Buczacz buckwheat groats were known throughout southern and eastern Galicia, and were even marketed in Bukovina. These groats, also known as *kasha* in Slavic and Yiddish, would be served in soup at the Jewish table, especially at the second meal of the Sabbath. The packing-paper industry that once existed disappeared by the end of the nineteenth century. An old cottage industry dealt in carpets for beds and sofas and tapestries for walls (in Polish *makaty, kilimy*). The excess agricultural produce of the surrounding villages was brought to the city, distributed to the urban population, to the rest of the country and exported abroad; goods for local use were imported from abroad, especially from the West. Exports, which were few in kind but large in quantity, were shipped directly to their final destination. Imports, however, were of many different kinds, each in small quantity, and thus were imported by small jobbers who in turn dealt with large wholesalers in Stanislav or Lvov.

6. The Economic and Social Role of the Jews

Podolia is part of Red Russia (Reisin in our sources). The Red Russians are part of the Malorussians (the people of Little Russia), Rusinim in Polish and Ruthenians in German. In the twentieth century people started to call the Malorussians Ukrainians.

Buczacz lies in a Ukrainian region. The owners of the large estates were Poles. The town, like most eastern Galician towns since the seventeenth century, was largely Jewish. Trade, except in pigs, was almost exclusively in Jewish hands and most of the craftsmen were Jewish. The Polish population grew in the days of the Austrians due to the bureaucratic apparatus that was introduced. Buczacz was not a royal town, but belonged to the landed nobility. Up to the sixteenth century, the town was owned by the Buczaczki family, followed by other families. In the seventeenth century it was owned by the Potockis, one of the great Polish families, whose power exceeded that of the monarch. Nobles preferred the Jews to the urban Christians, for they could exploit them more readily. Moreover, the urban Slavs (Poles and Ukrainians) were no competition for the Jews in financial matters, and they loved to drink no less than did the peasantry. The Armenians, who were the only competitors to the Jews, succeeded not only in gaining wealth, but bought land, joined the nobility and abandoned commerce. Potocki patronage proved expensive to the Jews; however, merchants who enjoyed such patronage could be assured of safe passage in transit and of security from the rapacity of the lesser nobility. In the first years of Austrian rule, which began in 1772, the town was in the hands of a cruel master, Michael Potocki; however, thanks to the Austrian sovereignty, the Jews were able to stand up to him and to prevent his interference in communal matters. The nobleman protested to the authorities and the dispute reached Vienna. Josef the Second's Vienna decided that the Jews, unlike the peasants, were not serfs of the estate owner. Vienna was interested in the Galician markets for its goods, and the Jews were favored dealers. The Jews, moreover, were the first to become accustomed to speaking German.

The emancipation of the serfs on the estates in 1848 posed a great economic problem for the landed nobility. They found a way out of their difficulties by leasing their estates to Jews. Once Jews were allowed to buy agricultural land in the 1860s, Jewish leaseholders and other wealthy Jews began to purchase estates. Prior to World War One, most of the large estates were in Jewish hands, whether by ownership or leasehold. In the Buczacz region, approximately one-fifth of the owners of large estates were Jews. Up to 1907, estate owners elected representatives to the Parliament as a special bloc. A score or so of estate owners was held equal to 12,000 taxpayers.

The Jewish percentage of landowners was higher than their percentage in the general population. In the Tarnopol region, the Jews constituted thirty percent of the landowners. At the beginning of the twentieth century, Polish newspapers bemoaned the shrinking of the homeland, claiming the land was passing into Jewish hands.

Prior to 1915 Buczacz was surrounded by Jewish large-estate owners and leaseholders, and by gentile estate tavern leaseholders and rural dairymen who had contracts with both the Jewish and gentile estate owners. The six or seven thousand Jews in Buczacz owed their livelihood to their agricultural surroundings. The Jews were the catalyzers of productivity in the agricultural estates. Besides grain, alcohol and cattle, which were export products for generations, Jews encouraged cultivation of pulses, as well as poultry-raising for export (first of eggs and later of meat). In German newspapers a dozen years before World War One, Buczacz Jewish merchants advertised live fattened chickens, two or three in a cage, for sale to private buyers, with the health of the fowl guaranteed. When Ukrainian peasants joined the keen competition among these merchants, they undermined the Buczacz standards. They prevented the advertisers from keeping their word by shipping live "carcasses," thus tainting the name of Buczacz throughout western Germany. Butter purchased by the Jews from estate dairymen and, in small quantities, from peasants, was also exported. With the reunification of Poland, the farmers' cooperative took most of the trade away from the Jews. Just as export trade was in Jewish hands, so was import trade. Jews were agents for Austrian, Czech and German commercial and industrial firms. Thanks to connections with western countries, many emigrated to the West. Before 1915, craftsmen who lost their jobs, as well as bankrupt traders and storekeepers who could not reopen businesses under different names, emigrated to foreign lands. (A common trick before 1915 was for a bankrupt husband to reopen his business in his wife's name.) Competition between Jews and Poles and between Jews and Ukrainians was already in evidence under Austrian rule. At first the Christian craftsmen and tradesmen failed. Of one nobleman who opened a nail factory and a noodle factory, it was said that his noodles were as hard as nails and his nails were as soft as noodles. The Jews could overcome competition with private Christian entrepreneurs; however, a dangerous enemy of Jewish commerce arose in the guise of a Polish-Ukrainian cooperative movement. The nationalistic press preached severance from the dispensable Jewish middleman. This propaganda had an anti-Semitic coloring as early as the Austrian period. It was highly successful in the reunited Polish Republic, especially among the Ukrainians who were more closely bonded to the territory than were the fewer Poles. The Polish government settled peasants on the estates of large landholders, Jewish estates being the first to undergo agrarian reform. This land, the source for Jewish livelihoods for four centuries, was gradually pulled out from under their feet. Emigration to any country willing to accept Jews (including Erets-Yisrael) grew.

7. Buczacz Town Plan and Sites

Buczacz was surrounded by a wall, a rampart (*waly*) and a mote. When the threat of the Turks and Tatars passed, the town spread beyond these barriers, which eventually disappeared. However, the educated eye will recognize the nucleus of the town that was once surrounded, even if examining a small-scale map of the town. This nucleus was situated at the angle between the west-bending Strypa and a small stream that runs into the river in the northwest. There, at the point where the river valleys meet the stream, lies a plain part of which was used for the town market, known as *Rynek* in Polish, *Ring* in German and *ringplats* in Yiddish. Mikolai Potocki built the town hall here in the 1860s, one of the few distinguished edifices that Podolia can boast of. About one hundred years after it was built, the building burnt down and was later restored, but it lost its original splendor. The church that was built by the same nobleman is notable for its images of the Virgin Mary, regarded as works of art, and for its wood carvings. Besides the square area of the market, the old nucleus consists of only a few small streets. The new town and its suburbs spread into the valley on both sides of that same small stream named the Potok, to the west of the Strypa, and along the crossroads connecting to Buczacz: to the west the road and the railway lead to Monastrishtsh (*Monasterzyska* in Polish), to the east the same road leads to Chortkov, to the southwest the road leads to Podhayits (*Podhajce* in Polish) and to Berezhan (*Brzezany* in Polish), to the northeast it lead to Strusov, Mikolintsa and Tarnopol. Due to the narrowness of the river valleys and the stream, buildings in the town were constructed on the valley slopes. Houses were built close to each other and few had surrounding gardens, especially in the Jewish neighborhoods. This density is well mirrored in the Shbush (Buczacz) descriptions in the tales of S. Y. Agnon, the great son of this small town.

M. Y. Braver

[Page 44]

History of the Jews in Buczacz
Translated by Adam Prager

1.

Buczacz was founded at the end of the 17th century,[1] but before it became a town it was a village known for its fortress and palace, which was built in a characteristic medieval style. The village of Buczazc was part of the aristocratic Buczaczki family's estates. The Buczaczki family, whose coat of arms was "abdank," excelled in defending Poland's eastern borders and spreading Catholicism and western culture in those areas. The earliest records concerning this aristocratic family which built the palace and the fortress go back to 1260 and 1379. One of the noblemen of the Buczaczki domain, the starosta [governor] of Halicz, Michael of Buczacz, received from Vladislav by way of tenancy the village of Zloczow. Rent was 100 grzibni and the only condition was that he live there on a permanent basis.

After some time Michael handed over the Zloczow village to the Sjonski family, which founded the town of Zloczow there in 1441.

The last member of the Buzcazcki family was Katerina, the daughter of Jacob. Jacob, who died in 1501, was a voivode [governor] in Belorussia. Katerina handed over the estate as a dowry to her husband, Jan Taburovski, as well as the Filaba coat of arms; the Taburovskis accepted the family name of Buczaczki. At the beginning of the 17th century the Buczacz family estates fell into the hands of the castellan from Kamenets, Janrze Potocki, who married the daughter of Mikolai, Katerina. And her brother Jan Krzishtoff Buczaczki, who was known for his fierce struggle against the Calvinists, died leaving no heirs. From that time on the Buczaczki estates were in the hands of the Putocki family, who further developed the estate and perfected the fortress. The one who particularly enlarged the city was the voivode from Bratslav, Stefan Potocki, who also broadened and perfected the palace and fortress.

Jews had lived in Buczacz since its estate days. After it became a town their numbers grew. In official documents Buczacz's Jewish community is mentioned from the year 1500 and onwards.[2] At the beginning of the 16th century, Poland held fairs in Buczacz which were important for its trade with countries to the east. During this period the Jews had close trade relations with the merchants of Krakow and especially with the famous wholesaler Jan Banner.[3] Likewise, Jewish wholesalers in Buczacz had trade relations with Turkey. We know, for example, that in the year 1578-1579 the Jews of Constantinople together with two Jews from Poland – one of whom was from Buczacz – brought to Lvov 391 barrels of wine from Lamesia out of the 813 barrels that were imported that year.[4]

In the middle of the 16th century the noblemen of Volin, Podolia and Ukraine began an extensive settlement campaign. During that period they founded a few towns in which many Jews chose to settle. These were Jews from various districts in Poland and especially from towns where their lives were a continuous conflict between themselves and the townsmen. The latter were against Jews living among them and persecuted them. The Jews, tired of the incessant friction, gave up their positions and emigrated to the eastern regions and settled in the new towns which by law were private estates of the noblemen.

These noblemen were interested in the development of their towns and therefore gladly bestowed upon the Jews many privileges. Here there were no restrictions concerning trade, work, settlement conditions and housing. All the trade as well as crafts and industries based on agricultural products were in the hands of the Jews. They also had the right to vote in municipal council elections and were exempt from all taxes and payments to the crown treasury. All this was arranged in order to provide them with convenient development conditions. The Jews of these towns represented the urban middle class, a class that every owner of a private town wished to have.

Buczacz was one of these private towns that in the 16th century absorbed a large number of Jews, who in turn founded a community. This community, like those in other cities in the eastern parts of Belorussia and Podolia, was affiliated with the regional center in Lvov. We know that in 1521 King Zygmunt the 1st ordered that taxes decided upon in Bidgushets were to be paid by the Jews of Buczacz to the Jewish collectors.

According to Polish law from 1539, Jews in Poland were divided into two groups: the crown's Jews and the estate owners' Jews. Thus the Jewish communities in the private estates – till then under the crown's jurisdiction – passed over to the hands of the aristocracy, who had the greatest authority in all matters concerning governance and law. The Jews were given rights and engaged in all trades, crafts and even industry based on agricultural products. However, the nobility were authorized to cancel these rights – an authority that was formerly in the sole hands of the crown.

In matters of taxes, and especially the head tax that was imposed in 1549, the private Jews were also under the crowns' rule. In the wake of the head tax, Jewish communities in the towns of the aristocrats, including Buczacz, were attached to the communities' organization – to the state committees and to the Council of the Four Lands – that existed from 1581 to 1764.

The communities in the private towns in most cases enjoyed special support from the towns' owners who were, as stated, very interested in their development. Thus these communities overshadowed those they originated from and even played a larger and more important role as regards Jewish autonomy than did the mother-community. They especially held key positions in the organization of the district committees.

Buczacz was handed down from one noble family to the other via commercial transactions, marital relations and inheritance. However, the constitutional basis for the Jews' life in the town remained unchanged during these transitional periods. In the middle of the 17th century the Cossacks raided Buczacz (the calamities of 1648). The Jews fought alongside their fellow townsmen. Armed with rifles and gunpowder and sometimes manning the cannons, the Jewish population defended the town together with the Christians. The town suffered a great deal during the Tatar wars (1655-1667), and the Turkish wars (1672-1675), when Sultan Muhamed the 4th put Buczacz under a long siege after conquering Kamenets-Podolskiy. In Buczacz in 1672, under the great linden tree behind the palace, the Sultan dictated severe surrender and peace terms to King Michael Vishniovitzk (1669-1673). Poland relinquished Podolia and the Ukraine to the Turks and was committed to pay an annual tax.

The Jews of Buczazc went through a difficult period during the years 1648-1676. However, in 1648 the Cossacks failed to conquer the city, which fended them off and withstood them due to its strong fortress. The Cossacks were forced to retreat and had to make do with burning the surrounding villages.

After a while life returned to normal.

Ulrich Werdum, who visited Poland in the years 1670-1672, relates his impressions of Buczacz, which he visited in 1672, in his memoirs:

"Buczacz is a large and amusing (possierlich) town spread over mountains and a valley with a lake to the West. The town is surrounded by a wall; its houses are well built. It has three Catholic churches and a Ukrainian monastery, now run by the Dominicans. The Armenians also have a church, and the Jews have a synagogue and a well-kept fence-encircled cemetery with beautiful large trees growing in it. The castle is made of stone, as are its fortresses. It lies on the top of the mountain where the Stripa River, originating from the village of Zlotnik 6 miles away, flows at its sides. The river supplies the power for 10 to 12 water-mills placed beside each other. The town of Buczacz is the estate of Lord Potocki. At the beginning of the raid, the Cossacks and the Muscals set fire to the whole town, which has now been rebuilt, especially by the Jews. They (the Jews) are numerous here, as in Poland and Belorussia."[5]

Later on the Jews suffered greatly from the various armies passing through and the many invasions by Poland's enemies. In the year 1648 many Jewish refugees from the Ukraine who were fleeing from the Chmelnitski gangs found refuge in Buczacz. Among them was R' Yaakov Eliyahu Ben-Moshe Meir of Sharigrod, who was chosen to be the community's rabbi.

Faced by the danger of the Turkish invasion in 1674, the Jews of Buczacz took part in a joint meeting of nobility and state and municipal officials to discuss defense procedures. Special supervisors were chosen for each of the town's quarters. In the Jewish quarter, the community leader R' Yerakhmiel was chosen.

In 1675, when the Turks attacked the town, the aristocrats and townspeople succeeded in fleeing into the fortress. The town was burnt to the ground and many Jews that failed to escape were captured by the Turks outside the fortress gates and slaughtered on the spot. Those in the fortress defended themselves gallantly, maintaining their resistance until the army arrived under the command of Jan Soviski the 3rd, who drove away the Turks.

However, the town's relief did not last long. A year later (1676), the Turks lead by their commander Ibrahim Shaytan invaded Zhorbano. Again Buczacz was conquered and ruined completely, not one house being left. However, Jan Sobiski succeeded in defeating the Turks near Zhorbano and dictated to them the Zhorbano peace terms, according to which Turkey was compelled to return two thirds of the Ukraine, leaving only one third to Turkish rule. All annual tax payments were cancelled and the issue concerning the return of Podolia was postponed for future negotiation.[6]

After the wars with Turkey, the Jewish population of Buczacz and its surroundings dwindled to such a degree that the Polish aristocracy of the Halicz district (Ziemia halicka) ordered their delegates in Warsaw to ask the king to release the Jews of Buczacz (including Jews of Tarnopol, Podheytse, and the rest of the district's towns) from all head tax (poglowne), for "the Halicz Law commands every man to stand beside his fellow man,"[7] Also, in the year 1713 when Buczacz Jews suffered greatly from Russian invasion, the Vice-Minister of Finance Pshendovski released them from paying the head tax.

When the war ended, Jan Potocki rebuilt the town. In 1684, Buczacz (according to the traveler Daleyrac who visited Poland that year and saw Buczacz), was a town built of large, high-storied houses. The Jews were living in the center of town in houses not yet restored, while the castle and fortress were completely rebuilt. During those years – in the second half of the 17th century – the large synagogue of the Jews was built next to the Stripa River. The situation of the Jewish settlement improved and it became financially sound.

The official documents concerning the community's privileges that were destroyed during the catastrophic years were renewed by Stefan Potocki on May 20th and they are a carbon copy of the privileges that were given years before to Chortkov and Stanislavov, also by the Potockis. They are actually no more than a confirmation of the rights given in the past. At the head of the document it is emphasized that Stefan Potocki is renewing and authorizing the rights given the Jews by the former town owners.

According to the bill of privileges, Jews are permitted to reside in the town as well as to deal in crafts and wholesale and retail trade, excepting Christian religious articles. Due to their bad state following the fire, they were exempt from all city and castle taxes for 12 years. At the end of this period, they are to pay one taller for each house whose front faced the street and half a taller for an extension. According to the old arrangements, the Jews were given free passage through the area between the church and the synagogue built by their fathers. Furthermore, Potocki gives them more land in order to expand their cemetery, and the right to construct a building for the caretaker, who will be free of all tax payments. The bill of rights frees them for good from payment of general taxes such as corvee, tithe, castle maintenance duties, and cattle tax. However, like all the other townspeople, they had to pay road maintenance expenses. The Jews are not subject to the municipal law courts but to the Buczacz castle commissioner. They have a right to appeal before the town owner, but are under no obligation to present themselves on Sabbath. It is forbidden to hold them in a cold prison, except for penal crimes. It is forbidden to hold the weekly market day on a Sabbath. Conflicts and trials between Jews are under the jurisdiction of the Jewish rabbinic courts.

Jewish butchers are exempt from supplying pork to the castle. However, they must supply the castle annually with one stone[8] of tallow and a large haunch of meat every week to the deputy starost [governor].

Jews are permitted to purchase houses from Christians, to build breweries and wineries, to produce salt and liquors, while fulfilling their obligations as in the past. They were also given the right to keep taverns. In another bill of privileges from 1706, it is emphasized that the rights of the Jewish craftsmen are equal to those of the Christian craftsmen. They must be members of the general craft guilds and pay all general taxes. However, as Jews they are exempt from all religious duties of the Christian craftsmen, such as churchgoing, participation in religious processions, and obligatory candle contributions to the church. But they must pay all candle fees, including tallow expenses, etc. to the castle and the church. (In 1799, the Roman Catholic church filed a complaint in the municipality against the Jewish and Christian furriers for not contributing their share of tallow. In that year there were fourteen furriers in Buczacz, eight of whom were Jews. The Christian furriers claimed that due to their modest numbers, and the bad state they were in, they could not provide their proper share. They suggested that the Jews, being more prosperous, contribute all the tallow. The mayor ruled that both Christians and Jews must give their share. {Baracz, p. 97-98}. On May 19th 1799, the community requested that Jews not be punished bodily but rather be imprisoned and that the communal leaders be present at their trials. This request was granted by the authorities.)

The 1699 statutes state that the Jews of Buczacz will have the same rights and freedom as the Christian townspeople, It is stated explicitly that a Jewish treasurer will be chosen who will be present when the town collects taxes from the Jews. Furthermore, the Jews must join in defending the castle in times of danger Buczacz Jews were also given the right to be elected to the town's council elections.[9]

This bill of privileges, approved by the town owners that came after Stefan Potocki (approved on Oct. 2nd 1737 by Mikolai Potocki, and on Oct. 3rd 1768 and March 26th 1777) determined the relations between the Jews, town owners and townsmen, enabling the Jews to live in a safe environment. In 1723 Potocki had declared in a special article of the bill of privileges, which was presented to the town hall, that there was to be a guard in the market composed of four people, two of whom must originate from the Jewish community. Potocki also tried to improve the financial state of the town and supported the Jews, whom he believed to be the sole factor for the town's financial development.

Due to these conditions, Jewish trade grew in the well-known markets of 17th century Buczacz. Besides trade, industry and crafts, the Jews also leased taverns in the suburbs and nearby villages. Furthermore, many of them engaged in crop and animal trade, especially in bulls and horses. Among the Buczacz Jews there were also wholesalers who conducted large-scale business ventures with foreign countries.

2.

Community life in Buczacz developed in the same fashion as in other communities in Poland. At the head of the community stood a committee consisting of:

1. 3-5 community leaders responsible to the authorities, and elected each year. Once elected they swore allegiance to Poland and were only officially installed after the voivode of the state and private towns gave his consent. In Buczacz, for example, consent from the town owner or his empowered assistant was necessary;

2. 3-5 respected citizens, c) members of the community committees. The community officials were a rabbi, religious judges, preachers, community scribe and the synagogue caretaker. All matters between the community and authorities were taken care of by the intercessor (syndicus).

In addition to the above, the community had a doctor, a pharmacist, a medical assistant, a midwife, guards, tax collectors and messengers.

Within the community there were many societies, such as the khevra kadisha [Jewish burial society], and the craftsmen's guild which took care of its interests among the Christian guilds, in the municipality and within the community.

In 1658 on the initiative of the Belorussia nobility, regional committees were established in Saymek, Vishnia, followed by formation of the Lvov regional committee including the communities of Brody, Zhulkva, Tismanets, Borodshin, Rohatyn, Lisko, Zloczow and Buczacz.

The Lvov community conducted all state committee matters to such an extent that the town leaders enjoyed control (hegemony) without letting the rural communities take part. However, with Lvov's weakening due to the political upheavals after the wars of the 17th century, the rural communities took control from the Lvov leaders. The community of Zhulkva, which was a branch of the Lvov community (przykahalek) succeeded, with support from the town owner, King Jan Sobiski, to free itself completely from Lvov's authority. Furthermore, it started taking over the regional committee. Together with Zhulkva, the communities of Brody, Tarnopol and Buczacz also made themselves heard. Buczacz's rabbi was chosen as the regional rabbi. Following the wars, many Jews from Lvov left for other towns due to the poor financial situation; this made it hard for those who stayed to pay taxes. Matters reached such a state that the Belorussia nobility complained in Saymek, Vishnia in April 1701,[10] stating that due to the mass migration of Jews to Podolia, where they were free under Turkish law from head tax, all the weight fell upon the few Jews who stayed behind. Therefore, taxes should be decided upon according to population size. The Lvov Jews especially suffered; they were forced to pay 1/7 of the head tax for all the Lvov region.

The issue concerning tax distribution was taken care of only in 1716, from which date the Belorussia Jews and the Podolia Jews paid their taxes separately.

Within the Lvov district a harsh power struggle amongst the Jewish communities took place. Slowly the rural town representatives succeeded in taking over most of the region's top positions. In 1664, Buczacz members of the regional committee who met in Swierz with representatives from Zhulkva, Przemishl, Yaborov, Kolomea, and Brody attacked the Lvov community, which consequently was forced to relinquish its monopoly and to attend to the views of all other representatives of the regional committee. Buczacz's representative in this committee was the town leader Rabbi David Preger, a prominent figure not only in the history of the Buczacz community but also in the history of the autonomous institutions of Polish Jewry in general.

David Ben Yitskhak of Prague, popularly known as R' David Preger of Buczacz, was one of the community and regional leaders. In 1676 and 1679 he signed a promissory note, borrowing a sum of 7200 Belorussian tallers from Gabriel Miltner of Breslau, to be paid back in four installments in 1682, 1686, 1688 and 1689. He participated in the Council of the Four Lands.[11] Preger died in 1697.

In 1700, in addition to two town leaders from Lvov, there were already seven representatives from the communities of Brody, Zhulkva, Stri, Tismanitse, Tsernalitse, Kosov, and Zalushtse in the regional committee. In 1720, the Buczacz representative played an important roll in the regional committee at Kolikov. This committee consisted of five representatives from Zhulkva, three from Brody, and one each from Bohorodatsani, Stri, Rohatyn, Zlotchov and Buczacz.

In this period the Buczacz community was headed by R' Aryeh Leyb, a wealthy and pious man, who was called by the people "R' Leibush the head of state."

R' Aryeh Leyb was the son of R' Yitskhak of Yaborov (Yakhorover) and the son-in-law of R' David Ben Aryeh-Leyb son of Shmuel-Tsvi Hirsh, the author of *Sheagat Aryeh* [Lion's Roar], who was head of the rabbinic court of Brisk deLita and a distinguished citizen of Zamosc.

R' Aryeh-Leyb had much influence over his community and was its representative for a few years at the regional committee. Thanks to his activity and energy in public matters, he became one of the committee's spokesmen and, later on, its head.

In 1720, when Hagaon R' Yehoshua Falk, author of *Pney Yehoshua* [The Face of Joshua], was in danger of losing his rabbinic chair in Lvov, R' Aryeh stood up for him and convened the regional committee at Kolikov in his interest.

As is known, R' Yehoshua Falk (1756-1681) was chosen after the death of the "Khakham Tsvi" in 1718 as the rabbi of Lvov and vicinity. However, a short time after his being chosen, a certain wealthy man tried to gain the position for his son-in-law, R' Khayim Ben-Lizaral, who was the grandson of the Lvov Rabbi R' Pinkhas Moshe Kharif. His father-in-law, who was mediator for the voivode Yavlonovski, succeeded in buying Yavlonovski's help as well as the support of some of the community leaders. Thus, In 1720 when R' Yehoshua's rabbinical appointment ended, the community did not renew it, but chose R' Khayim Ben-Lizaral to be the rabbi of Lvov and vicinity. The choice was approved by the voivode Yavlonovski.

R' Yehoshua was forced to leave Lvov and moved to Buczacz, the home of R' Aryeh Leibush, his father-in-law. R' Aryeh Leybush's daughter, Shifra, was married to his son, R' Yissakhar Podhitse.[12]

R' Yehoshua Falk turned to the regional communities of Lvov, who decided in his favor and did not recognize R' Khayim as the regional rabbi.

At the regional committee session that convened in Kolikov at the initiative of R' Aryeh Leibush' on July 17th, 1720, R' Khayim was ostracized. This verdict stressed that "we, the region's citizens, are independent of the sacred community of Lvov and of any rabbi it might choose. However, all the communities of the region consider themselves subject solely to R' Yehoshua, who may settle in any of our communities and where he settles will be the seat of rabbinical authority."

R' Yehoshua settled in Buczacz for another reason too. The starosta in Buczacz, Kinovski, was in dispute with the voivode Yavlonovski, a fact that ensured R' Yehoshua's safety.

R' Yehushua resided in Buczacz until 1730 when he was invited to be rabbi in Berlin.
During the struggle of the region against the Lvov community, R' Aryeh Leibush played an active roll and contributed much to its independence.

His eldest son, Zekharia is the author of *Menorat Zekharia* [Zekharia's Lamp] (1776) and Zekharia Meshulam (1778).

During these years there resided in Buczacz a wealthy man, R' Shimson, and his wife Reyzl, daughter of R' Efraim Fishl, head of the rabbinic court of Kolomea (died in 1783).

In 1752 this couple had a son named Meshulam. He was the well known Gaon R' Meshulam Igra. He spent his childhood in the home of his rabbi, the rabbi of Kolomia.

His father, who saw that his son was destined to greatness, gave him a basic education and then provided him with well-known tutors. At age nine the son already amazed his teachers with his shrewdness and knowledge of the Talmud. In 1761 he gave a Sabbath sermon at the great synagogue in Brody in the presence of the town rabbi, R' Itsikl Hamburger (R' Yitskhak Halevi Horovits). At the age of 13 he married the daughter of the wealthy town leader of Brody, Shmuel Bik. However, after a short time his wife divorced him and in 1768 he married Rivka Esther, daughter of the Rabbi of Brody, R' Yitskhak Horovits. In 1768 R' Meshulam Igra became the rabbi of Tismanitse and maintained close contact with the rabbis of his hometown, Buczacz, until 1784 when he left to serve as rabbi of the Pressburg community.

Up to the end of the 18th century the rabbis of Buczacz were:

1. R' Yaakov Eliyahu Ben-Moshe Mak, who escaped in the 1648 calamities from Sharigrod, and was a rabbi in Buczacz;
2. R' Elkhanan Ben-Ze'ev Volf, author of *Dat Yekutiel* (Zhulkva, 1696); his son, R' Abele, was the son-in-law of the Parnas of the Council of the Four Lands, R' Tsvi Ben Shimshon Maisels of Belz, who was active in the meetings of the Council during the years 1667, 1678, 1690, 1691.[13] His grandson, R' Shimshon Ben-Yaakov, was a rabbi in Zhulkva.
3. R' Moshe, a native of Zhulkva, was head of the rabbinic court of Buczacz for several years, and was afterwards chosen to be a religious court judge in Zhulkva;
4. Up until 1740, R' Aryeh Leibush Bar Mordekhai Madrish Auerbakh was a rabbi in Buczacz;[14] he was an uncle and rabbi of R' Meir Margolius author of the responsa *Meir Netivim* [Illuminator of Paths]. One of his daughters married R' Naftali Hirts Broda, head of the rabbinic court in Kolinits, and second to R' Khayim, one of the worthies of Zhulkva. In 1740 R' Aryeh Leibush was chosen rabbi in Stanislav where he served in the rabbinate until his death in Stanislav in 1750;
5. Meir Ben Hirts, who was also a state rabbi and in 1775 signed a census list of Jews in Buczacz and vicinity;[15]
6. R' Tsvi Hirsh Ben Yaakov Kara was born 1740 and died in 1814 in Buczacz.

In 1794 after being invited to serve as rabbi in Pressburg the Gaon R' Meshulam Igra spoke to the rabbis of the regional towns, who came to visit him in Tishminitse in order to depart from him: "I appointed to this region the Gaon Tsvi Hirsh Kara, head of the rabbinic court of Buczacz, who was an outstanding teacher. Address all difficult problems to him." From then on all the distinguished rabbis of Galicia turned to him with all their questions and doubts.[16] R' Tsvi Hirsh corresponded with all the great rabbis of his generation, such as R' Jacob of Lisa, R' Aryeh Horovits of Stanislav, R' Efraim Zalman Margolius of Brody, R' Yehoshua Heshel, head of the Tarnopol rabbinic court. After his death, his responsa *Neta Shaashuim* (Zhulkva 1829) was published.

3.

During the days of struggle with the Sabbateans in the eastern areas of Poland, the Jews of Buczacz were influenced by this movement.

As we know, in these parts the Sabbatean movement had a considerable stronghold, which succeeded in infiltrating into the circles of rabbis and scholars. The Sabbatean teachings were brought here by Jews from Turkey who settled in Kaminets-Podolsk at the time of the Ottoman conquest and who succeeded in spreading Sabbateanism among the Jews of Podolia. Besides communities such as Busk, Glinyani, Tishiminetse, Horodenka, Nadvorne, Podheytse, Zbaraz, Zloczow, Kamyunka and Rohatyn in which there were many Sabbateans, followers of the movement were also to be found in Buczacz, an important center for this sect. In their early years they operated in secrecy without raising suspicion, content to distribute words of heresy and recruit followers. They held constant contact with Shabtai Tsvi's emissaries, at first with Khayim Malakh, who was born in Poland and set out for Turkey at the end of the 17th century where he joined Shabtai Tsvi. He later returned to Poland in 1700 by way of Vienna and Berlin in order to strengthen the belief in Shabtai Tsvi.

On this trip he visited mainly in Belorussia, assuming that the sect had already become established there and had many followers. He visited Zhulkva, Horodenka, Podheytse and Buczacz. His sermons won many converts who believed his words.

After the failure of the Hasidim who emigrated to Erets-Yisrael headed by R' Yehuda Khasid, Khayim Malach visited Poland in 1715 for the second time. However, this time R' Khakham Tsvi warned his brother R' Shaul, head of the rabbinic court of Krakow, of this sect and especially of the "Bad Angel" Khayim Malakh.

After Malach left Belorussia, the Sabbateans of Buczacz were in contact with Moshe Meir of Kamionka – one of the sect's most prominent propagandists in Poland, with his brother-in-law Fishl (Fayvl) of Zloczow and with the preacher Yissakhar of Podheytse. We can also assume that they were in contact with the known Sabbatean of Zhulkva – Yitskhak Kadeyner. From testimonies concerning the Buczacz Sabbateans that were given in 1726 in a Buczacz house of study, we hear that "two of the treacherous movement members that were in Buczacz went to Nadvorne and exchanged wives with each other." In Nadvorne "all the heretics were followers of Shabtai Tsvi."[17] Among the Buczacz Sabbateans in the mid-18th century were Mordechai Ben-Moshe and Yissachar Ben Natan. These two were involved also in the matter concerning R' Jonathan Eybeschuetz [1690-1764] and his book "*VeAvo Hayom El HaAyin*," which raised quite an uproar among the rabbis and leaders of Polish Jewry in the years 1751-1752 due to its Sabbatean character. In a testimony given in 1752 by Natan Levi before a body of rabbinical judges in the rabbinic court of Brody, we hear from Natan Levi that "a citizen of Buczacz, whose name was Mordechai Ben-Moshe, came to Stanislavov as a spokesman. I pointed to the words of heresy in Eybeschuetz's book in order that he understand, for which he thanked me and confessed and attested to his sins, for he was a believer in such heresy until that day. He added these words: "These teachings I have learned from R' Yissakhar Bar Natan of Buczacz and these writings are sent to him by R' Yonatan of Prague." These writings were sent by him and were spread by him and his friends all the way to Salonica.[18]

Remnants of these Sabbateans joined Jacob Frank's group following his arrival in Belorussia.

A fable spread among the people stating that Frank was born in Korolovka, one of the suburbs of Buczacz. However, this is only a myth. It is true that he was born in Korolovka, but not in a suburb of

Buczacz, but rather in the small town of Korolovka where his cousins were still residing in 1756. We do not know how many followers he had in Buczacz, but we can say for sure that there were Frankists there at the time. It is known that the majority of his supporters came from Busk and Glinyani, which is the reason why they requested from the Primas Lubinski, in an official request dated May 16th 1759, that they receive a permanent foothold in Busek and Glinyani, making it into an autonomous district of sorts.

One Buczacz Frankist we know of is "Itsik Meir Bashush Zlatshover Hadar of the sacred community of Buczacz" from a testimony[19] given on the 2nd of Sivan 1756 before the rabbinic court of Satanov concerning the lechery in Lantskron. He brought to R' Shlomo Segal of Lantskron Sabbatean writings, among them Jonathan Eybeschuetz's book "*VeAvo Hayom El HaAyin*".

It is interesting that there were no Buczacz Jews among the Frankists who converted in Lvov following the historic dispute in that city from July 17th through September 10th 1759.

In the 18th century the financial situation of the Buczazc Jews was good enough to enable them to trade according to the 1699 statutes. However, one cannot deny that most of the population suffered from the tax burden that was laid upon the Jews at the time. During the years 1713-1714 the Jews of Buczacz paid 1200 gulden for head tax alone.[20] In addition to this the community paid interest on its debts and collected various other taxes.

Their representatives in the regional committee watched over their interests and joined with the representatives of Zhulkva and Brody to achieve independence from the Lvov center. It is interesting to point out that whenever the appointment of a state rabbi was on the agenda, Buczacz always put forward a rival candidate. In the latter half of the 18th century, a prominent tobacco merchant named Avrahamtshik of Buczacz imported tobacco from Turkey for a well known Polish tobacco company. He was a partner of Fayvel Ben-Shimshon (Samsonowicz) of Kamenets-Podolskiy.[21]

In 1765, the census of Jews in Buczacz recorded 1055 persons (988 adults and 67 children); in the surrounding vicinity there were 303 persons (278 adults, 25 children). A total sum of 1358 Jews (1267 adults, 91 children).

After the death of Stefan Potocki in 1727, his wife Joanna of the house of Sieniavski administered Buczacz till her death in 1733. Her heir, Mikolai Potocki, advanced the town – he built the city hall in Gothic style and founded the first high school [gymnasium]. The Jewish community was pressed financially and borrowed from him 1000 gulden at 10% interest. The loan was effected by the communal leaders.

Lazar Falkov. Yaakov Ben-Yaakov and Yosef Ben-Betsalel. On August the 10th 1747, Potocki ordered the community to provide substitute payment; namely, to give the Greek church (on a permanent basis) 250 liters of tallow in three payments per month.[22] However, the community did not agree with this demand and was forced by a court ruling of May 10th 1758 to pay the debt.

In 1772 with the first division of Poland, Buczacz was annexed to the Kingdom of Austria and its fate was that of all the communities in Galicia. In the first division Buczacz belonged to the Zalshatsiki district and later on to the Stanislavov district.

4.

At the outset of Austrian rule, the district administrator Kulmanhueber cancelled all the taxes that the Jews paid to the town owner Count Piotr Potocki according to Polish law, and also the right to collect certification fees for the election of the Buczacz rabbi. Austrian law did not permit collection of such fees by town owners. Potocki protested a number of times at the Kaiser's court. The Lvov governor advised him not to disturb the Kaiser's court in such a matter. However, he finally succeeded in his appeal; the Lvov governor was ordered to investigate and in the meantime to continue as in the past.[23]

According to the statutes of Josef the 2nd from May the 27th 1785 it was determined that the rabbi of Buczacz would be the regional rabbi. Of course the Jews of Buczacz suffered from the new statutes that reduced their financial possibilities. Especially harmful was the prohibition of estate, and winery leasing that was enacted in 1784. They were also prohibited to lease taverns (propinacje). In June 1778 the community appealed to the authorities for protection against "the cruel persecutions of the estate owner Count Peter Potocki." At the time Potocki requested from the central authorities to permit him to collect taxes from the butchers that were due to him by right of the statute and his being the town owner. He also requested that the heads of the community provide him with only the taxes concerning kosher meat. In July 1778 the governor replied that the situation would stay as it is until the final arrangement is decided upon.

Despite this reply, Potocki requested in September 1778 to hasten the conclusion of this dispute between the community and himself since the community was collecting sums that belonged to him, thus causing him great losses.

Despite attempts made by his attorney Patsintski to solve the matter, the dispute went on for some years. In the summer of 1786 Potocki once again appealed to the central authorities to decide upon the matter, for the community was collecting the krupka [grain] taxes, thus causing him great financial losses. He demanded that he be compensated retroactively and that he be allowed to collect taxes in the future. The Governor replied on December the 6th 1786, stating that he must wait for the final arrangement concerning the community's debts and their liquidation.

Meanwhile, Potocki reached a "secret arrangement" with the Jews concerning leasing, which by law was forbidden to the Jews. This became known to the authorities and in 1787 the town owner Potocki was fined for giving leasing privileges to the Jews of Buczacz. His sentence was printed out and sent to all the courts of law "that all shall see and beware."[24]

At the same time, the Jewish population of Buczacz grew, since many Jews were leaving the villages for the towns. They were forced to leave their homes because by the law of 1789 Jews who did not engage in agriculture were not authorized to live in the country, However they were permitted to deal in any craft and to trade. At the head of the Buczacz Jews stood three men who received authorization from the authorities. As part of the reforms that the Austrian government initiated among the Jews of Galicia (following Herts Homberg's appointment as the Inspector of Galician Jewish schools), 48 elementary schools were opened in 1788. One was a boy's school in Buczacz that existed until 1806.(Homberg's family in Krakow took the family name Autor.)

During these years, there lived in Buczacz R' Pinkhas Eliyahu Horovits author of *Sefer HaBrit*. His father Meir and his mother Yente were from Vilna. In 1776 their son was born in Lvov, through which they were passing on their way to Buczacz, where they wished to settle.[25] However, they called him "Vilna" after his father's descent. During his youth he wandered throughout Galicia and Germany and later on moved to Buczacz.Here he lived for some years, and started writing the book which was to stimulate the young to study secular subjects. He was one of the first heralds of general education in Galicia and Poland. His book also found acclaim among Jewish circles in other countries, and due to its clear and popular style was even translated into Judezmo in the Middle East. In spite of his inclination toward secular sciences, he stayed faithful to religion and tradition and stated this in his book.His sole purpose was to encourage Jews to study general studies, which he saw as necessary for the full understanding of Jewish texts. In the early 1790s he left Buczacz because of an eye condition attributed to eye strain caused by overwork on his book. He moved to Buva and after some years went to Pressburg, where he finished his book; it was published in Brin in 1797. His book is actually a popular encyclopedia of sorts for general knowledge, dealing especially with natural history. In the second part of his book "*Divrey Emet*" [Words of Truth], one can find correct views regarding Jewish life in Poland. He especially gave a realistic description regarding the dismal condition the Jews were in and preached in favor of changing their economic structure by means of productivisation. This would erase idleness and unemployment, and would raise their status vis a vis the gentiles. His book played an important role in furthering general knowledge among Jewish youth, which read the work in secret and drew from it their secular education. Pinkhas Eliyahu Horovits died in Krakow on April the 21st, 1821.

During this period heavy taxes were levied on the Jews. Particularly onerous were the taxes on kosher meat and on candles. According to the law of August 28th 1787, Galician Jews were ordered to take German family names by the first of January 1788. With this there began the process of the germanizing of the Jews; rabbis were commanded to conduct all their affairs in the German language alone.

The head of the community at this time was Rabbi Meir Schneier. He not only conducted the affairs of his own congregation with great energy, but carried out many important tasks for the benefit of all Galician Jews; they recognized him as one of their chief representatives. Taken by surprise by the law issued in Vienna on February 18th 1787 which made Jews individually liable to serve in the military, representatives of all the communities (at the initiative of the Lvov community) decided to propose to the central government the payment of a ransom sum in place of personal military service. For this purpose a three-man delegation was sent to Vienna: the Lvov rabbi Rabbi Tsvi Hirsh Rozanes, the representative of the Brody Jews, Rabbi Yaakovka Landa, son of the Gaon R' Yekhezkl Landa (author of *Noda be-Yehuda*), and R' Meir Schneier of Buczacz – proof of how greatly the Buczacz community was honored among Galician Jews.

In June 1790 the above-mentioned representatives traveled to Vienna and presented their appeal for the easing of restrictions on the practice of their occupations and businesses, for the return of their right to sell alcoholic beverages in towns and villages (abolished in 1797 with the consequent economic ruination of thousands of Jews), for the restoration of their jurisdiction (through the rabbinical courts) over matters of religious law such as marriage and divorce, and for instituting, in place of conscription, a system of paying a recruit-tax, it being difficult for Jews to observe their religious duties while serving in the military; the Jews are ready to pay a ransom-sum to replace conscription.

After making two more appeals in July, repeating their earlier requests, they were successful in their intercession.On July 29, 1790, Kaiser Leopold issued an order exempting Jews from military service, but stipulating that the community supply the required number of recruits from local volunteers or from abroad, or pay the sum of 30 florins per head so that the authorities could purchase other recruits.[26]

In May 1790 gymnasium [high school] students were accused of attacking Moshe Berkovits, a Jew, and stealing some of his belongings.The municipality, together with the community representatives Berish Hofman and Reuven Shternbaum, investigated the charge and concluded that the students were innocent.[27]

At the outset of the 19th century, the Jewish population increased considerably. In 1812 there were 352 Jews in Buczacz, 696 men and 768 women. Altogether, there were 1464 persons.[28] Most of the Jews dealt in trade and tavern keeping, occupations in which, however, Jews were under serious restrictions. Also in this period Buczacz was the commercial center of the estates.Here was concentrated all crop and cattle trade along with trade in all other agricultural products, all run by Jews. The community was in debt from the days of autonomy in Poland, but slowly managed to pay off the sum of 10,675 gulden. Eventually, they became administratively sound. In 1831 a cholera epidemic caused the death of 600 Jews. This was also the year in which the great synagogue burned to the ground.[29] With the help of Mikolai Potocki the synagogue was rebuilt in the town's center. However, on July 29th, 1865 a huge fire burst out in which the synagogue together with 220 houses were destroyed.

The community did not suffer from domestic conflicts between the misnagdim and the hasidim on the one hand, and between the above two and the maskilim on the other.

A distinguished and highly moral individual who had great influence over the community was R' Avraham David Ben-Asher Wahrman, who served as Buczacz's rabbi from 1813. R' Avraham David Wahrman, whose father was Anshil (Asher), son of R' David and whose mother was Rekhl, daughter of R' Avraham Rekhlis, was born on the sixth day of Adar 1771 in Nadvorne. His father was a man of his word, hence his nickname, Wahrman, later became his surname. R' Asher was a great scholar and a merchant, a distinguished citizen in his land. In addition to Jewish studies, his son was taught arithmetic, German and Polish. It proved difficult to find a teacher for the son by the time he reached the age of nine – he was that advanced. (Another young man at the time who excelled in his studies was Shlomo Kopler, who years later became a tax farmer with control of the candle tax and oppressed Galician Jews no end.)In 1780 the Gaon Meshulam Igra visited Nadvorne and was amazed at the boy's knowledge of the Talmud and predicted a great future for him as a Gaon. At the time, word about the boy came to the ears of R' Tsvi Hirsh Kara of Buczacz who wanted R' Avraham David for a son-in-law and visited Nadvorne to arrange for a marriage agreement with the boy's father. After his marriage, while staying at his father-in-law's house, R' Avraham David befriended Rabbi Khayim, who was later appointed head of the Czernowicz rabbinic court (author of *Be'er mayim khayim* on the Torah).

Already in his youth R' Avraham David corresponded with R' Yaakov of Lisa (author of *Khavot daat*), who was known for his critical acuity and who found fault in all the contemporary authorities. However, he greatly respected R' Avraham David as well as the Gaon R' Neta, head of the Podheytse rabbinic court and a well known cabalist. R' Avraham David delved deeply into the Kabala. In 1791 he was appointed rabbi of Biazlovits, where he broadened his studies not only in the sea of talmudics and exegetics, but also studied mathematics, astronomy and natural history. He did so, in his words, to answer heretics – the early talmudists also did not neglect worldly subjects and useful sciences.

With particular devotion he also gave himself to the study of cabala. During the period in which he occupied the Biazlovits pulpit, he became acquainted with R' Levi-Yitskhak of Barditshev who visited the nearby village of Romalov and was deeply impressed by R' Avraham David's personality and belief. R' Avraham David was one of the Tsadik R' Moshe Leyb of Sasov's students, and one of his followers.

The influence of hasidism was strongly felt in his writings, especially in *Birkat David* (published in 1805).

In 1814, after the death of his father-in-law, he inherited the former's rabbinical post. However, the community of Biazlovits was not willing to part with him. But Buczacz townsmen came in the night with wagons and moved R' Avraham David and his household to Buczacz bodily.

In Buczacz he had lasting influence over his community, and especially on many scholars who studied under him. These included R' Shlomo, head of the rabbinic court of Skala (author of *Bet Shlomo*), and R' Khayim Ben Shlomo, head of the rabbinic court of Czernowicz, supporters of Besht hasidism. He attacked R' Yekhezkl Landa (author of *Noda Be-Yehuda*) for his opposition to hasidism, and the authors of *Siduro shel shabat* (Puritsik 1818), *Be'er mayim khayim* (Czernowicz 1820, 1849), *Shaar hatefila* (Sodilkov 1833). [?He attacked] R' Shmerl, head of the rabbinic court of Rimolov, R' Moshe of Budzanov, R' Berl, head of the rabbinic court of Bayan, R' Fayvl Schreier, head of the rabbinic court of Bohorodtsani (authors of *Giduley hakodesh*, *Mikdash me'at*, *Mishmeret hakodesh*, *Asefat zkeynim* and one of the first Khovevey Tsion [Lovers of Zion] in Galicia.

During the same period, R' Wahrman was in close contact with Efraim Zalmen Margoliot of Brody, under whose influence hasidism grew and became more entrenched in Buczacz. Because of his closeness to hasidism, R' Wahrman's status as rabbi of Buczacz was compromised. The maskilim and the misnagdim, whose numbers were large, and who were represented well in community institutions, resented R' Abraham David Wahrman's hasidic leanings. They especially resented his introduction of half-day long prayers inspired by the Ari and the *Zohar*. Leading the opposition to him was the community leader R' Avish Shtern, founder of a synagogue in his name, known for his scholarship and one of the wealthiest men in the land.[30]

The maskilim would make no concessions to R' Wahrman, and one of them even submitted a memorandum to the state authorities in which he described the "deceitful acts" of the Buczacz hasidim. In the memorandum it is stated that the rabbi was deposed from his post because of his hasidic sins – something we do not know from any of the descriptions of his life.[31]

He was also accused of being a healer of the sick, and of hiding deserters from military conscription, smugglers and plain thieves – all out of pity for those fleeing their pursuers.

He died on the 29th of Tishri 1841.[32] Large numbers of hasidim attended his funeral and on his grave they swore loyalty to his principles. A mausoleum of especially large dimensions was erected over his grave, to which thousands of Jews streamed.

R' Avraham David Ben Asher Wahrman wrote eleven books.[33] His life was marked by great love of the people of Israel and by great enthusiasm. He held that through Torah man comes nearer to his inner self.

The increase in the number of hasidim led to conflict with the maskilim. Seeing that the head of the town supported them and the hasidic rabbis, the maskilim turned to the state authorities and pointed out the damages the hasidim were causing to the state.

On August 1841, Yosef Tefer, a Buczacz maskil, submitted a detailed account of the doings of the hasidim in Buczacz, and especially bitter complaints against the rebbe, who was the son and heir of Rabbi R' Avraham David Wahrman.[34] The memorandum tells us that he held the key to the mausoleum of his father, R' Avraham David. Anyone who wished to visit was required to donate a sum for his widow and a contribution for Erets-Yisrael. According to Tefer, his son was the one who added the surname "Wahrman" to his original name. Tefer recommends that the authorities demand a report on all donations for Erets-Yisrael and also suggests that he be prohibited from assembling his hasidim and from conducting prayers on his father's grave, and that an end be put to the deceitful acts performed there.

For this purpose a specially authorized official should be sent to dismantle the mausoleum and to remove the gravestone which stirs the hasidim to perform their demonic dances. However, the town owner and the local authorities are indifferent to all of this, since the flow of hasidim into the town means money in its coffers. Tefer himself used to be a merchant in Buczacz, where he was born and raised, but moved to Tarnopol and is happy for having left the hasidic hell in Buczacz. But the fate of his brethren prompts his concern. The hasidim scorn work and education and they neither know how to be nor wish to be useful citizens. Their rebbe preaches sectarianism and a life of idleness, as opposed to Tarnopol, where Jews work and earn the respect of their fellow citizens.

5.

Perceptible changes took place in the community after 1848. The influence of the maskilim led to improvements in education. While Buczacz did not play as important a role in the haskala [Enlightenment] movement as did Tarnopol, Brody, or Tishminitse [Tysmienica], it already contained many circles which encouraged aspirations towards education and cultural progress among the Jews.

Within the community, administrative control was in the hands of the haredim [Orthodox]. There were twelve synagogues in the town and thirty-six minyanim [quorums]. No rabbi was appointed after R' Wahrman's death. Rabbi R' Tsadok Rinek served for several years. After 1853, Rabbi R' Avraham Ben Tsvi Hirsh Teumim, formerly rabbi in Zborov (author of *Khesed le-Avraham*], served as rabbi. He died in 1862.[35]

Thanks to its stratum of maskilim and to the legal status of Galician Jewry, Buczacz Jews occupied an important place in the municipal administration. Of the thirty members of the municipality, 12 representatives were Jewish; nine were Poles and nine were Ruthenians [Ukrainians].

When Jews were allowed to own real estate after 1860, Buczacz Jews also requested that they be allowed to purchase real estate.

In 1860, two Jews, Feuerstein and Hofman, asked to have estates which they had bought illegally, registered in the land registry.[36]

In the constitutional period of Austria beginning in 1867, Buczacz began to fill an important role in the life of Galician Jewry. Buczacz was united with Sniatyn and Kolomea to form a single electoral region with a large Jewish population. This made it possible to elect a Jewish representative to the Galician Sejm and, later, to the Viennese parliament. In 1868 Dr. Maximillian Landsberger was elected representative to the Sejm and from there he went as representative to the Viennese parliament. In those days delegates were not elected directly but by regional parliaments (Landtage). Dr. Landsberger completed his studies at the University of Vienna, and afterwards became a well known lawyer in Lvov, where he was active in community affairs. In 1840 he took part in founding the committee for building a reform synagogue [bet kneset leneorim 'synagogue for the enlightened'] in Lvov. But this did not prevent him from opposing the maskilim and cooperating with the Orthodox Meir Mints in 1842 in a community issue. It is no wonder that an organ of the progressive maskilim in Vienna published a report from Lvov accusing Dr. Landsberger and Dr. Mahl of having joined them out of personal motives, since the authorities had not elected them to the community council, where maskilim were the majority. In the years 1848-1863 he was a member of the Lvov city council and from 1865 also a parnas [leader] of the Lvov Jewish community.

After 1856, the year in which Mark Dobes, the Kolomea[37]-Sniatyn-Buczacz delegate to the Galician Sejm died, Dr. Landsberger was elected in his place; he was elected a second time in 1867 and served until 1873. Actually he was a delegate only up to 1870. In that year the Poles left the parliament because of disagreements with the central government over Galician autonomy. Landsberger left the parliament together with the Poles, leaving Galician Jewry without representation in the Viennese parliament until 1873; in 1870 he also gave up his mandate to the Galician Sejm.

Helped by an alliance with the Ukrainians, Dr. Oswald Honigsman (1824-1880) was elected in direct balloting as delegate from Kolomea-Buczacz. He was a native of Risha who had completed his studies at the University of Vienna. In the years 1861-1866 he represented the Jews of Lvov on the Lvov municipal council together with Dr. Landsberger, Dr. Kulisher and Mark Dobes. In 1861 he was chosen to represent the progressives on the Lvov community committee and in 1867 he was selected in Brody to take the place of Meir Kalir in the Galician Sejm. In a debate in the Sejm on the abolition of restrictions upon Galician Jews, he stressed that he spoke as a Polish assimilationist. Despite such views, after his election as a parliamentary delegate he joined the other Jewish delegates from Galicia – Dr. Joachim Landa (Brody), Nathan Kalir (Brody) and Herman Mieses (Drohowic) – in the constitutional party (Verfassungpartei), not like the delegate from Krakow, Albert Mendelsburg, who joined the Polish fraction. This Jewish separatism continued until 1879. In the elections held in 1879 the Jews of Buczacz-Sniatyn-Kolomea chose as their delegate the Krakow rabbi, R' Shimon Shreiber, who joined the Polish fraction.

Following his death in 1883, a meeting of voters decided to suggest the candidacy of the renowned Viennese rabbi and author, Dr. Joseph Samuel Bloch, who was born in Dokla and was famous at the time for his courageous and proud struggle against Prof. Dr. Rohling and his book "*Der Talmud-Jude.*" The Jewish political organization in Galicia, *Shomer Yisrael* [Guardian of Israel], understood this candidacy as an action against them, and turned to the Jewish voters in the Kolomea-Sniatyn-Buczaczdistrict in order to present a candidate of their own. Also the Polish press attacked Dr. Bloch's candidacy on the grounds that he was a Viennese rabbi who neither knew Galicia nor spoke Polish.[38] Dr. Bloch, on the other hand, stated that he would join the Polish faction in the Parliament. Counter to the decisions of Shomer Yisrael, the Main Voting Committee of Lvov, and the wishes of the authorities, Dr. Bloch was elected a delegate to the Viennese parliament. He received 1460 votes as opposed to the 983 votes for the university professor from Krakow Dr. Warschauer. In 1885, elections for the new parliament were held. Once again Dr. Bloch met with the opposition of official circles. On May 2nd, 1885 a voting committee announced Bloch's candidacy at the Buczacz synagogue. The Central Voting Committee in Lvov put forward their candidate, Dr. Emil Bik. The election struggle was a fierce one. Dr. Bik, besides having the support of the authorities, the community leaders and the mayors, had large sums of money with which to buy votes. In Buczacz, Mayor Berish Shtern declared that Bloch would not receive over one hundred votes.[39] Dr. Bloch was promised by the Galician governor that his representative would be allowed to be present at the polling booth at the time of the elections.

When Dr. Bloch arrived in Buczacz, he was forced to stay in a private home because the district minister forbade the hotel owners from entertaining him. Berish Shtern added to the voters' list names of deceased citizens and was confident Bloch would fail. He did not hesitate to inform the Christians that Dr. Bloch was anti-Christian. Dr. Bloch writes in his memoirs about election day in Buczacz, a day on which the Jews of Galicia openly and daringly opposed the community and municipality leaders and fought for their public rights.

The delegate of the national central electoral committee, Jan Dubrzanski, a well known anti-Semite, declared at the voters' assembly: "If you vote for Dr. Bloch, you will live to regret it. Not only the town, but every single voter will feel the wrath of the entire country."

The Jewish mayor of Buczazc told the Christian inhabitants that the Jews were defending Dr. Bloch because of his hatred of Christians and because he wanted to imprison two respectable Catholic priests. Public notices, written by Jewish lawyers, appealed to the fanatic Jew-haters to fight the battle of the Jewish delegate, Dr. Emil Bik.

"On election day and on several days preceding it, I was in Buczacz. Two days prior to the elections, Jewish voters still hadn't received any identification cards or ballot slips. During these two days (Saturday and Sunday) all the Jewish voters assembled before the town hall awaiting these papers. They did not budge for a moment. Sabbath prayers were recited under the stars. But Mr. Mayor (Shtern), who with my help was saved in the past from bankruptcy, did not want to give out a single card. Telegrams were sent to the district governor and the governor of Galicia, who gave orders to provide the voters with the proper documents. The Mayor "complied" – he handed out 20 ballot slips."

"The struggle commenced anew. Voters ran to the district governor, who ordered that they immediately be given identification cards and ballot slips -- on condition, however, that the distributed ballots all bore the name of Dr. Bik."

"One man who was acquainted with the electoral regulations went to the district governor in order to demand a copy of his identification papers. He received a slap in the face instead.

"However, the Jewish voters were not deterred and did not move from the field of battle".

"They kept on demanding identification cards and ballot slips. The gendarmes intervened and tried to drive away the grumbling crowd, but to no avail! When the gendarmes threatened with rifles, the crowd bared their chests and cried, 'Shoot!'"

"The struggle lasted two days. After repeated protests before the prime minister in Vienna and the district governor, the Jewish voters finally received 450 identification cards and ballot slips."

"On Monday morning everyone assembled at the synagogue and swore to God and their fellow townsmen that they would give their vote to the candidate of the Jews, Dr. Bloch. Everyone went to vote, not a single soul stayed behind. The results, which were counted behind closed doors, found 306 in favor of Bloch and 503 in favor of Bik. It should be stated that Buczacz had only 300 Christian voters. Mr. Shtern's trickery, once again, did not fail him. I was defeated."[40]

However, the votes of the citizens of Kolomea were the decisive ones. Dr. Bloch won the elections by 28 votes.

In the Jewish streets of Galicia, you could witness the hustle and bustle of Jews happy and proud over their victory and Dr. Bik's defeat. For they saw Dr. Bik as a mere tool used by the Polish Galician authorities to undermine the success of a brave Jewish opponent of the anti-Semites.

These elections signaled the path of Galician Jewry in the future, and were a prelude to the national struggle of the Jewish people seeking national and civil recognition in 1907.

In 1891 Bloch again fought to gain the mandate in the district of Kolomea-Sniatyn-Buczacz. A wealthy candidate was put up against him in these elections as well. Leon Meizlish,[41] who resided in Paris and had financial means, was chosen at the advice of the rabbi of Belz, Mordechai Pelets (grandson of the Warsaw rabbi, R' Dov Berish Meizlish). He had the support of the Belz rabbi and President of the

Makhzikey Hadat [Defenders of the Faith] Yitskhak Shreiber of Drohowic.Meizlish lost even though the elections cost him 800,000 gulden.He didn't dare to come to Buczacz. The assimilated Jews who grouped around the periodical Ojczyzna [Native Land] supported the candidacy of the Christian Count Starzinski

On March 4th –5th Dr. Bloch was elected. He received 2128 votes, Count Starzinski 1778, and Meizlish 97. However, on October 22nd, 1895 Dr. Bloch relinquished his parliamentary seat and Dr. Maximilian Trachtenberg, mayor of Kolomea, was chosen in his place. Trachtenberg served as a parliamentary delegate until 1901. In the last parliament prior to the amendment of the electoral law in 1907, the representative of the Jews of Kolomea-Buczacz was Dr. Nathan Zeinfeld.

In the second half of the 19th century, the Jewish population of Buczacz grew. However, their percentage in the total population decreased.

In 1870 Buczacz counted a population of 8,959, out of whom 6,077 were Jews (67.9%); in 1900 in a population of 11,755, 6,730 were Jews (57.3%).

In 1892, with the help of the Baron Hirsh Fund, a Jewish school was founded with 262 pupils. In 1907, 180 pupils studied at the Baron Hirsh Fund school. In 1908, the gymnasium [high school] had 696 pupils, of whom 216 were Jewish.

The economic picture had not changed. Most Jews made a living from various forms of commerce. Export trade (grains, agricultural produce and timber) in particular grew. Many Jews also engaged in crafts. At the end of the 19th century factories and workshops were built that provided work for many Polish Jews in the manufacture of bricks, lime, soap, candles and in operating water mills and breweries.

In the seventies, the maskilim of Buczacz founded the "Bet HaMidrash" Library and the Lacznosc [Contact] Club, which were centers for the best of the Jewish intelligentsia. Among the lovers of Hebrew literature and the maskilim in Buczazc we should mention Wolf Bik, Berish Bochheim, Abba Shtern, Ezra Danberg, Pohorila – a Hebrew author and translator, Yaakov Frenkel, Pesakh Frits, the playwright David Anderman[42] who wrote Emuna VeHaskala (Drohowic 1887).[43]

With the upsurge of the Zionist movement in Galicia in the late 1880s, even the most prominent public personalities of Jewish Buczacz were impressed with the idea of the return to Zion. From a nationalist point of view, the first seeds of national awareness were sown in the electoral struggles of 1883 and 1885.

Despite this revival, no movement was founded that could unite all Jews around the Zionist movement, which was already active in other eastern Galician towns. In 1892 efforts were made to found a Zion Society and slowly the Zionist idea started to spread among all classes of Jews, especially among the young. They understood that a change in the life of the Jewish people was necessary, and in order to achieve such a goal the Jews needed to unite. In 1893, the Zion Society was founded. On April 31st, 1894, the first public meeting was held; Dr. Tsipper and David Maltz spoke, explaining the essentials of Zionism. At this meeting it was unanimously decided to broaden the Zion Society; a committee was chosen which was empowered by the executive committee headed by Wolf Tseimer to organize the society on the basis of properly written statutes.

In addition, two meetings were held at the club of the Jewish intelligentsia, "Kesher" (Lacznosc), in which Dr. Tsipper and Dr. Maltz discussed the Zionist plan and answered questions during the debate. Also attending these meetings was the head of the Jewish community, Abba Shtern[44], who was mayor from 1879.

Following this meeting, the executive committee issued a circular that was composed by the Hebrew author, Yitskhak Fernhof:

"Brothers! From the day the people of Israel went into exile and ceased to be a nation settled on its own land, ever since our dispersion among the nations, scattered to remote lands and distant islands, we have been hated and oppressed for no reason. Even in these days of freedom and liberty when there is one constitution and one law for all – on paper, we are still persecuted. For not much has changed and we continue to be exploited and fractured, harassed by the anti-Semites from without and by our own disunity from within. The people has given its support to various parties and if our enemies shoot their arrows of hate at us for doing so, at least we are not guilty. But if we allow differences among ourselves to consume us and destroy every remnant of national feeling, our sins will be beyond forgiveness. Thus to you, our brothers, we call out: 'Awake! Let us be truly united! Let us bridge the great gap that divides the tribes, that separates the younger generation – lawyers, doctors, writers, merchants – from craftsmen of all kinds. Don't scorn your neighbor, but rather with national feeling unite behind one idea as our ancestors did – which is what preserved them throughout the ages despite the hostile designs of their enemies. Let us walk hand in hand; let us learn to value ourselves, to recognize our talents. If we say to Zion, 'You are my people', no weapon will defeat us. Therefore listen to what the Zion Society says: 'Unite in every community and become one deeply unified association; help one another; feel responsible for your oppressed brothers who go up to our Holy Land to work the soil. Let every one do what he can to help his brother generally. My aim is to unite you in spreading and extolling knowledge of our national goals to our people in a wholly non-partisan manner. The means by which they can achieve this goal are as follows:

  1. Foster the study of Hebrew and broaden knowledge of the history of the Jewish people and its literature.
  2. Give talks and lectures on the above goals.
  3. Celebrate anniversaries and holidays of our literary history.
  4. Found libraries and establish reading rooms. Let us have friendship and togetherness as we move toward our goals.[45]

These words were directed also to the Jews in the vicinity, calling them to join the nationalist movement and to found Zion societies like the one in Buczacz.

At its first general meeting on June 17th, 1894, the society was already organized according to set statutes. On this occasion Dr. Gershon Tsipper and Rabbi Mendel Leibush Landa of Przemyshl spoke in Yiddish and Hebrew. Both of them succeeded in recruiting many new members. The first committee was chosen, with Wolf (Wilhelm) Tsimmer as President, Shmuel Taller as Vice-President, Yehoshua Hollander as Treasurer, the Hebrew writer Yitskhak Fernhof and Fishl Engelstein as Hebrew Secretaries, Dr. Zigmund Goldshtaub as Secretary in the Polish language, and Yaakov M. Fernhof, Moshe Wisser, Shmuel Neiman, Arnold Ringel, Shimon Hecht and Ayzik Bergshtof as committee members.[46]

In that year the Zion Society had 300 members. The society developed nicely thanks to Dr. Goldshtaub, Shmuel Neiman and Yitskhak Fernhof, who spread the Zionist idea in study houses and synagogues, as well as among circles of the Jewish intelligentsia, who were quite indifferent to Jewish matters.

The Zion Society also founded a "Bet Mikra" [study program] for high school students. They met daily for Hebrew and Jewish studies under Mordechai Kanfer, who was also a Hebrew writer, and Yitskhak Fernhof.[47] Together with the founding of branches of the Zion Colonization Company in Vienna, a branch called "Erets-Yisrael" was also founded in Buczacz. Its active members included Wolf Tseimer, Anzelm Muzler, Arnold Ringel, Shmuel Taller and Yitskhak Fernhof.

In 1898 there were 150 members in the Zion Society, at whose head stood Hirsh Shtern. The finest of the youth and of the Jewish intelligentsia joined the Zionist movement. In the early 1890s a workers' association was founded by Dr. Anshl Muzler, but it failed to gather the Jewish youth around it.

Buczacz became one of the most important Zionist strongholds of eastern Galicia, giving the movement many hardworking activists.

Endnotes

1. In the 16th century, 46 cities were built in eastern Belorussia with the aim of creating a complete chain of fortified cities to serve as a line of defense against Tatar incursions into Poland.

2. I. Schipper, *Studia nad stosunkami Zydow w Polsce podczas sredniowiecza.* Lwow, 1911, p. 155.

3. Idem., p. 36.

4. I. Schipper, *Dzieje handlu zydowskiego na ziemiach polskich*, Warsaw, 1938, p. 87.

5. Xawery Lisicki, *Cudzoziemcy w Polsce.* Lwow, 1876, p. 182.
    5a. *Acta grodzkie i ziemskie*, Lwow, 1931, vol. 24, p. 380, no. 198, ##2,3.
    5b. Idem. p. 368, no. 205 1/5, #39. "boskieto jubet prawo kazdemu subvenireblizniemu."

6. In 1699 in the peace treaty signed at Karlowitz, Podolia and a third of the Ukraine were returned to Poland.

7. *Les anecdotes de Pologne ou Memoires secrets du Regnes de Jean Sobieski.* Paris, 1699, vol. 2,

pp. 228-230.

8. Ancient Polish measure equal to about 25 pounds.

9. A copy of the ordinances is in the Viennese internal affairs archive, carton 279, vol. 4.

10. *Acta grodzkie i ziemskie*, vol. 22, ed. Prohaska: Lauda Wiscenskie, no. 67, p. 364; notice to the Sejm delegates from
    18th April 1701.

11. Israel Halperin, *Pinkas Of the Council of Four Lands*, pp. 156, 159, 169, 184, 206, 212, 213, 215.

12. Aryeh Leyb had three sons:
    1. Zekharia Mendel who was the student of R. Yehoyshue Falk and later rabbi in Podheytse (author of *Menorat Zekharia* ???, 1936)
    2. Naftali Hirts Mendel was the son-in-law of Rabbi Avraham of Stanislav and father-in-law of Rabbi Jacob, Head of the rabbinical court of Lithuania and author of *Khavat-Daat* [Opinion]
    3. Akiba, who was a well known man of means. As to his two daughters, Shifra was married to the son of Rabbi Yehoyshue Falk and the second to Rabbi Tsvi, Head of the rabbinical court in Manastirziske.

Here is the family tree of Rabbi Aryeh-Leybush.

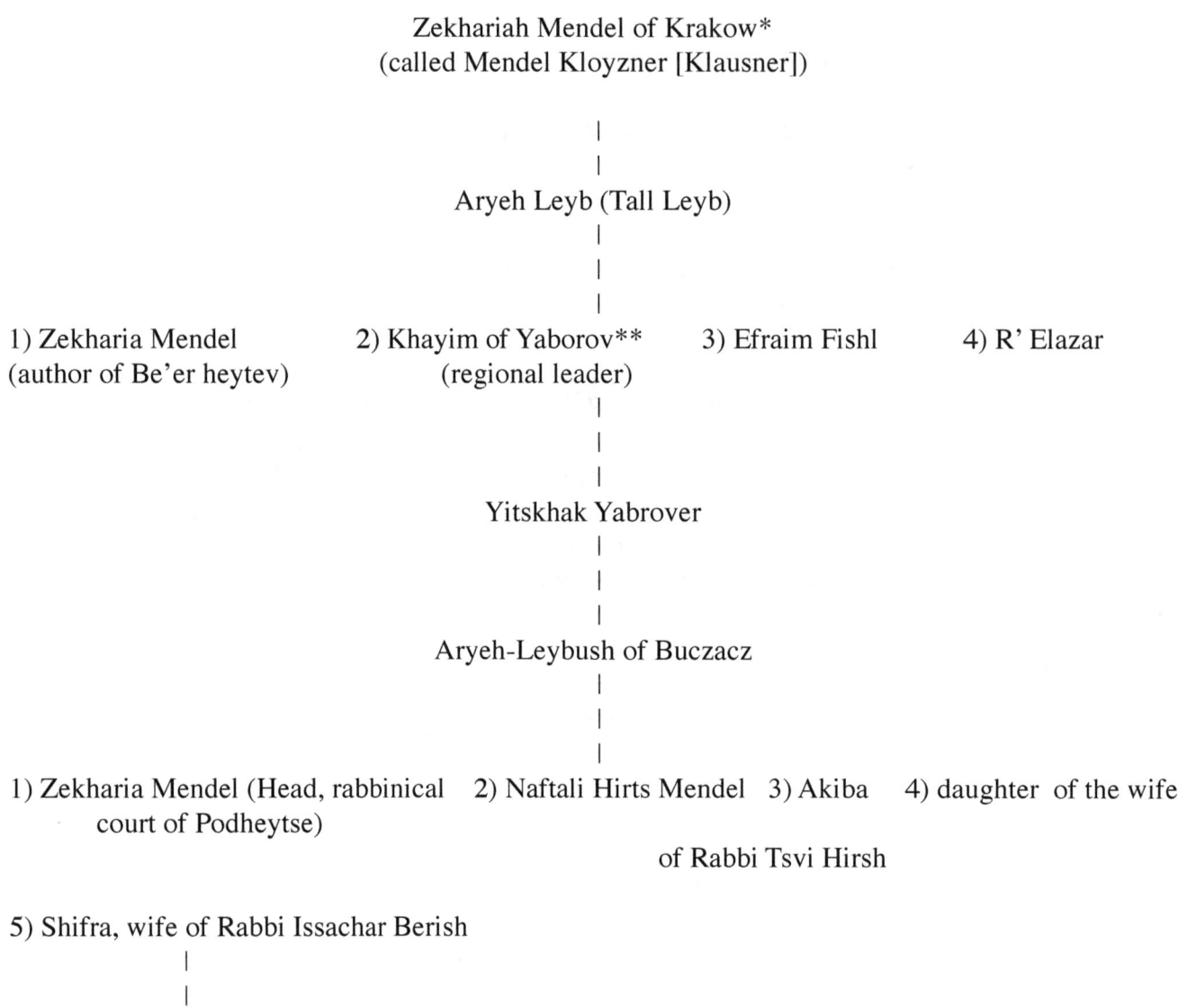

5) Shifra, wife of Rabbi Issachar Berish
|
|

1) Tsvi Hirsh Rozanes, Head of the rabbinical court in Bulikhov and, after the death of the Gaon R' Mordechai Ze'ev Orenstein, Head of the rabbinical court in Lwow.

2) Sarah

* In his old age he emigrated to Erets-Yisrael, becoming a prominent person in Jerusalem.
** He lived in Zhulkov and was a regional head in the province of Lwow. He took part in the council meeting at Kolikov in the month of Shevet, 1689 and was one of the leaders of the Council of the Four Lands in the years 1673, 1683-1689.

13. Israel Halperin, *Pinkas Of the Council of Four Lands*, pp. 109, 160, 163, 166, 215, 216, 221. XXIII-498.

14. Head of the rabbinical court of Bomberg and surrounding region. He was the brother of the mother of the Gaon R' David Openheim, head of the rabbinical court of Prague and son of Rabbi David, son of the sister of the author of *Torey zahav* [Pillars of Gold] (Ephraim Zalman Margoliouth, *Sefer maalot hayokhsin*, pp. 72, 78.

15. Majer Balaban, *Spis Zydow I Karaitow ziemi halickiej*, Krakow, 1909, p.4.

16. Tsvi Hurvits, *Sefer kitvey hageonim* [Writings of the Highest Rabbinical Authorities], Piotrkow, 1928, p. 199. In the court house of Buczacz an interesting Polish document was found; dated 20 Tammuz 1785, it is signed in Polish by Rabbi Tsvi Hirsh, son of Jacob Kara, and by the rabbinical judge Akiba of Podheytse. In it a Buczacz resident, Khayim Gabriel ben Pesakh of Trambubla, declares his wish to increase the dowry which his wife, Luba bas Arye, received from her father and to will it in his will. See Appendix 5.

17. G[ershom] Scholem, "Brukhia, Head of the Sabbateans in Salonika," Zion, 1941, p. 193.

18. Printed in: Moshe Arye Perlmuter *Sefer avo hayom 'el ha'ayin' shayukhuto le-r'yonatan ibishuts* [The Book Avo Hayom "El Ha'ayin" Attributed to Rabbi Jonathan Eybeschuetz], Jerusalem, 1942, p. 52.

19. Jacob Omri, *Sefer hashimush*, pp. 5-7.

20. *Pinkas of the Council of Four Lands*, p. 269.

21. I. Schipper, *Dzieje handlu zydowskiego na ziemiach polskich*, pp. 263, 313.

22. See Appendix 4.

23. Archive of the Ministry of Internal Affairs, Vienna. Galician Protocol Books 1776-1777. From September 1776 no. 48. Decret an das galizische Gubernium ado. 23 August 1776.

24. Pilleriana, 11 October 1787.

25. Gershom Bader, Medina vekhokhmeho, New York, 1934, p. 80. He reports that he heard these things from his grandfather who knew Pinkhas Pav.

26. Archive of the Ministry of Internal Affairs, Vienna. vol. 4, 11 carton 2579.

27. X. Sadok Baracz, Pamiatki Buczaczkie, Lwow, 1882, p. 36.

28. Vol. 41. carton 2582, no. 143, ex October 1812.

29. X. Sadok Baracz, p. 37.

30. Rabbi Alter Meyer, "Rabbi Abraham David of Buczacz," Haaretz 17th December 1946.

31. Tefer's memorandum is given in Raphael Mahler, Der kamf tsvishn khsides un haskole in galitsye, New York, 1942, p. 248.

32. This is the inscription on his gravestone:

Crown of the Law
Zion
Gaon of Israel

Hidden Light, Lofty and Mysterious
Sacred Light, Light of the World
Faithful Shepherd, Prince of Peace
Glorious Holiness, Of Infinite Knowledge
Pure Light, Sanctuary
Preacher of the Book, Emerald and Diamond
Honest and Faithful, Truthful and Complete
David King of Israel Doer of Many Deeds
His Holy Soul went forth on the 29th of Tishri, 1841
Our Holy Rabbi, Great in His Generation
Righteous Foundation of the World
Our Father Abraham David Our King
Our Teacher, May He Be Remembered Forever
He Was a Crown to the Rabbinate for Fifty Years
May His Soul Rest in Peace
(Printed in Eliyahu Tsvi Shmerlir, *Sefer Toldot HaRaba"d*, Lwow, 1890 [a rare book].

33.
1. *Daat kedoshim* (Lwow, 1871, 3 parts on the halakhic laws regarding slaughtering and unclean animals;
2. *Mishmeret hakodesh* (Lwow, 1879);
3. *Eshel Avraham* (Lwow, 1872);
4. *Birkat David* (1805);
5. *Makhaze Avraham* (Lwow, 1872);
6. *Imrot tehorot* (Lwow, 1879);
7. *Tfila leDavid* (Lwow 1886);
8. *Tehila leDavid* (Lwow, 1872);
9. *Divrey avot* [*beyur al masekhet Avot* (Lwow 1876) ;
10. *Eshel Avraham* [*Beyur al haHagada shel Pesakh*];
11. *Ezer mekudash* [*al Shulkhan HaArukh*] Even haezer (Lwow). A number of manuscripts remained in the hands of the family in addition to the above items.

34. In a memorandum he is called R. Abraham David Kara, but this is an error. He was the father-in-law of Rabbi Kara.

34a. *Allgemeine Zeitung des Judentums*, 1853, no. 34, p. 426. An article from Buczacz. After the attempted assassination of Kaiser Franz Josef the First, the congregation held a prayer meeting in the synagogue. Rabbi Tsadok Rinek spoke and he printed his address in a pamphlet which he sent to the Kaiser's mother. Rinek received a letter of thanks from her.

35. He was the son of the daughter of the famous Gaon R' Jacob of Lisa.

36. Archive of the Ministry of Internal Affairs, Vienna, vol. 42 Besitz.

37. After his death, the mayor and the city council of Kolomea asked the Representative for Galicia to exempt the Kolomea-Sniatyn-Buczacz region from holding elections. It could be expected that a Jewish delegate would be elected, since most of the region was Jewish. It was therefor preferable to first change the election laws and to stipulate that the results be valid only if a third of the votes were those of Christian citizens. An article from Kolomea in *Allgemeine Zeitung des Judentums*, 1865, p. 338.

38. *Israelit*. Lemberg, 1883, no. 9.

39. Samuel L. Bloch. *Erinnerungen aus meinen Leben*, Wien, 1922, p. 231. A Hebrew translation by Sh. Shalom was published in Tel-Aviv.Dr. Bloch writes in his memoirs: "On my way to Buczacz I spent several days in Stanislaw as a guest of the Halperin and Lipe Horovitz families. There I met Horace Shor, a likeable young maskil, liberal in his thinking, and a friend of that "outstanding" mayor of Buczacz, Berish Stern. This young man whispered to me: 'Honorable Dr. Bloch, why nurse illusions.What use to you are the voters if Berish Stern sits near the ballot box and counts the votes together with the District Representative. He has told me that you won't get more than a hundred votes'." (The above citation in Hebrew is found in the Shalom translation of the Bloch memoirs, vol. 1, p. 172).

40. *Zikhronot* [see footnote 39 above], pp. 173-4.

41. In these elections, the masses sang a satirical song in Yiddish. The first stanza was;

Kinderlekh getraye / Di gantse khevraye / Mir zoln ale iber a yor derlebn/Men darf shoyn geyn / Tsu Mayzles levaye / Un far Blokhen di shtim opgebn.

[Faithful fellows / The whole gang / Let's wish ourselves many happy returns / Now we have to go/ To Maizel's funeral / And to give our vote to Bloch.]

42. He moved to Brody in 1888. He died in Vienna on the 9th of Menakhem Av 1924. In 1913 he visited Erets-Yisrael.

43. The bookseller R' Alter Miller also lived in Buczacz in these years. He was the father of the well known learned orientalist Professor Ts. H. Miller (1846-1912).

44. Przyszlosc 1894, p. 151.

45. *HaMagid*, 1894, vol. 25, p. 205; Przyszlosc 1894, no, 19, p. 225

46. *HaMagid*, 1894, vol. 25, p. 205.

47. *HaMagid*, 1894, vol. 25, p. 349.

Appendices

1. List of Buczacz town owners.
2. The 1699 Statute.
3. Statutes regarding Jewish craftsmen.
4. The community's commitment to supply tallow to the Ukrainian church (1747) [this appendix is absent from this book both in Polish and in Hebrew]
5. A certificate of ownership from 1785.

List of Buczacz town owners
[appears in Hebrew only]

1. Gabriel Bucacki Starosta of Kamenets 1260.
2. Mikolau Viboda of Podolia.
3. Jerzy.
4. Jan.
5. Mikhael Castellan of Halic, fell in 1438 in a battle with the Tatars.
6. Teodor Starosta of Kamenets, fell in the battle of Wallachia in 1450.
7. Jan Mikolai, also called Muzylo.
8. Jakob Castellan of Halic.
9. Jan.
10. Mikhael Starosta of Sniatyn.
11. Jakob Khashman of Pluck, with whom ended the male line of Bucackis.
12. The town became the possession of Katerina, wife of Jan Taburovski, who died in 1547.
13. His son Jacob, who was called Bucacki.
14. His son Jan Krzishtoff (1572-1612).
15. His brother Jan.
16. Jan's wife from the Potocki family.
17. Stefan Potocki, died 1631.
18. His son Jan Potocki died in 1673.
19. His son Stefan gave the town and the Jews statutes. He died in 1727.
20. His son Mikolai left the Catholic church and joined the Ruthenian [Ukrainian] church, He died in 1782. He gave over the town in 1770 to his relative Jan Potocki.
21. Jan Potocki.
22. His twin brothers Kaytan (1751-1814) and Pavel (1751-1818).
23. Grandson of his brother Dominik Potocki, Adam Potocki died in 1870.
24. His sons Emil and Artur until the outbreak of World War One.

The 1699 Statute
[translated from the Hebrew translation of the Polish original]

Stefan Potocki, owner of Potok and Buczacz, guardian of the supreme realm, Starosta of Tarambubla, Kaniuv, etc., etc.. I hereby announce to all those who must be informed that the Jews and their community in the town of Buczacz have lost, due to the destruction brought upon by the enemy, the statutes regarding the privileges they were given by the previous town owners. I therefore am renewing them and permitting the Jews to settle in my aforementioned estates. They are allowed to live in Buczacz, to freely engage in trade and crafts according to their professions and needs.

To these Jews I hereby first of all give a winery for the period of 12 years with the condition that they are exempted from all obligation to the castle. When this period is over, they are to pay one taller for each house and half a taller for each auxiliary structure [batim akhoriim 'outhouses'?]. I permit the Jews, according to the previous statute, to use the road that passes through the church walls and the priests's house and leads to the synagogue situated by the Stripa River. I also hereby permit the Jews permanent use of this synagogue, which their fathers built at their own expense, Furthermore they may use the cemetery situated at the outskirts of town and may, if need be, enlarge it by 10 cubits and build a surrounding wall. They may also build in this cemetery in the customary manner a house, and settle in it a resident who will be exempt from all obligations and taxes.

The Jews are not subject to the town's laws and to its jurisdiction. Judgement of misdemeanors as well as of serious crimes will be made by me, and in my absence by the castle commissioner in Buczacz. The Jews must abide by his word in the case of a complaint against them until such a time as the laws and privileges are decided upon regarding all of the towns of His Excellency the King.

If it so happens that in my absence the Jews find my commissioner's ruling to be excessively harsh, they are to be given the right of appeal before me! Nor should they be forbidden recourse to the judgement of their rabbinic court, depending on the nature of the matter concerned.

Furthermore, the Jews of Buczacz are to be exempted of all duties to the castle and the economy that are usually performed by their fellow townsmen. Jewish butchers are exempt from slaughtering swine for the castle. However, it is the duty of each and every one of them to give a stone of tallow annually, and to slaughter animals [behemot 'cattle'; 'animals'] whenever so required.

They must give my podstarosta ['sub-head of castle'] in Buczacz a haunch of meat every week.

The weekly fair is not to be held on the Sabbath, nor are Jews to be tried on that day. They are not to be imprisoned in a cold cell except in cases of theft or penal crimes.

In municipal matters concerning bills and accounts, a leader of the Jewish community [parnas], elected for this purpose, is to participate. The hospital and the homes of the rabbi and cantor are exempt from all taxes. The Jews of Buczacz are also entitled to purchase houses from their Christian fellow townsmen. They may establish breweries and wineries. According to the old custom, they are to pay 6 gulden for each barrel of wine that contains 10 jugs, and 8 gulden for each barrel of beer. They are to be exempted from pasture fees as well.

They may purchase anything and engage in wholesale and retail trade. The Jew must not hinder any purchase by a Christian just as a Christian must not hinder any purchase by a Jew. Those who will hinder the affairs of another will be fined 10 grzibni.

I also hereby warn the Jews from attempting to purchase any ritual objects of the church. All other types of trade are permitted.

In times of enemy attack they must participate in the defense of the castle.

In order to give greater validity to these paragraphs and conditions, I hereby sign in my own hand with my customary signature.

Given in Buczacz on May 20th, 1699.

Stefan Potocki
Straznik* Vilki* Koronzi

* High-ranking warlord.

Statutes regarding Jewish craftsmen
(translated from the Hebrew translation of the Polish original)

Buczacz has many craftsmen of different religions, such as the Polish, the Greek and the Jewish. It has tailors, furriers, whitewashers, shoemakers, locksmiths, butchers, and those who belong to other guilds, among whom there are many Jews. Anyone is permitted to come and settle in Buczacz on the condition that he join the guild of his craft. Once a Jew becomes a guild member, he is authorized to sell any product. The Catholic and Greek are accustomed to contributing tallow and are required to join in church processions and requiems, from which the Jews are exempt. However, Jews who are members of a guild must pay the guild any sum that Christians are asked to pay.

They must also give donations for the purchase of tallow for the church and for all other needs.

Given in Buczacz on November 8th, 1706.

Stefen Potocki

A contractual certificate from 1785
(translated from the Hebrew translation of the Polish original)

A memorandum regarding the matter signed upon by the witnesses whose names appear below:

There appeared before us Khayim Gavriel Ben Pesakh of Tarambubla, a resident of Buczacz, who said to us: "I took from here as wife Liba Bat Yitskhak Leyb when she was still a virgin and now she is my wife – wed under the canopy according to the laws of Moses and Israel – and now that I have seen her devotion to me, I wish to increase her original dowry before the witnesses whose names appear below according to the law of possession or contractual ownership.

He declared before us that according to the original ketuba [marriage contract], he Khayim Gavriel Ben Pesakh said to his wife Liba Bat Yitskhak Leyb: "Become my wife according to the religion of Moses and Israel and I will take care of you, maintain you and provide your apparel according to Jewish custom which obligates one to provide for his wife and clothe her, and I will give you a dowry worthy of you according to the ten commandments in the amount of 200 Polish gulden for household maintenance, clothes and all your other needs as well as a pleasant home such as is fitting for the aforementioned bride Liba. What she brought with her from her father's house in the way of money, home utensils and linens, Khayim Gavriel evaluates at 100 gulden, equal to 200 fine silver gulden, and now that the aforementioned Khayim Gavriel wishes to increase the dowry and in effect has increased it, and it will come to a sum of 670 gulden, excepting the 200 gulden and the jewels she brought and all the jewels and clothes which now belong to her and those she will receive in the future from her husband.

The aforementioned also agreed that he and his heirs will pay her from his entire present and future estate the above dowry and certainly the original dowry and the additional one, even including his clothing. This dowry is valid and certified according to all the rabbinical statutes.

We received these instructions from the aforementioned Khayim Gavriel for his wife Liba Bat Yitskhak Leyb with a kerchief [mitpakhat 'kerchief held by both parties to a contractual agreement'] and in order to make it valid we sign below on this day the 20th of Tammuz takm"h according to the Hebrew calendar and the 20th of August 1785 according to the Polish calendar here in Buczacz.

Hirsh Kara, Head of the Rabbinical Court in Buczacz
Dayan [religious court judge] Akiba of Podheytser
(S. Baracz, Documents of the Buczacz Court, pp. 22-24)

[Page 74]

The Righteous, Illustrious Rabbi, Our Rabbi and Teacher, Rabbi Avraham David of Blessed Memory, President of the Court in Buchach

Translated by Betsy Halpern-Amaru

(The chapter is taken from the book, *Dor Deah*, written by Yekutiel Kammelhar and published in Risha[1], Galicia.)

And there came forth a shoot out of the stock of our teacher and rabbi, Rabbi Shmuel Edels (Maharsha), of blessed memory, an illustrious, holy rabbi, a pillar of instruction and marvelous posek – our illustrious rabbi and teacher, Avraham David of blessed memory, the author of *Da'at Kedoshim*, president of the court in Buchach, who is remembered with holy feelings yet today in his city as "the Zaddik."

He was born on the sixth of Adar in the year 5531 (February 20, 1771, NP) in the city of Nadvorna[2], to our teacher, Rabbi Asher Anshel, an "eminent scholar" (indeed, he would refer to his father by that title), and to Marat[3] Rachel, of blessed memory, his righteous mother. As he grew to a lad, he demonstrated wonderful, outstanding abilities and, throughout the city and its environs he was renowned as a "wonder-child." By the time he was nine, he was already very erudite in Talmud (Shas) and the Poskim[4]. The great rabbinic scholars were amazed by him and rejoiced in the glorious brilliance of the lad, Avraham David. One of them, the master and sage, our great illustrious Rabbi Meshulam Igra, of blessed memory, president of the court of Tismenitz[5] was once in Nadvorna. In the year 5540 he set out in his carriage, hoisted his standard onto the wheel of the wagon, and upon seeing the prodigy, extended his hand to him and brought him up into the carriage where he spoke with him about his studies. He asked him various questions and the young lad gave proper and profound responses. He believed a great future awaited the genius and that he would become "a rabbinic authority in Israel and a wonder to all the learned of that generation."

The illustrious rabbi, our teacher, our rabbi, David Shlomo Eibenschutz, of blessed memory, author of "Levushei Serad," was teaching Torah to the young Jews in Nadvorna at that time. He put him to the test and commanded him to read several pages from some tractate. The lad read with such intelligence and great understanding that he was very amazed at the breadth of his knowledge and the sharpness of his intellect. Thus his reputation became known throughout the region. The illustrious rabbi, our rabbi and teacher, Zvi Hersh Kro, president of the Court in Buchach, heard of his reputation and traveled to Nadvorna to examine him closely. Thereupon he realized that he had not been told even half of what the lad was capable of. He came to agreement with his father, Rabbi Asher Enshel, of blessed memory, regarding a marriage; and he took his son, the wondrous lad, Avraham David, as a groom for his daughter. The years of childhood passed and when he became Bar Mitzvah, he also became one of the students of the head of community, our holy rabbi and teacher, the Magid, of blessed memory, from Nadvorna.

A year after his wedding, the illustrious Rabbi Meshulam, of blessed memory, from Tismenitz came to the community of Buchach, his birthplace. Members of his family lived there and he was given the honor of giving a d'rash[6] on the Sabbath. All the learned men and Torah scholars of the city came to hear. Among them was the young Avraham David, son-in-law of the president of the court; and he stood off to the side. The illustrious one presented his interpretation with such intricacies that all of the learned were exhausted from trying to follow and comprehend the acute depth of his presentation. As our illustrious Rabbi Meshulam gazed at the faces of the listeners to see if they understood what he was saying, he realized that there was not one man who had not been challenged beyond his ability. And he said: " Behold, only that young man standing in the remote corner can understand what I have to say."

He was still living with his father-in-law, the illustrious president of the court of Buchach, our rabbi and teacher, Rabbi Kro – author of "Netah Shaashuim," responsa addressed to the greats of that generation who were accustomed to coming to him to inquire in regard to matters of halacha – when the illustrious Rabbi Meshulam Igra, of blessed memory, president of the court of Tismenitz announced that he had assumed the position of rabbi for the Pressberg congregation. The rabbis of the area came to take leave of him and asked him to whom they should turn with their most difficult questions. He told them that he was leaving behind the illustrious Rabbi Zvi Hersh Kro, president of the court in Buchach, who possessed prodigious, extraordinary knowledge, and that they should turn to him with any matter that was difficult for them. Living in a city filled with wise men and scribes, he became even more proficient in Torah, his wisdom grew to even greater heights, and he thrived like "a tree planted by springs of water." There he also found a good friend who became like a brother, the youth Reb Hayim who subsequently became God's shepherd, the illustrious, holy rabbi and teacher, Hayim, president of the court of Czernovitz, of blessed memory, author of "Be'er Mayim Hayim," of "Siddur shel Shabbat," "Shaar ha'Tifila," and "Eretz Hahayyim." At that time he lived there in Buchach and the two of them were attentive friends until they became rabbis, shepherds of the God of Israel.

2.

When the prestigious rabbi, Rabbi Avraham David was twenty, he was appointed as rabbi, president of the court of Yazlovitz[7], which is close to Buchach. It was his custom in religious matters to write down in a page of a book all the teachings and legal decisions he had made in the course of the day and to review them before going to bed that night in order to see if he might have made any error in judgment. Consequently, he made it an inviolable rule to develop a new interpretation of eighteen halachot each week. In the course of years, he thereby came to initiate myriads of innovative halachic interpretations, treasures stored in manuscripts that he left after him. Lest someone should come to ask for instruction, he never drank alcohol. However, in order to fulfill the saying of Haz'al – "a person is required to become intoxicated on Purim" – he would wait until midnight, a time when he knew for sure that the people of the town were deep in slumber, and would drink a little honey water to fulfill the commandment of Haz'al.

His daily routine at that time involved the regular daily prayers, thereafter helping his son with his morning prayers, and then sitting immersed in Torah for fourteen hours in his beit midrash where he would provide instruction for each questioner. Day and night there was no break in this routine until his eyes would begin to fail. Not wanting to interrupt his teaching, he did not readily respond even then, because the Torah not only nurtured his soul and spirit, but also was a remedy for his body.

He heightened the spiritual level of the people of his city to the highest degree of pure piety. Once when the holy rabbi, our rabbi and teacher, the Maharam, of sacred memory, from Premishlan[8] passed through Yazlovits, he sensed the piety in every passageway and corner and said: "this is the power of the Rabbi, the Zaddik, Rabbi Avraham David who has been occupied in holy work here for twenty-four years.

He has breathed a pure, holy spirit into his reprimands and into his sermons on ethics and piety." It was also his custom when he would officiate at weddings that before beginning the first part of the ceremony, he would awaken the heart of each groom with his teachings about ethics, righteousness, and piety. Even once he became president of the court in Buchach, the future grooms from the community of Yazlovits would come to him for a blessing before their weddings and he would teach them ethics (Musar). It is told that one time the Rabbi Zaddik asked a groom who had come to be blessed if his father and father-in-law would be providing basic support for him after the wedding. He replied that his father would be giving him support for three years and his father-in-law for another three years. The Rabbi Zaddik responded lyrically: "My son, take care to watch over your learning with great constancy during those six years. The learning of one who "worries" is a pressed impression; the Torah that one learns when one is worrying about earning a livelihood is only a rubbing, an impression and is not absorbed internally. Therefore, during the six years that you have sustenance without worry, be zealous to learn Torah and this Torah will guide you in every way all the days of your life."

3.

Although the illustrious Zaddik, Rabbi Avraham David, was a disciple of the Maggid of Nadvorna in his youth, when he subsequently sat at the table of his father-in-law, our illustrious rabbi and teacher Zvi Hersh Kro, president of the court in Buchach, who was among the Mitnagdim, he left his Hasidism and went the path of his father-in-law who conducted himself like the gaonim before him. But it was the will of God that Rabbi Avraham David would also be one of the righteous men (zaddikim) of the generation and a worker of wonders. Thus, it suddenly happened that his only son, his first born, fell ill with a life-threatening illness (heaven help him), which the physicians despaired of healing. At that time the holy rabbi, the glory of Israel, our teacher, rabbi Levi Yitzhak, of blessed memory, from Berdichev and author of "Kedushat Levi," came to the city Rimalov 9 . The entire city was amazed at the coming of this Zaddik and worker of miracles to their land. The rabbi's wife told him that he should go with his only son to the Zaddik from Berdichev who would bless the child and cure him of his illness. Since the doing would take time away from his study of Torah, the rabbi did not want to hear this. So the rebbitzen went to the heads of the congregation and begged them that they entreat their rabbi to have compassion for her and for their only son and travel with him to Rimalov, to the Rav, the Zaddik from Berdichev. They did so. After much urging, the rabbi was convinced. Together with the sick child and accompanied by several other members of the community, he went to Rimalov, which was not far from Yazlovits. When they arrived at the lodging place, it was time for the morning prayers and the illustrious righteous rabbi, our rabbi and teacher, Avraham David, prepared for prayer. On his way to the Beit Midrash he met up with one of the attendants of the righteous rabbi from Berdichev and asked him when the Zaddik from Berdichev would be praying and when he would be able to come to see him. He answered him that the Zaddik from Berdichev stayed awake all night and only now would be lying down to rest a bit, and when he awoke he would prepare himself for prayer which itself would last until after midday. Thereafter he would be able to come to see him. And so it was. After midday the attendant came to his lodging to summon him to the Zaddik from Berdichev. When he came before him, the holy rabbi from Berdichev asked him why he had come and he told him that it certainly had been difficult to interrupt the business of Torah, but due to the great urging of significant members of his congregation, he had come to get a blessing for this sick son. The holy rabbi asked him: "And where is your sick son?" And he responded that the lad was here in the lodge. The holy rabbi from Berdichev told his attendant to bring the sick boy into his presence. When he was brought before him, the Zaddik from Berdichev placed his hands on his head and blessed him. He said to his father, the rabbi from Yazlovitz: "God, my he be blessed, would completely heal him and from your, this first born, you will be worthy to see sons and grandsons who are God-fearing and greatly learned in Torah..." (And so it was). When the holy rabbi finished his blessing, the illustrious rabbi, president of the court of Yazlovits, put forth his hand in greeting to make his departure and travel home, the holy rabbi said to him: "Why are you in such a hurry to leave, right when I have found a soul mate?" He greatly urged him to remain; and he acquiesced to the request. The holy rabbi of Berdichev told his companions to return with the sick boy to their home and the rabbi, president of the holy court, would remain with him for a few days to enjoy Torah with him. He blessed them and they returned home with the sick boy in whom signs of recovery were immediately evident. Their rabbi remained with the holy rabbi of Berdichev until after Shabbat. Then he was forced to travel with the holy rabbi to the community of Skalat. From there the holy rabbi of Berdichev did not let him return to his house, but rather had him come with him to Berdichev where he stayed around six weeks and learned from the holy rabbi Barzin Eylein (?). Thereafter the holy rabbi bestowed upon him a parting blessing and he returned to his place, to the community of Yazlovits.

Upon his arrival from Berdichev, filled with enthusiasm and spirituality, with "life" burning as coals, his first deed was to remove from his house every penny of interest that the Rebbizin had taken from her loans– she lent money to people from the dowry she had brought from her father's house. He called her and commanded her to do an accounting of all who had borrowed from her over the course of the years in which she had been making loans and return to them any interest she had taken from them. Neither protests nor tears by the Rebbezin helped; she was forced to do as he has ordered. Not a thing remained in their house. Indeed, she had to sell her own ornaments in order to have the full amount that she needed in order to refund the borrowers. Consequently, they were left bare and penniless; the income they received from the community was sufficient only for scanty rations and a little water; and she suffered everything in silence. Her husband, the righteous rabbi, began to occupy himself with kabbalah and entered the garden of the holy Zohar, the writings of Ha'Ari, and of our rabbi and teacher Hayim Vital, may his memory be blessed for eternal life. With storms of his spirit, he attempted to ascend to a level beyond his abilities; and the spiritual powers within him struggled with each other and in the struggling, they broke forth with no restraint to their boundaries. Thus, he went outside, wrapped in talit and teffilin and in the town center called on God to sanctify his name. When heads and men of his community saw this, they took him and brought him to the house of the illustrious, holy rabbi, Rabbi Moshe Leib Misasov, of blessed memory and he had influence over his spirit and brought the inner storms to quiet. So the illustrious rabbi, our rabbi and teacher, Rabbi Avraham David himself would tell it at the beginning of his book, "Tefilat L'David," where he blesses "gomel," and gives thanks to God. Thus he would say: I rested and was quieted by coming to my teacher and rabbis, the honorable, great rabbi, the famous Hasid, a holy man of God, our teacher the Rabbi Moshe Yehudah Labit, of blessed memory, who was the envoy of the Merciful-One. He drew over me immediate deliverance for the sake of kindness and graciousness themselves, not for my sake. As one removes paper from the flask, so he turned away the foolishness, the impatience, the confusions, and the discord that I had felt from beginning to end, with no inner peace between the way of Hasidism and that of Talmud – all this he removed from me". And he returned to his home healthy and whole.

4.

After the death of his father-in-law, the illustrious teacher and rabbi, Rabbi Kro, of blessed memory, president of the court in Buchach and author of the book of responsa, "Neta Sha'ashuim," on the 8th day of the month of Shevat in the year 5674, the illustrious Zaddik, president of the court of Yazlovitz, was accepted as a replacement for his father-in-law, i.e., to serve as rabbi of the community of Buchach. In coming there, he directed that all questions involving forbidden and permitted matters would come before him and he would respond to every questioner except in civil matters. For that area, he instead appointed his firstborn son, the illustrious Rabbi Israel Aryeh Leib, of blessed memory, together with two judges who would be judges of civil matters. Only when the litigants forcefully requested that only the president of the court would sit in judgment of their case, would he deal with civil matters. In such instances, the court would present the claims and counterclaims to him in the name of "Reuben" and "Simeon" so that he would not know who the real litigants were; and he would present his judgment in terms of "so and so is culpable and so and so is innocent.

He was only occupied with Torah and with work. At midnight he would rise to lament the destruction of the Temple and thereafter he would occupy himself until midday with Torah and with work, which in his mind was prayer. Then he would drink a bit of not very hot coffee, and so that he would be obliged to say the final grace after meals he would eat a bit of bread with dumpling (?). Afterward, he would consider town matters and in particular, creature matters, the many needs of the children of Israel who came before him with the bitterness of soul and hardships of their days to receive his blessings and he would pray on their behalf that prosperity would be realized in the midst of the land. After the afternoon and evening prayers he ate chicken for his evening meal – he personally slaughtered two chickens every week that he would eat at the evening meal during the week.

There were those who opposed him there on these matters, for the learned of the city of Buchach were opposed to Hasidism. Consequently, they could not tolerate that their rabbi, the president of the court, was a famous rebbe and zaddik who extended the morning prayer until after midday, prayed in accord with the Sepharadi manner, and used the prayer book of Ha'Ari, of blessed memory. In addition, they were also infuriated by the fact that he did not use the ritual slaughterers of his community, but rather himself slaughtered fowl for his own daily use. On this matter, he, of blessed memory, apologized to them when he mentions the issue at the end of his book "Tefila L'David [10]." Still, his holy words were of no avail in appeasing the anger and fury of the murmurers and complainers. They continued to murmur against him, but he was sustained, as it is said: "may his friends be as the sun rising in its might [11]."

5.

The illustrious righteous ones of the era corresponded with him with responsa and the great illustrious teacher and rabbi, Ephraim Zalman Margolioth of Brody, of blessed memory, wanted to expend monies from his own pocket to publish the new legal interpretations made by the illustrious rabbi, the Zaddik of Buchach. (As mentioned above, he was making eighteen such new interpretations each week). However, to his great sorrow, his intent to do so was never realized because the illustrious rabbi and teacher Ephraim Zalman died suddenly one afternoon. Report of the death of his dear, beloved, great illustrious friend, was extremely hard on him, for he was unable to publish his multiple, essential legal rulings.

He also was in correspondence with his son's father-in-law, the holy, illustrious Mameeri Derzin (?), our rabbi and teacher of blessed memory of Zdechovice. Once they had an argument over the proper scribing of the letter "chet" in books, tefilin, and mezuzot. Our holy rabbi offered the new interpretation that only the second foot of the "chet" had to be in the same form on makes with the letter "zayin." They dispatched multiple letters regarding this matter until finally the illustrious president of the court of Buchach wrote the following to the illustrious one of Zdechovice: There already was a controversy between ben Asher and ben Naphtali regarding the written form of the letters (as is known, in the time of the earliest of the Gaonim in the yeshivot of Tiberias). At that time a divine voice decreed in accord with the opinion of Ben Asher, and I, I am he, for I am Ben Asher [12].

He also exchanged letters with the illustrious Rebbe Elimelech, of blessed memory, of Dynov as well as with all the rabbis of the provinces who dispatched their questions in matters of law to him.

And over the course of his living there, the number of his students greatly increased. Among the most outstanding and well known are:

The illustrious rabbi, our rabbi-teacher, Shlomo Dremaur (?), of blessed memory, president of the court of Skala [13], author of "Responsa of Beit Shlomo" on the four parts of the Shulkan Aruk and who was renowned as an outstanding "posek."

The illustrious rabbi, our rabbi-teacher, Ephraim Elisha, of blessed memory, president of the court of Chernevtsy [14], who was a famous, holy Hasid.

The illustrious rabbi, our rabbi-teacher, Smeryl, of blessed memory, president of the court of Rimalov, author of "Iyun Tefila" on the siddur, based upon what he had heard from his rabbi, the illustrious holy one of blessed memory.

The illustrious rabbi and Hasid, our rabbi-teacher, Moshe, president of the court of Bedzonov (?).

The illustrious rabbi and Hasid, our rabbi-teacher, Dov, president of the court of Beien (?) of blessed memory.

The illustrious and famous rabbi-teacher, Shraga Feivel Shreier, of blessed memory, president of the court of Bogorodchany 15 who published the book "Daat Kedoshim" concerning ritual animal slaughter with his comments and notes under the name "Gedolei HaKodesh."

Translator's Footnotes:

1) Risha, Raysha, is identified as Rzeszow in G. Mokotoff and S. Sack, Where Once We Walked (Teaneck: Avotaynu, Inc., 1991).

2) Nadvorna identified as Nadvornaya.

3) I have not translated "marat" as Mrs. or Ms. – seems anachronistic.

4) Rabbinical scholarship dealing with application of and arbitration over points of law.

5) Identified as Tysmenitsa in Mokotoff and Sack.

6) Homiletical interpretation.

7) Yazlovits or Yazlivitz is identified also as Pomortsy in Mokotoff and Sack.

8) Identified as Peremyshlyany in Mokotoff and Sack.

9) Identified as Grimaylov in Mokotoff and Sack.

10) I think there is an error in the text here. It reads "Tefilah LaDor", but his book is entitled "Tefilah L'David."

11) The quote is from Judges 5:31. There are numerous citations of biblical phrases in the piece. I have put in quotations only where – such as here – the words are presented as a citation.

12) There is a word/name play here that I am not sure is conveyed well. His father's name was "Asher."

13) Identified in Mokotoff, Sack.

14) Identified in Mokotoff, Sack.

15) Identified in Mokotoff, Sack.

[Page 81]

Rabbi Meshulam Igra
Translated by Melanie Rosenberg

Rabbi Meshulam Igra was a master sage from Tismenitz who later became the chief rabbi of Pressburg. Even the most prominent of scholars could not fully appreciate the extent of his greatness: his talents rendered him the embodiment of Israeli brilliance. A number of wise men of great intellectual talents, shining suns emanating great light, were among the distinguished men of Israel of the previous century (according to our count). One of the most eminent personalities whose exalted brilliance and sharp wittedness merited high accolades of praise, was Rabbi Meshulam Igra.

Rabbi Igra was a scion of rabbis and great men of Israel (a descendent of the renowned Rabbi Yehoshua Heshel, author of "Meginei Shlomo"), but his father, Reb Shimshon, was a simple landowner from the city of Buchach in eastern Galicia, a chaste and honest man. Up until the last generation, elders of this city would speak wonders of his righteousness and integrity. In Buchach, the city of Rabbi Meshulam's birth, his father built a house adjacent to a Jewish-owned tavern whose proprietor permitted himself to keep the premises open on the Sabbath. Rabbi Shimshon was greatly distressed and tried time and time again to prove to his neighbor the error of his ways, reciting ethical parables and attempting to influence him to cease Sabbath desecration. But his neighbor the bartender scorned him and his example. Rabbi Shimson then went to the local rabbi and brought suit against his neighbor over monetary damages. When the neighbor received the summons, he was surprised and said, "At no time have negotiations ever taken place between me and Rabbi Shimson regarding monetary issues. What possible claim can he have against me in this regard?"

When the trial began, Rabbi Shimshon arose and proclaimed, "Our sages have said (Tractate Shabbat, 119, B) "No conflagration is to be found, except in a place where desecration of the Sabbath occurs." Since my neighbor the tavern owner desecrates the Sabbath, I fear that a fire will break out in his building and spread to consume my house as well. Therefore I demand that he do one of two things: either take upon himself the commandment to observe the Sabbath, or buy my house."

From this righteous man was born Rabbi Meshulam, of whom Rabbi Moshe Sofer testified "his two arms were as two Torah scrolls; it was impossible to grasp the enormity of his erudition and speed of intellect combined." (from "Sermons of the Chatam Sofer, vol 1"). And note this wonder: Rabbi Meshulam Igra was a "mitnaged" who opposed *hasidut*. Yet one of the greatest *hassidic* rabbis of his time, Rabbi Chaim of Chernowitz, (author of "Be'er Mayim Chaim" and "S'doro Shel Shabbat") in his book "Sha'ar Tefilah" ("Gate of Prayer") describes him as "the ultimate role model for his time, a mighty leader of Israel, a true genius, an ambassador of Torah, a light of purity unto the world, a crown of glory for Israel." For according to *hasidic* legend, Rabbi Yisrael Baal-Shem-Tov himself once visited the city of Buchach where he laid eyes upon the son of Rabbi Shimshon, then a boy of four. The creator and master of *hasidut* looked at the child's face and turned to those assembled, saying, "Look and you will see: this child possesses a new soul, noble and exalted, the caliber of which has not existed in this world for several generations..."

Still in his childhood, at the age of five, Meshulam astounded his community with his sharp intellectual perception. Once, as Meshulam sat with other children his age before their rebbe, the pre-school teacher listened as the toddlers read and repeated the verses (Genesis 37, 9-10) regarding Josef's dream: "Behold, the sun and the moon and the eleven stars bowed down to me...and his father rebuked him and said to him, What is this dream that thou hast dreamt? Shall I and thy mother indeed come to bow down ourselves to thee?" The children's rebbe then read them Rashi's commentary on these verses, focusing on Yosef's having dreamt that his late mother – represented by the moon – would bow down to him in future. From this our sages derived that within every dream there are elements which will not come true. At this, the young Meshulam sprung forward and asked his teacher, "Just because Yosef's dream included prophecies that were untrue, must we deduce that every dream contains elements that are untrue? Isn't this generalizing from the specific to the universal?" (such an axiom would defy *gemara* logic – m.r.)

The children listened to the question posed by their peer and were silent, not knowing what to answer, but Meshulam could not remain still. After several minutes he once again asked, "Why did Yosef see fit to mention that he saw the moon in his dream, thus raising his father's ire as well as serious doubt as to the veracity of the dream? Wouldn't it have been more convenient had he totally omitted mention of the word 'moon,' a clear reference to his late mother, and not opened room for doubt?"

"And yet," added the child, his eyes glittering and his face shining, "one question explains another: Yosef related his dream verbatim, without omitting a word, for he was aware that every dream has an element which is untrue. Had he omitted the word 'moon,' his father and brothers would have searched for other false aspects of the dream. Keeping that in mind, Yosef related the dream in its entirety, with nothing excluded. And from this, the fact that Yosef was steadfast in mentioning the word 'moon' in his dream, our sages learn that there are no dreams without inaccuracies."

In his early childhood, at the age of eight, this wonder child began to compile his Torah interpretations into a book, and by the age of nine was well-versed in whole commentaries of the Mishna and Talmud. At that point, it was suggested to his father that his dear son become engaged to marry the daughter of Reb Shmuel Bick, one of the officers and wealthy men of Brody. At the request of the prospective bride's father, Rabbi Shimshon brought his son to Brody and to the town's main Bet Midrash. Here, in the presence of all of the wise scholars of Brody, the nine-year-old boy delivered a deep *halachic* discourse and stood his ground in a Torah debate with the local rabbi, the eminent Rabbi Yitzchak Horowitz (who later became the chief rabbi of Hamburg). As each articulated and argued his points, it was the child who claimed victory over the elder. When Rabbi Yitzchak Horowitz returned to his home, his young daughter came to greet him. He placed his hand upon her head and blessed her, saying, "May it be Thy will that you should marry a great man such as the delightful child who triumphed over me now in *halacha*."

Thus the young Meshulam became engaged to marry the daughter of Reb Yitzchak Bick, and when he reached Bar Mitzvah age, they were wed according to the laws of Moses and Israel. During his youth, he became renowned not only for his genius but also for being a *tzadik*, a righteous man. Yet his intense piety did not appeal to his young wife, the daughter of the officer and nobleman, and she began to demand a divorce. His father-in-law Reb Shmuel also became convinced that the match was not a successful one and began to urge him to grant his wife a divorce. Rabbi Meshulam acquiesced. A short time later he married the daughter of Rabbi Yitzchak Horowitz, the rabbi of Brody. Thus was fulfilled the rabbi's blessing for this very wise and righteous man.

During this time, a heated argument broke out between the notables of Brody and her sages regarding the matter of a particular divorce. Some ruled that the divorce was null and void, others championed its validity, and among those arguing the issue was the 19-year-old Rabbi Meshulam. The sages of Brody, who enjoyed a reputation for their great Torah erudition, decided to request an opinion from Rabbi Yeshiah Berlin, the chief rabbi of Breslow whose incredible knowledge of every aspect of the Torah was known to the sages of his generation. Each of the Brody scholars wrote his own answer to the question at hand, and each of these letters, among them Rabbi Meshulam's, was sent to Rabbi Yeshiah Berlin. Rabbi Berlin poured over each viewpoint, one by one, and when he finished reading the answer given by Rabbi Meshulam, he cried in wonder and admiration, "This is an elderly man who has attained great wisdom! His intellect and keen insight are so profound that he could rival many of the great sages of yore."

Rabbi Yeshiah Berlin was intrigued to discover the identity of the author, someone whose name or existence he had never been aware. At that very time, Reb Shmuel Bick, the officer from Brody, happened to be in the city of Breslow. Although he was there on business, Reb Shmuel saw fit to pay a proprietary visit to the rabbi's home. Rabbi Yeshiah received him happily, and in the course of conversation asked if perhaps he knew a certain wise scholar in his city named Rabbi Meshulam Igra.

"Yes," replied Reb Shmuel. "He's still quite young, around fifteen or so."

"So young?" cried the rabbi in astonishment, "And I had no idea of his existence!"

"May I ask why this interests the rabbi?" queried Reb Shmuel. "How many wise young scholars are there right here in Brody whom the rabbi of Breslow has never heard of?"

"What are you talking about 'wise young scholars,'" retorted Rabbi Yeshiah, "Rabbi Meshulam is a mighty genius, one of the few truly profound scholars of our day."

Upon hearing the words of this distinguished, elderly rabbi, Reb Shmuel Bick suddenly grasped his chest and collapsed to the ground in a faint.

After he came to, Rabbi Yeshiah asked him, "What made you faint?

"This young, mighty genius was formerly my son-in-law, and I convinced him to divorce his wife, my daughter," replied Reb Shmuel with a bitter sigh.

"If you once held such a precious, blessed vessel in your home and you yourself banished the holiness from the house, " said Rabbi Yeshiah, "then you deserve to faint a second time!"

Rabbi Meshulam Igra's reputation preceded him, and in time the Jewish community of Tismenitz, a city of scholars and writers and one of the nine largest communities in the Lvov district, turned to appoint him president of the area's regional rabbinical court. At that point he was all of seventeen years old! Rabbi Meshulam was as meticulous in his study of Torah as he was great in his knowledge and thoughts, never ceasing for a moment to serve the community, any time or place. Even as he traversed the path from his home to the Bet Midrash and back, he would be murmuring words of Torah, probing and postulating, discerning new interpretations, his lips moving to recite entire pages of *gemara* and Talmud as well as commentaries by Rambam and other *halachic* sages. Once, it is told, when the rabbi was walking through the marketplace, completely absorbed in pondering *halachic* issues, he was struck to the ground by a team of horses who raced by pulling a carriage. The townspeople who witnessed this dangerous, frightening occurrence raced to save the rabbi's life. As they pulled him out from under the wheels of the carriage, they heard him mumbling,

"And from this, we must decide whether the approach of Rabbi Avraham Ben David of Poshkira (the RAB"D) is more appropriate than that of the Rambam."

In Tismenitz, Rabbi Meshulam found ample ground from which to disseminate Torah in Israel. From the town's yeshiva of higher learning which he established, scores of Torah scholars went forth to the people. Many of these scholars themselves became great lights in the celestial heavens of Judaism, such as these notable rabbis: Rabbi Mordechai Bennet, the rabbi of Nikelshporg, Rabbi Naftali-Tzvi Horowitz, father of the *hasidic* dynasty of Rashpitz, Rabbi Frenkel-Teumim, the rabbi of Lipnik, Rabbi Yaakov, the rabbi of Lisa, who called his rabbi, Rabbi Meshulam, "Rabeinu Tam," and many others.

And so Rabbi Meshulam was able to find contentment in Tismenitz, where he succeeded in glorifying and advancing Torah. Large, important communities with major Jewish centers came to offer him positions as the head of their courts. Yet he refused to leave Tismenitz. Where his greatness reigned, he exuded humility, telling his students that so limited was his knowledge of Torah and *halachic* innovation that he was not worthy of his post as the president of a rabbinic court in a city of the Jewish world. Rabbi Alexander-Sender Margalioth, the rabbi of Sotonov (author of "T'shuvot HaRA"M"), one of the leading religious leaders of the time and a friend and colleague of the author of "Nodah B'Yehudah," used to say that he was strong enough to fight a Torah battle against the famed Rabbi Yehonatan Ivshitz, but not against Rabbi Meshulam Igra. Yet nevertheless, when the notables of the Three Communities (Altona, Hamburg and Wandsbek) approached Rabbi Meshulam and offered to have him assume the position of his father-in-law Rabbi Yitzchak Horowitz, he demurred, saying, "I am not able, nor worthy or entitled to sit upon the seat of the righteous sage Rabbi Yehonatan Ivshitz."

And when the community leaders pressed him, claiming that they would consider it a great honor for him to assume the position of his father-in-law in this rabbinical court, Rabbi Meshulam dispatched them to his wife, the daughter of Rabbi Yitzchak Horowitz, for her opinion. Naturally, the rebbitzin readily agreed to move from tiny Tismenitz to those three metropolitan communities, especially to greater Hamburg where her family was living. The messengers of the Three Communities returned to Rabbi Meshulam, their faces shining with joy, and reported, "Your wife agreed. Now there are no objections remaining to the Rabbi's acceptance of our offer."

Rabbi Meshulam nodded and said, "My wife, may she be blessed with long years, is worthy of being the rebitzen of the Three Communities just as she is worthy to be the rebitzen of Tismenitz. And I, small and young, know and recognize my paltry worth. Why, I am not even worthy to serve in the rabbinical hierarchy of the little town of Tismenitz, which deserves better. How much more do I lack the merit to serve as the president of the rabbinical court of the Three Communities…"

And so Rabbi Meshulam Igra remained in his post in Tismenitz for twenty-seven years, and may well have continued there into his old age. Yet at that time, a royal edict came forth obligating all Jews to be conscripted into the military. The Jewish community of Tismenitz, like other communities in Galicia, was required to supply a certain number of conscripts each year. The leaders of Tismenitz were apt to overlook scholars for this task, preferring instead to send in their place ignorant, uneducated youth. Rabbi Meshulam lashed out vehemently against this practice: in the city's batei midrash he attacked the communal leaders who carried out this practice, accusing them of being slave traders and responsible for the bloodshed of innocent people. Rabbi Meshulam rose to publicly rebuke the community leaders, his words stinging in reproach, "There is no discrimination in the law. All of Israel, including talmudic scholars, all must obey the law of the land and be drafted into the army. And if the government demands of us only a certain number of people, then we must cast lots among all those Jews who are eligible to serve in the army. Whoever has the fate to be chosen, whoever he may be – even the greatest scholar of our times – he must enter and serve within the military."

Rabbi Meshulam stood up and swore, "Even if the die is cast for my only son, Yitzchak Eliyahu (his father attested to the fact that his son's sharpness of intellect outreached his father's, yet Yitzchak died at a young age), then I will personally turn him over to the serve in the army."

Their great rabbi's words, however, were met with scorn by the community leaders, who refused to pay heed to his message. Thus Rabbi Meshulam decided that the time had come to leave Tismenitz, and when offered the post of chief rabbi of Pressburg, he agreed.

It is told that when Rabbi Meshulam set out from Tismenitz to Pressburg, the notables and officers of Pressburg organized welcoming delegations to greet the rabbi along the route. On the way they stopped at an inn to eat and rest before the rabbi's arrival. There they treated themselves to a fine meal, all the while singing the praises of their new rabbi and his phenomenal knowledge and piety. From time to time, one of them would go out and scout the area, seeking signs of the rabbi's arrival. "Why is it taking the rabbi's wagon so long to get here? Why is he so late?"

Meanwhile, at the very same inn a man and his wife sat inconspicuously eating a meal of dry bread. One of the notables of Pressburg struck up a conversation with them and asked, "Where are you from?"

"From Tismenitz," answered the man.

"And where are you headed?"

"To Pressburg."

"What's your name?"

"Meshulam."

The questioner understood that this was indeed the new chief rabbi of Pressburg, Rabbi Meshulam Igra, who always fled from false honor and had no desire to enter the city with jubilant fanfare.

Yet honor seeks out those who shun it. When it became known to the notables of Pressburg that their rabbi was present at the inn, they immediately hoisted him and his wife upon a grand carriage and prepared a majestic entrance to the city.

And there, in the city of Pressburg, Rabbi Meshulam Igra established a grand Yeshiva which trained a cadre of the finest rabbis and educators who went forth to teach Torah and become lights unto the dispersed of Israel. Rabbi Meshulam Igra became renowned as a wise sage among sages, the rabbi of the children of the Diaspora.

HaRav Y. L. Maimon

[Page 87]

Rabbi Abraham David
Translated by Jessica Cohen

Rabbi Moshe Leib of Sassov was a devoted follower of the *tzadik* of Berditchev. His student, Rabbi Abraham David, who later became the Rabbi of Buczacz, pleaded with his rabbi to permit him to travel to Berditchev, for he longed to observe the tzadik's ways closely. But his rabbi refused to comply with his request. "We read in the Book of Daniel," he said, "of the court attendants, 'who are unable to stand in the king's court.' Our sages interpreted this to mean that against their will they abstained from laughter, sleep and other things. And the work of Rabbi Levi Yitzhak is, that he burns with an eternal flame. Everything he does deepens his burning soul. Therefore, no one can stand close to him unless he is certain that he will be able to resist laughing when he sees the strange movements of the holy man as he prays and as he eats." The student promised the rabbi that he would not laugh, and so the rabbi of Sassov gave him permission to travel to Berditchev for the Sabbath. But when he saw the tzadik sitting down at the table and his strange grimaces, he was unable to control himself and burst out laughing. He was immediately seized by a kind of madness and the laughter went wild and did not stop, until they had to take him away from the table and send him with a guard to Sassov when the Sabbath ended. When Rabbi Moshe Leib saw him, he wrote to Rabbi Levi Yitzhak: "I sent you a whole vessel and you returned it to me shattered." The illness continued for thirty days, and then Rabbi Abraham David was suddenly healed. Since then, he holds a thanksgiving feast every year, and during the feast he tells all the details of the tale, and concludes with the quote: "Give thanks to God for He is good, His kindness endures forever."

(From " Or Haganuz " by M. Buber, p. 228)

[Page 87]

Rabbi Shalom Mordechai HaCohen Schwadron
Translated by Melanie Rosenberg

Rabbi Shalom Mordechai Hacohen Schwadron was considered to be the "Mashiv," the ultimate rabbinical authority of his generation. He was recognized by the top rabbinical leaders of the day as a giant in the realm of Jewish education, renowned for his greatness in Torah knowledge and spiritual piety. Devoting these talents to the perfection of *halachic* understanding, the rabbi became the highest authority ("posek") on questions of Jewish observance. No less a personage than the distinguished "Mashiv," the sage Rabbi Yosef Shaul Natanzon, looked upon Rabbi Schwadron as his spiritual successor, saying, "I see no one in this generation who is a *Talmid Chacham* of his caliber."

Rabbi Shalom Mordechai Hacohen became the "Mashiv HaDor," the ultimate rabbinical authority not only for the rabbis of Galicia, Poland and even Lithuania, but for the entire Disapora. The reputation of the sage of Barzhan reached far and wide, and from his 6-volume book "Responsa from the RASH'AM"(Rabbi Shalom Mordechai) as well as "Ways of Peace" we note that he received difficult, complex questions on educational matters from petitioners as far distant as America, Australia, China and Japan. Leading rabbis of great stature, among them Rabbi Meir Arik of Tarnov, also turned to him, acknowledging his superior authority on educational matters. Rabbi Shmuel Yankel of Radomishlah and Rabbi Nachum Weidenfeld from Dombrova, the Admor (*Hasidic* master) of Sanibedg and other celebrated rabbis, also considered Rabbi Schwadron as the highest "posek."

In the educational world, great importance was attached to his works "Mishpat Shalom" ("Laws of Peace") on "Choshen Mishpat" (a section of the Shulchan Aruch), which offered interpretations on the Shulchan Aruch, and "Hagahot V'Hidushim al Shas Ohr haChaim" ("Interpretations of the Talmud, Ohr Ha Chaim"), "Darchei Shalom" ("Paths of Peace") on Talmud and its commentators, "Hagahot MRRSH"G al HaShas" (Interpretations of Rabbi Shimon Greenfeld on the Talmud). Yet it was the publication of three additional compositions by Rabbi Schwadron which aroused the greatest notice in the world of Torah and education: "Da'at Torah" ("Torah Wisdom") on the laws of kosher slaughter, "Galui Da'at" ("Manifesto") on sections 61-69 of the Talmudic book "Yoreh De'ah" (dealing with issues of ritual slaughter) and about the laws of kashrut. Yet a wave of criticism followed the publication of "Galui Da'at." Several leading rabbis of the day took issue with Rabbi Shwadron's tendency towards leniency in various matters. One prominent opponent was Rabbi Tzvi Hirsh Shapira, author of "Darchei Tshuvah" ("Paths of Repentance"), head of the rabbinical court of Monkatch, who claimed that certain of Rabbi Schwadron's rulings were based on very shaky foundations. In a show of great humility, Rabbi Schwadron responded by stating that his publication solely reflected his own personal opinion and that each and every teacher was entitled to make authoritative decisions based on his own conviction. Yet in practice, educators in Israel looked to Rabbi Schwadron for instruction, holding his directives as holy. Further credence was given to his stance with the publication of a special addenda to the book "Galui Da'at" called "The Final Pamphlet." In this work, the rabbi took on his detractors, clarifying the interpretations and directives in question and posturing a firm premise for his positions.

Rabbi Shalom Schwadron was also distinguished in his knowledge of Jewish legend and was well-versed in all sources of research and interpretation. He became renowned for his original ideas in Jewish thought, as presented in his book on Torah, "T'chelet Mordechai." Further, he was an eloquent orator, famed for emoting pearls of wisdom which left a lasting impression upon his listeners.

Rabbi Shalom Mordechai Hacohen merited great respect for his activities on behalf of public welfare. As deeply involved as he was in the education world, he would leave the four walls of the yeshiva in order to voice his opinions on matters of importance to the community. He assumed bold stands on issues which he deemed to be crucial to the needs of the time.

In 1902, Rabbi Schwadron issued an appeal on behalf of supporting yeshivot and Talmidei Torah (the school system) which began with the verse, "and the Cohen (high priest) went out unto the people." Even at that point, he was keenly aware of the urgency to organize the *haredi* public to strengthen their educational establishment. He was tapped to come to America to reestablish the post of chief rabbi of the New York Kollel, yet fully cognizant of the significance of that city's large concentration of Jews and future as a major Jewish center, Rabbi Schwadron felt himself too elderly for such a prestigious post and suggested a younger rabbi in his stead.

Rabbi Schwadron established a yeshiva in Barzhan called "Tushiah" ("Wisdom") with the goal of making it the first in a wide network of yeshivot. Indeed, a number of outstanding, erudite Torah scholars emerged from "Tushiah" to bolster the spirit of Torah in Jewish communities throughout Galicia. The rabbi was committed to the improvement and innovation of education in the *heder*. Toward this aim, he commissioned a renowned *haredi* pedagogue, Dr. Yosef Zeliger, to develop a blueprint for a new, more sophisticated educational curriculum. Yet the entire project was squelched due to the rigid opposition of certain noted *haredi* circles, with the *admor* (master) of the Belz *Hasidim* at the helm.

In 1908 a major assembly of rabbis was convened in Lvov devoted to making financial arrangements for the Galician Kollel (yeshiva) of Rabbi Meir Ba'al HaNes in the Land of Israel. Deliberations from this gathering were prominently reported in the Jewish media of the day. Due to the vast spectrum of ideological stands represented among the delegates, the fear of dissension was noticeably present. For this reason, the participants voted unanimously to select a capable chairman acceptable to all: Rabbi Shalom Mordechai Hacohen Schwadron, the sage of Barzhan. So effective was the rabbi's leadership that just before the conference ended, a prestigious admor approached him saying, "Please, Rabbi, give me a blessing." To the astonishment of those gathered, Rabbi Schwadron responded by reciting the traditional priestly *cohen* blessing.

In his behavior and his daily conduct, Rabbi Schwadron showed no hint of favoritism or partiality. In his study of Torah, he was humble and took advantage of no man. At the venerable age of 70, the rabbi himself rose to take books from the shelves, never demanding the services of others. Exhibiting humility and simplicity, he avoided lording authority over others. Each morning he would step outside his home to scatter seeds for the birds and chickens. Rabbi Schwadron was also honored and respected by those outside the Jewish community: judges from the district court would frequently consult with him on particularly complex judicial matters.

His home was the headquarters for the Central Committee, and here he tended to hundreds of inquiries and petitions daily regarding questions of what is permitted and what is forbidden, religion and law, *kabbala*, ritual slaughter, rabbinic ordination, the freeing of *agunot*, and more. Great was the rabbi's diligence in addressing these matters, as well as his rigorous tenacity towards learning. He was accustomed to making a schedule each day, assigning hours to the study of *gemara*, *shulchan aruch*, and other commentators. He never missed his regular daily lessons which included 25 chapters of Bible (Prophets and Writings), one section of *mishnayot*, and 18 pages of *gemara*.

He was born in 1835 in one of the villages in the Zelochov district in eastern Galicia. His father, Reb Moshe Hachoen, a serious scholar in his own right, was committed to securing an outstanding Torah education for his son from very early childhood.

Rabbi Schwadron's first teacher and rabbi, Rabbi Ashkenazi, noted that while he originally related to young Shalom Mordechai as a student, he later became a close friend. Eventually the tables turned completely and Rabbi Ashkenazi acknowledged his former pupil as his own rabbi.

Rabbi Schwadron's first rabbinical post was in the city of Potok-Zloti from 1867-1871. From there he was appointed as head of the Rabbinical Court of Yazlovitch. Seven years later the rabbi became the head of the Rabbinical Court of Buchach. Following that, he served for a period of 30 years as the head of the Rabbinical Court in Barzhan prior to his death in 1911. His predecessor in the post was the distinguished sage Rabbi Yitzchak Shmalkis, the head of the Rabbinical Court of Paramishleh and author of the book of Responza "Beit Yitzchak."

Moshe Tzinovitz
Moshe Tzinovitz

A lesson at the Beit Midrash This picture was drawn by Eliezer (Lazar) Karstin in the year 5666 [1906] (he was born in 1868 in Kovner. He taught drawing at Bezalel in Jerusalem before the First World War. This drawing is taken from his book of pictures).

Next to the pillar from left:
Head of the Yeshiva Rabbi Abraham Leiblin, author of "KeKaf Mezukak."
The next three men are unidentified.
Standing: Haim Shapira, grandson of Rabbi Yosef Stern on his mother's side,
and grandson of the Rabbi of Czortkow Rabbi Yeshayahu Meir Shapira on his father's side.
Sitting, second line:
The first is unidentified; the second – Peretz, the attendant at the bath-house;
third: Itzi Schechter; fourth: unidentified; fifth: Yakov Levi, a merchant.

The tombstone of Rabbi Yitzhak Kahen (father of Yisrael Cohen)
Next to the tombstone stand his widow and the cantor

The wall of the Great Synagogue

[Page 89]

Synagogues in the Town
Translated by Adam Prager

In Buczacz, as in all the towns of Galicia, there were many synagogues, study houses, small synagogues (kloyzim), and prayer rooms. Here two of them will be discussed.

"The Great Synagogue"
Buczacz's synagogue had a unique character which distinguished it from all the other synagogues in eastern and western Galicia.

In the center of the town there stood in all its glory a magnificent building, built in a special style: a square building with a large fortified wall. The width of each wall at the bottom was approximately five meters and the height approximately thirty meters. On each wall rose buttresses of stone with arched porches between them and a vaulted roof above, the highly skilled craftsmanship of architectural artisans from Italy. The mayor Graf Potocki, known by the title Starosta Kaniowski, had invited them to build his executive residence in the Baroque style. (One of the finest buildings in Galicia, it is known as the Buczaczer Rathaus). The architects invested all their skills in these two buildings.

The building was constructed in 1728, 218 years ago, as the numbers etched on the wall of the building give evidence. They are engraved on a stone over a small window near the entrance to the women's section of the synagogue. The date is inscribed in Hebrew and in Roman numerals – MLCCXXVIII, that is 1728. On the outside eastern wall under the roof there is an inscription stating that in 1748, twenty years after the building was completed, the external walls were plastered thanks to a gift from Esther-Malka Beer (a generous woman who bequeathed gifts to a number of charitable institutions).

All around the square edifice's walls there were sealed transparent windows. The interior hall of the building was decorated with paintings, flowers and cherubs. These were noticeable on all sides of the hall. On the western side were the two-story high balconies of the women's section of the synagogue, which looked out over the splendor and beauty of the interior.

Huge copper chandeliers, created by volunteer artists, hung on all sides of the sanctuary, illuminating it with their brilliance and luster.

At the eastern wall the doors of the Holy Ark shone, the work of artists of our town, and above the doors were the Ten Commandments with a Torah crown over them.

On both sides of the stairs leading to the Holy Ark stood two iron rams decorated with engravings of flowers; on their heads were two metallic palm trees, the work of a craftsman. During the First World War a Russian general took away one of these palm trees for a Moscow museum.

The marble pulpit in the center of the sanctuary held a chair for Elijah. Made by an artist, it added splendor and beauty to the hall. All who entered the synagogue were impressed and moved.

Aside from the gold and silver Torah ornaments, I must mention: a) the sink and its copper pedestal. b) the copper basin, with its carved pictures by an artist, which served for the washing of the hands of the Priests (Kohanim) before mounting the podium. c) a copper Hanukka menorah a cubit in size and width. d) an old manuscript prayer book with painted letters on parchment containing hymns for all the summer sabbaths and various special prayers (including one for sick children). It was bound in wood and leather and was written 150 years ago by one of our town's scribes.

Some of these artifacts were sent by us in 1930 to the regional exhibition held in Tarnopol, where they generated great interest among both Jewish and Polish visitors.

In 1920, after the First World War, the walls and ceilings of the inner sanctuary were repainted, within and without, by expert painters. The townspeople donated generously for this costly renovation.

The fate of this magnificent synagogue was the same as that of all the synagogues in Nazi Poland; it was razed to the ground.

The Old Study House
Above all I shall mourn the loss of the old study house and especially the great treasure of books it held. This treasure was most unique both in quantity and quality. One could find not only volumes of the Babylonian and Jerusalem Talmud in various editions, not only midrashic, exegetical and halachic literature, but philosophical works from the Golden Age in Spain; grammar, astronomy and engineering books could be found as well. There were many dictionaries like the complete Shulkhan Arukh and even Joseph Perl's Megale Tmirin ('Revealer of Secrets') was to be found, in addition to old manuscripts. This old study house was situated next to the entrance to the Great Synagogue (a magnificent building, built 205 years ago by architects from Italy who were invited by Graf Potocki to build the tall and stately executive residence and who built the two buildings).

This study house was the stronghold and holy of holies of the town's Misnagdim. Here they followed their own customs with great strictness and conservatism, rising for prayer at the first light of dawn, paying close attention to dagesh kal and dagesh khazak [weak and strong stress in certain letters]. Forty years ago the Massorah [the traditional annotation to the scriptural text] was known to the three pillars among the worshippers, the elders Reb Osher, Reb Yaane Melamed and Reb Ayzik (known collectively by the biblical phrase "oshir yaane azus" ['the rich man answers harshly' – Proverbs 18:23]). They were most scrupulous in reciting the Shema prayer in time [Hebrew "krias-shma" and Yiddish "krishme" – Deut. 6, 4-9 and 11, 13-21, and Num. 15, 37-41] and in observing the rest of the Ashkenazic customs according to the Massorah and the Shulkhan Arukh.

The image of the Gabai, the irascible Reb Yoysef, is alive before my eyes. He would scan the catalogues of book stores from the world over and especially those of the Krakow bookseller Reb Arn Foyst [Aaron Faust], searching for old books lacking in the library of the study house. If he came across such items he would order them regardless of expense.

Who was the one who used to roam the study house all day finding great pleasure in acquainting himself with each and every book it contained? It was the youth Shmuel Yosef Czaczkes, compared to none in his love for books. This great love won him much respect. The Gabai assigned him the task of arranging and cataloging the books of the library. He was only twelve at the time, but he carried out the work successfully exhibiting great knowledge and exactitude.

Indeed, the old study house and its treasure of books were nourishment to the youth's mind – the solid basis of his development. This treasure fed quite a few well known individuals who were the pride and honor of the town. Allow me to mention the writer Itzi Fernhof, author of Sifrey Shaashuim ['Books of Delights'], David Tsvi Miller, a great scholar, expert in ancient languages and, especially, a relative of his, Shmuel Yosef Czaczkes, known and honored as S. Y. Agnon.

David Neuman ("Davar" Supplement 08.28.38)

More About the Old Study House
I do not doubt that in his childhood Mr. David Neuman heard the rumors and the tales concerning the antiquity of the study house in his town, the story of Graf Potocki and the architects he brought from Italy. Such rumors were widespread throughout all the small towns of Poland and Lithuania, and all of us heard them while growing up.

However, it is a fact that on Shabat Khazon in the year 1865 a big fire broke out in the town of Butshatsh (as it was spelled then). By the testimony of the writer in HaMagid (no. 34, 1865), nearly all the houses of the town "including the Great Synagogue, two small synagogues, and a score of study houses with their libraries were burned to the ground. For this we are deeply grieved – the writer continues – for all those precious books that were burned. Everyone knows of the beauty and value of the books from the synagogue of the late Dr. Meir Sheiner; there was also a lovely collection of books in the small synagogue of Dr. Avish. There were many books in study houses and books were also lost in the homes of individual members of the community. The late Isaac Tsvi Hacohen owned a valuable library. Many of the books belonging to the Head of our town's Religious Court [av bet-din] were destroyed, as well as the manuscript of his Torah research which he had composed with great zeal. The distinguished and learned head of our town's Congregation Eydas Yeshurun, Rabbi Wolf Pohorila, lost many of his books, including his own Hebrew compositions, with their wisdom and enlightenment, a loss not to be calculated. We are now a flock without a shepherd. We have no synagogue, no study houses and not a book to look into..."

I cite this selection, important in many ways, for if on one hand it denies the antiquity of "The Old Study House," on the other hand it supports Herr Neuman with regard to the scholarship and the many precious books that were in Buczacz prior to the great conflagration of 1865, after which date books definitely continued to accumulate. The town was rebuilt and "The Old Study House" with it, keeping its original name. The elders [gabaim] spent much time buying books in all fields of Torah and modern scholarship. In that old study house, "stronghold and holy of holies of the town's Misnagdim" – in which one could also find a copy of Joseph Perl's Megale Tmirin! – Agnon the child absorbed his knowledge and acquired a fundamental mastery of various fields of Torah, for him a pure and faithful source from which he draws and creates his unique works of art, his tales of Hasidism and the Hasidim...

Michal Rabinowitz Jerusalem

It is worth noting that in the article in HaMagid which Michal Rabinowitz cites, we can identify the tearful, broken-hearted figure of Berish Shtern. Two months before the fire he wrote that he was not conveying bad news in HaMagid for the first. He went on to write of fires in Brod, Kolomea, Horodenka, Tarnopol, Khorostkov, Czeshnov, Kozlov and on the spirited aid given by inhabitants of his city headed by the District Commissioner Foyle and the head of the community, Reb Pohorila. He reports on the campaign of assistance in Brod, where the recluse Reb Meir Kalir himself collected donations for the fire victims (HaMagid No. 28, 1865). And two months later he mourns for his own hometown. Berish Shtern was later known as a leading citizen of Buczacz, famous for his part in parliamentary elections where he supported the government and opposed the Zionists. His portrait was artfully drawn under the name of Sebastian Montag in the stories of Shay Agnon (in "Our Youth and Our Old Age" and also mentioned in "A Simple Story").

(Sabbath Supplement of Davar, No. 4933 [9.9.1983])

D. Sh. (Dov Shtok) [= Dov Sadan]

[Page 92]

The Buczacz Community
Translated by Adam Prager

A

Several towns in Galicia have through the years acquired a special status, religious, general or a combination of the two. Events that took place in them and noteworthy individuals who lived in them distinguished these towns from the rest. However, Jewish history has left its mark, for good or for evil, in almost every city and town at one time or another. Towns can be compared to human beings. Like us, they depend on luck, and just as the enlightened ones among us are few so are those unique towns or villages that become the center of the nation. It is as if these special towns were destined to fulfill an exemplary role. For this reason, our creator has bestowed upon them majestic landscapes, verdant forests, winding rivers, mountain ranges, beautiful valleys and ancient ruins. These towns are also known for their great families and individuals, and for historic political decisions and critical moments. For it has been said of towns: "God is only with the wise, the heroic, rich, and dignified."

Galicia has few towns of this kind: Lvov, Brody, Tarnopol, Zhulkov etc. One of those towns is Buczacz, lying between Stanislavov (which leads to Lvov) and Tarnopol. However, Buczacz's dignity and reputation can be credited solely to itself. Almost all Jewish spiritual trends swept through this town and left their mark. Or perhaps it was Buczacz that left a mark on these trends by lending them a personal touch and hue. For it is a town built on tradition, as well as being honored with a considerable number of Jews. In 1765, the Jewish population of Buczacz reached 1055. From that time on it only grew. In the 17th and 18th century Russian-Bratslavian [Russian Orthodox?] area, Buczacz was the leading community. Following the region's partition, the Buczacz rabbi became the religious leader of one part. Buczacz sent a community leader (who was also called "the head of state") to the Russian-Bratslavian state and also to the Council of the Four Lands. The community leaders, David Prager, who participated in the sessions of the Council in 1664, and Arieh Leib Ben-Yitskhak, who was a Council member at Kulikov in 1727. Are well known. Among the noteworthy Buczacz rabbis we should mention R' Yaakov Eliyahu Ben Moshe Mak; R' Elkhanan Ben Ze'ev Wolf, whose son R' Abale was the son-in-law of Tsvi Meisels, the famous community leader, who was a member of the Council of the Four Lands; R' Tsvi Hirsh Ben Yaakov Kara, author of *Neta Sha'ashuim*; his son-in-law R' Avraham David Ben Asher; and R' Avraham Ben Tsvi Hirsh Teumim, author of *Khesed Avraham*.

Buczacz was characterized by people like R' Avraham David Ben Asher (1770-1840). His life history and philosophy constitute a very important chapter in Buczacz' history. We shall, however, suffice with a concise account of his story. As a boy he already drew attention to himself by his great Talmudic erudition and sharpness. Tsvi Hirsh, author of Neta Sha'ashuim, chose him as a son-in-law for his daughter. At twenty he was ready to serve as the rabbi of Yazlovitsh. Buczacz was a town of scholars and Talmudists who did not believe in the tsadikim and their miracles. The war between the Talmudists and the hasidim reached its peak at that time, and it greatly troubled R' Avraham. When his son fell ill, his wife and friends urged him to bring the sick child to R' Levi Yitskhak of Berditshev. After refusing for a long while, he finally consented. From that day on he was a different man. He was greatly influenced by R' Levi Yitskhak, who helped him in reconciling his Talmudic and hasidic views, positions that were polarized in his town. The hasidim could not imagine a greater joy, for many of them feared his mastery of the Talmud and rabbinical law. Nevertheless, after he inherited his father-in-law's position, everyone marveled at his religious knowledge but opposed his way of life, his following the teachings of the Baal Shem Tov. In the practice of rabbinical law, he would draw his judgment from the Talmud and from rabbinical authorities [poskim], and not from the principles of the Kabbala. His wide-ranging literary work was basically rationalistic, Talmudic and exegetic. His essay *Da'at Kedoshim*, as well as *Eshel Avraham*, was incorporated as an independent section of the *Shulkhan Arukh*. In addition to all of his other books, he wrote a Kabbalistic commentary named *Birkat David* [David's Blessing]. At one point in his life his reason was somewhat shaken, and according to tradition he was cured by the rabbi of Sasov. He acted as Buczacz' rabbi till the day he died, approximately fifty years, and bestowed his spirit upon the town.

Many legends grew up around R' Avraham. People would say of him that he never went to sleep until he had reinterpreted 18 halakhot (religious laws) and that he had no idea what a coin looked like. When a gravestone was erected for him after his death, the word *malkeynu* [our king] was etched on it, Immediately someone reported this to the authorities; however, by the time they arrived to investigate, the letter kaf had been altered to pey, forming the word *mealfenu* [our teacher] (though missing an alef). Since that day, none of his successors were given the title "Rabbi." Instead they received the more modest title: "dayan" [religious judge].

B

The peace treaty that ended the war between the Turks and the Poles is considered by historians to this day as "the disgraceful peace treaty of Buczacz" (1672). According to this pact, Podolia and bordering Ukrainian lands were annexed to Turkey, which held them until the Karlowitz peace agreement (1699) [between Austria and Turkey], thus laying the foundations in these places during a 27-year period for the Shabtai Tsvi movement and later on for the Frankist movement. During this period the Jews' political and, to a large extent, financial situation was very good. It seems that the Jews of these conquered lands were satisfied with their conquerors to such an extent that the Poles began to suspect a secret liaison between the Jews and the Turks. During this time, eastern Jewry was experiencing a blood transfusion within the Podolian communities. This fact has not yet received the attention it deserves. This coming together of two sections of the Jewish people helps us to understand the nature of Jewish Galicia, its participation in the messianic movements, the rabbinical conflict, the ways of hasidism, the evolution of the haskala [enlightenment], etc. The Shabtai Tsvi movement was not brought to this district of Galicia by individual missionaries alone, but also by transient Jews from Turkey who came to settle. Even Yaakov Frank, founder of the Frankist movement, who was born in a small Galician town, spread his word and acquired his following after returning from where Shabtai Tsvi started his movement, bringing with him all of Shabtai Tsvi's flock. In Buczacz there were several people who referred to them disparagingly as "Frankim," The original meaning was forgotten as time went by. But it is most probable that those still called by the name were descendants of movement members or of those who immigrated from Turkey, for all Ottoman Jews were called "Franks." The persecution of the followers of the false Messiah were so fierce and their ostracism so severe that in time all memory of them were lost and their names were forgotten. All that remained were bits and pieces of rumors regarding such and such a person who was believed to be of Frankist descent. Great efforts were made in ridding the community of this affliction, Buczacz leading the way in this campaign. Existing letters and documents show just how wary and suspicious the Jews of Buczacz were regarding contact with this movement, and how they even warned others of them. This suspicion was aimed at the hasidism as well. The Jews of Buczacz saw it as a continuation of the messianic movement and so hasidism never established a stronghold in the town. In time, of course, hasidic chapels [kloyzim] were founded; however, they never had decisive influence, neither during community elections nor in the shaping of the towns' character.

C

The town of Buczacz lies in a mountain valley; the Strypa River flows through it and ends by falling into the Dnestr River. The town is centered in a crater between two plateaus. The main street and the market are situated at the lower part of the valley, while the side streets seem to climb up the slopes, the houses appearing as though placed one above the other. Bridges span across the river, which flows through the entire town. When the winter ice begins to melt, the cleaving ice-blocks produce thunderous sounds that frighten the townspeople who live by the river. Often, a bridge is damaged, thus preventing passage between the two parts of the town.

In the narrow town square stood the Town Hall (Ratusz), one of the most magnificent buildings in Galicia built in true Baroque style. Previously it was a square building abounding in ornamentation.

After the fire it was badly damaged, however it still partially retained its original shape and engravings. On the way to the railway station, one can see on the right the remaining ruins of the castle built in the 14th century and conquered and demolished by the Turks. Later on, Nikolaus Potocki restored and lived in it. Also the Roman Catholic and Greek Orthodox Churches stood out and everyone spoke of their beauty and interior splendor. Buczacz boasted of several other historical ornaments as well. During World War Two, part of the town was destroyed; during the past twenty years, it has been restored and rebuilt.

In the cemetery there were ancient graves and tombstones, some bearing famous names, others anonymous. There were mausoleums of tsadikim and gravestones recording miracles and calamities. I believe that even the town elders would have lost their way in this labyrinth of graves. Since some of the pinkasim [record books] were lost or burned, it was very difficult to retrieve from the depths of oblivion the town's history, which was waiting to be drawn out of these silent tombs.

Most wondrous was the Old Study House that, according to the etching upon its walls, was built over 210 years ago by Italian architects whom Count Potocki had invited to build his magnificent palace. It was not just any study house but the stronghold of the mitnagdim, a center for the opponents of Kabbala and hasidism. Those who studied and prayed there were a consolidated ideological group that occasionally left its mark on the town. They were Ashkenazim. Not "Ashkenazim" in the sense of being 'Germans, reformers'; on the contrary, they were pious Jews, strict regarding all Jewish laws, major or minor. They uncompromisingly followed the strict Ashkenazic system which teaches according to the pshat [literal meaning]. The allegoric and esoteric were foreign to them, and altogether proscribed. A large group of them would convene in the Old Study House on Saturday afternoon to hear one of the talmidey khakhamin [learned men] teach the weekly portion together with an explanation of the *akeda* [the sacrifice of Isaac]. While doing so, he would introduce opinions and explanations of philosophers who supported his position as well as of those who did not. A large treasure of books, a true archive, was to be found in the Old Study House. This was no chance collection but a well-planned one. Besides the well known sacred texts which were acceptable to all, such as the Tanakh [Bible], the Talmud with all its commentaries, the Midrash [homiletic interpretation], the Shulkhan Arukh [Jewish code of laws], and the poskim [rabbinical arbiters], you could find Hebrew research and philosophy books from all periods, books on grammar, engineering, astronomy, dictionaries and even rare manuscripts dealing with medical research in the middle ages. Not everyone was permitted access to all of these book, some of which were held behind lock and key. However, it should be stated that books dealing with hasidism, kabbala and esoterica were hardly to be found. Being the largest and most convenient library, everyone used it; in addition to learning Torah, they developed a certain style and direction. In this study house, S. Y. Agnon spent many an hour, and imbibed its spirit. Up until the Shoah, you could find his notes and comments in the margins of the volumes he studied. I also found there writings of the Malbi"m [Meir Leibush Ben Yekhiel Mikhal – a rabbi and exegete of the Tanakh (1809–1879)], in his own hand, on one of the books in the Old Testament.

D

Buczacz – surrounded by mountains. One of these mountains is named Pedor. At its edge there was a forest. It was traditionally believed in town that the Frankists consulted secretly in the valleys and in this forest. This is where these zealots assembled prior to the famous public debate in Lvov. Under the shade of these trees they sharpened their blasphemous tongues, cursing the Jewish religion and libeling its leaders and their Torah. However, they were not the only ones who took refuge under the shady trees. Up on the plateau one could find innocent dreamers among the intellectuals, dreamers of new gods and reformers of the world. Throughout all the generations thinkers struggled with their thoughts in this forest. Hasidim, mitnagdim, intellectuals, anarchists, socialists and Zionists, including the youngsters of HaShomer HaTsair – the Zionist movement that was founded at the end of World War One. At dawn or at night, all would visit this forest, opening their hearts and roaring out the anguish of their troubled souls. Here merry and sad folk songs, songs of rebirth and hasidic songs were sung, planting seeds of joy in young Jewish souls. A net of legends and events spread before the hiker along the paths of the mountain and forest. Desires and dreams from the past, not yet extinguished, were secretly reincarnated within him. A sense of something not yet brought to completeness always filled the air of this pleasant place. The winds that blew there would grow sevenfold, rain stormed frequently and whoever walked alone there would, against his will and despite the spacious and colorful scenery around him, fall into deep sadness. However, during those wonderful sunny days when nature displayed a scented green landscape across the plateau and down its slopes, the music of the forest resounded everywhere and Jewish young men and young women strolled off to read *Jean Cristophe* [Romain Roland's romantic novel] and returned full of faith in man and his world.

However, a Jew in Buczacz, a town full of tradition where erudition and character went hand in hand, could not help but feel a certain flaw, as though one of its strings had snapped. Some personal or public prayer, past or present, remained unanswered and continued to hover in the air. It is possible that this is the case in every Jewish town in exile [ba-gola] that plucks the plumage of its youth. Maybe this feeling originates from the state of perplexity felt by every young Jew who grows up in his surroundings, is nourished by them and in turn gives much of himself, only to suddenly be at a loss: where now [le-an]? Even this beneficent mountain can only give its visitors what it has always given. Whatever the case, even in a town of scholars and fine individuals such as Buczacz, life in exile will always be flawed. When, following an absence of several years, I visited Buczacz and tried to fathom it, I became aware that, indeed, an unfulfilled wish encompassing generations was reflected in the town's inhabitants and life style. S.Y. Agnon, born and bred in this town, attempted to mend this flaw, which is as fine as the defect in a choice citron, by means of artistic design. In the artistic sphere, these Jews excelled in both the sacred and the secular modes. However, in his great novel *Oreach Nata LaLun*, this ever-present flaw and incompleteness that has been Buczazc' imprint is again projected. Maybe the reason for this was Agnon's re-encounter with the town.

A thin layer of mystery and innocent dreams surrounded Buczacz. Basically, however, Buczazc was a rationalistic town, if one may refer to a whole town in such a way. From the character of its rabbis and scholars, the quality of its hasidim and mitnagdim, the aims of its intellectuals [maskilim] and the causes of all its wars, we learn one thing. This was a town that failed to lend an ear during the last generations to the kabbalists and mystics, ignoring tsadikim and the like. However, Buczazc did not possess a bloodless radical rationalism of dry bones. Tanakh [Bible] and grammar studies [dikduk] were common in town, as well as study of Agada and Midrash. One of Buczazc' writers was Itsi Farenhof, author of *Sifrey Sha'ashuim* and, in contrast to him, the learned scholar, David Tsvi Miller, who specialized in ancient tongues.

Itsi Farenhof was a man of aspirations and initiative. His love of Hebrew was profound and his taste was excellent. He set out to plough the fields of Hebrew literature in Galicia and succeeded in making a small furrow. Unlike other literary experiments, his was especially interesting and unique. The small pamphlets *Sifrey Sha'ashuim* were issued speedily throughout the Hebraist world. Writers such as Tshernikhovski, Klausner, Berdichevski and others contributed poems, articles or reports. To this day these small pages exude pure intimacy and good will, the Hebrew beautifully styled and modern. – Professor David Tsvi Miller was a great authority in Arabic culture and ancient tongues, an expert in Assyriology and taught these languages at the University of Vienna. He translated into Hebrew the Hammurabi Code, studied the structure of Biblical verse and deciphered its laws. He was a teacher at the Viennese Seminary [bet hamidrash havinai] founded by Shilink and Weiss. On reaching old age, he was awarded a rank of nobility by Kaiser Franz Josef. – Last but not least: Agnon, who dwells within us and represents the grandeur of Hebrew literature.

Buczacz' spiritual decline started long before World War Two. The young left, some to Erets-Yisrael, some to America and the rest to other countries. The languishing yeshiva students grew old and cultural activity dwindled. Nevertheless, the town's strength had not yet diminished completely; it was still capable of supporting many generations to come. One could compare it to a very wealthy man who has lost his fortune, but the remnants of whose wealth are still scattered about.

Beautiful and gracious Buczacz now lies in ruins. Bestial occupiers have poured their poisonous wrath upon its Jews, trees and rocks. This is how it was portrayed in a letter by Dr. Avraham Khalfon, one of its last Jews:

"Buczacz exists today only as a geographical fact. The town has been destroyed. Only two Jewish families remain and there are no Jews in the rest of the region. The streets of the town are covered with weeds and thistles. The houses were demolished, the synagogues are used as public lavatories. The cemetery was ploughed over by army excavations, its tombstones used to pave the "Pig Market." The high school [gymnasia], the elementary schools and other important buildings were destroyed. Over ten thousand Jews, inhabitants of Buczacz, were put to death by various means. Their bodies were buried in mass graves on the Pedor, the Bashtim, and in the forests and fields –."

Let us be consoled in that a small portion of the teachings [Torah] of the Study House [Bet Midrash] of Buczacz reached Erets-Yisrael and lives in its children and children's children!

Israel Cohen

[Page 97]

The Hasidim of Buczacz
Translated by Adam Prager

A wonderful era of the Hasidic way of life has vanished and with it have been lost certain Hasidic personalities whose like shall never appear again in the fashion and in the surroundings in which we knew them during our youth. When I recall those days, I feel the urge to cry out: Happy is the man who has witnessed all this!

The town of Buczacz was well known for its extremes. Its Hasidim were very zealous and its misnagdim were very strict. The stronghold where the main Hasidic strength lay was the Tshortkov kloyz [small synagogue]. The most prominent and most powerful figure among all the kloyz's Hasidim was Reb Yoshe Preminger, the recognized spiritual leader and the ultimate paradigm of the complete Hasid. The Hasidic spirit and atmosphere of the Tshortkov kloyz were felt far beyond its walls.

Hasidim of other rebes [Hasidic rabbis] came to pray at Reb Yoshe's kloyz, the most famous of whom were the learned and great scholar, the Hosyatin Hasid Reb Velvl Tirkl and Reb Yitskhok Zaydman [Isaac Seidman] and his sons, the last of the Vizhnits Hasidim. The latter left the kloyz after taking the initiative to establish the Vizhnits kloyz, which in the course of time itself became a center for Torah and Hasidism.

Among one hundred who prayed at the kloyz approximately 80 were certified teachers.

One instance of the beauty of Hasidism is revealed when Hasidim ascend to the highest reaches of heaven to worship the Creator with joy, namely on days of rest. Such days were quite frequent. Besides the holidays and the first day of each month [rosh khoydesh], where the content of Hasidism was expressed, there were also saints' memorial days [yortsaytn shel tsadikim] such as Hoshana Raba [Feast of Tabernacles], the third day in Kheshvan, the nineteenth day of Kislev, etc. On these occasions great feasts were held, although what truly mattered was not the food but the atmosphere. The celebration would start with a quiet melody (nigun) which would slowly turn into full-voiced singing accompanied by fervent dancing, the atmosphere becoming more and more ecstatic. While watching the dancers at such moments you could not but feel that they had left all earthly matters behind, so to speak, and had ascended to higher realms. We, the boys of the kloyz, would wait in great anticipation for these hours of joy. The most fascinating moment was when Reb Yoshe Preminger would tell his wonderful stories about tsadikim. S. Y. Agnon and I never missed an opportunity to listen to these tales, for they were told with great artistry, the characters becoming vivid and real to his audience. He had the rare gift of causing his hearers to break into a Hasidic dance when he finished telling his story.

At commemorative feasts such as these it was usual for amusing "incidents" to occur. I recall one Faybish Hirsh Shor, who used to stuff himself during meals. On one occasion a quite lavish dairy meal with pancakes, dumplings and what not was prepared. What did the Hasidim do? They prepared a dish of goose cracklings [gendzene grivn] " ('fried goose skin') to which Faybush Hirsh, as always, helped himself again and again. No one made any effort to restrain him since everyone except him knew in advance about the hoax. No one can describe Faybish's disappointment at falling for the practical joke and finding before him a table sumptuously laden with dairy dishes.

Among many important and honored Hasidim one figure stood out, that of Reb Hirshl Aberdam, a rich Jew and zealous Hasid. When some of the young members of the kloyz started joining circles of the haskala and the Zionists, Reb Hirshl took advantage of being called to read the lesson from the Prophets [maftir] at a Sabbath morning service to pound on the dais and declare in an aggressive and militant tone that something horrid had happened: The young men of the kloyz had gone to graze in foreign pastures. He named those involved, including S. Y. Agnon and myself, insisting on our being expelled from the kloyz.

Shortly after this incident S. Y. Agnon left Buczacz and emigrated to Israel, and I myself left as well. When I happened to bump into Reb Hirsh Aberdam in Vienna during the war, he expressed his deepest regrets to me over that incident, begging my forgiveness for the wrong done us.

In my eyes the life of the Buczacz Hasidim was a pure inexhaustible spring.. Every name I recall is a whole world in itself.

I remember Reb Hirsh Yidl Boyer, a learned scholar whose particular weakness was being critical of others. Once he said to Reb Yitskhok Zaydman: "Do you know the difference between you and me? When you recite the Eighteen Benedictions [shmoyne esre], your mind is in Vienna, whereas mine is only in Troybokhovits, which at least is not as far."

Reb Hirsh Yidl suffered a lot from coughing attacks. When the Hasidim raised a toast and expressed the wish that these attacks end, his reply was: "God forbid, may I cough for many more years to come." On one occasion he said that he had a mind to order mirrors from his son, Monish, who was a furniture dealer. He would hang them in the kloyz so that those who entered could see their faces.

Earlier I mentioned the Hasid from Hosyatin, the incomparable Reb Velvl Tirkl, who was a taverner. On Sabbaths and holidays it was customary among the Hasidim to meet for a drink at his house, where there was always an atmosphere of excitement. On Simchat Bet-Hashoeva ['Feast of Water Drawing'] and on the eve of Simchat Torah ['Rejoicing of the Law'] before the hakafot ['circling with the Torah scrolls'], just before midnight, they would march from his house singing and dancing all along the town's streets to carry out the hakafot.

One day Borekh [Baruch] Schnaps, a Talmud teacher and a cheerful type, being somewhat drunk, insisted on destroying the Town Hall. Moyshe [Moshe] Pines, who lived in this building, begged him to spare him and his family.

In the later years there also appeared the Kupichinits Hasidim. Yossi Bokhhaym [Bochheim], who was both a modern man and a zealous Hasid, deserves to be mentioned. On the twenty-first day of Kislev, at the birthday celebration for the old rebe, Reb Yitskhok Meir (of blessed memory), the above-mentioned tore a note of 10 crowns in two. One half he gave them at the start of the dancing, the second half was to be won when it ended. That same night his new shoes were completely worn out from the intensity of the dancing.

Nisn [Nissan] Pohorila was the wealthiest man in town and he prayed at the study house of Reb Itsi, grandson of the tsadik from Buczacz. Once during a quarrel over some insignificant matter, he called R. Itsi an ignoramus [amorets (in Yiddish)], to which R. Itsi answered loudly: "Beggar"!

I would also like to mention my grandfather Reb Alter Shochat (May he rest in peace). My grandfather (of blessed memory) was not in the habit of drinking, nevertheless he was the most joyous of them all.

Hasidim would say of him: Reb Alter Shochat is getting drunk.

Lastly I must mention that Reb Yossi Preminger was overcome by his fatal illness at the Tshortkov kloyz, and was carried by Agnon and myself to his house. We lay him in his bed from which he never arose.

Shimen Horovits [Simon Horowitz]
London

[Page 100]

The Jewish Awakener
(Der Jüdische Wecker)
Translated by Jessica Cohen

"*Der Jüdische Wecker*" was first published in Stanislaw and then in Buczacz in 1905. Following are correspondences about life in the town during those days, which were printed in the newspaper and translated into Hebrew.

Stanislaw, 3 Kislev 5666 (1905)　　　　　　　　　　　　　　　　　　　　　　　　**Issue 10**

The Buczacz Zion Group
Buczacz, First day of Kislev

Here in the town of Buczacz on Monday, the victims of the pogroms in Russia were mourned in the Great Synagogue. The synagogue was packed full with some five thousand and nine-hundred men and women. Dr. Schor, the Stanislaw district president, gave an extremely impressive speech. All the townspeople fasted, recited "*Va-Yachal*" and the congregation's cantor sung the "Thirteen *middoth*" prayer, "*El Maleh Rachamim*" and "*Av Harachamim*."

Dr. Schor spoke again at the "Zion Association" house in the presence of all the members, the town president Mr. Abisch Stern and the citizens' leader Bernhard Stern.

The Zion Association collected three-hundred and seventy crowns from its members, and another five-hundred and fifty crowns from outside the synagogue, to benefit the orphans and widows.

Our thanks to Dr. Schor for his work for the benefit of all.

With blessings of Zion, "The Zion Group"

*

Stanislaw, 22 Tevet 5666 (1906)

Issue 17

In Buczacz on Sunday, 10 Tevet (January 17th), there was a public meeting with many attendants for the purpose of recognizing the Jewish nation. The meeting was conducted by a committee established for this purpose, composed of all sectors of the population. Mr. Yitzhak Webber, the *maggid* from Koloma spoke at the meeting. The meeting was held based on Article 2, because the District Governor was unwilling to give permission to hold a public meeting, thereby further proving that he treats us as Jews, a sign that he sympathizes with our ideas.

Abraham Horn

*

Stanislaw, 16 Sivan, 5666 (1906)

Issue 29

A truly noble man, not only from birth but also due to his good deeds, his ideas and his gentle and honest sentiments, Edward Ritter P. Gniewosz Aleksaw, has died in Vienna.

We, the Jews, have suffered a great loss in his death. He was a great friend of Israel and a brave fighter against the anti-Semites.

When the Baron Hirsch was about to establish in Galicia an institute in which he had invested millions, he turned to the section leader, P. Gniewosz, and it was he who advised him to establish a network of public schools in Galicia and Bokowina. And he also cooperated with him as curator and vice-president. He fought for the emancipation of Galician Jews with all his might.

The Jewish delegates laid a wreath on his bed, with the inscription: "To the brave fighter for equal rights for the Jews. Galician Jewish delegates."

The Buczacz community also sent a delegation, lead by the mayor, A. Bernhard Stern, who laid a wreath in the name of the Buczacz community, with the inscription: "To the honorary citizen of the town of Buczacz, in memory of his great deeds for the benefit of Buczacz."

The manager of the Baron Hirsch institute issued an order to all his schools to hold mourning prayers in memory of the noble man.

"Laziness is the mother of all evils" – this is apparent. The Jewish population of Buczacz represents more than sixty percent of the town's population. Forty-two teachers teach in the town schools, and yet there are almost no Jewish teachers among them. And, after all, there are a number of young Jewish women in the town who have completed their studies to be teachers, and even so they can not get a teaching position in the town schools. And if they do obtain a teaching position, they are sent to some distant village in a rural area, where the pay is poor. The meager salary they receive is not enough even to pay for the most basic expenses. If they could get jobs in the town itself, they could subsist while eating at their parents' tables.

And no one is to blame for this other than the negligence of our brothers, the citizens of the town, who do not stand up for their rights. The town management – which includes a few Jewish members – would not have opposed this. However, to our regret, every one of the Jews of Buczacz is a world unto himself, and takes no interest in the general affairs. One could say that if the Jews of Galicia in general are drowsing, then the Jews of Buczacz are sound asleep and snoring loudly... and thus they are missing out on anything that relates to the good of the people of Israel, even when it concerns the good of their own brothers.

How the Jews of Buczacz can be awakened from their slumber, I do not know.

And those who see the many soda stores in town, might think that the townspeople are so enthusiastic that they have to cool themselves off by drinking cold water. But the indifference and coldness of our brothers, people of Israel, in this town, contradict this assumption. And who knows whether perhaps it is the excessive drinking of soda water that has brought on their inactivity.

*

Stanislaw, 6 Tamuz 5666 (1906)   **Issue 32**

Buczacz. This past Sunday, the Buczacz "Zion Association" held a memorial service for the Bialistok casualties in the Great Synagogue. The cantor and his choir prayed "*El Maleh Rachamim*" and sung "*Av Harachamim*" and the famous Jewish scholar, Dr. Rokeach, eulogized the dead. His warm and touching words brought tears to the participants' eyes. The synagogue was full of men, women and children, and was also attended by all the members of the presidency and the community president, Rabbi R. Abisch Stern, as well as the Jewish citizens' leader, Bernhard Stern.

                                                                                                              The "Zion" group

*

Buczacz, 3 Elul 5666 (1906)   **Issue 40**

Resurrection of the Dead
(A letter from Buczacz)

Our representative, Dr. Nathan Zeinfeld, has finally made his voice heard. Until now he has abided by the rule, "a fence around wisdom is silence." Now, before the elections, he has decided that he would at least like to "choose death with dignity."

[translator's note: unclear]. We do not wish to contemplate the way he has behaved until now, but he has now done "an act" for which he deserves commendation.

As is known, the Polish club cheated us, they promised the Jews eight seats. And when the district was distributed, it turned out that the Poles had made a mockery of us. We had only five definite seats, and three that were doubtful. Buczacz was joined with Tlomatz, Sniatin, Zalchetzki and three rural villages. Now there is no doubt that no Jew will be elected here. And I am not surprised that the Jews of Buczacz are silent, for they are silent about other matters too.

And I am even less surprised at the Buczacz Zionists. By removing the Hebrew secretary from the association, because he protested the Jews' Polish politics, they proved that they are politicians... Whereas the Jews of Zalchetzki and Sniatin, I do not understand at all – why do they not hold a protest meeting against joining the three rural villages.

And so our Dr. Zeinfeld addressed the Lvov community with a letter, proposing to convene a gathering of the communities in order to consult over the reaction to the new decree issued by our Polish brother.

The Lvov community has accepted the proposal, and it will convene a "community day" of Galicia during the second half of September. All the Jewish communities, with no exception, will be invited to the occasion. Furthermore, all the Jewish representatives in parliament and in the national representative house in Galicia. Will shall live and learn.

I am a man of little faith, but for now we will stand aside and see how things turn out.

A landlord from Buczacz

(in the same issue)

The theater troupe "Itztrubal" is in Buczacz at present. They have set up at the "Abar" hotel, and are performing a series of plays. They are presenting the well-known plays: *Kol Nidrei, Gavriel, Isha Ra'ah, Akedat Yitzhak*, and so forth. The "Itztrubal" troupe has a good reputation. It always has several formidable forces. In the next issue, we shall write further on the matter. For the time being, a few words will suffice. We have already written about "*Kol Nidrei*" a few weeks ago. At that time, we noted that the playwright Y. Sarkanski was not an appropriate poet to depict this tragedy. However, with his keen sense he managed to select good material, and we accept his gift with love. The troupe performed the play with talent. Young Mr. Leibgold, as the head of the inquisitionists, Mr. Orich as Bartala, Mrs. Steif as Elvira, and Mr. Adler as Benedictus, all played their parts with understanding and great emotion. The audience was riveted and gave their full attention to the plot of the play.

Incidentally, we will devote a special article to the audience, where we will take it to task.

*

10 Elul (1906)   **Issue 41**

From the Jewish World

There was a meeting in Buczacz on the matter of the *etrogs*, and all the *gabbaim* from the Batei-Midrash, the *kloisim* and the *minyans*, as well as private individuals, swore that they would not use any *etrogs* other than those that came from Eretz Yisrael. And all the *etrog* merchants will only bring *etrogs* from Eretz Yisrael from now on.

From the Jewish Theater

The troupe "Itztrubal" (*tanentzapf*) has captured the hearts of the Buczacz audience. On Saturday evening and Sunday evening, they performed "Daughter of Jerusalem" and "Mishnah for the King." The theater was filled to capacity. The actors demonstrated their full force and ability, and the audience was completely satisfied. We shall not discuss the plays themselves at present. There is no room for that, perhaps another time. We have said previously that, until this day, we have had no real poets, poets who would draw from their own spiritual sources, from the spiritual source of the people, and create Jewish-national plays which would have the power to seize the soul of the spectator and take hold of his heart. Mr. Auerbach, in his "Daughter of Jerusalem," integrated Shakespeare, namely *Romeo and Juliet*, and also plucked a few feathers from "Love of Zion" by Mapu, thus creating a new play for the Jewish theater. The actors were excellent. Young Mr. Leibgold as Cohen, Mrs. Steif as Tirtza and Mr. Orich as Na'aman truly excited the hearts of the audience, and the other actors were also noteworthy. Mrs. Steiner played Katora with great understanding, Mr. Leibgold senior and Mrs. Feder molded the characters of Ovdan and Macha beautifully. Mr. Steiner as the prince was excellent.

In Feinman's "Mishnah for the King," young Mr. Leibgold played Sebastian and Mrs. Steif played Miriam with great emotion and enthusiasm which left a deep impression on the spectators. Mr. Orich as Alonzo was quite good. Sarafina and Ferdila, the slaves of Sebastian, were played by Mrs. Feder and Mr. Leibgold senior, to the audience's satisfaction and enjoyment, as always. Mr. Adler as Don Antonio and Reiles as Don Fabio played their roles fairly well.

To our regret, the Jewish audience is interested in such scenes. Scenes which are a necessity of the reality in any Jewish play. But this is no fault of the actors. In every Jewish play there must be a few slaves and maidservants who play at marriage like a cat plays with a mouse, and the audience enjoys this and is full of laughter. Even the ostensibly intelligent people take pleasure in these scenes, which would be unbearable to a delicate soul! Only dancing and twirling in great quantities – this is what they desire. Shalom Aleichem's "*Shvitat Hakaparot*" to them is a comedy so comic as to bring one to tears. Who is at fault here – the playwright or the audience? We believe that only the audience is to blame.

It is clear that the theater is no place for sour faces, but rather, as the poet says: "The stage is the judging place of the world." The actors must satisfy the landlords, for they wish to live, and they always give the audience more than they take from it. The troupe will remain here for a few more days and promises some more good plays. We shall live and see.

On Saturday evening they will present the most famous play in the world, "Mammon, the God of Money, or the Treasures of Korach."

The management has ordered new sets for this play.

*

Buczacz, 17 Elul 5666 (1906)　　　　　　　　　　　　　　　　　　　　　　　　　**Issue 42**

From the Jewish World

There are four diseases which are prevalent in our town of Buczacz: Typhus fever, rubella, diphtheria and whooping cough. To our regret, the diseases are showing signs of epidemics. The schools have been closed and bathing is forbidden in the Stripa, based on the assumption that this is the source of all these diseases. However, it is strange and dangerous that the municipality allows water from the Stripa to be poured on the streets, for this spreads the germs even further. Lavatories should be built in the lot where the burn victims (from the fire two years ago) live in seven caravans, so that they will not have to pollute the lot, where children from the Baron Hirsch school play. Likewise, the streets should be cleaned every morning, rather than only once a week. There should be a committee of landlords to oversee the cleaning in a stricter manner and if, God forbid, these things are not done, we are in danger of these four diseases taking over, God forbid, for the entire winter, and there will be more victims. Remember, Jews, that "protect your lives" is a great rule in the Torah.

The High Holy days are approaching, the Jewish soul must be clean, and it is good to have a healthy soul in a healthy body.

During the holidays the Batei-Midrash will surely be full of people coming to pray, may the evil eye have no power, and this might also be a cause for the diseases to spread. There must be more "minyans" to avoid crowdedness.

　　　　　　　　　　　　　　　　　　　　　　　　　　　　　　　　　　　　　Zvi L-L

With feelings of love and affection, I bless my friend b"d the venerable author Mr. Haim Czaczkes Halevi and his dear forefathers, on the occasion of his marriage to Ms. Idel Kahn from Podwoloczyska.

[The Jewish Awakaner]
edited and printed in Buczacz in 1906

Hapanas [The Torch] was a Hebrew supplement to the
newspaper, Der Wecker, issue 63, on 22 Iyar, 5667

Buczacz, Tishrei 5667 (1907)   **Issue 45**

The Jewish World

Our village (or, as the Jews of Buczacz proudly refer to it when traveling, "city") has been blessed with a *yeshiva*. And when I say *yeshiva*, you must not think that an actual *yeshiva* has really been established and that students are already studying Torah there – this is not the case! There is no need to always accept everything as it is written, sometimes one is permitted to use cunning language, and the *yeshiva* mentioned here is no more than various discussions about establishing a *yeshiva*. The idea is to establish a *yeshiva* here like the ones that exist in all the Jewish diaspora in Galicia, Stanislaw, Borodshin. The teachers are in an uproar, claiming that their livelihood is about to be lost because their students will be taken away and given to the "yeshiva," where the tuition will be half-free, and the Jews of Buczacz are most eager to buy things cheaply. The same commotions that were raised against opening the "Tripa Psol" school, are now being waged against the *yeshiva*, which has not yet been created. Its existence is evident only in various posters and announcements, "calls to action" in the matter of the "yeshiva," thought up by a few *avrechim* who eat at the tables of their fathers-in-law and who play at "wolf and goats" on the tables of the Mishnah.

(an anonymous young man)

*

Buczacz, 7 Marheshvan, 5667 (1907)   **Issue 47**

Buczacz. Hashem has finally taken mercy on our dark village and sent down two great luminaries. The "small luminary" is the one from Washington and the "big luminary" is, to differentiate, the *yeshiva*. From now on the Jews of Buczacz shall have plenty of light. For this world and for the next world.

The person in charge of the small luminary from Washington is a great "goy" and the person in charge of the big luminary is a small Jew, with all due respect.

In order that the Jews may have a place to pray, because there is a shortage of synagogues in the town, small and tiny synagogues, Batei-Midrash, small Batei-Midrash and various kloises of all types, they have established the Kapatchintzi klois.

*

Buczacz, 28 Marheshvan, 5667 (1907)   **Issue 50**

Announcements
Benjamin Baran, Buczacz

Lending for very cheap prices the finest books in the jargon, by famous authors such as Mendele Mokher Sefarim, Peretz, Sholem Aleichem, Spektor, Dinezon, Reisen and Shalom Asch.

Booklet 4 Has Already Been Published
HaYarden, a Magazine

Devoted to Literature, Science and Affairs of Life
By Dr. Elazar Rokeach

Content of Booklet 4

A) Henryk Ibsen by Mordechai Kemper. B) Tears, a poem, S.Y. Czaczkes. C) Avrech – a drawing, Avraham Lebensrat. D) Albert Messin and the Symbolists, Azriel. E) Poem, Noah Sabin. F) "A quick look," Zvi Srapstein. G) The Pogrom in K., Noah Sabin. H) Will you Understand me, S. Kemach. I) Poem, S.Y. Czaczkes. J) Velvil Seberzier, Meir Ben Mordechai Weissberg. K) Contemplations, Azriel. L) In memory of the painter Adolf Mendel, Noah Sabin. M) Persimmon, Azriel. N) *Shneihem Hishalchu*, S. Halatnikow. O) Complaints, Mazal Tov. P) Holdover of Wages, Ben Zion Fredkin. Q) Bibliography.

Booklet price is 50 heller   For yearly subscribers 6 – A.
                                        For six months 3 – A.

First Year Booklet 4
5666 (1906) Menachem Av

HaYarden
Literary and Scientific Magazine

Editor: Elazar Rokeach
W. Dratler Printing House in Buczacz

Typeset with brand new machinery, letters for *lashon kodesh*, Yiddish, German, Polish, Ruthenian, offers his services for printing essays and books in Yiddish, Hebrew, German and Polish – all for reasonable prices.

*

Buczacz, 16 Adar, 5667 (1907)   **Issue 61**

From the Jewish World

Last Monday, the religious studies teacher of our community, Rabbi Gaon Yehiel Michal Brimer, died at the age of eighty-four. He was the son of the Rabbi Gaon Moshe Brimer, senior president of the Rabbinical court from the community of Bodzanow, author of *Sefer Zichron Moshe*. The late R' Yehiel Michal served as a rabbi for sixty years. Previously, he was a rabbi in Melnica for forty years, then he came to our town and became the religious studies teacher for over twenty years. He was a great scholar, sharp and proficient, as he proved in his proofreading of his father's book, *Zichron Moshe*.

He was always a well-liked and peace-loving man. He was eulogized by the Rabbi of Monasterzyska, the Rabbi Gaon H. Lipa Meisles, and by two of our town judges, Rabbi Yosef Preminger and Rabbi Feibel Wilig. May his soul be bound in the bond of everlasting life.

The Election Movement

Buczacz. The election movement began its activities last week. The *Rada Narodowa* [National Council] appointed a committee of twenty members two weeks ago. Dr. Kzizanowski was chosen as chairman, and his deputy is Dr. Auschnit. Eleven Jews joined this committee as members, including five Zionists.

The unaffiliated citizens, on their part, held a voters' rally last Sunday and elected a special committee made up of thirty-five members. And indeed: ten Poles, ten Ruthenians and fifteen Jews, including five Zionists, seven Socialists and three independents, and they are about to approve another five Zionists. One Ruthenian priest is among the thirty-five. Dr. Peller was chosen as committee chairman, his deputies are Dr. Maglanizki and Mr. Yonas Neiman. Dr. Nacht was chosen as treasurer. It is still unclear who the first committee will nominate as candidate. It is said that the mayor, A. Bernhard Stern, is favored for the position, however he has not yet officially announced his candidacy. There are other rumors, namely, that Gniewosz, our neighbor from Potok Zloty, desires to honor us with his representation. However, we do not know how much truth there is to this rumor. The *Rada Narodowa* intends to offer as our candidate Stefan Maisa. Let us hope that our Jewish voters will manage to run a Jewish candidate in this voting district, and fight for his success.

The second committee wishes to establish contact with Dr. Birenbaum (another Matityahu) and offer him the candidacy. The Socialists have declared that they are willing to elect him, although the Socialist Party directorate favors Dr. Yarosawitz, who served previously as a delegate from the Borszczow district.

*

Buczacz, 22 Adar, 5667 (1907)   **Issue 62**

From the Election Movement

Buczacz. The committee of unaffiliated citizens sent a telegram to Dr. Birenbaum to offer him the candidacy. Dr. Birenbaum replied that he will come to Buczacz in the middle of March.

The Zionists in town have been placed in an odd position due to various causes. Some of them, who are members of the unaffiliated committee, are obliged to join forces with Dr. Birenbaum, because they negotiated with him previously.

In the meantime, the Zionists-Day determined last Sunday to present the candidacy of Rabbi Gedalia Schmelkes from Przemysl in Buczacz. Things will likely be settled and both candidates, who are not simply status-seekers who seek prestige at any price, will reach a compromise. But one thing causes us pain, which is that we have remained in *Rada Narodowa* as a herd with no shepherd. Ever since Lewenstein was insulted in such an offensive manner that he was forced to leave the *Rada Narodowa*, we are truly left as a ship in the midst of the ocean.

It is interesting to see how our Polish brothers, the *Rada Narodowa* members, refer to their Jewish brothers: Poles who have stood on Mount Sinai. Prince Statariski calls them simple Jews, whereas Mr. Abrahamowitz calls them by the name "Members of the Old Pact." Who knows what name Staialowski would have given them if he were also involved.

*

Buczacz, 12 Iyar, 5667 (1907)   **Issue 63**

Buczacz. The Jewish National party candidate, Dr. Birenbaum, came to Buczacz last Friday, and received a respectful and enthusiastic welcome from the Jewish population. On Shabbat afternoon he spoke before a crowd of voters and presented his platform, which made a great impression on his supporters. The resolutions he proposed were met with great admiration and his candidacy was unequivocally approved.

It is hard to predict whether he will be elected. The most difficult business is prophesizing. After all, it is not known at all which methods the opposing camps will employ against him. There are many emissaries there…

The District commissioner invited our community leaders to meet with him and told them that he would like the well-known Marshall of Snyatin, Stefan Maisa, to be elected and that our mayor, Mr. B. Stern, should give up his candidacy. This means that our mayor is no longer an option.

The end of our mayor's candidacy is extremely tragic! Tragic in every respect. Gloomy from every direction. A disappointment from all sides. If he had given some of his power to the circles closest to him…he would be worthy of congratulations. We do not deal with politics, to the right nor to the left, but our heart aches to see such power, such intelligence, go to waste – with no results. This is even more true when we notice how many people in his opposing camps should have been grateful to him, should rightly have given him many thanks.

Man is ungrateful, that is an old refrain, however "He who is subjected to this, his heart shall break in two."

*

Buczacz, 26 Iyar 5667 (1907)   Issue 65

Buczacz

Dr. Birenbaum's supporters are diligently organizing propaganda for him. Mr. Leibel Teubisch also gave a propaganda speech for Dr. Birenbaum. The Ruthenians have their own candidate, Dr. Yarisawitz from Vienna, who is also a socialist, and therefore the socialists support him too. They are also developing vibrant propaganda.

The government candidate, Mr. Stefan Maisa, gave his election speech on Tuesday the 7th, to an audience of invitees in the *Rada Paviatowa* hall and presented them with his platform.

[Page 109]

Professor David Zvi (Heinrich) Mueller
By G. Kresl
Translated by Betsy Halpern-Amaru

1.

For years after the death of Mueller, legends and stories about the "illui from Buczacz" (born June 7, 1856) circulated in my surroundings, which was also the locale of Mueller in the days of his youth. Lacking central figures after World War I, Jewish Kolomyya loved to cling to well known, world famous personalities of the Jewish past of which Kolomyya, in the course of its history, had been an honorable part of. Consequently, during my childhood I heard endless stories about the Rav of Kolomyya, Rabbi Hillel Lash (Lichtenstein), a Hungarian whose influence on the Jewish world extended from Kolomyya to Jerusalem and Petah Tikvah. (His son-in-law, Rabbi Akiba Yosef Schlessinger was one of the first settlers of Petah Tikvah). Similarly, it included Mueller, the "illui from Buczacz" who had been "acquired" as a son-in-law by a wealthy man in Kolomyya and from there, made his way to Tcherniketz and subsequently to Vienna where he became one of the greatest scholars of oriental studies.

Mueller left behind a survivor in Kolomyya, indeed one who remained there up to the last years of the Jewish community. She was his first wife whom he had been forced to divorce for reasons of his heresy and, who, in the course of time became a grocer in the city. Since Solomon Bikel provides an excellent description of this tragic drama in his biography of Mueller, which touches on Kolomyya,

(Title in Yiddish, chapter 2), there is no need to say more about it. Nonetheless, I cannot forget what the Zionist teacher and rabbi in the same area, Zelig Gross, z"l, once told me: Consider! – Rabbi Hillel Lichtenstein and Mueller both happened to be together in Kolomyya – there are no greater extremes than these two, one, among the religious fanatics of the nineteenth century, and the other, a young "illui" who became a heretic. Each of them had a part in the establishment of the new yishuv in Eretz Yisrael: one in Petah Tikvah, the other, through his students and the students of his students who went to Eretz Yisrael and participated in the formation of the spiritual nature of the Yishuv.

I was young and did not grasp the full meaning of the words. Only after many years did the depth of his words become clear to me. By then I could no longer engage in conversation with this distinguished man, for the Shoah had put an end also to his life.

2.

As rich as Mueller's biography is in drama, in details it is poor. It is barely possible to sketch the events of the early years of his life clearly. A brilliant well read, young man, whom the wealthy considered an ideal match for their daughters. He was "purchased" by one of them, understandably, on the condition that he would continue with his traditional Torah studies. However, it quickly became clear that the very essence of the "purchase" entailed a "bad bargain". As one might assume, an illui such as he could not restrict himself for long within the walls of the traditional House of Study (Beit Midrash). This was the era of the flowering of the Enlightenment, when the greatest of Hebrew authors and poets were at the height of their fame: Smolenskin, Y. L. Gordon, and Lilienblum. It goes without saying that the closest to Kolomayya was Smolenskin and therefore the "Shachar" in Vienna. There were no few travelers going from one place to the other, who, in the course of traveling, would bring with them copies of the "Shachar" which, like no comparable journal, inflamed the hearts and souls of such young men.

Mueller was not able to hide his attachment to Haskalah for an extensive time and the end was not long in coming. He divorced his wife and rich in-laws, and turned, understandably, to the "big world" whose center was in the heart of Galicia, that is, the capital city, Vienna. Although the move was only from Kolomyya to Vienna, it involved a huge leap for a young man as deprived as Mueller. He made his to the nearest station en route to Vienna, i.e., Chernovtsy. This capital of Bukovina had drawn many of the Galician maskilim in the previous century and had become an intellectual center in a number of academic areas. Living there in those years was the Hebrew poet and maskil from Zolochev, Israel Halevi Teller, as well as Mueller's uncle who had a son with longings similar to those of Mueller. The three – the two cousins and the Hebrew maskil – did not yet know the destiny that lay ahead of them. At least two of them would wander to Eretz Yisrael and fill important positions there: Teller as a teacher and educator in Rehovot who would raise a young generation of teachers and community workers in Eretz Yisrael; and Dr. Schwartz, coming to Israel by way of Kushta, would become not only one of its most important physicians, but also one of the Jewish community workers in the old Hebrew yishuv (the recent new one had not yet come into being), to whom a memorial stands in the royal court in Kushta. All initiatives passed through him and even the purchase of the land for Petah Tikvah was not accomplished without him. A quick look at the Jerusalem newspapers of the time, at the essays and histories of the Hibbat Ziyon movement by A. Droynov makes the great extent of Schwartz's role in the growth of the yishuv quite evident.

In the meanwhile Mueller and Schwartz studied everything that was required for entry into the "tent of real learning" – the university. Actually, Mueller did not need to do much in order to reach this hoped for goal. About this youngster from Buczacz, Teller states "he did not come empty-handed to Chernovtsy: an outstanding scholar of Mishnah (Shas), expert in Tanakh, grammar, and Hebrew language; and when hiding in the attic of his father's house, he had also had learned German, Polish, French, English, Russian and Greek..." (*On the Early Days*, vol. 2, p. 166). Like others who had moved from the Beit Midrash to secular studies, he saw Braslav, the site the rabbinical school of Frankel-Graetz, as a lighthouse that mated these two worlds that still wrestle each other with open enmity in the cities and towns of Eretz Yisrael. However, he remained in Braslav only for a short time. It became clear that the real heights of Braslav were not the imagined ones that floated before the eyes of the young men of Israel in the towns of Russia and Galicia. He was not attracted by rabbinics the way he was drawn by Torah in the modern sense of scientific study. He went on to the universities of Vienna, Strasbourg, and Leipsa, where he immersed himself in study of the languages of the orient and the oriental world.

These were the days of the flowering of oriental studies in Europe and the West. The masters of this subject were disseminating their knowledge in the learning centers that Mueller now attended. Foremost among them were Nildaka and Felisher ; and the former even included the Bible and related languages within the perimeters of his work. Mueller was an attentive student to his teachers and he even pursued areas of study that up until that time had remained closed to others, specifically, the area of the languages of south Arabia. At this point in time, it was not an acknowledged field of study, but rather, concealed and hidden in the Arab desert and its wildernesses, it was one no western scholar had yet explored. The "illui from Buczacz" was now joining a small select group of researchers who were primarily seeking to bring languages hidden and buried on monuments and inscriptions in the wide area of south Arabia out of oblivion. Adventuresome and courageous travelers, among them the well-known Eduard Glazer, risked their lives to recover and bring back to Europe great amounts of epigraphy that was until then unseen by human eyes. Such travelers and researchers now needed experts in oriental languages who were gifted with a degree of mental acuity that was not found in the world that had brought such inscriptions to light. Mueller now became one of the greatest, important authorities on deciphering the enigmas of south Arabian inscriptions. In a short period of time, he acquired a world reputation as a specialist in this area with a wealth of essays, research studies, and articles. Such material involved only the very specialized. Moreover, within that narrow circle, he was so outstanding that the University of Vienna was no longer able to hide itself from his great scholarly achievements. The University of Vienna promoted him and granted him a prestigious academic title that even the liberal Vienna of Franz Joseph did not lavish upon Jews – the title of Full Professor. Moreover, this was achieved without any of the corruption or flattery of the source of the title such as was common even among the great and good scholars of those days.

Indeed, such a promotion would not even be taken for granted today; in those days, seventy to eighty years ago, it was so rare as to be almost non-existent. The recognized fact that he came to such a high position without denying his Jewishness was acknowledged in his own day. Thus, it was written about him in those days: "The well known scholar, Dr. David Mueller of Vienna, who taught until now as an untenured instructor in the University, within the division of ancient thought and Semitic languages, has been promoted to the level of Full Professor. It is known that this scholar is one of a very select few. Yet with all his knowledge and the high estimation with which he is held in the scholarly world, he has not turned away from his people and his Torah and he is one of the distinguished authors.." ("HaZiphirah," 1885, p. 34).

3.

Although Mueller was now absorbed in the world of the orient, the admiration and love he felt for Peretz Smolenskin from the days of Buczacz and Kolomyya still burned in his heart. When he arrived in Vienna he admitted to Smolenskin as well as to others that he was not disappointed in the hero he had imagined. To the contrary, he attached himself with much affection to Smolenskin. Through his days of wandering within the universities of the west he had realized his dream of secular study. Moreover, the other dream of the young Hebrew intellectual (maskil) was also now realized through his association with Smolenskin. The "Shachar," the warm hospice of the best of Hebrew writers and intellectuals in the 1860's and 70's, now became the Hebrew hospice of Mueller. Here he revealed not only the breadth and depth of his knowledge in all areas of talmudic literature, but also his sharp critical sense, and not least, the beautiful, superior style of his Hebrew.

Without a doubt, the most preeminent of the research articles that Mueller wrote for the "Shachar" is a comprehensive, sharp critique of Solomon Buber's edition of Pesikta (vol. 2, 1871, p. 385-95 reprinted in his German book, German Title, Vienna 1907, pp. 132-141). It was uncommonly audacious for one to take position against a scholar as recognized as Rabbi Solomon Buber, to point out errors in his edition, and particularly, to critique his grasp of the intertextual references within the midrashim of this work. Moreover, the major thrust of the essay was an attack against Buber's concealment of the source for much of his work, specifically, the work of Y. L. Zunz in his book of interpretations. With heartfelt words, Mueller protected the name and honor of the great work of Zunz against those who took from it generously without any acknowledgment. Delving into the deep water of talmudic and midrashic literature in this essay, Mueller appears to have revived his Beit Midrash days in Kolmyya and Buczacz. Indeed, in a reference to the critique, one as well known as R. Isaac Hirsh Weiss commented that it was correct and to the point ("Dor, Dor v'Dorshov" Part 3, vol. 4 p. 246, n. 9).

Although Mueller's Hebrew writings extend over decades, they are fewer than those he wrote in the vernacular. (Nonetheless, the number is greater than that attributed to him by G. Rosenmann in his article on Mueller in (Yiddish Title), vol 17, translated in Hebrew in Sefer Hazicharon of the Vienna Rabbinical Seminary, Jerusalem 5706, p. 26). When Smolenskin died and his family was destitute, it was Mueller who recruited a group of those well known in the Jewish world to help the family of the writer. Certainly Mueller sustained his hidden love for Hebrew literature, for its writers, and not the least, for the Hebrew language. That he himself did not acquire an eminent place in the scholarship on Hebrew language was due to the subject of his research and the nature of Jewish studies during that era. Since oriental studies was viewed as a branch of general science,, within the scope of subjects that comprised "Jewish studies" Mueller's reputation was almost unacknowledged. The situation did not change when Mueller began devoting himself to research on the Bible. Critical study of the Bible was unusual in Jewish scholarship whereas it was a most respected branch of general scientific, i.e., Christian, scholarship.

Certainly, within the oriental world there was ample room for the Jewish world. Generations of Jews lived in Arab speaking lands, including south Arabia. Mueller particularly tracked the Jewish perspective – hence his concern with the several versions of Eldad the Danite and his research on the various customs intertwined within the stories of Eldad. This was but a small particular in a huge field; it is not surprising that he was "swallowed up" there and his work did not become known except to a few experts here and there. By now he had in a sense become custodian of research on south Arabia, be it in dealing with the finances of scientific explorations or in processing the results of these scientific explorations. Glazer's travels were made possible because of Mueller's connections with powerful circles (this time in France!); and in this capacity Mueller is to be credited for the first monumental book about the Negev, southern Israel, and Transjordan written by the well-known Czech scientist, Eloise Mussel (*The Rock of Arabia*, 4 vols.) Until recently this book was known only to a very few expert scholars. Now, since we have entered the area around Elat, it has become an enlightening work that solves a number of problems that were previously troublesome. Certainly, work in this area was generally associated Mueller's research on south Arabia. But, without a doubt, what was functioning here, knowingly or unknowingly, was the pull of the same love of Hebrew – the love for the land of Israel.

Mueller's Hebrew writings are few. But Hebrew readers seek them out, view him as one of their own, and even take pride in his accomplishments and conquests in the field of oriental studies. From time to time brief articles about him, describing his steady rise in scholarly circles with warm praise, appear in Hebrew newspapers. These Hebrew readers are far from Mueller's field of interest; but he exists and certain scholars bother to publicly inform the Hebrew readers about him. One such scholar, for example, is Mueller's friend, the renown scholar, David Kaufman of "Hashachar" (9). Similarly, later on he wrote in a more popular form an article about Mueller's book on the prophets in Yiddish Title.

Not long after this, Mueller, distant from his brethren and his readers who heard from and about him only second or third hand, would enter the "service" that would involve an honored position within the life of our community during the last two generations, specifically, the "service" of teacher in the rabbinical seminary in Vienna.

4.

The belated opening of the rabbinical seminary to the hundreds of young men from the cities of and towns of Galicia who flowed to the schools either of Braslav or Berlin is a puzzling fact that has not yet been properly explained. However, when the deficiency was repaired and a seminary was established in Vienna (in October 1893), it was filled with young men from Brody, Bazaschan, Drogobych, Levov, Zholkava, Borislav, Pashmishal, Zabrze, Kolomyya, Buczacz, – and I count here only those participating in the first year of studies. There was no town in Galicia that did not send its young men there. Of course, students from other regions of Austria-Hungary also came, but they were always fewer in number and it was common knowledge that the Galicians came with the Talmud in their hands.

Mueller was called to serve in this seminary as an instructor for Hebrew language, grammar, Tanakh, and in addition, the other subjects involved in the oriental studies that he had taught in the University of Vienna. Here, and only here, did he from the outset find students from his own native land and background. Therefore it is no wonder that from the start of his teaching appointment, the other seminaries began to lose their Galician students. The atmosphere in this seminary was not an easy one, for one third of the teachers were from a totally different environment and their academic approach was strange and foreign to students of the Galician schools. Nonetheless, the students quickly became acclimated. Particularly influential was the personal magic of the eminent teachers of Hungary and Slovakia – the Rector, A. Schwartz, Abraham Bichler, and Rabbi Meir Ish-Shalom.

Certainly the other seminaries produced rabbis personally and professionally of excellent quality. However, an examination of the roster of students permits one to say, without exaggeration, that no other seminary turned so many minds and hearts toward the Zionist movement, the Land of Israel, and Hebrew education. Subsequently, Bichler left for London and Rabbi M. Ish-Shalom died. Avigdor Aptowitzer and S. Kreuss replaced them. With the arrival of these new powerful teachers, a kind of balance was achieved between the teachers – two from Galicia and two from Hungary. Just recently in his recollections of Mueller (*Batzron*, vol. 19, pp. 7-9) Rabbi S. Kreus increased the tension between the teachers from Galicia on the one hand and those from Hungary on the other. The source of this tension is readily clear. Aptowitzer, a faithful student and disciple of Mueller who assisted with the first of the scholarly publications about Mueller (see *Maznayim*, vol. 16, p. 122) provides a clear example of how easily one learned, indeed, with enjoyment as opposed to the exhausting method of Kreuss which bursts through every line of his scholarly publications. As is known, Aptowitzer introduced the study of Hebrew as a language to the seminary, an innovation that was unheard of in any other rabbinical seminary of that time. The extent to which Mueller's approach to Hebrew and an Hebraic atmosphere extending from Tanakh to modern Hebrew literature was influential is readily apparent. This had in fact been the love of his youth. However, estrangement from and natural warfare against such a youthful love was common in those days, indeed not only in those.

The Galician students were faithful to their teacher from Buczacz; and as we will soon see, the influence between these students and their teacher was reciprocal, be it in Torah, in scholarship, or in life.

Certainly, it is not necessary to state that Mueller's approach to Bible, the subject in which he immersed himself as teacher at the seminary, was not the approach of Christian Bible scholars and researchers. It was a trick of fate that this scholar, in whom Hebrew, particularly biblical Hebrew, was a living language, was viewed by Christian scholars as a flower breaking into a territory that did not belong to him. However, even before the seminar had begun, Mueller was known as one of the most important researchers on Gaznius's medieval biblical dictionary. This dictionary had gone from the possession of the learned Christian Radiger (Gaznius's son-in-law) to a modern adaptation by Parnatas Buhal. Mueller's participation on the project, however, had essentially been in the area of oriental languages. Specifically in that realm non-Jews were ready to grant him wide breadth in which to distinguish himself. When it came to the Bible itself, he was so ill received that he subsequently had to write a special essay in defense of himself.

This issue requires us to advance to the subject of Mueller's biblical research. In that area he is credited with a great discovery in the area of biblical rhythm. Certainly Mueller's readings of Bible were more natural than those of non-Jewish scholars for whom language difficulties obscured broader general content. It became clear to Mueller that he had found a principle in the construction of prophetic verses, that from the perspective of beauty and ring was not like the rhythm of general literature which is based on long and short syllables. It became clear to him that the principle of this rhythm operated not only in the words of the prophets, but also in ancient Greek literature, in hieroglyphics, and even in Ben Sira. He worked and reworked this principle until he had established a wealth of evidence from all areas of ancient world literature and published it in two volumes entitled Yiddish Title (Vienna, 1895; Mueller's student, Michael Berkovitch who was Herzl's assistant and his first Hebrew translator, produced an excellent abstract of the work in a series of articles called, "Siphre Haneviim B'zurotam Hareshona" (The Initial Form of the Prophetic Books") that was published in "Zephira" 1896, Folio 70, 71, 75, 88, 100).

Innovation or not, there can be no doubt that only a Hebrew speaker, favored with an ear for the particular hidden and concealed emotions of our language, would have able to develop this principle in the manner in which Mueller had done.

5.

Exactly two hundred years ago, in 1753, R. Lowth's book on biblical poetry was published. Even today there are few analyses of biblical literature comparable to this book which awakened interest and drew attention to a recognized phenomenon in Bible that Lowth called "Parallelism." The essence of parallelism involves not only similar ideas expressed with different words, but also includes contrasting conceptual parallels even though that parallelism and meter contrast with the previous concept. Mueller continued to develop this principle of parallelism and found that no small number of the words of the prophet contained a conceptual meter not only in terms of the division between stanzas, i.e., in the depth and short breadth of the stanza, but also in the interrelationship between stanzas. When one sets forth multiple chapters of the Prophets in two parallel rows, the great extent and breadth of the parallelism becomes clear. The first stanza of one column and the "response" of the other is the primary, fundamental structure of the biblical rhythm. There is no better example of this than the following one taken from the first chapter of Amos.

3	6
Thus said the Lord	Thus said the Lord
For three transgressions of Damascus	For three transgressions of Gaza
For four, I will not revoke it.	For four, I will not revoke it.
Because with threshing boards of iron they threshed Gilead.	Because they exiled an entire population Which they delivered to Edom.

4	7
I will send down fire upon the palace of Hazael,	I will send down fire upon the wall of Gaza,
And it shall devour the fortresses A	And it shall devour its fortresses

5	8
I will break the gate bars of Damascus	I will wipe out the inhabitants of Ashdod
And wipe out the inhabitants from the Vale of Aven.	And the sceptered ruler of Ashkelon

And the sceptered ruler of Beth-eden
And the people of Aram shall exiled to Kir
Said the Lord.

And I will turn My hand against Ekron
And the Philistines shall perish to the last man
Said the Lord.

9
Thus said the Lord
For three transgressions of Tyre
For four, I will not revoke it;
Because they handed over an
entire population to Edom
Ignoring the covenant of brotherhood.

11
Thus said the Lord
For three transgressions of Edom
For four, I will not revoke it;
Because he pursued his brother
with the sword and repressed all pity
Because his anger raged unceasing
And his fury stormed unchecked.

10
I will send down fire upon the wall of Tyre
And it shall devour its fortresses.

12
I will send down fire upon Teman,
And it shall devour its fortresses.

It is possible to continue with verses 13-15 paralleling verses 1-3 in chapter 2.

Multiple examples are brought by Mueller in his book, German Title (Vienna, 1898), and two supplements, German Title (Vienna, 1907). All of them demonstrate the inner rhythm that rings for any ear in the chapters of the Prophets. Consequently, there is no need to disrupt verses in the manner that gentile scholars of biblical meter, especially the most famous of them, Severus, had done. Mueller was sharply critical of the "discoveries" of the gentile scholars who found long and short syllables – not only in poetry, but also in prose – and even more that they invented and related verses and emendations of verses to what they had "discovered" in a way that would have repulsed a beginning student of Hebrew. Mueller fostered students who continued in the same direction. Especially noteworthy were Michael Berkovitz and P. Perles who demonstrated that the principle was widespread in areas that even Mueller had not paid attention to.

Mueller's books were not able to awaken the interest – either in a positive or negative sense – of Christian biblical scholars. It goes without saying that the Jewish scholars were all on his side and David Kaufman even published great praise of Mueller's discovery in Yiddish Title (subsequently included in his collected writings, vol. 1 Frankfurt, 1908, pp. 379-393). Such was not the case with gentile scholars who viewed biblical research as their personal domain. There were those who reacted with sharp words, scorn, an abundance of suspicions of the lowest sort (Rudolf Samand particularly excelled at this). Mueller suffered greatly from the negative treatment of the gentile scholars, particularly those whom he respected. In his third and last book devoted to this subject (the title of which is mentioned above), he responds to the most positive and negative of their reactions, and also delineates the history of his discovery and its influence on the literary scholarship of ancient literature.

There is much humble bitterness in this composition; needless to say, he did not restrain from responding to his opponents as they deserved. He showed the gentile scholars who had scorned him and his teachings to what extent they were not equipped to grasp the spirit of the Bible and ancient Hebrew poetry, and the degree to which these were coordinated with the complementary effort of collecting what had been said by the early (*Rishonim*) and later (*Aharonim*) commentaries and thereby the full extent of biblical interpretation which is indeed enormous. He returned again to analysis of the substantive charges of his critics and, with additional examples, proved, against claims and assertions of all sorts, the efficacy of his methodology and the principle he had discovered. Mueller was absorbed in this task for ten years. After that the storm abated and the power of the discovery was lost and forgotten: except for a very few, all the general books on Bible that include multiple details that are insignificant in the history of biblical research barely mention Mueller and his great contribution in uncovering the inner principles that function in ancient Hebrew prophecy.

6.

A man such as Mueller was not able to stagnate and be satisfied with his unmatched achievements in oriental studies. To the contrary, as he grew older he continued to acquire knowledge and even entered into the newest area in oriental studies – hieroglyphics. In those days it was still a young science that had not yet established firm, solid foundations. Mueller, who had used ancient Babylonian literature as a basis for the method he used with biblical meter, found yet another way to relate the Bible to this ancient literature that had been newly revealed after thousands of years. He published a scholarly edition of Hammurabi's Code and even added a Hebrew translation relating it to the Bible (Vienna, 1903; a large portion of it is included in B. Z. Dinberg's *Yisrael B'Artzo* [Israel in Its Land], Vol. 1, Book 1 Tel Aviv, 1934, pp. 78-87).

The era in which Mueller's book on Hammurabi's Code appeared was the era of the polemic over "Bavel and Bibel" that had been aroused by the anti-Semite, Franz Delitash. Many Jewish scholars then opposed Delitash and contradicted his claim that the biblical narratives lacked originality and were dependent on Assyrian and Babylonian literature. The only one of the Jewish scholars who was fully qualified to respond to Delitash's slander was Mueller. However, Mueller was not a polemical person. Still, there was no more proven weapon against this hostile scholar than Mueller's book with its multiple facts. Specifically, in publishing the full text that made Hammurabi's Code understandable, it demonstrated the great cultural differences between the biblical world and Mesopotamian literature. Everyone could now be convinced of the ethical and cultural height of biblical literature and of the great distance between it and the world that Delitash praised and glorified to the German Kaiser and the German community that suddenly had become so enthusiastic about the loftiness of Mesopotamia.

This was a great service on the part of Mueller even though it was never basically intended for such. In the haven of his university and seminary teaching he never ceased work on texts, innovations, and activities to promote research and scientific trips to oriental lands. He devoted his last years to the scientific legacy of Edward Glaser as well as expending much energy on Mussel's travels and book, *The Rock of Arabia*. Mussel's expression of gratitude for Mueller's very real assistance which appears at the beginning of all four volumes of his wonderful book suggests that Mueller was especially interested in the results of research and travels among the Bedouins of the Negev and Transjordan, their languages and stories, and, not least, in the landscape of Israel. Together with this he assisted Reuben Brainin who sought to develop a forum in Vienna that would unite east and west in the context of a common Hebrew background. In "East and West" Mueller published a little linguistic article that demonstrated the extent to which he was situated in the Hebrew world and how close its affairs were to him. Who would have guessed that the symbol of our market, "the flying camel," was also due to Mueller's Hebrew research which fully explained and demonstrated the relationship between this symbol and similar ones in the oriental world.

With a good reputation, Mueller died at the age of sixty-six in Vienna on the twenty-first of December 1912. He left behind multiple books and research articles that have made him long remembered. He also left behind hundreds of students who have spread out over the Jewish world and continued his tradition, the tradition of scientific learning, and lastly, his great affection and love for the Land of Israel and our Hebrew language.

[Page 118]

A Letter from Professor Mueller
By David Zvi Mueller
Translated by Jessica Cohen

Vienna, April 12, 1893

To my dear honorable uncle, the eminent and great scholar *ksh"t* [honor the glory of his name] *mohr"r* [our teacher and master, rabbi] Yehuda Farb *n"y* [may his light shine], greetings!

First of all, I thank you profusely for your honor's letter, which gave me much happiness. May God lengthen your years and protect you from trouble and may your old-age be blessed and good.

Today I received a letter from my brother *n"y* from Stryy, and enclosed in it was a letter from my dear mother [may she live], in which she writes that a bad rumor has reached the town of Buczacz and that slanderers have slandered me and have spoken ill of me, and that she would rather die than endure this. And I, in my innocence, do not know the meaning of this and I do not know what sin I have committed, I have not stolen horses nor written false bills nor spoken evil of D' and his teachings. Quite the opposite, I am the strong pillar on which the house of Yehuda leans and all members of the Vienna community respect me, and through my doing the name of D' is sanctified. I have also been chosen to serve as a teacher at the study house for rabbis which has been founded and which I helped to found and to glorify Torah. Who is this man who has the impudence to say evil things of me which hurt my dear mother's heart and your heart, my dear uncle? They are slanderous liars who wish only to violate my honor out of malice.

I request that his honor my uncle write to tell me the root of the incident, tell me who laid the venomous seed and I shall prove his falsehood to his face. And I shall present trustworthy witnesses such as the honorable Rabbi *avda"k* [presiding judge of religious court] of Vienna, Dr. Gidemanen or the rabbi of the Karlsroh community[1] who will be a teacher, like myself, in the study house for rabbies, and others like them.

And I do love and respect your greatness.

David Zvi Mueller

End notes
1. Reb Pohorila was a banker and a writer. He wrote Khomat anakh on the Torah and Shearit yehuda on the Talmud.

Professor Mueller's father

Professor
David Tsvi (Heinrich) Mueller

[Page 119]

Sigmund Freud's Family Tree
Translated by Alejandro Landman and Norbert Porile

Sigmund Freud's parents were born and lived in Buchach. His father, Jacob Freud, was born in 1835. He married at age 19 but his wife died prematurely. At age 42 he got married a second time, to Amalia Nathanson. They had 2 sons and 5 daughters, one of whom was Sigmund.

According to the accompanying family tree, the surname Freud is derived from Freide. This was the name of an important woman and the family adopted her name.

In 1812 an Austrian government official arrived in Buchach in order to fulfill a law requiring that all inhabitants have official surnames. Thus was born the surname Freud.

The accompanying family tree was prepared in 1914 on the basis of the gravestone inscriptions in the Buchach cemetery and other documents. Its preparation took several years and the genealogy was approved by the Freud family.

Translator's (NP) note. The above account contains numerous errors:

  1. Sigmund Freud's parents were not born in Buchach and there is no evidence that they lived there. His father was born in Tysmenitz and his mother in Brody, towns in eastern Galicia Freud's grandfather, Schlomo Freud, was born in Buchach but moved to Tysmenitz as a young man. Schlomo's ancestors, going back at least 4 generations, lived in Buchach.
  2. Jacob Freud was born on December 18, 1815.
  3. Jacob Freud married Sally Kanner in 1832. Thus he was 16 or 17 years old at the time of his first marriage. Sally died in 1852.
  4. Jacob Freud married Amalia Nathanson on July 29, 1855. He was thus 39 years old at the time. There is unconfirmed evidence that Amalia was actually Jacob's 3rd wife. He may have briefly been married to a woman with the first name of Rebekka between 1852 and his marriage to Amalia.

    Sigmund Freud was actually the oldest of Jacob and Amalia's children. He was born May 6, 1856.

    Freide was the name of Schlomo Freud's great-grandmother, a resident of Buchach.

The above information comes from "Freud and his father" by Marianne Krull; translated by Arnold Pomerans. W. W. Norton, New York, 1986. It is confirmed in additional biographical accounts of Freud.

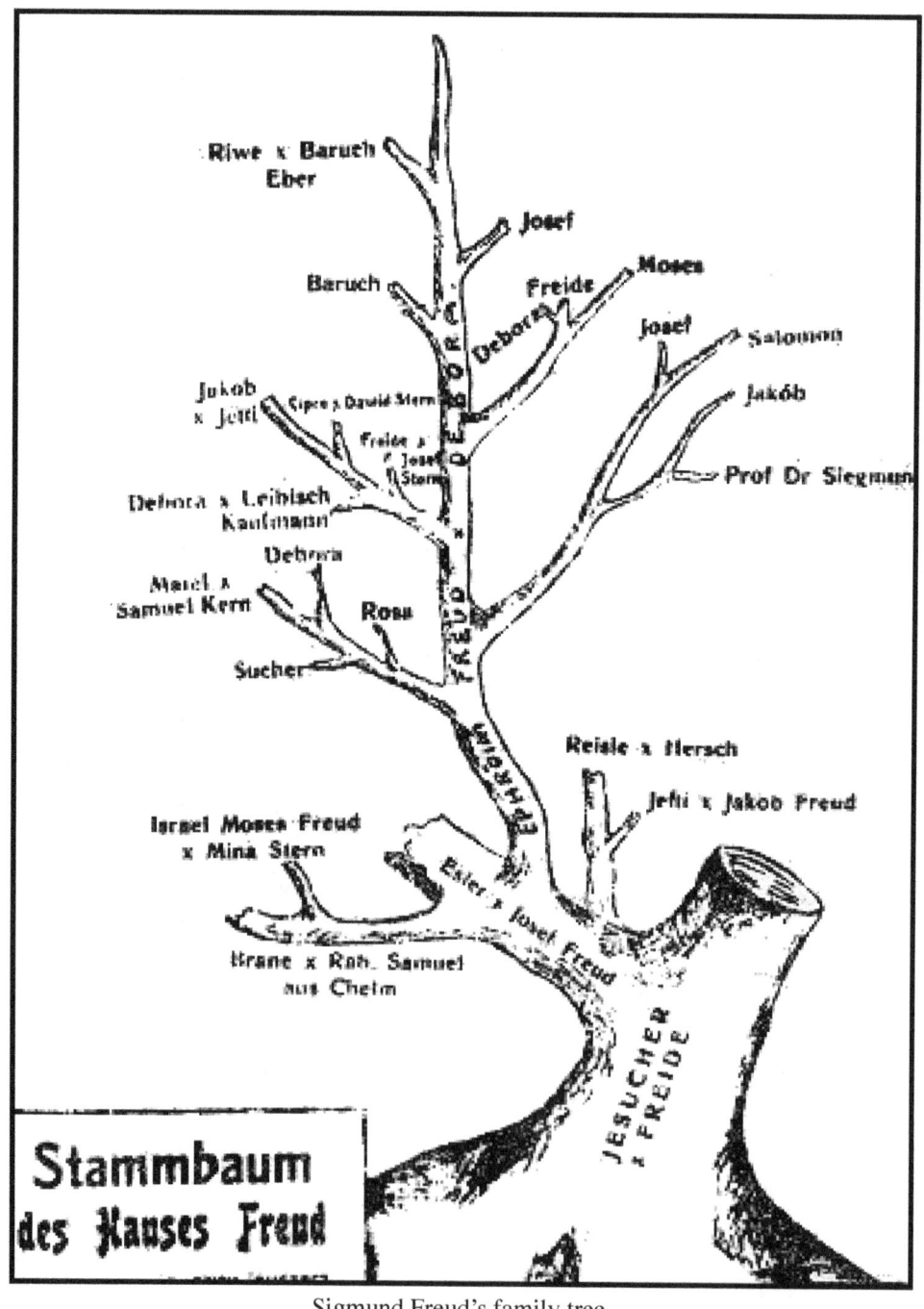

Sigmund Freud's family tree

[Page 119]

Encounters with Sigmund Freud
Translated by Alejandro Landman and Norbert Porile

My first acquaintance with Freud occurred in Hamburg on Grindel Street. In my youth there lived in my neighborhood a widow surnamed Bernis, who was related to the Rabbi of Hamburg, who in those days was the legendary "Haham" Bernis. When this woman learned that I was going to give some lectures in Vienna, she asked me to bring her greetings to her son-in-law, Prof. Freud, who lived in that city. Until that time, 1898, I had never heard of Prof. Freud.

I gave one of the lectures to the humanist association "Vienna". It dealt with the controversial drama "Yohanan" by Zoderman. This drama deals with the negative attributes of orthodox Jews from the viewpoint of their religious practices rather than with the antagonistic political attitudes towards them, which were already widespread at the time. In my lecture I criticized the position of modern Jews who tolerated such criticism, the negative attitudes that they displayed towards the Orthodox, and their indifference to the harassment of orthodox Jews.

Following my lecture we all sat down to a friendly meal. Freud acted as the host of this gathering. He expressed various thoughts about the subject of my talk and made several jokes related to religion. He suggested that many Jews resembled Yohanan the Convert: shaggy coats, unkempt hair, mysterious face. Freud preferred the man in the elegant tuxedo to the one dressed like a prophet. I thought to myself: how far has this man drifted from Jewish life that he can't accept the oriental trappings of his ancestors? I was not surprised, however, as it was known that in these circles, in which Freud was the leader, rabbis were not welcome at lectures. This organization did not want to appear to be too religious in order to be able to participate in the activities of the more liberal circles of the land. However, we cannot think of them as being truly anti-religious. Thus, Freud undoubtedly had an encounter with the Rabbi of Vienna, although it was only on paper in the form of a cartoon that appeared in the most important humorous newspaper in Vienna. In this cartoon Freud appeared in the guise of Rabbi Gidman out on his daily walk. The legend below said "Guy de Monpassant" and this statement certainly did not convey an impression of "preaching in the desert". I thanked Freud and gave him the greetings from Hamburg.

After working for several years in Vienna I once again attended a lecture to the above group. Freud was the lecturer and his topic was "Hamurabi, the ancient codifier". Now I could understand why Freud was so successful in academic life. He did not issue pronouncements and spoke not dryly but in an interesting manner that really struck home. The audience at this lecture was small although Freud's voice was best suited to this rather intimate setting. I had been told that Freud's lectures in North America were not very successful because he spoke in a low voice. Most of the audience could not hear him and there were those who attributed this problem to an illness. I was happy to note that all these tales were not true.

Freud utilized a type of trick in the above lecture that was widely used at that time. He said: "I have just remembered that I forgot to bring from home the pictures of the Hamurabi tablets that I wanted to show you." After the lecture I told him in a jocular manner: "You used the evidence of our Torah." I didn't find his approach to be reasonable. It was historically inaccurate as it elevated Hamurabi at the expense of Moses. On top of that, I said, "you forgot the pictures at home!"

Freud was at this time at the peak of his fame. He received many honors in America. "What do you know about Freud?" was the first question New York reporters asked visitors from Vienna. His theory was considered to be the most important discovery of the time, or at least the most important one made in Vienna. Nonetheless, the number of his American patients decreased substantially owing to the poor social conditions that developed first there and then in the rest of the world. Jokingly, but not happily, Freud spoke of the American millionaires who were coming to Vienna to shake his hand.

Some more time passed and I once again gave a lecture to the "Vienna" group, this time about the history of Jewish education. An interesting discussion took place at the reception which followed the lecture. Freud argued insistently that Jews had not made any significant contribution to knowledge. While stating that in medicine one certainly recognizes "the well known Mendelsohn, the friend of Lesing" he indicated that this was neither here nor there. The well known dermatologist, Prof. Shlema Arman, a colleague of Freud at the University, then took advantage of the deadly silence that followed Freud's attack on Judaism to reply. I was not surprised by Freud's attack since in certain circles in Vienna "Jews without any respect for their ancestors" amused themselves in self-destructive activities. Arman stated that while we Jews perhaps did not invent the generator or the auto, we did give to the world the "Tanach" and with it God. In my final summary I stated that I would go even further than Prof. Arman: I promised to gather proof that we Jews also invented the generator and the auto.

I kept my word and presented a carefully researched proof in a lecture entitled "Jews as inventors and discoverers", which was partially published in the newspapers "Ost und West" and Algemeine Zeitung das Judentum". In my lecture I spoke of Poper-Linkaus, inventor of the electric carriage, and of Sigfrid Marks, inventor of the first gasoline powered auto.

After several years Freud sent me his family tree and history and the preparation of this manuscript confirms the thoughts expressed here. I had no further contact with Freud until I visited Judge Julian Mak in New York. Mak's family members were friends of Freud.

While Freud's position on Judaism seemed pretty clear to me, I was surprised by the indications of his support of Zionism. I was further surprised when I learned that Freud was an honorary member of the Vilna organization for the preservation of Yiddish.

Freud's father moved to Vienna from the Galician town of Buchach. From Vienna he moved to Freishtad in Moravia. In Vienna, Freud's father was a commission agent, that is, he traveled to make purchases on behalf of Viennese merchants. His famous son, who was well aware of his exalted status, joined in his old age an organization that supported the language of his native land.

Dr. M. Grinwald
(Based on an article published in Haaretz on September 21, 1941.)

[Page 122]

Yitzchak Fernhof
Translated by Dr. Rose Shoshana Ages (Kleiner/Neufeld)

A

Fernhof's literary activity had its beginning at the end of the previous century, in Buczacz, eastern Galicia, a city noted for Torah and enlightenment. Jewish Galicia in those days was in the process of awakening from a deep sleep. A select group of writers, orators and community leaders had been instrumental in this awakening. Reuven Asher Broides, Berndstater, Silberbush, Ehrenpreis, Shlomo Rubin, Yehoshua Tahon, Naimark, Nathan Birnboim, Moshe Shulboim, Bernfeld, Shlomo Schiller, Shtand and others sounded a message of awakening to Galicia with vigor and warmth, each one in his own way. This message was heard at first only occasionally, and by the few.

However, in time the numbers of listeners grew and a movement arose that led eastern Galicia to a spiritual awakening. In her deepest recesses there was a longing for some sort of change. The air was still suffused by the spirit of the R'nk (Rabbi Nachman Krochmal), Shy'r (Shlomo Yehuda Rappaport), Yosef Perl, Shimshon Bloch, Yitzchak Arter, Latris and others.

Their books were found in attics, and they were read clandestinely. In the library of the old beis medrash [house of Torah study], in Buczacz, these people's research books stood in one row, and on the same shelves, as the books written by the pious and the followers of musar [moralists].

The R'nk was not held in higher regard than the Rambam, nor were 'Duties of the Heart' and 'The Akeda' given more recognition than 'The Eternal Paths.' The crown which had been removed from the head of Galicia decades earlier, still sparkled in a remote corner and awaited the hand that would return it to its former glory. The confidence in self which had faded, began to come to light and to reveal itself.

Indeed, the revival came about through physical and spiritual labour, because decades of inaction, the conservative way of life, and the strong attachment to tradition did their damage. Opposition to everything new, and to any attempt at innovation, was very great.

A war between fathers and sons was spreading. Religion struggled with knowledge, 'light' with 'darkness,' enlightenment with conservatism.

All these events, that were common at the time in the whole Jewish world, occurring on a large, or smaller, scale in different locales, were charged with dramatic tension in Galicia as well. Yet, as a result of these struggles there arose cells of revival, and corners of renewal, and leaders of an awakening, who unleashed a torrent of innovation in the frozen life of the Galician people of Israel.

Yitzchak (Itzi) Fernhof lived in these twilight years, when the creative powers of Galicia were awakened, and the light of YL"G and Mendele and Achad HaAm began to appear from afar.

He was not a high priest in the temple of creativity, but rather a Levite. He accompanied the great ones, and carried their musical instruments. But while accompanying them he also used to play his own music. His melody was unique, and at times even pleasant to the ear. There are times when he surprises with an original theme, and with sparks of true creativity. And he also had a measure of humility.

He spreads his wings and tries to fly, and more than once we even hear the wings flutter, but he cannot stay too long in that sublime air. He is drawn to the soil, to the earthly ambiance, which he captures in a realistic manner. And his Hebrew language is fresh, with striking expressions and innovations, even if here and there traces of the florid style of the haskala language remain.

An example of his linguistic talent can be noted in his article, Two Imaginations, which appeared in the second volume of the Book of Delights, in 1896. In that article we find several expressions that demonstrate Fernhof's original, and profound linguistic perceptiveness.

Describing how moved he was by Herzl's Judenstaat, and the dreams which reading this book gave rise to, he presents us with a vision of a kind of minor utopia. In this vision the names and the language used reflect a unique prescience. The word 'Judenstaat' is translated by him several times as 'the state of Israel,' whereas all the translators to this day have called the book "The State of the Jews."

When he imagines the state of Israel rebuilt on its original site, he says, among other things: "And my eyes will behold rabbis elected to the assembly houses, ministers of the interior, and ministers of foreign affairs, and ministers of the treasury." Ministers in the state of Israel are called by him: 'Sarim' [just as they are currently called in Israel – translator].

Surely, this linguistic intuition is not incidental for Fernhof. He dreamt a great deal about the state of Israel, and that dream is clothed in an original, prescient, Hebrew style.

B

Fernhof was the type of person who disseminates culture; he was a torchbearer, who teaches Torah to the many. The major characteristic of such a person, at a moment when he formulates a certain conviction, or a certain ideal, is that he does not rest, and is not silent, until he wins supporters for his ideal. As Fernhof had a great love for the Hebrew language, took pleasure in it, and excelled in it, his fervent wish was to transmit it to others.

He gave private Hebrew lessons in Buczacz*. Afterwards, when he was hired as a teacher at the Baron Hirsch school, in Zlochov (thanks to the recommendation of the linguistic scholar, David Zvi Heinrich Miller), he achieved part of his goal.

However, his success was short-lived. The Baron Hirsch schools, whose aims were admirable, were not welcomed by the Jews of eastern Galicia. Only a few of 'the enlightened', were happy to welcome them. The majority looked at them with disfavor. In their eyes the teachers, the students, and the parents, were regarded as 'destroyers of the covenant,' as instigators and agitators.

This kind of school was regarded as tantamount to a nest of heretics, a schoolhouse for the 'sinners of Israel.' Fernhof, who worked so hard to be accepted as a teacher at that school, where he hoped to broaden his activity and influence, was bitterly disappointed. He did, however, enter into the town's enlightened society, the society of maskilim, but he remained a pariah in the eyes of the pious, the zealous, and their followers. His plans became less ambitious. His dream evaporated.

A better fate was reserved for his second love, Hebrew literature. He loved the Hebrew writers, those from far and near, and cultivated an ambition in his heart to summon them all to one gathering place. He wanted with all his being to establish a place of honor for Galicia in the Hebrew literature that was undergoing a revival. He knew that the center of literary creativity was not in Galicia, but he wished to transform Galicia into an auxiliary center of literary creativity.

With this plan in mind he did two things: He himself wrote as much as was possible, and published his writing in different publications. In this way he acquired fame for himself and for his region. However, because he possessed a large measure of self criticism, he understood that his contribution, and that of others, were not sufficient to achieve his goal. He therefore established a journal in Buczacz by the name, 'The Books of Delights.'

This was supposed to attract the writers from other major Jewish centers and to publicize the special character of Galicia, since the stars of Galicia would shine alongside the bright lights of Russia... Indeed, this was a minor platform that resembles somewhat the 'penny books' of Ben-Avigdor. But despite everything it was an independent platform.

This minor platform succeeded so well that its few issues featured a concentration of famous writers, and those who were to become famous. Tchernichovksy published there one of his first poems, 'Let us go out, let us dwell in serenity;' Berdichevsky published a piece about the four leaders of the world of the chasidim, which enraged Galicia for a short time; Breinin contributed his sketch, 'My Grandfather;' Klausner offered an article on 'Original Literature' and on the quality of translations.

Even Sh. Ben Zion figured among the contributors. Needless to say the writers of Galicia brought their own spirit to this forum. With all the flaws that plagued these thin journals, they also represented the promise of a new era.

The new generation was influenced by them, and their simplicity was in a sense a novelty for the yeshiva students. However, these little journals ceased publication, and then re-emerged in Zlochov. But even there only two issues appeared. At this juncture Fernhof experimented with his friends by establishing new (literary) forums like 'The Jordan,' and 'The Young Hebrew.' He had a great desire to create, edit, and to include himself, as well as the writers of Galicia, in the new Hebrew literary life.

C

As previously noted, Fernhof continued to write and publish much in almost all the [Hebrew – translator] periodicals of his day. He wrote poems and stories, sketches and epigrams, critiques and articles on contemporary questions. He did translations and adaptations, editing and publishing. He tested his strength in many fields, because he never attained a state of complete self knowledge. He did not have a clear understanding of where his strength lay, and which literary path to follow.

All his life he reflected on his abilities and his talent. He experienced doubt, meditated and then wrote. It is especially these struggles, this self-searching, that touch the heart and make him an interesting subject. Today, about 30 or so years after his death, we know that there was a good and healthy kernel (of talent) in him, but it was wrapped in many shells. He was a writer with a soul and with insight, who used to tell it straight and simple. Of course, not all his stories are good, and the good ones are not all of equal value.

His first published book, 'From the Legends of Life,' was not well received by the critics. Brenner, Berdichevsky and others subjected him to severe criticism. Perhaps they were right, for in this work the lines were blurred between adaptation, translation and the original source. His style here showed negligence, and his ultimate purpose was unclear.

However, there is no doubt that the harsh critique was also influenced by the traditional bias toward the writers of Galicia, that was a type of convention in those days. This criticism hurt him very much, for it came from writers whom he admired a great deal, and whom he held in such high esteem. But this criticism also had a positive impact, and led him toward greater creative efforts, and toward better results.

Henceforth we see him in another light. In the series of stories that he wished to publish in a special volume, titled 'Mitnagdim'**, we sense a greater self assurance and a more mature power of expression. Here his soul as a writer found some comfort, and he was able to appropriate for himself an honorable and original place in our literature.

Chasidism and the chasidim were fortunate in having writers who depicted them either in their poems and prose, or in a serious, or amusing, story. There were many important figures who honored the chasidim with songs and praises, and there were others who poured their anger and their mockery on them. They were a worthy target for all.

This was not true for the mitnagdim, the brothers and opponents of the chasidim. The mitnagdim remained in the shadows. They were neither studied nor investigated. They were usually described as being of secondary importance, as dull, as obscure, as adversaries, whose purpose was to serve as a foil for the chasidim. They were incidental types, fleeting images, who do not live and exist in the story in their own right.

Then Fernhof came along and wrote a whole book by the name 'Mitnagdim.' Only two or three stories from this book were published in his lifetime. Most of them were found among his papers and are being published here for the first time. And here is what constitutes the book's innovation. In this book the mitnagdim and their movement are the focus of the stories. Here the chasidim serve only as background props. And this is not surprising.

In Buczacz, where the fundamental impressions of Fernhof's life were carved out, chasidism did not strike deep roots. In Buczacz he observed the mitnagdim on the street, in the study hall, during their conversations, during their Talmud study, during their quarrels, and during their peace making.

He grasped their world vision and understood their spirit and temperament. By delving into their soul, and analyzing their speech, he revealed a wonderful secret: Nothing separates the mitnagdim and the chasidim except their belief in the 'tzadik' [righteous leader, or rabbi, head of the chasidim – translator].

In essence, they resemble each other in their nature, and in the depths of their souls. The mitnagdim are opposed to the chasidim with a passion that is chasidic. They negate the teachings of the chasidic rebbe with the same fanaticism with which the chasidim absorb these teachings. Moreover, they are ready to punish the members of the 'cult', in the same manner that the 'cult' members are ready to punish their opponents.

In his description of these opposing images Fernhof rises many a time to the level of an artist, who sees into the hearts of his heroes and paints them with a skillful brush. For this purpose he has at his disposal various talents and abilities: A sharp vision, a fine style, mockery, humor, caricature, restraint and involvement in the lives of his heroes. These, and similar, means make the description simple, straightforward and exciting.

We feel that the mitnagdim also need 'tikkun' ['spiritual improvement' – translator], and Fernhof provided them with it. These characters are carved from the reality that existed in his day, and are not figments of his imagination. In the margins of the manuscript are listed names of people, residents of Buczacz, who served as prototypes for the characters in the stories.

It is evident that he did not invent 'acting figures' from his imagination, but took them from his own surroundings. First he studied the people whom he encountered, followed their movements and learned their traits, and only after he learned to know them very well, did he begin to shape and create them in the framework of his stories.

However, for all their realism, Fernhof was able to pour into these characters his own spirit, and to create them according to his own vision. Rabbi Moshe Baruch Hindes, the pedantic Rabbi Shlomo Zeev, Kalman Berish, and many others, are interesting types, whom Fernhof captured in both a realistic manner and through allusive references.

For him the subject of the mitnagdim became a type of citadel, the central focus of his creative ambition. After a period of struggling with writing, creating and publishing, it was as if he finally had found his literary path.

He wrote these stories with a passionate soul, for he saw his destiny in them. This was not another capricious undertaking, or a light diversion, but a mission.

In one of the drafts there is a short preface to this book. The preface is signed: 'Fernhof, Stanislav, winter of 5671' [1911 – translator] and here is what it says: 'Many have written, even in the last years, about the chasidim and the tsadikim, and have forgotten the typical mitnagdim who are fast becoming extinct. In the future our writers will be held accountable for the neglect and abandon of these figures.

The author of this book on the mitnagdim was raised at the feet of the mitnagdim and knows their nature, character, inner world, obstinacy, persistence in defending their existence and their disdain and scorn toward the tsadikim and chasidim... and that which he knows, he will attempt to convey.'

Here we see that it is not by chance that he wrote the stories about the mitnagdim, for he felt a need, and the ability, to write about those, whom Hebrew literature had disenfranchised and left to their solitude. He wished to remove the slander which had been attached to the mitnagdim, the allegation that they were dry, and limited to the study of Talmud and the performance of mitzvot.

In Fernhof's stories the mitnagdim are revealed as persons of understanding, who have a lyric vitality about them. Their exterior may be dry, but their inner self is the opposite. Try to deepen your contact with them, he wrote, and at once you will encounter vital Jews, with a rich spiritual life, marked by contradictions and an abundance of energy.

The mitnagdim are, as he noted in the margins of his draft, chasidim who do not believe in 'tsadikim.' Only this one point divides them.

Fernhof identified with them. His spirit clung to theirs, and it shaped their images from the inside, with a measure of loving kindness and grandeur.

Fernhof was not the founding father, but he was one of the builders (of the new) Hebrew literature. In several periods of our literary creativity, and in several chapters of its history his contributions are firmly established, as an editor, an intermediary, or narrator.

He left his imprint on the process of renewal of literary Hebrew creativity in Galicia and elsewhere. He included in his journals Hebrew writers from other countries. Among them were those from Galicia, who became later the support columns of Hebrew literature - Agnon, Barash, Rabbi Binyamin, Lifshitz and others.

Even if they belong to a higher sphere, and to another generation, they had, in their early years, basically absorbed the literary atmosphere created by Fernhof, Gershon Bader, Graber and others like them.

They took leave of him and moved on to greater depth and greater height, but they read Fernhof's work, collaborated with him, and absorbed the good that he transmitted to them as an intermediary and writer.

Israel Cohen

* S. Y. Agnon recalled for me a witty, and fitting, expression that he heard from Fernhof, in which there is a word play on opposites. When guests came to visit him, and he was in the midst of a private lesson, he would say to them [in Yiddish

– translator]: Wait a minute, I just have to give a (one hour) lesson...
** This book was published in 5712 (1952) by the Writers Association at 'Dvir.'

[Page 127]

Family Memories
Translated by Dr. Rose Shoshana Ages (Kleiner/Neufeld)

World War I destroyed our tranquil home. Many of my memories have now become dim. And the angel of death, who took away our father before his time, had also brought a sudden end to those memories.

Father was in the habit of speaking to us as he would to equals. He would share with us his impressions of things, his ambitions in life, and that which his eyes observed. He shared with us the beauty of nature, taught us how to enjoy life in its fullness, and how to endure life's difficult moments.

I shall never forget the hikes, during our summer vacations, on which father took us through the pine forests of the Carpathian mountains. He taught us how to climb the mountain cliffs, encouraged us to reach the peaks, and to observe the beautiful landscapes which unfolded before us. Father used to enthrall us with his poetic language, and therefore, it is no wonder that we, the children, were in the habit of expressing our feelings in a poetic, childish language before we even learned to write. Father enjoyed very much recording our rhymes on paper. He saved them, and even showed them to us when we grew up.

Only my big brother (Moomi) was to continue writing, while the rest of us were to become submerged in the practical world. Father was the embodiment of goodness; he never punished any one of us. However, the very fact that he was angry with us, or that his mind was not at ease, was in itself a great punishment for us.

With the help of my elderly mother, who survived the Nazi slaughter and lives with me, and with the help of a few of my father's friends, who are still living, among them Gershon Bader, Dr. Shimon Bernshtein, and Dr. Louie Launer, I am attempting to write a biographical sketch, that would be combined with my own memories of my father.

My father's birth date is the subject of controversy. According to the marriage certificate he was born in 1866. However, in his death certificate the date given is 1867, while according to the file card of the New York Public Library, which lists all of my father's books in its holdings, his birth date is 1866. This date seems acceptable to my mother, who wishes with all her heart to be regarded as a little younger than my father, at least on paper.

He was the son of Israel Fernhof, and Chaya, whose maiden name was Fliegler. They lived in Buczacz, Galicia.

Father lost his mother when he was seven years old. She was soon replaced by a stepmother. However, luckily, he was taken to the home of his uncle Fliegler, who actively supervised his studies. There he acquired a thorough mastery of the six books of the Mishnah, and its commentaries. He excelled in these studies, and also acquired a very good knowledge of the Hebrew language. Secretly he used to read anything he could lay his hands on, in Hebrew and in Yiddish. He studied German literature in the same clandestine manner. Before long he became an expert in the classic literature of Goethe, Schiller and Heine. His knowledge of written and spoken German was very good, even though he had to conceal this from his teachers and educators, lest he be caught in the act of pursuing these forbidden studies.

Even in the later years he was a controversial figure in the community, since he dared to publish in his "Sifrei Sha'ashu'im" (Books of Delights) a chassidic sketch by Micha Yosef Berdichevsky, who was still a young man at that time. Soon the young intellectuals of Galicia gathered around this brilliant autodidact. He became the head of a literary circle and began to write. His articles and poems were printed in the Hebrew periodicals which were appearing in Europe at the time. With these writings he became one of the founders of the new Hebrew literature in Galicia.

I should like to bring here a short biographical sketch, which had been printed on a postcard, with my father's photograph. This postcard, along with postcards of other well-known Hebrew writers of the day, was distributed by the publishing house of Abraham Robinson in Stanislav. The text of the postcard reads as follows:

"Yitzhak Fernhof was born in Buczacz (Galicia) in the year 1865. A man of diverse talents. In his childhood he recited many poems, and in the end he began to write stories, and sketches, which are characterized by their sharp observations and gentle humor. He was the first to lay the foundation of Hebrew literature in Galicia.

He skillfully edited the "Sifrei Sha'ashu'im", which helped greatly to spread the Hebrew language in Galicia, and to attract to it the young men whose learning had centered around the 'klois' (small synagogue and house of study). He was also the editor of "Ha-Yarden" (The Jordan), and "Ha-Tsair" (The Young Person). Several years ago his stories and sketches appeared in a collection called "Me-Aggadot Ha-Chaim" (From the Legends of Life). At present his book, "Ha-Mitnagdim" (The Opponents of Chassidim), has been submitted for publication. It is unique in its new approach, and is highly regarded by those who have read the manuscript.

As far as I can recall the original version of the book, "Ha-Mitnagdim," was submitted to "Ha-Olam" (The World), which was edited by Mr. Moshe Kleinman (may he rest in peace) in Moscow. However, during World War I this book, already in print, was lost during the chaos that reigned in Russia in those days, and its traces were never found. Fortunately, a damaged and imperfect copy of the original manuscript was found by my brother in the wreckage of our old home in Stanislav, and it was sent to me before the Nazi invasion, which reduced this city to rubble. Thirty five years later I see it as a debt of honor to assist with its publication in the state of Israel.

I also know that this would have been the fondest of father's dreams, who was one of the earliest pioneers of Zionism, a contemporary of Theodor Herzl. No matter where my father lived he was the head of the Zionists and Hebraists, and he filled our hearts, the hearts of children, with a love of Zion. Were it not for the wars we would have made aliyah to Israel as chalutzim, or pioneers.

His work in literature did not provide sufficient income to support my father and his family. There was the constant pressure of worrying about earning a livelihood for the family. My father thus became a flour merchant, and managed his father-in-law's flour mill, and the enterprises connected with his warehouse. However, in the meantime he acquired a reputation as someone proficient in Hebrew and German, and as an expert in the literature of the humanities. That is when the foundation established by Baron Hirsch invited him to join the teaching faculty of its schools, first in Zlochov, and ultimately in Stanislav.

After my second brother, Shmuel, was born, in 1894, and after I was born, in 1897, my father's financial situation became difficult, and he was forced to give private lessons, in order to support us, and in order to provide the best education for us. It was an education that he himself had never been given; he was obliged to acquire it through his own efforts, and under enormously difficult conditions – subjected to terror and fear lest his teachers catch him, for they regarded any time spent on secular studies as heresy.

How I admired my father when I'd see him tired from his teaching day at the school, and yet still playing with us and telling us wonderful legends, which he himself had created for us. Or he would read to us his own poems and sketches.

I also remember that father invited to our home people such as Sholom Aleichem, Reuven Brainin and others, who would be visiting our town as public lecturers. He would describe to us the greatness of those people, and it would leave a strong impression on us. Incidentally, he always used to serve as chairman at these public lectures. He would introduce them to the public in a beautiful and polished Hebrew, which was envied by many. Our home was always a meeting place for the leading figures among the Hebraists, for my father's pupils, and for his followers.

It was a great event in my father's life when he purchased his own home in the beautiful section of Stanislav, on Lipova Street 88, close to the magnificent gardens of the Elizabeth promenade. In this house he set up his library, of which he was so proud, and for which he was envied by all the book collectors.

All this was destroyed and demolished by the invasion of Petlyura's bands during the upheavals that followed World War I.

When that war broke out we, like many others, left our home in Stanislav, with our little sister, Klara, who was only a few years old. She was father's joy, and he saw in her the personification of beauty and charm. We fled from our town in a wagon, and on foot, through the Carpathian mountains to Hungary, and we were subjected to all the trials of the war. We wandered from town to town, and after many hardships arrived in Vienna.

Worries about making a living drained father's strength. He gave private lessons, worked for the Joint as a researcher, and did not shirk from any work, as long as he could feed his family. During that long war all his sons were drafted into the Austrian army and even he himself wore a uniform, despite the fact that he was already over 50 years old.

After the war he was again unemployed. He was promised the position of librarian at Vienna's Jewish community library. However, as on many previous occasions, he was now also obliged to face one disappointment after another. The Baron Hirsch foundation, which paid a low salary, warned father that they would cut off that salary if he did not agree to return to Stanislav to begin teaching at the school. It would be under the conditions of chaos and destruction which prevailed after the war. Since he always worried first about his family's welfare, he left his wife and his children to enjoy the comforts of life in Vienna, while he himself returned to the region of ruins that was now Stanislav.

All the communication lines to that city were broken, and only by chance did we learn about his death, six months after he had passed away. His death occurred on February 23. He died from a typhoid infection, in an isolated cubicle of the Stanislav hospital, far from his family, in his effort to spare us his painful suffering and loneliness. On his dying lips he uttered the name of his beloved daughter. At his grave site all his students and friends were present, but not one member of his family was there. Before me lies a copy of the Juedische Volkszeitung, of February 28, 1919 which contains an obituary for my father. I bring it here just as it appeared: "The new Hebrew literature, and Yiddish literature in general, have suffered an irretrievable loss. Yitzhak Fernhof is no more!

He was about 51 at his death. He was buried with his people, far from his family, a martyr of the great art of teaching, a martyr of his passionate love for his family, and his people. He labored some thirty years without a break, as a pedagogue and Hebrew-Yiddish writer. As a teacher at the local school, established by Baron Hirsch, he was one of its first founders and leaders, and he was the guiding light of the local society, "Safah Berurah" (Pure Language).

From 1896 to 1898 he published the periodical "Sefer Sha'ashuim." Among the first participants in this literary undertaking were such great writers as Shaul Tchernikhovsky, Mikhah Yosef Berdichevsky and Reuven Brainin. In 1906 he published here, in Stanislav, the Hebrew periodical "Ha 'Yarden". One also has to mention his book, "Me'aggadot Ha'chaim." His last big book contains stories, some of which had already been printed, about the lives of the mitnagdim. He composed several excellent textbooks for the teaching of Hebrew. He also contributed to various Hebrew periodicals.

Being that he did not have the means to bring his family from Vienna to Stanislav, after four years of wanderings, he ended up here living a lonely, isolated life from the end of August of the previous year.

Loved and honored by all the different classes of the Jewish public in Stanislav, he stood firmly by his duties until his last breath.

In the hearts of the young, who were undergoing a renaissance, and who felt gratitude toward him, he built for himself an eternal monument. May he rest in peace!"

Beneath this obituary appeared a poem, by the editor, Herbert Sfondson, which expressed the love of all my father's students and friends, in German. The Hebrew translation is given below:

Obituary

on the death of the teacher and unforgettable friend

Yitzhak Fernhof

On the day he was lowered into his grave
A clear and pleasant day in early spring,
the light of sunshine softened the earth
but a striking thunderbolt from the great heavens
stunned the hearts of all your students.
We rushed in shock to the graveyard
to the source of our friendship, the creator.
We followed you to the cemetery in tears
To a grave site narrow and dark.
The man who awoke our spirit is gone
His words stirred our hearts.
In the black dust, oh our teacher, you shall rest
You were the crowning glory of our soul
May your sleep be sweet! As in the past, so at present
We shall honor everything you have commanded us,
In the heart of the youth, whom you have taught,
An eternal monument you have built for yourself.

About 20 days before his death, on January 3, 1919, the same paper printed the following announcement:

"On Saturday, December 28, 1918, there was held at the local "Pure Language" society, a public examination of the 50 students in the first course that had been capably directed by the renowned Hebrew writer Yitzhak Fernhof. From the midst of the parents group, which was on this occasion moved to the point of tears, one father presented Mr. Fernhof with a silver cup, made by a craftsman, as a token of appreciation and thanks."

My brother, Dr. Moshe Fernhof, a writer and poet and known especially to the Yiddish writers of his time, has written a moving poem, in which he asks father's forgiveness. "Forgive us, father" that we were not able to stand by your bedside during your last days. The poem was published in a German newspaper in Vienna.

In his last letter to my sister, who was still a little girl and was making her first efforts at letter writing, father begged her to write him long letters. "What a beautiful thing it is when a father and his daughter understand each other well, and they discuss everything by means of letters, at a time when a person to person conversation, to my regret, is not possible."

Most of the things that father wrote in his youth were signed with the name Itzi, until professor Yosef Klausner convinced him to change his name to Yitzhak.

In the spring of 1938 I visited my father's grave at the old Jewish cemetery in Stanislav. It was an attractive stone structure, designed and built by a mason. This was a short time before Hitler's invasion, and my heart told me that this was the last time that I was going to have the privilege of visiting that site. Now, after the horrendous tragedy that fell upon the Jewish communities of Europe, when all the sacred sites of Judaism were destroyed, there is no more hope of seeing that grave.

This book, which contains the best of my father's writings, will serve as a monument to his memory. His words – they are his memorial.

William Fernhof
Woodridge, New York, 1949.

[Page 131]

How Buczacz Jews Voted in Austrian Parliamentary Elections
Translated by Adam Prager

In Galicia elections for the Austrian Parliament at the end of the 19th and the beginning of the 20th centuries were always accompanied by major scandals in which the municipal, regional and occasionally the central authorities were involved. The decisive factors that determined election results included forgeries, bribes, and threats. Voters were warned that if they did not vote as instructed from above, measures such as raising of taxes and cancellation of permits would be taken against them.* Forgeries in voter lists were apparent and no serious efforts were necessary to uncover them. Names of long-deceased citizens were added to the lists; people miraculously came back to life during election time. Some members of the ruling group would even vote two or three times. Most of the Jews in Galicia had two first names, enabling them to vote separately with each one. This was possible since the election committees consisted mainly of people from a specific party. With no representatives of other lists present, they were able to determine in advance the election results.

Moreover, great pressure was put on the voters by the Polish Club, whose rule in Galicia was unchallenged. Even though most of the population was Ukrainian, the Polish intelligentsia with the help of assimilated Jews and "Moshkes" (ordinary Jews) knew how to dominate the public affairs of the region and dictate to the voters the choice of candidates. The Polish rulers let nothing interfere with their goal and spared no means to reach it. The Polish Club was aided by regional officers, municipal heads, council members, and leaders of the Jewish communities, including Hasidic masters and their followers. The Polish press, whose editors included assimilated and converted Jews, also served the Club's ambitions. Woe to the man who dared submit his candidacy without prior approval from the

Polish Club. Such a submission was doomed to fail. No wonder then that nearly always the candidate chosen by the Club was the one elected. At times the Club did the Jews, who constituted 10% of the population, a favor by allowing the candidacy of a few assimilated Jews or of "Moshkes" that were loyal to the Poles.

In the electoral district Buczacz-Kolomyya-Sniatyn – all three comprised one region – the situation was similar to that in the rest of the Galician towns: the candidate of the Club, at times a Jew, was almost always chosen. However, in 1883 something occurred in the Jewish community that was an upheaval of sorts. That year the chief rabbi of Krakow, who for over two years had been the parliamentary representative of the Buczacz-Kolomyya-Sniatyn electoral district, died. Rabbi Schreiber was a loyal member of the Polish Club even though his insufficient knowledge of the official parliamentary languages prevented him from giving speeches in parliament and participating in debate. However, during votes he was always present and voted together with the Poles. On the Sabbath eve, a "minyan" was arranged for him in the parliament building to enable him to pray with a quorum while being present when voting took place. Following his death there was a parliamentary vacancy for a candidate from the above three cities. A public election committee was assembled immediately to choose an articulate delegate who could stand up and fight for the interests of the Jews. This committee had its eyes set on Dr. Joseph Samuel Bloch, a rabbi in Floridsdorf near Vienna, who consented to the committee's offer, adding that a parliamentary position would give him an opportunity to explain to the peoples of Austria – and to the Jews themselves – the truth about Judaism.

As election day approached, a great storm arose in the Polish press. The Jews were accused of betraying the Poles and were threatened with a national ban of the aforementioned three towns. To the Poles each mandate given by them was a reward for a favor done for them. Rabbi Schreiber was chairman of the "Makhzikey Hadat" ("Upholders of the Faith") Society. Aided by the influence of this society and the Rabbi of the Belz hasidic court, he contributed greatly in the various elections to Polish success. The Poles in return felt obligated to hand over the mandate of these towns to him. However, following his death a political figure appeared who was unknown to them and whom they did not trust, despite the fact that he expressed his willingness to join the Polish Club. The uproar in the press grew from day to day. There were also some Jews whose greed and lust for power drove them to bribery and incitement of the press against Dr. Bloch.

Approximately 14 days before the elections, a group of so-called prominent Jews met to protest against Dr. Bloch's candidacy, which was allegedly harmful to Judaism. They decided to demand that Dr. Bloch abandon his candidacy. The chief speakers and instigators in this group were Dr. Emil Bick, the president of the Lvov [Lemberik/Lemberg/Lviv] community and head of the "Shomer Yisrael" [Watchman of Israel] Society, and the preacher Levinstein, father of the parliament delegate Nathan von Levinstein. In their youth these two followed the German centrist line in politics, but were now Polish patriots. In their speeches they emphasized that the duty of the Buczacz-Kolomyya-Sniatyn Jews was to award a mandate only to natives and residents of the country, adding that choosing a man from Floridsdorf would only anger the Poles against the Jews.

A letter in this spirit was sent to Dr. Bloch. He answered immediately, stating that the "well known" gentlemen had approached the wrong man and should turn to the election committee of the three towns and warn of the dangers of Bloch receiving the mandate. He added that to his knowledge a few Polish delegates lived in Vienna without causing any harm to the daily national affairs of Galicia. He added that he had done nothing to receive the candidacy and was willing to forfeit it if the committee so requested. The Polish rulers and assimilated Jews of Galicia naturally found this response unsatisfactory. A national ban against Dr. Bloch was decided upon and the mayors of all three towns were instructed to announce the ban to all the voters. But none of this helped. Dr. Bloch won by a two-thirds majority and was chosen to be the delegate in the Austrian Parliament. Interestingly, Dr. Bloch was chosen without his voters knowing him and without their hearing any election speeches from him. He didn't even have the financial means of traveling to the election district.

The fact that right after the elections Bloch identified with Count Eduard Taaffe's government raised much anger and resentment among the Jewish gentlemen of Vienna. They believed that all Jews must stand by the German party. Thus, any Jewish attempt of reaching an understanding with the Czechs and the other Slavic nations undermined the supreme German rule and rendered one a bad Jew. The war against the Taaffe government was to their minds a Jewish issue. Because Bloch supported this government, he was endlessly persecuted. Indeed in Western Austria Jews contributed significantly to the spreading of German nationalistic thought until this policy boomeranged. Only after anti-Semitism among the Germans increased year by year and reached alarming proportions did these Jews slowly begin to understand and respect Bloch's political views.

Together with the formal announcement of his election, Dr. Bloch received funds enabling him to travel to the three towns, Buczacz, Kolomyya and Sniatyn, and introduce himself to his public. He was everywhere received with great enthusiasm; his entrance into the towns was like a legendary victory march. Horsemen in colorful attire on decorated horses paraded out to welcome him, and to the loud cheering of the crowd he was escorted to the city council where he was congratulated on his outstanding victory and where he gave his first speech before his supporters. There was great joy throughout the towns despite the fact that certain public figures such as mayors, their friends and other community leaders did not participate in the welcoming festivities.

Dr. Bloch's first parliamentary action in matters concerning the Jews was to raise the issue of the hunting of Jewish souls and their forced conversion to Christianity, for children were literally being kidnapped in Galicia. Word of stolen children was very common and was often reported in the daily press. Every Christian who had sinned or had committed a crime and wanted to atone for his sins could kidnap the first Jewish child he saw and present him as a sacrificial offering at the nearest monastery. The child would be doomed forever. This child represented the payment for the kidnapper's sins. What did he care about the parents and their grief? They were merely Jews. The authorities seemed to investigate such matters only to announce finally that there was nothing to be done against the church.

The parliamentary term ended with the coronation speech of Kaiser Franz Joseph the 1st. According to the law, new elections were announced. Dr. Bloch felt it was his duty to go to his electoral district to update his supporters concerning his actions in the parliament in which he had served for a year and a half. However, a Jew from Kolomyya named Vizelberg, a member of the community board and the city council, advised Dr. Bloch not to do so for his being reelected was unthinkable. Apparently Dr. Emil Bick took advantage of the situation to conduct intensive propaganda to win the support of the mayors, their friends and other community leaders. However, soon enough it became clear that Dr. Emil Bick's party was a party of officers without an army. A voters' assembly was held in the Buczacz synagogue where Dr. Bloch's candidacy was declared unanimously. Also in Kolomyya and Sniatyn the majority were in favor of Dr. Bloch. These moves obviously annoyed the Polish intelligentsia greatly and in the meeting of the national central elections committee in Lvov it was decided, contrary to the views of Franz Smolka, president of the Austrian Parliament and Count Potocki, to reject Dr. Bloch's candidacy and to impose on the voters an unwanted candidate, Dr. Emil Bick.

Even the Polish press instigated outrageously against Dr. Bloch and the Jews. For many years, Count Potocki was the governor of Galicia and developed friendly ties with many Jews. He supported Jewish cultural ambitions and sympathized with the Jews in their sufferings. Even the preacher Levinstein in Lvov used his synagogue to warn the Jews of their duty to vote only for the candidates chosen by the Poles.

The uproar over the elections spread throughout Galicia, dividing every Jewish community into parties for and against one of the candidates. The wit that was unique to Eastern European Jews became part of the elections and a weapon in the struggle. Two sayings in particular among those that passed among the voters merit notice. The Tora portion of the week read in the synagogue at that time was "Vayeshev" [Genesis 37-40] ('and he dwelled'), spelled vav, yod, shin, bet. These letters were read as an anagram for the words "Veylt Yosef Shmuel Bloch" ('elect Joseph Samuel Bloch'). Also used as evidence against Bick's party was the question: "How can a Jew give his vote to Bick when it is says in the Bible 'thou shalt not bow down'" – al tishtakhave – du zolst nisht bikn [bukn, Yiddish 'to bow down to' is in some dialects pronounced bikn].

The blind hatred with which the press persecuted Dr. Bloch caused much resentment among the Galician Jews and a few hundred Jews from Lvov appealed to the central elections committee of Galicia to certify Dr. Bloch's candidacy which was supported by almost nine-tenths of Galician Jewry. Their appeal, however, was to no avail. The central elections committee in Galicia decided upon the candidacy of Dr. Emil Bick. Dr. Bloch, who relied on Jewish votes, did not give up. He went to his electoral region to present a report to his voters. He first went to Kolomyya and Sniatyn and was once again welcomed by the cheering Jewish multitudes; the houses of the towns were festively decorated. Voters' assemblies in which he gave speeches were very successful despite individual attempts of obstruction. From Sniatyn Dr. Bloch planned to continue to Buczacz. However, the arrival of news, proudly presented by Dr. Bick, regarding Dr. Bloch's ineligibility to be elected forced the latter to return immediately to Vienna to investigate the matter. His name did not appear on any list, neither in Vienna nor anywhere else, meaning he had no right to vote or to be elected. This news struck everyone by surprise. In Vienna Dr. Bloch learned that he had neglected to keep his voting rights. Previously he voted in Floridsdorf which at the time was not a part of Vienna, However, by relinquishing his rabbinical post there and moving to Vienna to serve in the parliament, he lost his right to vote and did nothing to assure himself of that right in Vienna. Dr. Bick was quite happy to learn this, although his joy proved premature. The deadline for submitting appeals for corrections in the voter lists was not overdue and several days later Dr. Bloch's name was added to the Viennese voters' list.

Dr. Bloch returned to Galicia and on his way spent a few days in Lvov where Dr. Bick, aware of

Bloch's financial situation, tried to bribe him into selling his candidacy. Bloch, of course, rejected the offer outright but took the opportunity to suggest to his rival that they end the ugly mutual war that only benefited the enemies of the Jews. Furthermore, he invited Dr. Bick to accompany him to the electoral region and allow the voters to choose one of them as candidate. Dr. Bick was not enthusiastic about this offer. From his parliamentary experience he knew the voters were not on his side. When he tried to speak at Buczacz's great synagogue, there was no audience. When the mayor Berish Shtern promised to pay a gulden to each man who would come to hear Dr. Bick speak he was advised to dress the peasant boys in Jewish clothes and bring them to the synagogue.

Dr. Bick was well aware of the Jewish voters' views, but he believed in the ultimate strength of wealth among the Jewish population that suffered great poverty. Furthermore, he believed in the crafty election hypocrites who in each election always achieved their goals. His confidence lay in the fact that in all three towns he could enjoy the services of the mayors, members of the city councils and clerks of the local authorities who prepared the voter lists.

Berish Shtern once bragged out loud about the tricks he would use during the elections. Those who had two personal names he would list three separate times in the voter lists. If they were loyal to him, he would let them vote three times, while if they belonged to the rival party he would disqualify them altogether – an easy task, for he was the chairman of the voting committee.

With the approach of election day, the conflicts between the parties grew to quite monstrous proportions. Polish journalists swept through the region conducting propaganda in favor of Dr. Bick. Anyone who wanted to earn a few guldens was at his service. Even the central elections committee in Galicia sent a man to warn the voters against voting for Dr. Bloch.

In Buczacz the mayor Berish Shtern told the Christian inhabitants that the Jews were protecting Dr. Bloch because of his hatred towards Christians and that Dr. Bloch wanted to imprison two respectable Catholic priests. Public notices, written by Jewish lawyers, attacked Dr. Bloch and supported Dr. Bick.

A few days before the elections Dr. Bloch left Lvov and set out for Buczacz. Prior to his departure he visited the region's governor and demanded that his list receive appropriate representation in the local election committees in order to assure clean and honest elections. This was promised to him. On his arrival in Buczacz nearly all of the town's Jews were waiting for him at the railroad station. He was received by a cheering and joyous crowd, but was forced to take private lodgings since the regional officer forbade all hotels and restaurants to offer him a room. Inspection of the voters' list was impossible because it was delivered by the mayor Berish Shtern. Two days before the elections the Jewish voters had still not received I. D. cards and ballot slips.

During these two days – Saturday and Sunday – all the Jewish voters gathered in front of the city council demanding I.D. cards and ballot slips. However, the mayor refused to issue even a single card. (The demonstrators did not leave the premises even for a moment and conducted the Sabbath service under the stars.) After sending a telegraph to the regional governor, an order was given to comply with the voters' requests. However, the mayor issued only 20 ballot slips. The voters ran to the regional officer, who commanded they at once be given the necessary documents – although only those containing Dr. Bick's name. Once again war burst out. The voters were not deterred and did not leave the battlefield. The demands for the documents only grew as time went by. The gendarmerie intervened and tried to drive away the grumbling voters from the city council. But to no avail! The gendarmes threatened with rifles only to see the voters expose their chests and cry out: "Shoot!"

The struggle lasted two days and finally, after many protests before the prime minister and the regional governor, the voters received I.D. cards and ballot slips. On Monday the elections, which were to last two days, began. The mayor appointed two of his men to be representatives of "the Bloch party" and introduced them to the regional officer, who in turn appointed them members of the election committee. The Bloch party was without representation on the electoral committee, thus enabling Berish Shtern to carry out his plan without interference. Indeed after counting the votes for the first day of the elections, Dr. Emil Bick had received almost a two-thirds majority. The results from Kolomyya and Sniatyn weren't that satisfying either. Dr. Bick's agents and supporters rejoiced after hearing the results and Dr. Bick himself arranged a festive meal in Lvov to celebrate his victory. In Jewish quarters spirits were low. The Jewish leaders were in despair. Shtern's trickery had gained Dr. Bick's party a majority of approximately 450 votes and they were close to accepting defeat. However, after a secret conference at three A.M. it was decided to fight on. The motivating spirit for this decision came from a Pole, the writer Wisniowski, who personally supported Dr. Bloch. His reasoning was based on the fact that the voters who sold out to Bick's agents had voted under their supervision that same day, while voters voting according to their own free will had no one to press them, meaning they could have chosen to vote the next day. Assuming that these people were Bloch supporters, one could conclude that the next day would be Bloch's and therefore the struggle must go on.

The Polish writer's encouraging words introduced new motivation. Carriages were brought to transport suburban voters to the polling station. Women and children went from door to door urging people to vote. Some individuals such as teachers and butchers, who feared the community leaders, were in hiding. However, their own wives handed them over and they were taken to vote. There was great excitement. Women ran to their family graves to pray for Bloch's victory. Synagogues were full of praying crowds.

The Pole's wonderful idea proved to be correct. The majority of voters the next day were Bloch supporters. The promises of Bick's agents to build a synagogue for the Jews and a church with an organ for the Christians did not change people's minds. The Jewish heart was not for sale. At the election's end, the Jews' efforts on the second day turned out to be decisive. Dr. Bloch won by a small majority and was to be the representative delegate in the parliament. Word spread wide and fast. The expressions of joy throughout the streets of Buczacz, Kolomyya[**] and Sniatyn can hardly be portrayed. Joy and festivity were not witnessed in the towns alone but throughout all of Galicia. Everywhere Jews wanted to hear of the electoral struggle between Bloch and Bick, more than of the elections in their own regions.

It was a David and Goliath struggle. On one side stood the great power of wealth, the central elections committee, the mayors' and their clerks' violence, regional officers and the local election committees, the outrageous incitement of the biased press and the opposition of the Jewish community leaders.

While against them stood a man on his own, empty-handed, with nothing but the support of the Jewish voters.

However, Dr. Emil Bick, who had invested great sums in the election confrontation, refused to acknowledge defeat. He commanded the collection of evidence for acts of fraud committed during the elections and submitted an appeal to the parliament. Interestingly, this appeal included all the acts of fraud perpetrated by his supporters, such as counting votes of the dead, multiple voting of individuals, etc. Bloch's supporters submitted memoranda to the parliament which proved that acts of fraud were committed by Bick's party supporters. In the memorandum that arrived from Buczacz the violent acts by the mayor and the regional officers against the Jewish voters were described. The parliamentary certificates committee proposed to conduct an investigation and to submit a report before the parliament. The report, which was submitted 3 years later, confirmed only the acts of coercion and fraud of Dr. Bick and his agents. His appeal was rejected and by a majority of votes the parliament accepted Dr. Bloch's candidacy.

The electoral district of Buczacz-Kolomyya-Sniatyn, the most populated one in Galicia, had a Jewish majority. Every voter believed it was his right to demand of his representative in parliament that he stand beside him in all matters concerning his business. If heavy taxes were laid upon him, if a governmental clerk offended him in any way, or an anti-Semitic judge poured his wrath upon him, in all such cases a Jew would turn to Dr. Bloch for help. Also Jews from other parts of Galicia turned to Dr. Bloch for assistance. Day after day he visited the central authorities and various ministers lobbying for the sake of the mistreated Jews in Galicia. Although this sort of lobbying was burdensome and unpleasant, Dr. Bloch fulfilled his duty patiently and faithfully, reminding himself that "the needs of the Jewish people are great but their knowledge is small." He hoped that in the next elections the Jews would learn to appreciate his committed service and that no Jew would vote against him. However, even this hope proved false.

By the end of the year 1890 the parliamentary term had ended and new elections were set for the beginning of 1891. In the electoral district of Buczacz, Kolomyya and Sniatyn Dr. Bloch's rivals had long begun the process of undermining his third attempt for a parliamentary seat. Once again Dr. Emil Bick was the opposing candidate, although with the aid of prominent Galician Jewish figures a recurrence of the previous dirty struggle between the two was prevented. Dr. Bick was promised the candidacy for the towns of Brody and Zloczow on condition that he waive his right to candidacy for the three towns Buczacz-Kolomyya-Sniatyn, which Dr. Bloch would receive. This concession was correctly seen as a victory for Dr. Bloch. However, not for long. Suddenly a new candidate appeared who also believed that the mandate could be bought with money and taken from the hands of Dr. Bloch.

This new candidate was a Jew from Paris named Leon Meizlis, grandson of the famous Rabbi Horshai and son-in-law of the Russian millionaire Brodski. His candidacy was supported by the "Makhzikey Hadat" Society and by the Belz hasidic court. The aforementioned society published a weekly Hebrew newspaper. Two months prior to the elections the society turned to Dr. Bloch and asked him to donate 5000 guldens for the paper, a sum that weekly papers had to deposit as security at the law court. Since the society lacked this sum, they believed that by promising Dr. Bloch their total support he would provide it. Dr. Bloch, whose total belongings did not add up to this amount, naturally refused. Furthermore, he refused to collect donations from the Jews of Vienna for this purpose. This rejection brought about the candidacy of Leon Meizlis, representing the ultra-orthodox.

Leon Meizlis, with great confidence and enthusiasm, set out to achieve his goal. He visited the regional governor in Lvov and plainly stated to him that the mandate must be his and that he was positive he would get it even if it cost him 100,000 guldens. Meizlis spoke with such conviction that it was clear how certain he was of his victory. On his return to Paris certain doubts concerning his Austrian citizenship and right to be elected arose. However, Berish Shtern, the mayor of Buczacz, helped him in arranging all the necessary documents. Meizlis's representatives swept through the region distributing money, especially to the poor. He circulated defamatory leaflets addressed to both Jews and Christians. To the Jews he wrote that Dr. Bloch's deeds were always harmful to the ultra orthodox. His representatives traveling through the villages told the peasants that Dr. Bloch quarreled with Catholic priests in order to ridicule them before their congregations and added that if he were chosen for the third time he would probably become Minister of Labor and enact a labor law forcing all peasants to do hard labor for the Jews.

The agents would also claim that Dr. Bloch was planning to convert churches and monasteries into governmental warehouses. Such lies were spread widely among the peasants for many days. Peasants received wine in abundance. Christian propagandists were given large sums in order to unite all Polish and Ukrainian peasants in favor of Leon Meizlis. However, Meizlis's notion that with the help of the Christian vote he would succeed in overcoming Bloch was doomed to fail. The Jews weren't tempted by the large sums and they also knew how to treat Leon Meizlis. At Kolomyya he met with abuse and cursing that would have made any honest candidate resign immediately. He dared not even enter Buczacz. His men went out to meet him an hour's ride away from town, received his money and promised that his candidacy was guaranteed.

Thus was conducted the Bloch-Meizlis electoral struggle, one between two obviously unequal strengths. On the one hand there was a rich candidate distributing a fortune without achieving a thing. On the other hand was a man who knew how to fight against anti-Semitism and for Jewish rights. One could, of course, guess the results in advance. Bloch's victory was not doubted for a moment. However, in the midst of the campaign something unexpected occurred. The Polish priests, who were always known for their anti-Semitic views, decided suddenly to take the mandate from the Jews and to announce a candidate of their own. They told the peasants that there was no great difference between Dr. Bloch and Leon Meizlis and that good Christians must not vote for Jews whatever the case. Thus arose the candidacy of Count Starzanski, a Pole and a true enemy of the people of Israel. This candidacy was supported, of course, by the Polish central elections committee at Lvov. Also the Polish press, with its well known anti-Semitic editors and assimilated Jews, supported Count Starzanski and poured out daily words of slander against the Jews and against Dr. Bloch.

Clerks in the region began persecuting the Jews in various ways. The Poles were hoping to intimidate the Jewish majority with the incited drunken peasants. The Poles saw that the Jews were competing among themselves and believed that for this reason their candidate would receive the mandate. However, their assumptions turned out to be false. Even though Dr. Bloch had to fight now on two fronts he did not give up. Everywhere he went he was received with great enthusiasm. In Buczacz a great reception was held for him at the train station; clapping and cheering followed his speech. He was unanimously declared as the town's candidate. Indeed, the elections of the 4th and 5th of May 1891 proved that the Jews were committed to Dr. Bloch. He was reelected, receiving 2118 votes, Count Starzanski 1178 votes, and Leon Meizlis 97 votes.

Elections in Buczacz and Sniatyn were held without disruptions, although there were riots and bloodshed in Kolomyya where farmers supporting Count Starzanski went through town abusing Jewish voters. All shops were closed. One Jew was stabbed to death and others were wounded; the town's Jewish cemetery was desecrated. The rioters were later punished. Leon Meizlis the pathetic candidate who was mainly responsible for these riots and who wasted a fortune in order to receive 97 votes, fell ill a few months after his defeat and died.

****

Dr. Bloch's blessed actions for the Jews in the Austrian parliament were like thorns in the eyes of the anti-Semitic delegates headed by Prince Lichtenstein. These delegates were resolved to do anything in their means to bring about Dr. Bloch's resignation. They weren't content with the spreading of outrageous propaganda from the parliament's podium, but also reached an agreement with the president of the Polish Club, Mr. von Zlaski (who was known for his anti-Semitic views) in which he was to force Dr. Bloch to return his mandate. In June 1895 the head of the Polish Club suggested that Dr. Bloch give up his mandate voluntarily. He explained to Dr. Bloch that he gave his word to Prince von Lichtenstein to have this done. Von Zlaski continued to threaten that the mandate would be canceled completely if he refused to comply, for as president of the Polish Club he was capable of gathering a majority in favor of such a decision. Dr. Bloch had no choice but to surrender to the forces against him and to turn once again to the voters.

However, the attacks on him from the anti-Semitic party did not cease after his concession. The anti-Semites did all they could to prevent him from being reelected. Dr. Bloch could not imagine that under such conditions there would be Jews who would stand against his bid to be reelected, thus turning them into allies of the anti-Semites. However, one such Jew existed, the lawyer Maximilian Trachtenberg, a former mayor of Kolomyya.

The Prime Minister at the time was Count Badni who took upon himself to rule over Austria by Galician methods. The former president, Count Taaffe, often expressed his view that as long as there were anti-Semitic delegates in Parliament it was only fair and to the government's benefit that a man capable of standing up to them also be there. However, Count Badni had his own views. His statesmanship was based solely on power. This policy of his was a complete failure. His failures were so many that shortly afterwards he had to resign. He was successful, though, in one matter. He prevented Dr. Bloch from being reelected in order to save from disgrace the head of the Polish Club. An order was given to all the governors' clerks in Lvov to use any means possible against Dr. Bloch. Jewish voters left town during elections to avoid complications. Factory owners, who supported Dr. Bloch, were summoned by the regional officer and forced to pay large sums for election expenses for Dr. Trachtenberg. They couldn't refuse, for if they did their factories would be shut down for "sanitary reasons." Tax collectors warned voters against failing to vote for the government's candidate, Dr. Trachtenberg. A warning from a Galician tax collector could not be taken lightly. Gendarmes stood by the hall where the voting took place, preventing Jewish voters from even coming near it. Thus, Dr. Trachtenberg's victory was guaranteed.

Also the anti-Semites in Vienna headed by Dr. Karl Lueger, who was one of the Christian-Social Party leaders, did not stand by. Telegrams sent by them to various people in the electoral district contained promises of donating great sums for propaganda financing and urgent demands to fight against Dr. Bloch. Acts of violence during these elections and all kinds of trickery determined the election results in advance. Dr. Trachenberg received the mandate.

Liberal members of the Club were very upset by the way their president acted, but they were a minority. To protests of this sort, Zlaski once cynically responded: "I admit that Dr. Bloch has been of great benefit to the Jews and that he was essential to them, however I do not admit that the Jews' messiah had to be born right in the middle of the Polish Club."

The newspaper "Idishe Prese" wrote among other things: "Dr. Bloch removed from the parliament the "scientific" aspect of the "Jewish question," the "scientific" reasoning for the slander of Jews and Judaism. By this he earned a permanent place for himself. He has now left the parliament, the doors closing after him with a jarring sound. But in the very moment that they closed, there slipped back into the parliament the terrible demon of corruption. He is here once again, for the person who drove him out is no longer here."

Dr. Koppel Blum

* Closure of factories for "sanitary reasons," unlawful use of police force, etc.

** In Kolomyya a Bloch party was founded. It was named "The Good Youth" and had an agreement with Polish intellectual circles headed by the Polish writer Wisniowski. According to this agreement the Poles promised to support Bloch's candidacy on the condition that Bloch's party would support their candidate in the municipal elections that would take place shortly after the elections for parliament. This agreement was carried out fully.

Voters' meeting in 1907

A voters' meeting in 1907 [picture]. The candidate was Dr. Nathan Birnbaum (Mattityahu Acher), who appears in the middle of the assembly below; also Agnon is at this meeting. Here are some of the people who were identified:

Dr. Nathan Birnbaum (marked by arrow) Leon Wechsler
Farnhecht
Matisyohu Weinrib
Joseph Wahrmann
Samuel Hirsch Leblang
Dr. Feller
Samuel Teller
Bertshe Tanne
Leibush Glantser
Samuel Berger
Sh.Y. Agnon (marked below to the right)
Moses Gutwald
Zusia Avner
Khayim Kreminer
Alter Tishler (tinsmith)

Shvarts (tailor) (Prince)
Leyzer Horowitz
Khayim Shechter
Hersh Izner
Isaac Pohorile
Dr. Isaiah Hecht
Abraham Spirer
Joel Harzes
Betsalel Kreminer
Moses Joseph Gotfried
Solomon Frankel
Asher Zilbershein (brother of Dr. Zilbershein)
Heinrich Edelshtein
Mikhl Zisberg
Itshele Anderman
Moses L. Kornshpan
Leyzer Frifeld
Lucyow (Christian, socialist activist Nagurzenka)
Solomon Rosenblum (tailor)
Aaron Rauchov
Fibush Leibush Pohorile (grandfather of the translation coordinator)
Khayem Gaster
Hersh Ginsberg
Yosl Potoker (carpenter)
Ziskind Hertsman
Mordekhai Segal
Sholem Klemper
Abba Gross
Mikhl Haller
Isaac Hersh Visser
Isaac Balin
Jacob Nacht
Moti Kokols (on the cart)
Khayim Helitser
Kopl Hazokn
Eber Vitsinger
Khayem Bauchman (carpenter)
Ezekiel Sh. Rosenthal (carpenter)
Berish Hofman
Borekh Langberg
Isaac Cohen
Tsvi Heller, Leyzer Gotfried (on the balcony)
Ben-Zion Berler
Mendl Shternberg

[Page 142]

From My Memories
by Dr. Zvi Heller
Translated by Jessica Cohen

The situation of the Jews in the town and the surrounding areas was harsh, as it was in all the small and medium sized places in Eastern Galicia. This was because there was no industry there and the area farmers and Christian citizens were poor – and the few wealthy Jews handled mid-sized export business of agricultural produce.

Among the educated, the landlords and the common people, there were many who were courageous, independent, and willing to provide civil and political defense, throughout all the periods of enslavement to the Starosta (the district governor) and his servants in the community and the town, in the taxation and municipal tax offices.

In all the local elections, there were representatives of the opposition to the community and town rulers, although the famous electoral system in Galicia, and particularly in Buczacz, prevented any hope of victory. But in the elections for the parliament in Vienna, too, Buczacz was united with the town of Kolomei, one of the "Jewish" districts, because there was a slight hope for Jewish victory there.

It is worth noting that while in Kolomei, the national Jewish factors and the independent citizens had to wage their war for the Austrian parliament against powerful organizations of merchants and artisans, *Chassidim* and intelligentsia, who supported assimilation and the regime, in Buczacz the "mushkim" and their followers only existed thanks to the support of the district governor, with most of the Jewish population in town opposing them.

And this is why the Jews in this district were successful even decades earlier, when the reactionary electoral system was prevalent, in electing a Jewish representative, despite the severe pressure from the authorities in Israel and in the district.

The well-known Rabbi Moshe Sofer (Shriever) of Krakow was elected as the Jewish representative of the Buczacz Kolomei district in the Viennese parliament. After he resigned from this office, Dr. Josef Bloch, a famous national activist among Austrian Jews ran in the bi-elections. Dr. Bloch was the editor of the newspaper "*Jüdisches Wochenblatt*" [*The Jewish Weekly*] in Vienna, and he served as a rabbi in the town of Baden near Vienna. He was originally from the town of Sanz in Western Galicia. The opponents of the national candidate, Dr. Bloch, were the known assimilators Dr. Bik and Meisel, whose traitorous role was to break the unity of the Jews and thus enable the victory of the Polish *Szlachta* representative, Dr. Starzinski.

The Jews fought tirelessly against threats, coercion and persecution by the authorities, and Dr. Bloch was elected to parliament as the representative of the Jews of Kolomei and Buczacz, among whom were many notables, such as Yankel Farnhof and others.

This victory also strengthened national awareness and the fighting spirit of the Jewish masses in Buczacz, which lead to the re-election of Dr. Bloch as their representative again in the following elections, against Dr. Starzinski, whose influence among the authorities in Galicia and Vienna was powerful. When Dr. Bloch ran as the Jewish candidate for the third time, the authorities realized that it was not likely that the Jews of Buczacz and Kolomei would betray a Jewish national candidate in favor of a Polish Christian, and they ran a Jewish assimilator against Dr. Bloch – Dr. Trachtenberg of Kolomei who was, incidentally, a fine man and had excelled in his position as mayor, in the many good deeds he did for the area Jews. After the authorities increased their pressure on the Jews and endangered their economic status, Dr. Bloch decided to withdraw his candidacy, in protest.

The Jews of Buczacz did not lose their spirit, and in 1906 many townspeople joined the Jewish students and the Zionist intelligentsia, along with socialist and radical groups among the Poles and the Ukrainians, in a campaign for democratization of the electoral system. The elections for the Austrian parliament were therefore held in 1907 based on the new democratic law. But the Galician Poles artificially installed an electoral map system, in order to achieve mandates in Eastern Galicia, at the expense of the Jews and the Ukrainians. They had united under a joint protection pact, which gave the Zionists, with the help of the Ukrainians, two mandates from villages and small towns (from the Buczacz area, Dr. Gevel, an attorney and Zionist activist from Lvov, and from the Czortkow area, Professor Mahler, a scientist and Zionist activist from Prague). Together with the head of the Galician Zionists (Adolf Stand, who was elected in the Brody district) and Dr. Straucher, the Jewish leader of Bukowina, they created the National Jewish Club in the Viennese Parliament.

The Buczacz Jews in 1907 took upon themselves the difficult task of achieving victory in Buczacz for the national candidate, Dr. Nathan Birenbaum of Vienna (a different Matityahu), the well-known author and formerly the first secretary of Dr. Herzl.

In these elections, the Poles selected as Dr. Birenbaum's opponent the wealthy landowner from Wisa, and they attached the towns of Zaleszczyki, Sniatyn, Borszczow and Tlumacz to Buczacz, and they added many villages to this municipal district, in order to weaken the Jewish majority in the district.

In the picture in this book we see the enthusiasm of the masses, among them Jewish students and farmers, including Ukrainians. Next Dr. Birenbaum stands Leon Weksler, the political activist and longtime Zionist in Buczacz and Lvov (secretary of the central election committee) and secretary of the Jewish Club in the Austrian parliament in Vienna, as well as secretary of the national club of Eastern Galician Jews in the Diaspora. Leon Weksler, who passed away in Jerusalem roughly a year ago, was leader of the activity in Buczacz at the time.

The pressure applied on the voters from the municipality and the *Starosti*, the *Gendarmerie* and the tax offices, was harsh. In the elections, they used both physical force and the military: in Drohowitz the army attacked the Jewish voters, and over the bodies of three Jewish victims, the assimilator Dr. Lewenstein entered the parliament instead of the Zionist candidate Dr. Gershon Ziper. This happened in Buczacz as well. Army troops took control of the main bridge over the Stripa river, which leads to the municipal offices where the elections were held, to close off the route to the Jewish voters. In the town hall offices and the nearby firehouse, they gathered two-hundred people, mostly rabble, who drank brandy and ate sausage all day, and went in and out of the voting booth every five minutes and voted in place of other voters, who were detained by the bridge. They also voted in place of hundreds of deceased voters, who the mayor had placed on the voting list. And we recall Jakob Grosfeld's call in the city hall courtyard: "Cohens, come out, for the dead are coming." Many Jews dared to defy the army and forced their way over the bridge.

Dr. Birenbaum sent telegraphs to the interior ministers and the army in Vienna, protesting the fraud and the army units, but Galicia was abandoned to the Polish rulers, and Dr. Birenbaum received most of the votes, but was left out of the parliament. The protestations presented by Buczacz Jews to the parliamentary election committee were never reviewed. But in the second area of the Buczacz district, the election activity was run by the Zionist youth from Buczacz, including the author of these lines. With the help of the Jews in the towns and the village Ukrainians, we managed to elect a Zionist representative, Dr. Gavel. We also assisted the district of nearby Czortkow to elect Professor Mahler, as stated previously.

This situation engendered an increase in anti-Semitism among Polish teachers and students in the public *gimnazjum*. The students created a "club" with an explicit anti-Jewish agenda, and began to inform on their Jewish classmates' Zionist activities and on the distribution of Zionist newspapers and pamphlets in the school, as well as on their active participation in the elections. The *gimnazjum* administration organized disciplinary action against the heads of the Zionist Jewish youth, who happened to be our classmates – such as Zvi Heller, Laiser Gottfried, Haim Kriegel and others. The school administration received a Jewish informant's report from Jaslowicz, whereby the *gimnazjum* student Heller had given a speech there in the Beit Midrash during the elections, against the authorities and supporting immigration to Eretz Yisrael. The Jewish students went into defensive mode, and obtained the protocol book from a Christian student, a member of the "club" who opposed anti-Semitism and demanded that the educational authorities in Lvov prosecute the anti-Semitists. This counter-attack managed to weaken the anti-Semites' boldness, and the trial against the Jews ended with one student being expelled to a different *gimnazjum*, and light punishments for three others, even though it was known that the Zionist student organizations were located right across from the *gimnazjum*. During World War I, when I was on the Russian front, I met my acquaintance from Jaslowicz, who confessed to me, being as no one knew what the next day would bring on the front, that he had informed on me to the *gimnazjum* headmaster, because he was afraid that my Eretz Yisrael propaganda would "damage his livelihood" as an agent for tickets to America. In the town and the vicinity, we continued our political campaigns and national education, and in 1910, when the national census was held – my friends in Buczacz and I campaigned in support of registering Yiddish and Hebrew as our languages, in contradiction to the authorities' requirement that the Jews should record "Polish". Although our activity was illegal, because one was permitted to record only one of the official languages, the Jewish speech makers and the citizens performed their national duty and received administrative penalties, detentions and fines. Together with my friend Haim Avner, an attorney and a leader of the movement in Czortkow, I once traveled late at night in December 1910 to the distant towns of Wisnjowczik and Zlotnik, between Buczacz and Podhajce, and we got stuck in a frozen lake and only reached the town at midnight. All the local Jews were waiting for us anxiously, and when we arrived we went straight to the synagogue, where we lectured to all the town residents. In the gimnazjum, too, during that period, the Jewish students wrote in their declarations that Hebrew and Yiddish were their languages, despite the coercion and threats against the students and their parents, and despite the risk of expulsion from school or the danger of losing a year of study. There was also, of course, pressure on the part of the authorities, by means of influential Jews. Thus, for example, the Jewish mayor contacted Moshe Weisser, who was not involved in political activism at all, but was a decent and educated Jew and could serve as an example for others – and informed him that he had been elected, with his assistance, to the city council and that he would have to declare that his language was Polish. Moshe Weisser refused, of course, and did not receive the mandate offered by the squire.

In such an atmosphere of national tension, the year 1911 arrived, the year of the parliamentary elections. In order to prevent the claim of the Poles, that the Zionists are "traitors and enemies of Poland," who bring German candidates from Vienna, the Zionist center in Lvov decided to run only Galician candidates this time. Dr. Birenbaum and Dr. Raphael Landau, both from Vienna, who had left the Zionist movement and become "unaffiliated" activists, arrived in our district without permission from the Zionist center, but they were turned away. The center set as candidates for our three districts: 1) the Buczacz town district (comprised of five towns, including Sniatyn, Zaleszczyki, Borszczow and Tlumacz), the central Zionist activist Dr. Michael Ringel, who was then a young lawyer in Lvov; 2) the district of Buczacz and the vicinity – Dr. Saltz, the longtime Zionist lawyer in Tarnow, who was a *Hovevei Zion* leader and founder of the first Galician settlement in Eretz Yisrael, Machanayim in the Upper Galilee; 3) the district of Czortkow and the vicinity – Dr. Shmuel Rapoport, a religious Zionist activist, religious scholar and philosopher.

I was responsible for coordinating the affairs in the three districts and this was not easy, because of the scope and the amount of locations, but also because of financial reasons. Apart from the Czortkow district, where the candidate himself covered his own expenses, being a wealthy landowner, and apart form the final weeks in the Buczacz district, when the expenses were taken over by Dr. Ringel, who owned a "fresh" dowry – I had to raise large loans and bear this cost too. It is interesting that after a few weeks of activity, the chairman of the center, Dr. Gershon Ziper, came to Buczacz to prepare the declaration of candidacy for Dr. Ringel, who was completing his law exams at the time. When I came as the head of a delegation of the town elders and notables, to welcome Dr. Ziper at the train station, he was amazed that this Heller, with whom he had been corresponding for several weeks, as the coordinator of the three districts, where he was also obtaining large loans and using the Hebrew name of Zvi – was not, as he had thought, an elderly educated man and a wealthy merchant, but rather no more than a "studentil" of roughly 21 years of age.

Since Dr. Ringel happened to be related to the "ruling" family in Jewish Buczacz – the government was afraid that it would lose the family's traditional support and they had to run the head of the family against him, the mayor of Buczacz. And although he was not considered a serious or threatening opponent, he was an old expert at electoral matters of the known type. The army did not interfere this time, but local coercion gangs were formed, mercenaries and thugs and "protection men", whose job was to create an atmosphere of pressure and terror against the Jewish and Christian population. They used to pickpocket the voting certificates from the voters, without which they could not vote. We had to organize defense groups and attack forces against these gangs, from among the youth and the people. Groups of students from academic societies in Czernowicz and Tarnow were sent to help us. One of them, Dr. Eliyahu Tish, is now in Jerusalem. Another person who came to assist Buczacz was the old representative Ernst Briter, a liberal and radical Pole, who was a friend of Israel, who received the mandate in Lvov with the help of the Jews. He brought with him his entourage, which was known from the "popular" electoral war in Lvov. He was not afraid to barge into the offices of the authorities and the voting booth locations, and object to the many forgeries. He set up his headquarters in the restaurant belonging to our townsman Leib Roll, now in Israel.

We managed to gather most of the voting cards, but before our voters reached the voting booths, the gang members voted by means of forgeries of these same cards. And when my late father, Alter Heller (Haim Yehoshua) objected forcefully to these forgeries, as the representative of the Zionist party in the voting booth – the representative of the authorities threatened him, telling him that there was to be no shouting there and that if he personally knew the people who were repeatedly voting under false names, he should write down the facts and the objection in the protocol, and this would serve as the basis for an appeal.

The central regime, Count Bowzinski, was still afraid of the election results, and especially wanted to prevent a Zionist Ukrainian alignment in Easter Galicia, and Jewish voting against the government candidates in Western Galicia. He therefore made an agreement with the Zionist center and promised it 4 or 5 mandates, including one for Dr. Ringel in the Buczacz district and also for the candidates Adolf Stand, Dr. Reich, Dr. Ziper and Dr. Tohn. But the Count simply cheated the Zionist center, and after the Zionists did not receive the Ukrainians' assistance in Eastern Galicia and cancelled their separate parties in Western Galicia – the noble Count violated the agreement, betrayed the Zionist center, and by means of force, forgeries and threats, the Poles caused the Jewish candidates to fail, including Dr. Ringel, by appointing Stern Brish as the Buczacz representative to the parliament. He did not do anything and continued to fulfill this honorary role for a short while in independent Poland, because in Eastern Galicia, which was not yet an official part of Poland, election manipulation was not permitted and the government asked the Polish representatives from Galicia to participate in the first Sejm as a founding meeting.

In 1922 the first democratic elections restored the Jewish national representative to the Buczacz district (which was called the district of Tarnopol, Czortkow, Buczacz).

It is worth noting two characteristic details. When the Zionist parties in Galicia united with the economic unions and the professional unions with a Zionist affiliation, into one list and divided the districts between them, only the Buczacz district candidate asked to appear in his own town. Incidentally, he was the representative of the Zionist labor party – "*Hitachdut haPoel haZair – Ze'irei Zion* ". It is interesting that the ruling family accepted the fact that during that period only a Zionist could be a candidate, and they did not object to their townsman being the candidate. However, their dynastic approach led them to claim that their family also included Zionists. Most of this family voted, as Jews and good Zionists, for the official candidate for their town – and only a few could not overcome their tendencies and during the first months after the elections they regarded their chosen representative coldly. But gradually, all the circles of the town and the district, including the representatives of the authorities, got used to their representative, the young Zvi Heller.

The Buczacz *Landsmannschaft* in Vienna also reached a decision to congratulate their town, which had achieved a national representative. They sent a congratulatory letter to their townsman and the friend of their youth, for his election as parliamentary representative of his community and the district.

In 1927 there were elections in Poland again, this time under the reign of the *Sanacja* people, who had decided to obtain a majority in the elections, at the expense of the Polish opposition parties and the national minorities – including the Jews.

The Jewish club at the Polish *Sejm*, which comprised 34 representatives and 12 senators, decreased its presence significantly under this electoral system, and in Eastern Galicia the Jews "were left with" only 4 districts: Lvov, Stanislaw-Kolomei, Tarnopol-Buczacz, and Zaloczow-Brody.

However, since the author of these lines, as the candidate for Tarnopol-Buczacz, was known as an opponent of the "*ugodah*" (compromise) with the Grabski government, and as the oppositional representative against the Andke government and the *Sanacja*, there was a plan in the government to lead to his downfall and to appease the general Zionists in another district. However, after notice reached all the towns and villages in our district from the local and district authorities, "that this could cause riots, because all the circles and activists from the moderate parties and the opponent parties support Heller," – they were forced to abandon this plan, and the result was that the candidate in the Tarnopol district received more votes than any of the Jewish candidates, namely, over 30 thousand votes. A Zionist was elected in Krakow with 15 thousand votes, in Stanislaw with 25 thousand, and in Zloczow with 20 thousand. When the government counted the votes, they determined that the Tarnopol-Buczacz candidate had received all the Jewish votes, and in addition some 3,000 votes from Christians in various locations. This was proven by the excess of votes which the Jewish list received in the same places, which was more than the total number of Jewish voters. The Christians voted for the Jewish list as invalids, retirees, laborers, artisans, government and private clerks, and so forth, all of whom benefited from representative Heller's proposals and his parliamentary fight for their basic interests.

At the end of this term I did not run again, and the district of Tarnopol-Buczacz was left without a Jewish representative the whole time. World War II broke out and the town and vicinity were occupied by the Nazi forces and later annexed to the Ukraine as part of Soviet Russia.

The Zionist Movement in the Town

During the *Hovevei Zion* period as well, Buczacz was one of the first places in Galicia where the movement found support both in circles of the elderly, the *Chassidim* and the educated, and among the youth and the intelligentsia. During this period, a Zionist union was created, with two purposes: to assist the *Yishuv* in Eretz Yisrael, for which purpose it was in contact with the center in Tarnow under the direction of Dr. Saltz, and it also had a social cultural purpose. The establishment of the society created a sort of revolution in the town. Apart from Zionists such as Shmuel Teller, Yitzhak Hirsch Weisser, Hirsch Stern and his sons, Yakov Leib Alfenbein, Yisrael Shlomo Stern and others, the society was also joined by young intelligentsia, some of whom remained Zionists their whole lives, such as Dr. Sigmund Goldsteub (son of Israel Ber) who lived and was active in Sniatyn and his brother Leon (who is in Haifa), Dr. Farnhof, who was a representative at the First Zionist Congress and even young men such as Anshel Mosler and Dr. Rosenbaum, who did not have an ideological affiliation with Zionism, joined the first society in the town, and like Dr. Diamant Herman in Lvov, who later moved to the P.P.S. Dr. Mosler moved from the P.P.S to the Z.P.S as the founder of this movement, which was later succeeded in Galicia by the Bund. In this society there were lectures on Eretz Yisrael subjects and on general cultural affairs. It was located in a private apartment in the "Rink" and was abolished in 1902. After two or three years the Zionist society opened again, under the name of "Zion." Following the great shock of the Kishinev pogroms, there was another great national awakening in the public. There was a mourning and protest gathering in the synagogue, the students sung *"Eli Zion ve'Eria"*. During the gathering organized by the community in the synagogue in 1905, in honor of the Polish holiday on May 3, the Zionist youth stood by the gates and did not let the people inside. With calls of "all those who believe in *Adonai*, go home," the youth entered the synagogue, led by the student Sigman (now named Menatseach) and dispersed the audience, and Yosef Tischler (now an engineer in Jerusalem) and others collected contributions for the pogrom victims. The new Zionist society opened on Koljowa St., opposite Meir Torton's house. They had a Zionist *minyan*, including Ansel Friedman (whose son is in Eretz Yisrael) as a volunteer cantor, and on the Sabbaths and the high holidays, some of the Zionist landlords and the Zionist youth prayed there. Libusch Freid was chosen as the society chairman. He later lived in Vienna, and died on his way to Eretz Yisrael in 1939, on the shores of Haifa onboard a ship that was expelled to Mauritius.

The society was inaugurated with Libusch Freid's lecture on the Rambam. Local and guest lecturers came to the society, among whom was Dr. Avraham Silberstein, who was later an important activist and assistant chairman of the Zionist Congress tribunal. He died two years ago in Geneva, where he was active throughout the war years in assisting Hitler's victims in the occupied countries, as well as Jewish refugees. He came home often from Lvov. The lecturers also included many local students. Dr. Hillel Susman was sent to lecture by the local committee in Stanislaw, and he was received by a large audience in the house of Avraham Shomer. The anti-Zionists from the P.P.S society made demonstrative appearances at the gatherings, led by Dr. Ansel Mosler and Gotwald. Chairman Loser Eisenberg was chosen as president (whose wife is now on Kibbutz Mishmar Ha'Emek), and his assistant was the tailor Hofinger. After Dr. Susman referred to the Kishinev pogroms in his lecture, Mosler and others shouted "a worker was killed there." In all the commotion, the P.P.S people tried to disrupt the gathering and their deputy began to conduct the meeting. The student Matityahu Weinrab (later a lawyer in Snook) objected to this profusely, explaining that as long as there was a chairman, the deputy had no right to conduct a meeting. Eventually, the Zionists moved the lecture to the "Zion" society auditorium. During this period there were also many lecturers at the time of the World Zionist polemic in support of and against "Uganda." And of course, the vast majority of Buczacz Zionists objected to the Uganda program. One special event should be noted. An anti-Zionist by the name of Speigel, who was a Hebrew teacher in the area villages, together with his friend B. Sigman-Rodes (father of Dr. Menatzeach), came to the society. Speigel had immigrated to America and became one of the Reform rabbis there, who were anti-Zionists at the time. Several years later he came to Buczacz as a guest and gave a lecture at the society, where he spoke of the need to "disseminate the Jews" and of "the destiny of Judaism among the Gentiles." The well-known preacher Avramson (father of the poet Avramson from America) also came to Buczacz as a guest and Zionist lecturer.

And another odd occurrence: in the village of Osowcza, near Buczacz, lived a wealthy Jew by the name of Fikholz, who had an educated daughter who married a young yeshiva student, a great prodigy.

One of his classmates at the Beit Midrash was originally from Buczacz, and was later to become the Professor of Semitic studies in Vienna, Dr. Heinrich Miller. Fikholz's son-in-law suddenly left his wife and ran away. Many years later it was learned that he came to Rome, where he converted to Christianity, and some say he was known in the Catholic church as Houston Bramen. According to this rumor, in the infamous trial of Dr. Bloch against the anti-Semite Rohling, he provided our enemies with Talmudic material against the Jews.

The Zion society was also active in supporting Eretz Yisrael, and its activists bought and sold shares of the Colonial Bank in London. The youth, led by student Naftali Ben Dov (now Menatseach) collected contributions for the JNF. And thus we find in the Zionist newspaper Wschod, from 1905/6, lists of fund-raisers, donors and donations which were collected from individuals in the Zion society and in the Klois and from the JNF blue boxes.

The society was also active in cultural endeavors and in disseminating the Hebrew language, as well as in political areas, both local and national. According to the instructions from the central committee in Lvov and the regional committee in Stanislaw, protest gatherings were called for in Buczacz and in Oscjia Zialona (where the "Hatikva" society operated), to protest the conspiracies of Dr. Bik against Zionism. They sent the prime minister, Baron Geutsch and the Zionist leader Dr. Shalit in Vienna, resolutions calling for democratization of the parliament elections and for the assignment of an autonomous borough for the Jewish voters, in order to assure the Jews full representation and to prevent them from having to become involved in the national strife in Austria between the Poles and the Ukrainians, and between the Germans and other Slavs. It is worth noting that at the congress of Jewish official delegates in Lvov, even Brish Stern, the mayor, objected to Dr. Bik's offense against the honor of the Zionist movement, even though he was usually a supporter of the regime.

In around 1907, the Zion society moved to its new premises in Yosef Bergman's house (next to the Polish church), under the direction of Loser Eisenberg, who was later removed from office because he propagandized for his relative, the chairman, in the city hall, and in the 1907 elections he came out against the national candidate. All the Jews who were disloyal to the Zionists' political war also left the society at that time. The society began Zionist activities and acted under the direction of Leibusch Freid. They organized many lectures and assisted the youth in learning Hebrew. They also had guest lecturers such as Dr. Silberstein, Rosenman and others who studied outside of Buczacz. After the 1907 elections, the rabbi from Stanislaw and the Zionist leader Dr. Mordechai Broide (who later moved to Lodz and died recently in Jerusalem), came to lecture at the Hanukah ball in the Ukrainian "Besside" hall. When he gave details of his fight against the assimilators, who laid obstacles for our political fight, he hinted at the presence of the government representative, with regards to the role of the traitors in Stanislaw and in Buczacz in the Austrian parliament elections. He said that as far back as the Hellenization period, anti-Jewish actions had occurred not only under the duress of Antiochus Epiphanes, but first and foremost under the initiative of the Jewish assimilators, the traitors and the sycophants.

The Zion society also met at Wolf Horn's house, and at the time of the victory of the "Young Turks" party, they held lively arguments about the effect of this Turkish revolution on the Zionist aspirations for a Jewish state in Eretz Yisrael. Dr. A. Dretler (later an attorney in Lvov) lectured on this subject.

The Zion society then moved to the Sternberg house (in the Anderman Hotel). During this period the society chairmen were Bezalel Herzas, Zalman Hoenig (whose son is on Kibbutz Gan-Shmuel) and my father Haim Yehoshua Heller (Alter), who continued his position until the beginning of World War I and the escape to Vienna. A group of youngsters was very active at that time, including Hirsch Balin, who was known as *Gospodarz*, because he took care of the society's economy. Paul Eidelstein (now in Haifa) and Shalom Weinstock (who now lives with his family on the moshav "Beit-Shearim" near Nahallal, and whose name is now Yosef Heller) and Yakov Halpern. The latter planned his *aliya* together with myself. This pioneering plan came to us not only under the influence of my father, of blessed memory, and the Eretz Yisrael newspaper, "*Hapoel Hatzair*", but also probably from the fact that there were three of our townspeople in Merchavia, in Eretz Yisrael, at the agricultural cooperative which was conducted according to Dr. Openheimer's system. The farm manager was Shlomo Dik (who came back to Israel after Hitler and worked as an expert on large agricultural plans, and died in Paris), and two graduates of the agricultural school in Slowodka in our area. They were sent to Israel by the Baron Hirsch fund. Their names were: Fritz and Moirer, and I do not know what became of them.

In 1912/13, appointed by the Buczacz district committee, we collected a large sum of money which was enough to obtain two seats in the Tenth Zionist Congress, which was held in Vienna in 1913. We gave one of the seats to Shlomo Schiller, the well-known writer and teacher who was at that time in Eretz Yisrael. My participation in this congress in 1913 in Vienna and in the conference of Russian Zionists which was held there – as a very young man – suddenly introduced me to the world Zionist movement and its activists, and to the labor movement representatives from Eretz Yisrael. From there, I went directly to the military service in an officers' training school in Czernowitz.

Jewish Youth Movement

At the same time, there developed in our town a Jewish youth movement, whose founders and pioneers were from the youth who studied at the *gimnazjum*. During those years, the members of the Polish socialist movement, the P.P.S. – *Promien* – were very active in the Polish *gimnazjum* in Buczacz, and they published a newsletter named "*Latarnia*". This movement was led by the student Chlebek, whose father was the Latin teacher, a very popular and knowledgeable man. It was characteristic of him to reach an exchange agreement with his friend Munisch Boyer, also an "unusual" person: he taught him Latin while Boyer taught him Hebrew.

When a Galician minister (*Namiestnik*) once came to Buczacz, young Chlebek and his friends organized a political demonstration against him outside the district council building. The demonstration was dispersed by the police, and Chlebek was expelled from the *gimnazjum*. Prominent among the Ukrainian youth, was Nazaruk (son of a furrier), who later became a minister in the Ukrainian government. Together with Dr. A. Mosler, he organized the first agricultural workers' strike in the entire area, and they published the newspaper "*Sluzba Dworska*" and even caused severe welfare riots. Austrian army troops were then sent in to oppress the "revolution" and save the Polish landowners, the "Paritz".

However, at the end of that year, in which the Jewish members of the "Promien" organization graduated from high school, a great turning point occurred among the Jews. There was a national, Zionist awakening among the *Noar HaLomed*, which began to organize Zionist clubs for education and independent studying of Jewish affairs and Hebrew. The student Matityahu Weinraub, who was knowledgeable in Hebrew from his father Haim Weinraub, a great scholar, was active in Buczacz in this area. Our townsman Dr. Avraham Silberstein often came from Lvov, where he was active in the youth movement "*Zeirei Zion*", and he imparted to the youth of Buczacz knowledge of Hebrew and Jewish history, which he had written himself but not published, because the manuscripts had been destroyed during the Russian occupation and the First World War. Silberstein also lectured on various Jewish and Zionist subjects. Sigman-Menatseach, who inherited the Hebrew spirit from his father, the learned teacher, organized a group of friends, including Bleukopf, Smeterling (today an attorney in Jerusalem), and the students Schitzer and Schecter, who came to Buczacz from the village of Strosow as a "*hospitant*" in the *gimnazjum*. The youngsters would meet in Tischler's private room. Later they met the student Katz, who had moved from Zloczow to his relatives in Buczacz, and with his help they expanded the club, whose chairman was Tischler and his deputy was Manio Pohorile (today a government clerk in Jerusalem). Matityahu Weinraub organized different clubs for adults in Munisch Heller's apartment, and a club for youngsters, including Gottfried Laiser, Zvi Heller and their friends from the intermediate classes. Our meetings were held in the storage cellar of Y. A. Gottfried in the Ashkenazi house next to the Weksler Hotel. The third club was led by Yonah Heller from Bozanow, who was a prominent member of the orchestra in the *gimnazjum*, run by Professor Geziov. Heller, Tischler, Menatseach and Gottfried later moved to the *gimnazjum* in Brzezany, which for some reason became the destination for expelled Buczacz students. Silberstein administered courses in Hebrew, Tanach and history, in the apartment of the Pohorile brothers, Emmanuel and David (now Dr. Pohorile, an attorney in Tel Aviv and chairman of the Buczacz *Landsmannschaft* in Israel). There was also a club for self education with lectures and discussions on various scientific topics. A student named Tau came to Buczacz from Kolomei, he was a learned man and organized a club for lectures and sing-alongs. Young people who knew Hebrew, such as Tischler, Menatseach, Halfon, Zvi Malex (now a rabbi in America), Yosef Shneor and others visited the *Ivria* club on Shabbat, where they spoke only Hebrew for one hour with the adults, or taught Hebrew in the community soup kitchen. After all the difficult beginnings during the stormy period, the Zionist youth movement shifted to organized action in twelve clubs, eight for *gimnazjum* students according to age and class, and four clubs for young girls. The movement was directed by a local committee, whose chairman was Zvi Heller. Haim Avner was the deputy and Yitzhak Shneor was secretary. The movement was affiliated with the Zionist organization of the *Noar Ha'Oved* in Lvov, "*Tzeirei Zion*", and some of us would participate in the movement's national conferences in Lvov, which were called *wiecy* and which were a sort of seminar for ideological and practical studies for the counselors. Most of the Zionist leadership in all the parties in Galicia and Vienna stemmed from this circle, because these conferences were also the arena for the first signs of the ideological differentiation in Zionism. Our twelve clubs in Buczacz conducted extremely broad organizational and cultural work. The members were required to learn Hebrew and to read the newspapers "*HaShachar*" and "*Moriah*" and to study from the textbooks on Zionism written by Czaczkes-Kirton (now named Dr. Kosta, a physician in Herzliya), the book "The National Existence of the Jews" (*Byt narodowy Zydow*) by Shlomo Schiller, the history of the Jews and Eretz Yisrael issues, and the literature of Jews. The students of the upper classes also read "*Wschod*", "*Welt*", "*HaOlam*" and "*Hamitzpeh*". The members were examined on all this material by a member committee, and this was a condition for acceptance into higher clubs. Throughout the year there was also systematic organizational activity, in order to introduce the students from the lower divisions into the movement.

The movement concentrated its activity in the rooms of the Hebrew school "*Safah Brura*", which was located at first in the house of Freid and Eisenberg in Garbarnia, and then in the Kaner house, which also served the Zionists as an election office because of its proximity to the city hall. And finally it was in the rear house of Abish Dik near the Stripa river and opposite the public *gimnazjum*. Every Shabbat all the members of the movement congregated there and heard different lectures and interesting debates, which demonstrated the level of education and progress of the participants. The youth leaders and various Zionist activists came from here. The movement also operated a large library in different languages for different ages, and once a week the young boys and girls exchanged their books, and by means of pop-quizzes we tested whether they had read and understood the books. In the soup-kitchen there were Hanukah parties, beautiful plays and literary balls.

When we graduated from the *gimnazjum*, we founded an academic society named "*Hashmonaim*", which was affiliated with the "*Hasmonea*" society in Lvov. Our society took upon itself a large part of the Zionist work in town, and developed lovely social and cultural life. In the "*Hashmonaim*" society we created a large scientific library, which helped members, friends and supporters to deepen their knowledge of Judaism and Zionism, knowledge of Eretz Yisrael, Hebrew and Yiddish literature, and general sciences. The society parties gathered all the circles of town and the intelligentsia from near and far towns. I recall the grand Eretz Yisrael ball in the halls of the Ukrainian club, with the presence of famous Zionist economist David Treisch, who developed the special system for settlement and agriculture in Eretz Yisrael. The society members – the youths Miller and Heller-Anderman, who died in World War I; Dr. Yeshayahu Hecht, head of the *Hitachdut* party and its representative in the Buczacz community and city hall; Dr. Eliyahu Nacht, an attorney and Zionist leader in Drohowitz; Dr. Yosef Somerstein (a doctor in Vienna); Hindes, Nussbaum, Attorney Isio Spirer, Judge Cook and others – were killed during Hitler's time. Yitzhak Tischler and attorney Poldzie Marangel and our friend the activist in Buczacz, Haim Sinzia Frankel, died before the war. The well-known activist in Buczacz, Lvov and Vienna, Leon Weksler, died in Jerusalem. Dr. Avraham Silberstein, a delegate to the *Sejm* and deputy-chief of the congressional court, died in Switzerland. Dr. Avraham Halfon, the old Hebrew, a founder of "*Hathiya*" in Vienna, died in Hadera, after having managed to live in Israel for a short while, as a survivor.

If we are discussing the academic youth in our town, we should mention an amusing fact: since the Austrian system of law studies meant that the students of that division were only examined once every two years, some 100 law students in Buczacz also spent most of their time in Buczacz. In order to overcome their boredom, they created a club named "*Ha'alaburda*", whose members would gather in the evenings at Pyotrowicz's confectionery in Dr. Alter's house. The club, which ran for two or three years, was led by Waksler, Reiss, Frankel and others. The "*Ha'alaburda*" was organized on the foundations of a state: a government, with a royal court and a Chancellor at the head of the government; courts and legislation; university and examinations, in which "exam fees" were paid with confectionery cakes. In the exams, which had an amusing scientific nature, questions on legal problems were presented humorously. They were very interesting and attracted a large audience. But we finally recognized that this club did not have a positive influence on the academic youth and was distracting them from Zionist and cultural activities and from studying for serious exams. With the help of our Zionist society "*Hashmonaim*" and under its influence, we stopped the activity of the "*Ha'alaburda*" and its existence, even though most of its members were not party-affiliated and did not want to give up this social occasion.

Hebrew and Jewish Studies and Literary Endeavors in our Town

We shall not mention here all the various *"cheders,"* some of which had outstanding teachers and pedagogues such as Pesach Beuler, who was an expert in grammar, Tanach and literature, and whose daughter – Khaye Rol Beuler, of blessed memory, who was married to Arie Rol – died prematurely in Tel Aviv. She was very active here in assisting immigrants from Buczacz, and was the living spirit in the Buczacz organization. Other teachers included Baruch Koenigsburg, Haim David Becker, Leib Yazlowitzer, Barisch Rodes-Sigman, Mendele Melamed, and the teaching assistant Shalev Eliyahu, who we see together in one of the photographs with the students: Loser Heller, Nathan and Benjamin Anderman, Zelig and Leiser Gottfried, Osia and Shmuel Zeifer, Holtzstein (the photographer's son), Moshe Bertsneider, Shmuel Cohen and Shlomo Weisser, the son of the butcher Fischel. And it is a well-known fact that they did not dare to take photographs of the *cheder* students in every place in Galicia.

In most of the *Batei Midrash* and the *kloises*, individuals and groups studied Torah all day, and in many evening classes. The old Beit Midrash was an especially important place for the study of Torah and Jewish studies. The *mitnagdim* were concentrated there, prominent scholars led by Rabbi Mordechai Spielberg. They prayed there throughout daylight, and there were valuable books in the library. Interestingly, the library rules stipulated a special department whose books were accessible only to adults, and "youngsters" under the age of fifty were forbidden to read them. A notable scholar in this *mitnagdim* group was Avraham Freid, grandfather of Ze'ev On, a member of the Tel Yosef kibbutz and manager of the workers' society.

Among the students of this Beit Midrash were also porters and butchers, and also a few of us students, and of course there were landlords and young men knowledgeable in the Torah. Some of the volunteer lecturers and teachers who excelled in conducting their classes were Asher Miller, who taught Mishna on week days, at *Mincha* and at *Maariv*; Chaim Weinraub and others who taught "Ein Yakov" and "Akedat Yitzhak", and others who taught Tanach and literature. All these studies were conducted in the evenings and particularly during the winter months, on Shabbat evenings, while Midrash was taught on Shabbat mornings.

The Hebrew language, especially grammar and Tanach, was taught by several teachers and private tutors, who taught Hebrew, general education, classic German literature and calligraphy. Many students studied in the primary schools and in the Polish *gimnazjum*, at first in the "Basilian" monastery building and later in the beautiful government *gimnazjum*. Progressive Buczacz had long been notable for its professional Jewish intelligentsia, which was the fruit of independent, local nurturing: the physician Dr. Nacht and his sons, Dr. Stern, Dr. Marangel, Dr. Peller and others who were teachers, senior government officials, and even one female physician, Dr. Frankel (daughter of Aharon). And during the last fifty years there were hundreds of Jewish academics in Buczacz, including many young women (and many of them now work in their professions in Israel and America).

The pioneer in the instruction of the Hebrew language was Yosef Rosenman, and one of the first activists was Ms. Shindel Segal, who also taught Hebrew in her apartment in the house of Haim Neta Anderman Brink or in the soup-kitchen. At that time, Dr. Silberstein came from Lvov and began to teach in the public kitchen according to the "Hebrew in Hebrew" system.

During the years 1906-1907, the Hebrew enthusiasts from the "Zion" society, led by Yitzhak Hirsch Weisser, Yakov Leib Alfenbein and Matityahu Weinreib, as well as the youth movements, decided to create a Hebrew school named "Clear Language" (*Safah Brurah*), modeled on the schools which existed in other places in Galicia. They contacted the center for Hebrew teachers in Lvov, which was directed by Raphael Soferman (now a teacher at the Gymnasia Herzliya in Tel Aviv) and Zvi Sharpstein (now a teacher and writer in America), and asked to bring the well-known author and teacher G. Shofman, who lived in Galicia at that time, to Buczacz as the headmaster of the school. However, the teaching center recommended Berkowitz, a Hebrew teacher from Eretz Yisrael, who had evidently been in a position in Rohatin until that point, and is now a teacher in Hadera. The school was located in the "Garbarnia" house, in the Eisenberg-Fried house behind the Ukrainian church next to the market square. It then moved to the Kaner house near the post office and city hall, and later to the Abisch Dik house, opposite the *gimnazjum*. As headmaster, Berkowitz managed to expand the school, which was at first a school for kindergarten children and evening classes for the young people who studied at the Polish governmental, general-primary and secondary schools. Yisrael Farnhof (who was related to the author Yitzhak Farnhof) was appointed as a second teacher, and Berkowitz also acquired students from the senior classes in the *gimnazjum* and the students of the senior course.

Due to a severe conflict which developed among the teachers, part of the school board was opposed to Berkowitz. At that point, Farnhof, with the help of Yitzhak Hirsch Weisser, founded a separate school and Berkowitz moved to the court of Moshe Weisser, a Hebrew scholar (whose son Matityahu Weisser is in Tel Aviv), where he managed a school for young people. After a while Berkowitz returned to Yavniel in Eretz Yisrael, but he returned to Buczacz after a short period, married a wife from the Friedman family and opened a school in the form of a kindergarten. He then moved to Lvov as the director of a Hebrew kindergarten, and after not long he retuned to Eretz Yisrael. The Hebrew school deteriorated, and only after the war, during the realization of Zionism and the pioneering aliya, the study of Hebrew began to develop again, both in the pioneering youth movements and in the school directed by Farnhof and assisted by Haim Kofler and the teachers Ms. Gottfreid (daughter of Shmuel), Ms. Glanzer (daughter of the judge Glanzer and wife of Knobler) and others.

As I write of all these events, it is impossible not to mention the dear, kind young man, who was like a pleasant riddle to everyone in our town. I am referring to Shmulik Czaczkes, the famed author Shmuel Yosef Agnon, who lives in Jerusalem. His father was a learned man with great knowledge and a *Chassid* in the Czortkow *kloise*. Shmuel Yosef's uniqueness was evident from early childhood. He internalized knowledge and Torah in his father's house and in the kloise, but this framework became too narrow for him, and he desired spiritual and mental expanses in other places and in educated and progressive circles in Zionist organizations and clubs for studious youth. In the general great Beit Midrash for the landlords in Buczacz (directed by Rabbi Itzi, named after the *tzaddik* from the Wharman family), where my father, of blessed memory, was a *gabbai* for a long time – Agnon's grandfather, Reb Yehuda Farb, of blessed memory, and my own grandfather, Reb Mordecahi Heller, of blessed memory, would sit nearby a large window and pray. In this place I myself sat, as did little Shmuel, on small, low chairs during the High Holidays prayers, and we internalized the tunes and the beautiful prayers sung by the cantor and the *shochet* Getzel Golberg (his sons Alter and Yehosha and his daughters are in Eretz Yisrael, and his son Moshe, who was learned in the Talmud and known for his journalistic articles, was killed by the Nazis). In this Beit Midrash we both later met with Zionist landlords and young men, apart from my student circles and the young men from his *kloise*. In this Beit Midrash and in the nearby Fritzhand house, we initiated the custom of pledges for the benefit of the JNF during the *aliyot* on Simchat Torah. Shmuel Czaczkes liked to come to the "Zion" society often. He was friendly with a group of young men, such as Paul Edelstein, Shalom Weinstock, Yakov Halpern, Yakov Fischer (his daughter in Israel is married to Dr. Kornblit-Korn from the *Kupat Cholim* [sick-fund] center), and he was also close with the heads of the Zionist *Noar Lomed*, and particularly the Hebraists, including Yosef Tischler, Menatzeach and others. In the "Zion" society he published a newspaper named "*Shabbat-Oivest*" (Fruits of Shabbat), which was published in handwriting and in print. This paper contained discussions of the Messiah and Messianic beliefs, as well as poems and articles on other topics. When he came to the youth parties and especially to the Chanukah celebrations, Shmuel Czaczkes would secretly bring one of his poems, which would be read to the audience by a student. This may have been done out of modesty or perhaps out of fear from the *klois*. I recall that a poem of his was once recited by the student Halpern (brother of Ms. Salzman, who is in Tel Aviv), who drowned in the Stripa river. Many people at that time suspected that the young Shmuel Czaczkes was presenting poems written by his father, for who could believe at that point that this child was destined to become Agnon.

When he walked with his friends, Agnon would often break away from them for a few moments and disappear through the gates of one of the houses. When he returned, he would explain that he had suddenly been overcome with thoughts and ideas, and had gone inside to write them down in his notebook.

During that time there was a cantor and a choir in the Great Synagogue in our town, where the youth took singing lessons. Towards Passover, the cantor was preparing a new tune and he asked young Czaczkes, who had already become famous for his ability in this area, to write him a small poem for a melody he would compose. If I am not mistaken, the song was approximately as follows:

> *Pesach* was there.
> And if there are no more *matzot* and wine in my house –
> But the bread is no more.

Agnon was also involved in a different society of older intellectuals, such as Mordechai Kanfer (who teaches in the Baron Hirsch's school) and his son Moshe; Moshe Gotold (the local socialist); Teuber the old teacher; Itzi Farnhof, who was a Hebrew teacher in the village and then found acclaim with the publication of "amusement books." There was also Fischel Engelstein, who later lived in the colony of Buczaczers in the town of Metz in Alsace-Lorraine. Farnhof also published a pocket dictionary of Grazowski with translations into Polish, German and Yiddish, called "New Hebrew Dictionary." It was printed in Stanislaw, by Robinzon (now a book publisher in Tel Aviv). With the help of his son (now Dr. Farnhof, a doctor in New York) and his relative Dr. Kopel Schwartz, of blessed memory, our friend Yisrael Cohen published the late Farnhof's books in Israel. Young Czaczkes also published his articles and poems in "*Hamitzpeh*" ["The Observer"] and the editor of that paper, the author S. M. Lazar (whose son the journalist Dr. Lazar is one of the editors of "Maariv" in Tel Aviv), came especially to Buczacz to meet Czaczkes, whose articles made a great impression on him. When Rokeach came to Buczacz, Agnon was given an opportunity to expand his literary work. The author Rokeach came from Eretz Yisrael to Galicia via Romania, where he stayed and worked for a while. He began his activity in Stanislaw and then moved to nearby Buczacz. Rokeach and Czaczkes became very friendly, and they cooperated in publishing the Hebrew monthly "*Hayarden*" and the Yiddish weekly "*Der Wäcker*," both of which were printed in Stanislaw and in Buczacz at Helberg & Dretler's printers. These periodicals published many poems and articles by Shmuel Czaczkes. Yakov Kaner, who was later active as secretary of the youth movement in the *Poel HaTzsair* party in Galicia, was a technical assistant. "*Hayarden*" also published caricatures of Buczacz personalities. One of them had the following caption: "I am a tailor, I make clothes, whoever wishes shall wear them." Rokeach was also assisted by many people such as Kanfer, author Yitzhak Farnhof, and others. Rokeach moved from Buczacz to the town of Stri (due to financial difficulties and printing debts) and eventually returned to Eretz Yisrael.

Shalom Aleichem came to Buczacz on his literary tour, invited by Moshe Kleinman, editor of the "*Yiddishes Tagblatt*" in Lvov. He was supposed to visit Agnon, who also published his poems in this publication of Galician Zionists. However, the visit did not take place, and Shalom Aleichem left his card for Agnon before he left. He apologized for leaving without saying goodbye, but left a friendly suggestion: "Learn, learn a lot, for your actions will be rewarded." Rokeach also gave many lectures in Buczacz on literary and philosophical topics.

Three other societies were active in Buczacz until the First World War: a women's Zionist society called "Rachela," directed and activated by Ms. Dr. Peller, Gizella Stern (wife of Dr. Moshe Kanfer), the sisters Regina and Rosia Stern (daughters of the young Abisch), Toni Eisenberg, nee Edelstein (now in Haifa), and the young women Herzes, Hecht, Primazia Weinrab, Chana Blein, Hagar and others. It was a very active society, which arranged Hebrew lessons, parties, in which students and Zionist youth also participated, lectures by members and by students (Weinrib, Weksler Heller). Once they even brought Shlomo Schiller, the author and writer from Lvov. The members of "Rachela" collected donations for the JNF at weddings. The society met at Yakov Stern's house. It is worth mentioning a tragicomic incident, which occurred due to the cooperation between the members of "Rachela" and the students. Avramtzu Spirer (later a lawyer and head of the community in Jaslo), who was known as a practical joker, once arranged a game in which he placed a ring on the fingers of twelve "Rachela" girls, adding the phrase "with this ring I take you as my wife according to the law of Moses and Israel." It is hard to describe the panic and the scandal in town following this funny event, since the Rabbinate asserted that he must give an official get [divorce] to each of these young women.

For a number of years, there was also a society of trade assistants, within the *Poalei Zion* party, in Ehrlich Bringplatz's house, under the presidency of Berzio Frankel – son of Yonah (who was later director of the Joint in Munkatz and a lawyer in Lvov). Members included Yonah Kopfer from Monasterzyska, who was an accountant for the Eisenberg brothers, and a man from Tarnopol named Zalman Hertz, who worked at the Dretler printers and helped the *Poalei Zion*, and died in Eretz Yisrael. Among the activists were Anshel Czaczkes, Agnon's brother (now in Jerusalem) and others. The *Poalei Zion* party had ties with similar societies, such as "Achva" in Stanisalaw and Lvov. After *Poalei Zion* left the national Zionist movement and became an independent party with a class-based and Yiddishist character, the Zionist intelligentsia left it, and the Buczacz branch was closed down.

There was a workers' association for many years in Buczacz, named "*Bertrestwa-Briderlichkeit*" (unity), whose residence in the period before the war was in a house on Podhiezka St. It was a general workers' association with a cultural, social nature, for the class whose members felt the need for a special social framework, as they thought they had been excluded from the society of "landlord-like" youth (Zionist and Hassidic youth and the *Noar Halomed* organizations). This association developed and became a socialist organization affiliated with the Z.P.S. Since its members were only Yiddish-speaking Jews and their spiritual leader was Dr. Anslem Mozler, founder of the Jewish sector in the P.P.S. – named Z.P.S. – the Buczacz association also moved to the Galician Z.P.S., which later united with the Bund. The association was very active, mainly in the social and cultural areas. Among its leaders and activists were Moshe Gotwald, Zleznik, the members of the Duchovny family (one of whom is now in America and his wife is chairwoman of the Buczacz women's assistance organization), the Kitenflon brothers, Yonah Rosenblum and his wife, from the Kitenflom family (now in America), Zeifer and many others. Zlaznik Herman once organized a tailor workers' strike and set up a kind of cooperative – a joint workshop for all the strikers. However, this cooperative did not last long, because the workers went back to their tailors. Zlaznik remained in the cooperative as an independent tailor. After the war, Zlaznik was chairman of the society of artisans, "Yad Charutzim," which existed many years before the war and whose main role was to elevate the social standing of the artisans and obtain representation for them in all the elections for the municipality, the community, the tax board and the professional union, which was directed for many years by the Jewish tailor Nussi (Nathan) Pik. The artisans had welfare assistance institutes, both separate from and joint with other citizens, and they had a beautiful, large synagogue next to the *Ezrat nashim* of the Great Synagogue and opposite the old bathhouse, which was called "*Das sneiderishe shilachil.*" This synagogue was directed by Shimon Hecht, Fischel Skelka, A. V. Yurman, Fischel Kitenflon, Mordechai Winkler and others. Not far from there, on Mikolei Street, stood the Jewish hospital in a separate beautiful building. After the war, the hospital was directed by Arie Rol and his wife Khaye, nee Beuler (she died in Tel Aviv) and the physicians Dr. Nacht, Dr. Chalfon and Dr. Hirschorn. The latter two came to Israel as Holocaust survivors, and died here.

The butchers and carriage-owners represented separate ranks, and they included people knowledgeable in the Torah, and with social and cultural knowledge and aspirations. Some were also financially successful. Among the butchers were the Weisser and Peper families, and among the carriage-owners was the Goldberg family. Meir Goldberg provided his sons and daughters with an education, and his daughter is now a teacher in America, and is married to Professor Schotsman, also one of our townsmen who is active in America, who visited Israel to acquire knowledge of the land and the country at "Beit Berl."

There was also an anarchist group in Buczacz, led by the brothers Sigmund and Monia Nacht (sons of the doctor), Dr. Kanfer (who was later a teacher in Chelm and a journalist in Krakow in the Zionist "*Novi Dezianenik*" and moved to the *Poalei Zion* party), young intelligent store assistants, who gathered secretly in the forest near the Stripa river, opposite the black bridge, and once in a while they would include us students of the lower classes of the *gimnazjum* in the meetings. The Nacht brothers were known as pillars of the world anarchist movement and were active in Spain. The youngest, Monia (Max), still lives in America and recently gave a scientific lecture at the club of former Buczacz residents.

There were some individuals with vague socialist leanings in the Zionist movement and among the young men and landlords. My father, who was a merchant, *gabbai* of the Beit Midrash and chairman of the "Zion" society, also had a socialist outlook. This fact had a great influence on my characteristics and my way in life. The people also sensed this and presented my father, "the commoner landlord," as their candidate for the community elections, and he was their representative on the tax board and the local sick fund management, although he himself was distant from these things due to the worries of earning a living. He chose to devote his spare time to writing essays and poems in Hebrew, Yiddish and German, although he never revealed this in public.

The occupation of Buczacz by the Russian army during World War I and the Cossack reign over the town for several years, destroyed most of the houses and businesses. Many Jews died in the typhoid epidemic. Many died on the fronts, in deportations, or from starvation. Many went to Stanislaw or Lvov and other places, or moved to the Western areas of the Austro-Hungarian monarchy, such as Hungary, Czech, Moravia, Graz and Innsbruck. Some two-thousand people arrived in Vienna the capital and managed there. At the end of the war and after the further suffering during the "small" wars between Poland and the Ukraine, and between Poland and Soviet Russia, the soldiers began to return to our town from the army and from captivity and many returned from their places of exile. Hundreds of Buczaczers gathered in a café on Overdonau Street in Vienna, after I posted small announcements in the Jewish prayer houses and cafés, inviting them to the meeting. The participants included people from all ages and classes, including those who had lived in Vienna even before the war – the presidency was occupied by respectable activists from our community. The meeting had two purposes: a) to explain to our brothers in Vienna that they must return to the destroyed Buczacz to start a new life there. It was after the Balfour Declaration and the San-Remo Conference, where Eretz Yisrael was declared as our real homeland and it was waiting for enterprising, willing groups of people. There was great enthusiasm and understanding. We knew that Galician soldiers from the Austrian army, including some from Buczacz, were still in Eretz Yisrael: engineer Wildman (a senior clerk in the Mandate government), Dr. Smeterling (now a lawyer in Jerusalem) and Dr. Gutman from Stanislaw (now a lawyer in Jerusalem and former assistant mayor) and of course Agnon, and others. But the prohibition against aliya dictated by the Zionist executive cancelled this initiative. b) to establish a Buczacz *Landsmannschaft* in Vienna, in order to provide for those who returned and those who stayed. The organization was established, because some one-thousand Buczaczers remained in Vienna, and it was led by Leibisch Freid and others, and during the years before Hitler, our friend Yehezkel Ederer was elected as chairman.

After we returned to Buczacz, we began to work toward the restoration of the town and its Jews, and to rebuild the ruins of public life and the Zionist movement. This was a period of festiveness in light of the San Remo Conference resolutions, which the Jews interpreted as the establishment of a Jewish state, and the days of the great awakening of the national spirit under the regime of the Ukrainians, who were interested in the Jewish national movement and in establishing Hebrew schools, in order to release the Jews from the Polish influence. In the democratic elections, national councils were elected instead of the religious communities. These were lead by *"Tze'irei Zion"* circles and representatives in Czortkow and Buczacz, which were established in the area under the influence of the movement in Russia and the Ukraine, and which were pillars of the Zionist labor party, "*Hitachdut*", in Eastern Galicia.

Due to reasons of world view and from bitter experience, we decided to prevent the Bund's control over the workers and the "folkists" and among the artisans. We established a popular, inter-class Zionist association, which united within it both the workers and proletarian youth, and the popular ranks, who had been distanced from Zionism before the war, as it had been a movement of landlords and intellectuals and their children, and they therefore found their place in the anti-Zionist parties. We rented all the rooms on the ground floor of Dr. Auschnit's house on the *gimnazjum* street, and began the work of social merging of the boys and girls from all levels, by means of various activities: lectures, parties and communal studying in meetings, lessons and conversations. To our regret, the reluctance was mutual. The parents' objections on the one hand, and mistrust on the other, were an obstacle for us. Due to this lack of success, the path was reopened for the activity of non-Zionist circles and their followers among the *Noar HaOved*, with the help of "salon-communists" from among the students and the "red rabbis," graduates of the Beit Midrash, especially after our first pioneers from "Hashomer HaTzair" made *aliya*, as we were left with deficient resources.

The first "Hashomer Hatzair" groups from Buczacz and nearby Czortkow made *aliya* with the large wave of aliya of this youth movement from all of Galicia. They immigrated after spiritual preparation and agricultural *hachshara* [training]. We made many efforts to help them with the *hachshara*. I lived in Czortkow at the time, and I would come to Buczacz often, of course, to assist this pioneering movement. Our *hachshara* place in Czortkow, for example, attracted important figures among the youth, such as Dr. David Meletz's daughter and Gershon Ziper's daughter, who has been in Israel for a long time, and whose name is now Dr. Helena Flaum-Ziper. She worked at first at the National Library and now works for the Ministry of Foreign Affairs. This group of "Hashomer Hatzair" pioneers left Poland illegally, without passports, and was delayed for a long time in Slovakian Pressburg and worked hard to make a living, until they arrived in Israel and began immediately to work in road-paving and various public works. They worked on the Haifa-Jeddah road, under very harsh conditions, along with Egyptian laborers, and they suffered from dysentery, rheumatism, malaria, and so forth. Most of the group's members were the founders of Kibbutz Beit-Alpha, and some later moved to Ramat-Yochanan. This group included Zvi Neuman (now in Beit-Alpha, an agricultural expert and member of the agricultural center), Ze'ev Eiserzon (now named Ze'ev On), Ish Tel-Yosef, who moved to the "Gdud Avoda" and was among the founders of the large Kibbutz Ein-Harod and later among the founders of Kibbutz Tel-Yosef, together with his wife Yonah of the Budinger family, one of the first pioneers in Czortkow and now a well-known and experienced vegetable grower. Ze'ev Eiserson-On is one of the central figures in the labor movement, and director of the "Workers' Society"; Yehoshua Hoenig – one of the founders of Kibbutz Gan-Shmuel, who was the manager of the "Na'aman" factory and is now a manager of "Hamashbir Hamerkazi"; the agronomist Yakov Bleukopf, a teacher and agricultural counselor, and now director of a division in the Ministry of Agriculture. Yosef Held, Masha Antler and her husband Milek Hirschorn, who died defending his group in the War of Independence, all moved from Beit-Alpha to Ramat-Yochanan. Other settlers there included Hirschorn's brother, the physician Dr. Hirschorn, who died after a short life in the homeland, and my brother Mila (Shmuel) Heller, of blessed memory, the youngest member of the group. He fell prey to the harsh reality during an all-night guard duty near the camp on the Haifa-Jedda road, and was buried in Haifa in the old cemetery, at the age of 17 or 18. Yodenfreud – now a managing director of "Ha'Ogen" and the "Solel Boneh" shipping works in Haifa; and Leibel Ze'ev, one of the managers at the Kibbutz Artzi's "Na'aman" factory, who lives in Kiriat-Haim; Dov Kaner, who moved from road-paving work to Tel Aviv as an experienced construction worker, and the member Schopler (in Jerusalem). Some did not make it and left Israel: Samet and Nirenberg returned to Buczacz, Zelig Anderman went to cure himself of the severe malaria, came back to Israel after Hitler's Holocaust and worked in his profession as a pharmacist. Yisrael Neuman went to America, where he continues to be active as a friend of working Eretz Yisrael. Neuberger and Segal, who lost their Zionist faith, are now in Poland. From among the *hachsharah* members who did not make *aliya* at the time, Ze'ev Goldberg came to Israel later, and Willa Torton and Dr. Rega Zahler came as new immigrants, and are both government clerks in Tel Aviv. It is worth noting that even before this group, which was one of the pioneers of the Third Aliya, Buczacz pioneers made *aliya* during the Second Aliya, including Gershon Gafni (now a farmer in Israel) and Fritz and Moirer, who worked in the Openheimer farm in Merchavia, directed by our townsman the well-known agronomist Shlomo Dik.

After the first group immigrated, a young group of pioneers remained, and they continued their *hachshara* at the quarry works belonging to Itzi Hirsch Weisser. There was a group of 5 or 6 young candidates who worked at Folkenfolk in *Nagorzanka*, and another group of Weksler and Yisrael Neuman (Zvi's brother, who was later a lawyer in Buczacz), who cleaned produce for the Buczacz landowner A. Zelermeier. In one incident during their work, the group of pioneers – mostly *gimnazjum* students – were surrounded by Polish scouts, called *Harcerze*, with Professor Michelski from the public *gimnazjum*. Many were then expelled from the *gimnazjum* and others were tried in court for treason. But in the meantime, the war between Poland and Soviet Russia broke out, and the town was occupied by the Bolsheviks, and then they managed to destroy all the prosecution's material. When the Poles returned, the court was forced to release the defendants due to lack of evidence. These events weakened the movement. However, at the Shomer Hatzair conference which was held, if I am not mistaken, in 1921 or 1922, the anti-Zionist group appeared with anti-British slogans, and although the central leadership tried to silence this movement, it completely destroyed the Shomer Hatzair branch, and consequently the pioneer movement in Buczacz. Only after a certain period, during 1923-4, was there a reawakening of the aspiration to train pioneering *aliya*. This time it came from the Hitachdut party circles, under the welcome initiation and guidance of Yisrael Cohen (whose brother Asher Cohen is also in Israel), who is now editor of the party weekly, "*Hapoel Hatzair*" (it is worth mentioning at this point Yisrael Cohen's elderly mother, eighty years old, Ms. Gitl Cohen, wife of the *Shochet* and *Bodek* Yitzhak Cahn, who is in Israel).

The Women's "WIZO" activists, 1934 Seated, from right: A. Bilgrey, P. Marangel, A. Bazner, C. Rol, T. Hirschorn, P. Rosen. Standing, first row: Pohorile, Anmeldong, N. Nimand, S. Frankel, Bazan, Avner, Hirschorn, Hirschorn, S. Shechter Second row: Frankel, Horenstein, Chalfan (Gafner), Sigman, G. Glanzer (Knobler), Buchwald, Buchwald, Hertzman. Bottom row: H. Blai, P. Lustgarten, S. Horowitz.

The "Hashmonaim" Association

The "Mizrachi" Activists, 1934 Seated, from right: A. Halbrecht, S. Hoenig, Y. Silberstein, S. Silberstein, A. Stern, M. Frankel, Y. Katz.
Standing, first row: Orbach, M. Reich, S. Berger, H. Kopler, H. Warman, L. Ernstof, M. Bergman.
First row: Einslicht, M. Ehrlich, M. Blein, H. Neiman, Haken M. Hoenig.
Bottom: M. Silberstein, M. Hoenig, Y. Cohen.

The Committee of Young Merchants, 1939

The Noar Lomed Movement, "Tzeirei Zion-Hatikvah" P. Heller nee Anderman, Heltzer, Segal, L. Segal, L. Hirschorn, Birenbaum,
M. Saltzman nee Halpern, Reifeisen, A. Gottfried and Ederer

The Poalei Zion (Ichud) Association, 1934

The Hebrew teacher Yisrael Farnhof
with a group of students

The Zionist organization, "Achva"

Hebrew course for trainees
at the "Safa Brura" [Clear Language] School T. Feder, Tzvi Heller, Sarah Fischer, Clara Heller, Pepa Heller,
Zvi Malchas,
Izak Sheinberg, Prima Wienraub, Avraham Chalfan and his sister,
Naftali Menatzeach, Kleiner and Kreigel. Center: the teacher, B. Berkowitz.

The "Hechalutz" [the Pioneer] Organization in 1928

The "Hechalutz" [the Pioneer] Organization in Buczacz in 1930

The "Hechalutz" [the Pioneer] Organization in 1924
Seated: A. Rosenbaum, S. Goldberg, M. Heller, Yisrael Cohen, Chana Wiesinger, P. Margaliyot
Standing: A. Heller, H. Margolis, S. Karbas, S. Weisinger, P. Neiberger, H. Pikholtz,
A. Kopler, Antler, M. Landman, Asher Cohen

Pioneer Kibbutz "Solel"
Including: Y. Goldberg, Tunia Wirnik (Stempler), S. Meiberger

The First "Shomer Hatzair" Group (1920) Ze'ev On (Eiserson),
B. Nirenberg, M. Heller,
Zvi Neiman, W. Torton, S. Hirschorn, Y. Heller

Yisrael Cohen's group of pioneers, which was called "Kibbutz Hameshulash" ["The Triangle Kibbutz"] championed the slogan: "Language, People and Land." It introduced a vibrant spirit into the life of the youth and the pioneer movement in Buczacz. Its cultural activities were concentrated in its apartment in the Reinstein house, on the way to the train station. Many members of this group made *aliya*: Yisrael Cohen, Kopler (son of Chaim) who is on Kibbutz Mizra and others from this group – due to financial difficulties – were delayed in Vienna, including Weissinger, of blessed memory, who was later an officer in the police and in the army in Israel and second-in-command of the Be'er-Sheba military district. He was one of the first to settle there permanently, and drew several Buczacz immigrants to the capital of the Negev: Kreigel, a pharmacy owner, Berger, and the Miller brothers, owners of a furniture carpentry. This group also included Moshe Held, who is now in Tel Aviv and a member of the Buczacz *Landsmannschaft*; Shmuel Kerbes, Margalit, Landman, Fischel Neuberger. Upon arriving in Israel, the "Meshulash" group went to work on the farm belonging to our townsmen Gedalyahu Margalit in Petach Tikva. He was an experienced agriculturalist, owner of an estate in the area of our town, and made *aliya* after the First World War. He continued his work as a vineyard owner in Petach Tikva, and still lives there now.

Following is the Yiddish announcement which the "Meshulash" group published in Buczacz, calling upon residents to contribute to the *aliya* fund:

Buczacz, 21st day of Tishrei, 5675

Pioneer Kibbutz "Hameshulash!"
[Yiddish text through bottom of p.162]

After the group made *aliya*, Ze'ev Goldberg gathered some 20 young people who were not party-affiliated, and along with the remaining members of the Cohen group, organized a new pioneer *hachshara*. In 1925 these pioneers went to four *hachshara* locations. At the same time, the "Shomer Hatzair" also recovered and began its organizational pioneering activity.

There was also a sports club in Buczacz, Z.K.S., in which Zelig Anderman (now in Israel) was very active. Ze'ev Goldberg was secretary, and was sent by this club to Lvov, to train as a certified sports instructor. While there, he also made organizational and ideological contacts with the "Hitachdut" party and the "Gordonia" youth movement, and when he returned to Buczacz he became active in both these organizations, particularly in the area of pioneer *hachshara* for the youth, in the framework of "Gordonia," together with his wife Rosia Genzel and others – Yisrael Cohen's students.

Our town also had a branch of "Ezra" – the society for assisting pioneers – whose center in Lvov and whose leadership were mainly in the hands of the Zionist labor party, "Hitachdut." The chairman of "Ezra" in Buczacz was Sher (a member of the movement in Kopyczynce, who married the daughter of the shoemaker Zeideh Sternberg, and died at a young age). The secretary was Goldberg, and activists from all the Zionist parties began to collect money to help the local pioneer *hachsarah* and the members of the "Meshulash" kibbutz, who managed to reach Vienna after being smuggled over borders, and then arrived in Israel. The "Gordonia" pioneers made *aliya* in 1929, and at the same time as the members of "Hashomer Hatzair," who included Shumert, Schwartz, Karbas and others (in Ein Hamifratz and Mizra).

The "Hitachdut" was directed by the lawyer Shico Hecht, Haim Sinzia Frankel, Hirsch Nirenberg, Yosef Hornstein (son of Shimon), Gustav Flenboim, Rol and others. The "Hitachdut" was at first concentrated in the Zionist association in Dr. Auschnit's house and then moved to Zeide Sternberg's house, and from there to Yosef Gotfried's house, and finally to Hirsch (Hanzis)-Ginsberg's house (the Yitzhak Schulman house). The party was active in the fund work, in assisting pioneer *hachshara* and in the local elections, and its representative Dr. Hecht was elected to the community and Dr. Frankel to the municipality, Ze'ev Goldberg to the sick-fund management. In affiliation with the party, there were also departments for artisans and hired workers. The latter established a professional organization for egg-packing workers, of whom there were many in Buczacz.

The "General Zionists" party had public value in Buczacz because of its long-time activists. They were active in the funds, in assisting the pioneers, in providing for the Hebrew school. The representatives of this party were also in the community, the municipality and the merchants' union. Among its activists were the Knobler brothers, Pinchas Weinstock, Zvi Kalman, Pinchas Weinstock's brother-in-law (now in Petach Tikva, as Zvi Hinter, representative of the Zionist labor in the Petach Tikva workers' union), Yakov Halpern and Asher Katz, Yitzchak Katz, the son-in-law of Nissan Pohorile, Yisrael Farnhof, Medwinski (whose son is in Israel), Patznik, and Dr. Engelberg, who was the party chairman during the last period. The youth movement, "Achva," was lead by Dr. Geltner (now a doctor in Rehovot and director of the government hospital in Tzrifin), Shmuel Horowitz, Bleukopf, Kaner and others. "Achva" provided *hachshara* activities for its members.

There were also old-time activists in the "Mizrachi" party, such as: Yisrael Shlomo Stern and his son Abish, Mendel Reich, Munisch Frenkel, Yisrael Katz and others, who were active in various areas and particularly in the community. There was no "Agudath Yisrael" in our town, nor a unified Hassidic sect, and they represented all the orthodox people in the town. Silberstein and others were active in the "Mizrachi" pioneering.

The Revisionist party, which was established in 1926/7, was active in its separate areas and in its youth movement, "Beitar." The party chairman was the notary clerk Leib Zeifer, and among its activists were Hirsch Alner, attorney Yozek Stern, Anderman, Gottfried, Medwinski and Kirschner (the latter two are in Tel Aviv). This party was also active in pioneer *hachshara*.

Hesio Shetchel, Yosef Knobler, the "Wizo" representatives, and the youth and women's organizations, were active in the JNF committee. Dr. Henrik Gross was chairman of "*Keren Hayesod*" and its activists were Pinchas Weinstock, Medwinski, Farnhof, Haim Frankel and others. "Wizo" was lead during that period by Ms. Medwinska, the physician Dr. Wolftal, Ms. Khaye Rol and Ms. Bazner-Eisenberg (who is now on Kibbutz Mishmar-Ha'Emek with her son Bertek Bazner, one of the kibbutz founders).

The parties "*Poalei Zion Yamin*" [Right Zionist Workers], lead by Bernard Herzes, and "*Poalei Zion Smol*" [Left Zionist Workers], lead by Yitzhak Shtachel, were weak in terms of numbers, and therefore they had few activities and their existence was only slightly noticeable during elections. There were also "Bund" representatives. The communist group was stronger, mainly because its members came from the academic youth, particularly those who had returned with this spirit from the university in Prague, and also from among other students and even the local Beit Midrash students. They also included many "salon communists," who joined at a young age under the influence of friends, with no self awareness, and they quickly distanced themselves from any activities. But there were also those who stayed loyal under all circumstances and even when their lives were endangered. These young men, who came from wealthy and middle-class families, suffered intensely from the regime's persecution. Some of them left for Soviet Russia and others continued to be active underground in Buczacz, or reached Russia during the Holocaust and returned to Poland or Israel. Many came back from there disappointed by their ideals and the party. The communists, the "Bund" members and even "*Poalei Zion Smol*", created a neutral framework internally and externally, in the form of a cultural organization named "*Peretz Farein*," which was located on Branzki Street and which had a Yiddishist, combative, leftist image. They built a library and organized lectures, plays and parties. The members included Aharon Kopler and Yakov Klemper, but it was clear that the communists in this society overpowered their Zionist and Bundist adversaries and they controlled it.

The "*Yad Charutzim*" artisans' association was one of the oldest in town and encompassed craftsmen from all professions. The association was lead by Yitzhak Freund, Zelznik Herman, Sternberg Zeideh, Yakov Margolis and Alter Goldberg and his son. The association was also active in welfare activities and special institutions: a hostel for the poor, support for the needy and so forth, as well as in the professional field in the form of apprentices, distributing licenses for independent workshop owners, work relations and professional training for craftsmen and workers. During the elections they always sent their representatives to the community, the municipality, and the sick-fund, where their representative was once the chairman (Nathan Pik) and more recently the assistant chairman. During the last period before the Holocaust, a severe disagreement arose between the two leaders, Herman Zleznik and Freund – and the craftsmen ran separately for the community elections and split the association into two societies of artisans.

The Merchants' Association encompassed many merchants and shopkeepers and they met in the cooperative bank, *Bank Zaliczkowy*, at Yakov Stern's house. The association was led by Yitzhak Katz and the bank, which gave loans for all types of commerce and craft, was directed by Katz, Michal Kornovelia, Yakov Margalit, Alter Goldberg, and the manager and secretary was Haim Frankel, M.A. The merchants' association was very active in defending its members from the taxation burden during the "Grabski" period, on issues of licenses and so forth.

During that period there was also a wonderful Hebrew school directed by Yisrael Farnhof and Haim Kopler, Ms. Gottfried-Sapir and Ms. Lustgarten.

All the youth movements and pioneer movements gave Hebrew language lessons. Some of the teachers were volunteers. There was also a "drama class," led by Kalman Freidman (who tried to work in his profession as a soap and candle manufacturer in Eretz Yisrael, and returned to Buczacz), the pharmacist Zelig Anderman (now in Israel), Herzas Bernard and his wife from the Shenberg family (now in Israel), Adella Pines and others. In our town there were several public libraries during that time. A Zionist library, whose books came from the community, from the pre-war libraries, and it was probably located in the "Zion" society or in the "Kehila" [community] halls; a Hebrew library, which was located in the *kehila* corridor, and was given special care; a "Hitachdut" and "Gordonia" library and internal libraries in each of the other Zionist associations, such as the "Peretz" library and the "Shomer Hatzair" branch library. This branch was called "For the *Shomri* Youth," and it operated as a branch of the association center, which was located in Lvov for legal reasons, *Opieki nad mlodzierza szomrowa,Tow*. It functioned as an association of adults in support of the youth, and was directed by attorney Yosef Koch and Dr. Zvi Heller. Although they themselves were members of other parties, they gave their names officially, in order to enable the "Hashomer Hatzair" its legal existence and activity.

The hospital operated until the period of the Holocaust, as it was constantly an exemplary institution and a pillar for the people's needs in times of sickness. It was directed at that time by David Neiman, Arie Rol, Ms. Paula Marangel, Manish Frankel, Zvi Nirenberg and others. The physicians were Dr. Nacht, Dr. Hirschorn and Dr. Chalfan.

The orphanage, which was created for World War I orphans, operated in Buczacz until the Second World War broke out and was an exemplary institution. It was located on the Pedor Mountain in a beautiful and hygienic environment, in small pretty houses and excellent air. The public committee was directed by Professor Yitzhak Flik, Ms. Paula Marangel (Dr. Marengel's wife), Ms. Dr. Gross and a few activists who were dedicated to their welfare duties. The household was managed by Ms. Weissinger (whose sons and daughter are in Israel). The pedagogic administration was run by Ms. Pepa Anderman, who is married to Neiberger, and they are both still in Poland.

The children were given national Eretz-Yisraeli education and learned Hebrew. All their spiritual and physical needs were taken care of. There were, of course, other welfare institutions, including the society for dissemination of hygiene among Jews, "T*ow. szerzenia hygjeny wsrod Zydow*," a branch of the center in Lvov, which was active in Galicia in similar ways to the activities of "Oza" in Poland and the entire Jewish world. The association was given educational materials for the masses and hygiene means (sheets, soap, etc.) from the center, and it distributed them among the needy. It also received sports and exercising equipment, and arranged lessons for both youth and adults. Herzes, Goldberg and others were active in this area.

In this context we should mention the beautiful recreational places in our town, of which there were many, however they were seldom used due to the concepts of time and lack of understanding on the part of parents. The town was in a valley between the two ends of the Stripa river, and the crowdedness caused poor hygiene conditions. On the other hand, the town was surrounded with beautiful mountains and forests, a wonderful view and clear air. Apart from the "Basta" mountain (formerly a Polish fortress), with the train bridge under which the beautiful river ran – downhill there was a poor Jewish neighborhood and the Jewish cemetery. Opposite this was the other mountain, the Pedor, which the river surrounded on three sides. The Christian cemetery was on this mountain, as well as an area of villas, mainly owned by clerks and the Polish intelligentsia. There were lovely forests there. All this area was a wonderful place for hikes and for the social life of the youth and its organizations, a place for adults to take walks in the evenings, and a place for recreation and convalescence for people suffering from lung disease and exhaustion, during the day. The Stripa river at the foot of the mountains was a place for bathing and "ocean" sports, for sailboats and even bathing. The other beautiful place was in the city park, "Topolki," near the large flour-mill belonging to Count Potozki. This mill was leased by Jews – Moshe Gottfried, Avraham Freid and others. It was the only sports area for the Jewish youth, where they played "*Semal and Palstra*," to which the parents severely objected as they saw it as mischief on the part of the children, who played instead of learning, and even placed themselves in physical danger by the beatings they would give and receive during the game. There were also regional exhibitions organized in Buczacz. In 1905 there was a large and successful agricultural exhibition. The exhibition hall – a large wooden building – was later purchased communally by the Jews Shlomtzi Schulman, Pik and others. Another building which was open for purchase by Jews in the town was a large building for performances and gatherings and a theatre auditorium, in the beautiful place in the town park. A "dramatic" detail is worth recounting: after the Yiddishist conference in Czernowitz, the authors Shalom Esh, Y.L. Peretz and Nomberg came to our town, following the recommendation of the famous conference initiator, Dr. Nathan Birenbaum. A welcoming party was gladly arranged for them, in the form of a literary ball in the aforementioned auditorium, even though the town was mostly Hebrew in its spirit, and Zionist in its ideology. For many years a rumor went through our town, whereby Shalom Esh, who did not know the character of the town or the organizers of this ball, supposedly attacked the Hebrew language in his speech, which caused one academic, a fanatic "Hebrewist," to jump up on the stage and slap Esh on his face. This rumor has not been sufficiently confirmed.

This park was also a place for recreation, especially for the Jews, who organized celebrations of various kinds there. A coffee-house, which was established here by our friends Arie Rol and Medwinski, served as a fine committee-house for our public meetings and gatherings.

[Page 166]

From the Days of my Youth
By Dr. Naftali Menatseach
Translated by Jessica Cohen

A cold winter day. I am standing on one of the streets of Buczacz with my father, of blessed memory, and with his childhood friend Reb Mordechai Kamper, a Hebrew teacher at the Baron Hirsch Primary School. We are discussing my entering this school. It was my first visit to Buczacz, and it is ingrained in my memory. I went there from my home village of Pauszowka in the Czortkow region. Kamper recommends that I enter his school. But I am not inclined to do so and I do not wish to stay on my own in the unfamiliar town. Father, of blessed memory, accepted my refusal and we returned to our beloved village, where I spent my first, happiest childhood years. Approximately ten Jewish families lived in the village, all of whom made their living from commerce. There were also a few landowners. There was a small stream in the village and a large lake on the outskirts, where I would bathe with my father, of blessed memory, and with my friends, but regrettably I was unable to learn the art of swimming.

During the winter, I liked to go sledding down the mountain, and when the snow melted at the beginning of spring and the blocks of ice floated on the stream, I liked to sit on a block of ice and sail across the water...And when I fell into the stream, which was not deep, I did not despair, but rather got up onto another block, until I happened to hear Mother or Father calling, and then I would hurry ashore. I may have been slapped by Father, who was never idle and would give me a piece of his mind… In our large garden next to the house there were fruit trees, and at spring time I would enjoy the blossoming of the cherry tree, and the apple and pear trees. It was a great pleasure to climb the cherry tree and pick the beautiful juicy fruit and put it straight into my mouth. And how I loved going up to the wild-berry bushes and picking and eating the sweet, tart berries, an act which my mother, of blessed memory, said I excelled at as early as the age of two. And the best of all was the giant pear tree, full of juicy "Emperor pears," whose taste, the taste of heaven, still lingers in my mouth. And there was also a forest in the village, where my friends and I would walk on Shabbat and that was our Oneg Shabbat, which would conclude with a visit to Count Wolenski's fruit orchard, whose Jewish lessee would sell the fine apples, pears and plums. There were also pink rose bushes growing there and we would buy good fruit and roses and bring them home, and our mothers would make an excellent kind of confection from the roses, similar to jam, which is good, as is known, for times when there is no need to use it, or as the saying goes: "may we never have need for this confection…"

Lag Ba'Omer was a great occasion for children. We would climb a mountain which we referred to as "Mount Sinai," armed with bows and arrows, and would have target practice. Then we would take out of our backpacks, which we brought from home, tasty biscuits, eggs and preserved cherries, and after saying the boreh pri ha'eitz and boreh minei mezonoth blessings, we would dine to our hearts' content on these delicacies. And the merry winter holiday was Tu Bi'Shvat ("Arbor Day") on the fifteenth day of the month of Shevat, which promised the enjoyment of Eretz Yisrael fruits such as figs, dates, carobs and almonds.

After returning to the village from Buczacz, my father placed me in the first grade of the village school. A gentle young village teacher taught us in Ukrainian and Polish. She tried to arouse our interest in the studies, and I did indeed find some interest in them, however my position as the only Jewish child in the class of "shkeitzim", whose language I understood only a little, was unpleasant for me. And the foreign languages were not attractive to me either. I therefore left the school and stayed in my father's house, where I continued my religious and secular studies as before. Besides Hebrew, I also studied German, Polish and arithmetic. I recall that when I was six years old, I would tutor my late brother Israel, who was five, in Hebrew writing.

My father, Reb Avraham, son of Nathan Rodes, a Buczaczer, who moved to the village of Pauszowka after his marriage with my mother Chaya Esther, daughter of Shlomo, tried his hand at first in commerce, like the other village Jews, and we had a general store. However, my father was not especially successful in his business, and gradually moved to the profession of teaching. He would teach all the Jewish village children from age 3 until their marriage (18 to 20, approximately). The content of the studies was: Hebrew, from the alphabet to the Tanach and Talmud, and German up to reading Schiller and Goethe and learning them by heart. His educational activities also included helping to write love letters from the groom to the bride in German, and letters to the father-in-law in Hebrew.

Most of the students were from the Zonensein family and the head of the family, Reb Moshe Zonensein, owner of an inn, was a learned and educated Jew, and wrote poetry in Hebrew and German. Some of his sons and grandsons are in Israel.

When I reached my second grade studies, I finally moved to the town of Buczacz and entered the second grade of the Baron Hirsch Primary School. The beautiful blonde teacher, Mrs. Langer, wife of the headmaster, had complete control over me there. This teacher managed to make the studies pleasant for the young children, and she would speak Polish and sometimes a little Yiddish with us. I recall that when I had to write an exercise in school and my pen nib broke, the teacher gave me a new nib and, pinching my arm, said: "here is a pinch and a nib for you" [in Yiddish]. A "Rabbi's wife" such as this was likely to be beloved by the students more than a tutor with whip in hand at the ready.

At the same time I would also go to the cheder. In the winter I studied with the teacher Rabbi Meir on the Nagorzanka, and we would descend the hill in the evening, at eight, heading towards the town. We would go to the "animal market" near the soup kitchen, from whence we would go home in groups. Once, we reached the "animal market" and I was intending to walk home with a group of friends who lived nearby the great "Black Bridge," which crossed the Stripa river. However, imagine my surprise and amazement when I saw all my friends capturing pigs, which always wondered around there, and riding them home... I, who was reluctant to ride such an unclean beast, had to walk home on my own to my residence with my Aunt Chana, of blessed memory, and pass through the main road near the cemetery's stone wall. It was snowing heavily and I walked through the snow, daydreaming. And suddenly, I was horrified! A figure wrapped in a white prayer shawl appeared before me. It was none other than a "dead man" risen from his grave in the cemetery, approaching me. It did not take long for me to realize what this image was, I fell to the ground... When I awoke, I found myself in bed in my aunt's house. It turned out that an acquaintance had passed by in a sled and found me laying on the road, and had taken me on his sled and brought me home to my aunt... During the summer, I studied in a different cheder with a "tutor" (not a rabbi), Shmuel Horn, the brother-in-law of Dr. Peller. He was addressed by the students as "teacher", rather than "rabbi." He had a beautiful young daughter named Bertha, and I met her years later in Vienna.

I left Buczacz again after one year of study and returned to our quiet village, where I continued to study diligently with my father and teacher. Eventually, the rural idyll ended because we moved to the city, and I then entered the Baron Hirsch Primary School again, in the forth grade, where I studied together with my friend Yosef Tischler. Apart from general studies in Polish, we also learned German and Ukrainian. We learned Hebrew from a text book in Polish translation, and Hebrew grammar from the teacher Mordechai Kamper, mentioned previously.

The bridge on the way to the primary school and the "Sokol"

The market stalls next to the city council

On a Zionist celebration day

There was also a teacher of religion, meaning, Jewish history taught in Polish, who was the elderly teacher Reb Moshe Chaim Teuber, who had a long white beard and wore a black "prak". He was a teacher who had become licentious, and according to the gossip about him, he secretly smoked cigarettes on Shabbat. We had to learn the lessons by heart, word for word, from the Jewish history book, and mercy on us if we missed a word, God forbid... After the fourth grade of the primary school, we had to pass an exam in order to transfer to the gimnazjum. To my misfortune, the exam was given on Shabbat Chazon, the evening of Tisha Be'Av, and there was also a written exam. I was a religious boy, who kept all the mitzvot and was strictly observant, with short side-locks on my head – I was faced with the severe transgression of writing on Shabbat! The battle within my heart was difficult, but I gave in to the demand of my parents, of blessed memory, and I was also somewhat influenced by the bold approach of my friend Yosef Tischler to this severe transgression.

We passed the exam successfully and were accepted, with good fortune, to the gimnazjum, and once again I was tested by having to wear the goyishe uniform and cut off my side-locks. I lacked the courage for this operation, but my educated uncle Z. Rosenberg, of blessed memory, who later emigrated to America, stood by my side and took care of the arrangements. He led me to the barber, where I went through the "shearing" and returned home with my side-locks shorn, put on the blue uniform and went out with my uncle for a trial walk through town. In this way, I was admitted to the society of gimnazjum "students" in the highest educational institution in our town, where my fate was to battle the anti-Semitic teachers and fight for my survival, as I had to give private lessons to the school students and contribute to the support of my family, because my father, of blessed memory, continued to teach. My friend Yosef Tischler and I were among his students. We learned the Bible, Prophets, Talmud and Hebrew as a living language. I used the book "A Speaker of his People's Language" at that time, and in order to make the studies easier I put together a Hebrew-German dictionary from the textbook. This pamphlet disappeared over time.

I loved the Hebrew language and studied it with dedication and diligence. I found the Talmud studies difficult, especially as I had to study in the evenings when I was sleepy and exhausted from hard day's work. However, one thing would encourage me on those winter evenings of studying, which was an evening meal of hot potatoes and a cup of tea, after which I was able to continue my studies. I learned a few tractates, but I did not internalize the Aramaic language well.

My father, of blessed memory, used to pray at the great Beit Midrash (Sephardi version) next to the Great Synagogue. I was bar-mitzvahed at that Beit Midrash, and I would always pray there on Shabbat and holidays with my father. Rabbi Demata would also pray there, and the Beit Midrash attendees would sit and study diligently. I recall two prominent scholars, one was the grandson of the great tzadik from Buczacz, Rabbi Yisrael Leib, who was short and hunched, but his face was noble. The old-timer scholars would address him with various questions, especially when they were stuck with some serious problem. The second was a blind man, Chaim Raphael, and when someone would read to him from the Gemara, he could explain every single thing and could also continue reciting by heart from the place the reader had stopped. From among the town's most educated men, I recall S.Y. Agnon's father, who was a merchant and an educated man. It appears that it was he who paved the way for his young son in the field of Hebrew literature and lit the spark of poetry in his heart. I also recall Matityahu Weinraub's father, who was a scholar and was fluent in Hebrew and German. There was also the Zionist scholar Leibisch Fried, as well as David Neuman and Ginsberg, may they live long, who are now in Israel. There were also Jewish socialists such as Gottwald, who was associated with the Zionists, and a militant socialist from the town's group of assimilators, Mosler, a leader of the movement in the region, who also exerted great influence on the Ukrainian peasants.

On week days I would usually pray not in the large Beit Midrash, but in the old mittnagdim Beit Midrash, because I had to get up early and prepare to go to school. Therefore, I would pray early in the morning with the old-timers. As I stood in one corner of the Beit Midrash, immersed in my prayer, a young religious scholar with side-locks and a long coat stood at the other corner – it was S.Y. Agnon, who was destined to become the greatest Hebrew writer of our generation.

My love for Zion began when I was very young, in my childhood village, in the fields, gardens and forests of Pauszowka. During those days, I read a pamphlet published by "Hovevei Zion" in Odessa, which was very influential on me. During the First Zionist Congress my father, of blessed memory, would read reports from the congress in "HaTzfira" with me, about Dr. Herzl's speeches and his opponents... On Shabbat afternoons my father would attend a Hebrew speakers club in the "Zion" group, and he would come home and tell of how they spoke Hebrew for a whole hour, which made a great impression on me. During that period I would hike through the forests of Podlesie and Fedor in the environs of Buczacz, and I would read the historical stories of S. Friedberg about "The Kingdom of the House of David," Mapu's "Love of Zion" and also "Religion and Life" by Reuven Asher Broides, "The Book of Wandering" by Peretz Smolenskin, and amusement books by Yitzhak Farnhof. Zionist preachers would come and give sermons in the Great Synagogue and I waited impatiently for the preacher to finally start talking of the love of Zion and Eretz Yisrael. I particularly recall the preacher Abramson, who I believe was from the Ukraine, and who was the father of the Hebrew writer H. S. Ben-Avram, who now lives in Israel. He was a prominent Zionist national speaker, and how happy I was to hear him speak out against the Uganda plan, for I suffered the pain of "Zion Zionists", who were outraged at the "Ugandists." At that time, we read the Hebrew newspaper "Hamaggid", which was published in Krakow, and later "Hamitzpeh" and "Hatzfira". We also read the official German Zionist newspaper Die Welt, and later the Polish Wschod and Moriah.

Our "practical" Zionist activity began from the forth division of the gimnazjum, and consisted of founding Zionist circles among the unassimilated students. In these circles, we studied the history of Judaism and Zionism (using V. Sapir's book) and Eretz Yisrael studies. In particular, the students organized activities for JNF fund raising, distributing collection boxes to all sectors of the Jewish population and in the synagogues and study houses. Our first counselors and teachers were Matityahu Weinrab and Avraham Silbersein, of blessed memory, students of the upper classes in the gimnazjum, and after completing their studies at the gimnazjum – as academics. I recall how my friends Avraham Chalfan and Zvi Anderman (who is now a Reform rabbi in America) and I studied the book of Jessayahu with Silbersein, including learning entire chapters by heart. Silbersein also gave Chalfan lessons in Polish on Jewish history, from a book which would be published as a textbook by the "Zeirei Zion" center, which was a Zionist organization of Galician high-school students, from which Hashomer Hazair stemmed at the end of the First World War. Silbersein taught "Hebrew in Hebrew" to the gimnazjum students from all classes, both beginners and advanced students. His influence on us was great and he instilled in our hearts a significant affinity with Hebrew culture, for he was a philosopher with extensive knowledge of Jewish culture. There were some contrasts and a kind of completion between the two leaders, Avraham Silbersein and Matityahu Weinrab. The latter was an expert in Torah and Talmud and was warm-tempered, an enthusiastic Zionist and an exciting orator. He was a prominent Zionist activist, founder of the women's society, "Rachel," together with Dr. Peller's wife, and was very active there. This society conducted Zionist lectures. And I recall a lecture by Shlomo Schiller, who was invited especially from Lvov. Matityahu Weinrab's friend and partner in Zionist activity was Leon Weksler, an extremely talented orator, who was well-known as a popular speaker.

I would like to recount some events which are ingrained in my memory from those days. Once during the morning break from classes at the gimnazjum, my friend Manio Pohorile came over to me, alarmed, and said: "Did you know – Herzl has died!" It was a blow to the Zionist ideology which nested deep in our young hearts and it was impossible to accept this terrible news.

I was deeply impressed by the mourning assembly held in memory of Kishinev after the pogroms. This moving ceremony was held in the Great Synagogue, and besides the recitals of "Yizkor" and "El Male Rachamim" [prayer for the dead] by the cantor, some of the Zionist leaders participated in the ceremony as speakers, and the student choir sang Yehuda Halevi's "Eli Zion Ve'Areyah".

In 1906 a Hebrew author, Eliezer Rokeach, came to Buczacz. He was the uncle of former Minister of the Interior, Yisrael Rokeach, and came from Eretz Yisrael through Romania (see his description in Silberbusch's memoirs and in Moshe Smilenski's "The Family of Earth"). Rokeach quickly made contact with the intellectuals of Buczacz, especially with Mordechai Kamper, the Baron Hirsch School teacher mentioned previously, who had socialist tendencies. He also contacted the young poet, who was a rising star, Shmuel Yosef Czaczkes (Agnon). Together with them, Rokeach established a Hebrew literary journal, "HaYarden," and also published a weekly, "Der Waker" (the Arouser). In my estimation, these two intellectuals, Rokeach and Kamper, had no small influence on their young friend, the dreamer, who was taking his first steps in the field of Hebrew literature. Agnon would stroll with his two elderly friends in the "Schulgas Forest" and they would discuss literary and cultural issues, matters of great importance. I recall a literary lecture given by Agnon, a kind of essay on the new Hebrew literature, which was full of pearls of wisdom and brilliance.

Rokeach's lectures on Eretz Yisrael and Hebrew literature were scientific and in-depth, but the lecturer would flit from one subject to another and would strew his talks with the ideas of Aristotle, the Rambam, Schopenhauer, Nietzsche and Wagner. I remember one sentence from one of the lectures, when he was intending to compare and contrast Schopenhauer and Wagner: "Schopenhauer musizierte in der Philosophie und Wagner philosophierte in der Musik" ("Schopenhauer made philosophy into a kind of music and Wagner made music into a kind of philosophy"). I recall Mordechai Kamper's literary essay in "HaYarden" on Henryk Ibsen.

It would be appropriate to describe our gimnazjum teachers a little. There were a few Jewish teachers, and among the Christian teachers there were many enemies of Israel, but this did not prevent them from secretly accepting gifts, in cash and deeds, from the Jewish students' fathers, in order to sweeten the children's fate in the progress of their studies. An exception to this was the Latin and Greek teacher, whose name was Chlebek. He was a Pole, with white hair, dressed in old-fashioned "Schlacziz" clothes, a kind of short, green zupitza which reached down to his knees, and folded boots. He was a philologist, and besides the European and classical languages, Greek and Latin, he also knew Sanskrit and Semitic languages, including Hebrew, which he learned from Munish Bauer, the former Beit Midrash attendant, who became heretical. And the latter studied Latin and Greek from his student and teacher, Professor Chlebek. Chlebek would show the school students the similarities between Hebrew and the Arian languages, Latin and Greek, and Sanskrit. For example: the word "Ra'ah" [saw] is in Greek "hora'u", "har" [mountain] is similar to "horus," "shakaf" [transparent] to "skuapeo", "yayin" [wine] to "oyanus" and so forth. He would speak Hebrew with me, and would tell me to translate into Hebrew the lesson I had translated from Polish to Greek, and of course I would do so willingly. Once a supervisor came to visit the gimnazjum and when he saw my notebook, he asked: "What is this script doing in the Greek class?" Chlebek replied: "This student knows Hebrew, and I suggested that he translate the Greek into Hebrew."

In the upper classes of the gimnazjum, when we had to write an essay on a topic of our choosing, I abided by the following rule: begin every essay with a Hebrew saying. For example, I began the essay on the function of blood in the body with Hebrew and Latin characters: "Blood is the soul." I recall the teacher Kironski, who was a Greek teacher. When he entered the classroom we were in danger of being tested on our ability to recite a lesson from Xenofon or Homer. My friend then asked me to ask the teacher what he thought of some idea from a Jewish philosopher, a Talmud scholar or the principles of Judaism, as compared to the ideas of Socrates, Aristotle or Plato. The scheme was successful, for the philosopher teacher with his great mind, would delve into the ocean of Greek learning and extract several ideas from Greek wisdom. He would not have time to finish his lecture in one class and would have to continue the next class. With this trick, my friend and I escaped the hassle of a recitation exam a few times. I also recall another Latin teacher by the name of Rembetz, who had an awkward, fat body, and who was very fearful of the socialists and the anarchists. He called me an "anarchist" – I do not know where he got this opinion from.

Our serious cultural life occurred outside of school, in the general and Zionist cultural clubs, where we heard lectures on topics from general literature or historical subjects, or Hebrew literature. In those days I would prepare my homework together with my friend Manio Pohorile, who now lives in Jerusalem. Along with other friends, such as Zvi Heller, Schenberg, Guttfreud and others, we would give Zionist parties, especially Hebrew literature parties. Once we held a party in honor of Ahad Ha'Am's anniversary. I knew that Bialik had written a poem "To Ahad Ha'Am." However, I was unable to locate a book of Bialik's poems in the entire town, so having no choice, I had to sit down and write a poem for Ahad Ha'Am. And thus Ahad Ha'Am was saved from having no poem at the party held in his honor. All the Zionist gimnazjum students were organized in clubs with counselors from the upper classes, including myself.

Apart from the "Zion" group, in which the Zionists were organized, there was also the "Ivriya" club, where the young Hebrew teacher Yisrael Farnhof was especially active. They held various lectures on historical, Zionist and Jewish topics.

The Zionist activists in Buczacz tried to establish a Hebrew school in town. We attempted to bring in an external teacher, in addition to the local teachers. I found out that the writer G. Shofman was living in Lvov, and also engaged in teaching. I quickly wrote to him and invited him to come to our town and serve as the teacher in the Hebrew school about to be established. I received a rapid response on a postcard, with the words: "I will not move from here." Some time ago, when I visited Shofman, he reminded me of his words: "Do you remember what I wrote to you from Lvov: 'I will not move from here'..." "What a wonderful memory you have" I replied. In 1907, the expert teacher Baruch Yitzhak Berkowitz, who now lives in Hadera, was invited to Buczacz by the Galician teachers organization.

In 1907 I left Buczacz, due to the oppressive gimnazjum teachers, and moved to the town of Brzezany. There, I continued my studies and my Zionist activities, in the framework of the "Zeirei Zion" organization of students, and in "Ha'Ivriyah", under the guidance of the Hebrew teacher Zvi Sharpstein, now a professor at a teaching seminary in America. And on the holidays when I came to the home of my parents, of blessed memory, in Buczacz, I took part in "Ivriyah." My friend Yosef Tischler, who came to his parents' house on holidays, would also be active in "Ivriyah," and I remember one lecture he gave on "the Jewish Legend." After completing my gimnazjum studies in 1909, I had to decide which profession was most suitable for me in Eretz Yisrael before entering university. I asked for advice at the "Hovevei Zion" office in Jaffa, whose secretary was then S.Y. Agnon, who had made aliya two years prior. I received a reply with advice to study medicine, but Agnon wrote on the margins of the card: "Stay where you are and seek out a living there." This angered me, for I viewed it as an insult to my heart's desire to make aliya to Eretz Yisrael. And when I met Agnon here I asked him why he had given such as response. He replied that during those days they were not issuing propaganda for making aliya, due to the harsh conditions in Israel. Agnon later immortalized that conversation of ours in his book A Guest for the Night, in a conversation that occurs between the narrator and Dr. Milch.

After I left Galicia in 1909 and moved to Vienna, I of course continued my Zionist activities, in the JNF and the Eretz Yisrael office, and I took part in founding the Hebrew academic society "HaTchiah," together with my friends from Buczacz, Avraham Chalfan and Zvi Anderman. We later founded the Hebrew Association, but that is a separate episode in the history of Zionist youth who moved from Buczacz to Vienna.

My parents moved from Buczacz to Vienna in 1915 and I lived there with them until coming to Israel. Later, I visited them frequently here in Hadera, until their deaths in 5702.

[Page 174]

The First Hebrew School in Buczacz
Translated by Jessica Cohen

In October of 1907, I was invited by the Hebrew school committee to accept the position of headmaster of the school which was to be established in the town (the members of the committee, if memory serves, were Itzi Hirsch Weisser, Bezalel Herzes, Matityahu Weinreib and Jacob Leib Alfenbein). Upon my arrival in Buczacz, I found the committee members, who were holding office in Itzi Anderman's hotel, busy registering students. A young man stood beside them, his face blushing like the cheeks of a young woman. He was greatly enjoying the events, as if it were for his particular satisfaction that the parents were coming to register their sons for the new Hebrew school. It was Shmuel Czaczkes (the author S. Y. Agnon). The committee announced that it had hired an assistant teacher: a private Hebrew tutor in the town, whose livelihood would be damaged when the school opened, and they therefore found it befitting to take him on as an assistant teacher in the school. I visited the teacher, Rosenman, in his home. He was a learned man, a kind of *talmid hacham*[1], his face emanating a childish innocence and a delicate soul. He expressed his fear that he would not be able to manage a class, for he was not accustomed to that. I assured him he would have my complete assistance. The committee rented an apartment, brought in used benches and a blackboard, and the studies began.

A few days after my arrival in Buczacz, two students from the upper class of the *gimnazjum* came to see me. Their names were Naftali Menatzeach (Sigman, now a physician in Hadera) and Yosef Tischler (now an architect in Jerusalem). They asked if I would be willing to accept a group of students from the upper class at the *gimnazjum* to study Hebrew, new literature, grammar, the Book of Prophets and so forth, as well as a group of young women who had graduated from the *gimnazjum* but were still at a beginner level of Hebrew. Of course my answer was: yes! They told me that they had decided to speak only Hebrew amongst themselves and now, with the opening of a Hebrew school in their town – their longtime aspiration – they had decided to propagandize the Hebrew language. They would walk through the neighborhood streets and speak Hebrew out loud. The public would hear and would know that our language was being resurrected. I explained to them that indeed that was one of the school's duties, but we should not be too hasty. If they waited a short while, within a few months they would see the teacher walking with the school students on the main roads, speaking Hebrew and singing Hebrew songs. We would also produce historical plays for the public in Hebrew, and it would be a natural, inartificial presentation. But they were insistent, they had made a decision that could not be changed. The student Naftali Menatzeach was particularly stubborn, he was an uncompromising radical fanatic. The second student, Yosef Tischler, was also a fanatic of the Hebrew language, but slightly more moderate. He was a sort of *talmid hacham* among the students. His knowledge of the Hebrew language was greater than that of his friends. And "the words of wise men are heard in quiet."[2] As a Hebrew teacher, I stood ashamed before these pillars of fire. I said to myself: if only there were more fanatics such as these in Israel! These *gimnazjum* graduates perceived the new Hebrew school as a small temple, where the teacher was the High Priest serving in the holy temple, and when he touched the school it was as if he were touching the apple of their eye. Their love for the Hebrew language knew no boundaries. The Hebrew school served them as a symbol of the Hebrew national and cultural revival.

The religious people were opposed to the school from the first. Their attacks were particularly directed towards the head of the school committee, Itzi Hirsch Weisser, who was an enlightened religious Zionist. They spoke badly of the teacher, for being shaven and perhaps also irreligious. The sacred language was taught bareheaded in the Hebrew school (the Tanach was taught with covered heads). The teacher walked with his female students along the main roads, speaking the sacred language openly. And the head of the committee took out his anger on the teacher and the older female students, for not coming to study Hebrew, but rather to socialize with their friends the *gimnazjum* graduates. Matters even reached the court, and the head of the committee was punished for insulting the senior female students. He began to interfere with the internal affairs of the school, to judge what was permitted and what was not, and what he was permitted to do and what he was not. Fortunately for me, the students' parents were on my side and did not allow the school to be turned into a *cheder*. The *gimnazjum* students stood by my side as a rock, defended their school and teacher and repelled all the attacks.

Several of the school graduates are in Israel: Dr. Naftali Menatzeach, Dr. Avraham Halfan (both in Hadera); Dr. Zvi Heller and his wife Dr. Esther Pnina Heller nee Anderman, his sister Dr. Pnina Neuberger (Tel Aviv), his younger sister Dr. Clara Kaner (Haifa), Chaya Rol of blessed memory, nee Biler, Dr. Emmanuel Pohorila (Jerusalem), Dr. David Pohorila, Attorney, Dr. Nussia Meibaum nee Tzeler, architect Yosef Tischler (Jerusalem), Dr. Pnina Shapira (Kiriat Haim).

For Chanukah, I prepared a play with the school students, "Chana and her Seven Sons," as well as recitals and songs. Two days before the play, I received a notice from the district governor, prohibiting the production of the play, because it was "anti-Polish." I immediately went to see the mayor, Barris Stern, a learned Jew, whose attitude toward the school was positive and supportive, despite being a pillar of the authorities. I showed him the governor's notice and the text of the play in Hebrew, which was an historical play from the time of the *Hasmoneans* and had nothing to do with the affairs of Poland. The mayor went to see the district governor, showed him the text of the play in Hebrew and asked him what was the meaning of the prohibition. The governor showed him an informant's letter claiming that it was an "anti-Polish" play, and asked the mayor to provide him with a Polish translation of the play by the end of the day. The translation was provided, and the play went on to be presented as planned. The informant's letter was the best possible propaganda for the school. The mayor and the Jewish and Christian government officials came to the play. The finest of the town's citizens came and the auditorium was full to the brim. When the informants realized that their scheme had failed, they published a manifest to the residents of Buczacz, by the name of "*Shema Yisrael*," which was full of curses and abuses, and defamations of the teacher who was seducing the town's children away from traditional Judaism. They sent one copy to my parents in the *moshava* of Yavniel,[3] to influence me to renounce my evil ways, otherwise I would meet with ill fate. The opponents' acts strengthened my spirit even more in my determination to hold strong and not to flee the battle.

When I came to Galicia in 1906, the Hebrew school was still a newborn. The school was not built on firm ground. The school committee did not collect funds to reserve for times of recession. It did not sign annual contracts with the parents, so that they would pay for the holidays as well. As it happened, when everything ran smoothly, there was money to pay the teachers. But some of the parents removed their less advanced sons from the Hebrew school a few months before the exams in the public schools, as they were concerned that they would not be able to pass the government exams. The school's income decreased and there was no money to pay the teachers with, which was an obstacle for the development of the Hebrew school in Galicia. The committee did nothing on its part to fill the void, and its claims of having nowhere to obtain money from, did not satisfy the teacher nor his empty stomach.

A similar thing occurred in Buczacz. As long as the school attendant delivered the money he collected from the parents to me (many parents would send the tuition with their sons directly to me), there was money to pay the teachers, the janitor, the rent and the other expenses. I would present a monthly report to the committee. However, when the head of the committee ordered the collector not to deliver the collected money to me, but rather to him, he stopped paying salaries to myself and the attendant and did not pay the rent. When I asked the head of the committee where the money he had collected was and why he was not paying the salaries and the rent, he turned to me and said: how can you demand an account from me? The head of the committee was certain that he had grasped the bull by its horns. I had no choice but to turn to the parents and ask them to send the tuition directly to me, otherwise I would be forced to close the school. When the head of the committee realized that his control had been lost, he summoned a parents meeting and invited all the opponents of the school. He also invited the head of the teachers' organization and brought along a teacher who was to be given the position of headmaster instead of myself (I do not wish to mention any names, since I had a previous disagreement with the head of the teachers' organization and with the aforementioned teacher). The meeting was stormy, curses and insults flew over my head like hail. I requested permission to speak, so as to reply to my critics, and was not granted it. This created an even greater storm. The head of the teachers' organization and the teacher sat in anticipation of the moment when the crown of headmaster would be removed from my head and assigned to the awaiting teacher. And then came a man with a letter and delivered it to the head of the teachers' organization, and invited him and the teacher sitting by his side to accompany him. Upon their departure, the meeting dispersed. It was said that one of the parents had gone to the mayor and told him about the scandal, and he had summoned the head of the teachers' organization and the teacher, and warned them that they should leave the matter alone, because they might be about to unwittingly destroy the school. The head of the school committee returned home with his tail between his legs, for his honor had departed from him. And I was released from my shackles. I became free to realize my aspirations and my plans to establish the Hebrew school on a sound foundation, both materially and pedagogically, which would not be subject to fluctuations and shocks. This affair became well-known in all the Galician towns, from one end to another, and was the talk of the day, not only amongst the teachers. I met with M. Lipshitz, who later became the director of a *Beit Midrash* for teachers operated by the *Mizrachi*[4] in Jerusalem, and he told me: "We in Lvov knew of the scandal occurring in Buczacz. And we knew how the scheme was undone."

The years 1907-1908 were full of bitterness for me. But they were also years of much experience, during which I became familiar with the ills of the Hebrew schools in Galicia, but also with their healing methods. Difficult pedagogical problems presented themselves and demanded solutions. The Hebrew schools in Galicia were schools only by name; in reality they were places of Hebrew lessons for only one or two hours. One group left and another came. I was faced with the question of how to create a comprehensive Hebrew school.

In November of 1908 I traveled to Palestine to visit my parents and take a rest from my wrath and anger. I gave the task of running the Hebrew school in Buczacz to one whom I had educated as a teacher in Rohatin and later in Buczacz, Yisrael Farnhof. In Palestine, I visited schools, in particular nursery schools. In April 1909 I returned to Buczacz. I rented a large garden with fruit trees and shady trees, from Moshe Weisser. I built a large, spacious shed in it. I announced that I was opening a "kindergarten" for ages three to seven. Two days before the opening, I received a notice from the district governor that I must dismantle the shed within 24 hours, otherwise the municipality would dismantle it, at my expense, and I would have to pay a fine. This time too, I went to the mayor, showed him the notice, and explained to him the purposes of the kindergarten and the educational value of preparing children for school, and that it was the first Hebrew-Polish kindergarten in Galicia. There were almost no Polish kindergartens in the entire country. The mayor went to the district governor and asked him why the notice had been given. The governor showed him an informant's letter, according to which I was intending to open a *cheder* opposite the council house and the national bank in town (the word *cheder* was a derogatory word among the Poles, implying a place of dirtiness and lack of order). Of course, the kindergarten was opened on time with no obstacles. The informant's letter only managed to create wide publicity for the new kindergarten.

Some two months after the opening of the kindergarten, I notified the chairman of the "Organization of Hebrew Schools in Galicia," Dr. P. Korngrein (who later became a judge in the Tel Aviv District Court), of the opening of the kindergarten in Buczacz. I mentioned that I was willing to allow female graduates of the Hebrew schools in Galicia the opportunity to receive a practical education in my kindergarten. I requested that the school organization send a delegation to visit the kindergarten and ascertain whether it was worthy of its duties. The organization sent Dr. Moshe Yisrael Ratt to visit the kindergarten. Dr. Ratt heard the children speaking, telling stories, singing, making crafts, playing and talking Hebrew among themselves. He asked me how many years these children had been studying in the kindergarten. I told him that the kindergarten had only opened some three months prior, and he thought I was fooling him. After that visit, the school organization published a notice in the newspaper, calling on headmasters of Hebrew schools in Galicia to send their outstanding graduating female students to Buczacz, to receive an education in nursery school teaching, and to later open kindergartens in all the towns of Galicia (one of those educators, Pnina Stein, has been operating a kindergarten in Tel Aviv for several decades). That year, the editor of the newspaper "*Ha'Mitzpeh*" in Krakow, Dr. S. Lazar, published an article in his paper in which he described the great shortage of teachers in Galicia, and asked the headmasters of the Hebrew schools to enable young people to train themselves as teachers, under their administration. In a letter to the editor, I replied that I was willing to do this. After the editor of "*Ha'Mitzpeh*" conducted an investigation and ascertained the quality of my school, he published an article in his paper about Mr. Baruch Berkowitz's school in the town of Buczacz, and called on young people who wished to train themselves as teachers to travel there and be educated at the school. (One of those young people, who has been in Israel for several years, is the Hebrew linguist Nissan Bergreen, author of the grammar book "The Theory of Forms.")

In 1910 the Organization of Hebrew Schools in Galicia held a "Day of Hebrews" in Lvov. I was invited to participate in this occasion. I replied to Dr. Korngrein, the chairman of the organization, that I was willing to come and bring with me "an exhibition" of the work of the children in my kindergarten. I asked to be informed whether they would provide me with a space to present the exhibition. The response was positive. When I arrived with the exhibition at the "*Tikvat Zion*" auditorium, where the "Day of Hebrews" in Lvov was to be held, they showed me the area they had assigned for the exhibition. I took out the children's works and began to arrange them. The exhibition made an indescribable impression! Each of the representatives wanted to take one of the children's works, to show the people of their towns the wonders of the kindergarten in Buczacz. And thus the town of Buczacz became a small center for Hebrew education in Galicia. The years 1909-1912 were glorious years for the school and the kindergarten in the town of Buczacz. They represented a certain compensation for the years of suffering and anger during 1907-1908.

In July 1912, I traveled during the vacation to the village of Mikoliczin Wirmaczia, in thug the Carpathian Mountains. There I met the Zionist leaders from Lvov, Dr. Michal Ringel, Dr. B. Hausner, Jacob Bodek, and the writer Eliezer Rokeach. They asked me why I had chosen the distant town of

Buczacz, of all places, as a location of educational action, rather than Lvov, the center of Zionism. The Zionist organization could be of assistance to me and could be useful for extensive educational activity. When they tried to convince me to move to Lvov and begin everything afresh, I told them of my educational plans. I told them that the kindergarten I established in Buczacz was not an end in and of itself, but rather the means to a greater end. The kindergarten would be the foundation for a comprehensive Hebrew school: an elementary school and a Hebrew-Polish *gimnazjum*. Dr. Ringel replied: in that case, there is all the more reason for you to move to Lvov. The Zionist organization will help you with everything. In September, I moved to Lvov. The Buczacz episode was over, and a new episode – the Lvov episode – began. Some of my dreams in that realm came true in Lvov. In 1914 the First World War broke out. Lvov was conquered by the Russians, and "during war, the muses are silent," as the old Greek saying goes. As a result of my endeavors, a board was chosen which included Zvi Karl (who is now in Tel Aviv), his brother-in-law Dr. Teuber, and the Zionist Shlomo Ducker (now in Tel Aviv), and they opened a Hebrew-Polish elementary school. I managed a kindergarten and a Hebrew school. I also gave lessons to teachers, both male and female, and to kindergarten teachers. The Jews of Galicia experienced much turmoil – the conquering of Galicia by the Russians and its liberation, the pogroms conducted by the Polish armies and the "Holertziks" against the Jews of Lvov and other towns after the end of the First World War, the collapse of the Austrian monarchy, the Bolsheviks' storming of Galicia in 1920, their approach to Lvov – all these forced me to comply with my parents' request to return to Palestine. In 1920, I returned with my family to Palestine.

The history of the Hebrew schools in Galicia, the great educational activity carried out by the teachers for the benefit of the students, by means of the Hebrew schools, as well as the results which were later discernible among the Hebrew youths who left the schools, the *gimnazjums*, the universities, and came to Palestine to participate in building the country – all these deserve to be recorded as memories for the next generations.

Baruch Y. Berkowitz
Jerusalem-Hadera.

Endnotes

1. *Talmid hacham*: lit. "wise student" (Hebrew). A phrase used to describe a scholar of Jewish law [tr.]

2. Ecclesiastes 9:17 [tr.]

3. *Moshava*: The earliest type of Jewish settlement in pre-state Israel, originally agricultural [tr.]

4. *Mizrachi*: An international religious Zionist movement, founded in Vilna in 1902 [tr.]

[Page 179]

Histadrut Hechalutz in Buczacz
Translated by Jessica Cohen

In 1923, the foundation of the Hechalutz[5] movement in Buczacz was reestablished, after an intermission of over two years since the Third Aliyah[6] group made aliyah in 1920. The main impetus came from a few young people, centered around Yisrael Cohen, who were very active in operating the *Hechalutz* movement in our town.

But before I describe *Hechalutz*'s methods of action and status in our town, I must preface by mentioning two organizations, one political and one cultural, which existed during this period in Buczacz. For these organizations constituted an embryo from which *Hechalutz* emerged, and also because most of the *Hechalutz* founders were active in these organizations. I am referring to the *Hitachdut*[7] party and to the *Ivriya*[8] association. I shall not go into details about the *Hitachdut*, but I shall devote my words to the *Ivriya*.

The establishment of *Ivriya* stemmed from an essential need to concentrate the supporters of the Hebrew language and culture, who were scattered with no contact amongst them. The founder and active force in this association was the Hebrew teacher, Yisrael Farnhof. Among the organization activists were Dr. Silberstein, Yisrael Cohen, Ms. Khaye Roll, of blessed memory, Gitta Glantzer, Ms. Enmelding, L. Hartzman, Chaim Weisenthal, Arieh Frankel, Moshe Held, and others.

The organization was active in a variety of areas. They laid the foundations for a Hebrew library, which helped to form Hebrew reading groups. Lectures were delivered in Hebrew on Jewish and general topics. There were training courses in various subjects. The association's impression and influence were discernible beyond the boundaries of the organization.

There were also serious efforts to establish a theatre group, with the assistance of Kalman Friedman. One play, by the name of "Shaul and David," was extremely successful.

I recall a series of lectures given by Ms. Roll about S.Y. Agnon. There were a number of people in Buczacz for whom the Hebrew language and culture was an essential need, such as Dr. Khalfan, of blessed memory, who was permeated with Hebrew culture and who would express his affinity with the language at every opportunity.

I recall a typical episode, during the opening session of the newly elected community assembly (if I am not mistaken, this was in 1924). Dr. Khalfan delivered a welcoming speech in Hebrew, which was of course received enthusiastically on the part of the language loyalists, and unwillingly on the part of the assimilated. At that point, he was nicknamed by Mr. Yakov Stern, "der Dr. mit di brayteh paschin"

Histadrut Hechalutz, which was established, as was previously mentioned, in 1923, was affiliated with the *Hechalutz* center in Lvov. The movement aimed to propagate the idea of labor and agricultural training, imparting the language and values of the Hebrew culture, and primarily: making *aliyah* to

Israel and personal fulfillment of the ideology. The path of the Buczacz *Hechalutz* movement was not easy at first. The decline in the public affairs of the Jewish community, which prevailed after the period of flourishing following the war, as well as the signs of assimilation which were revealed during that period, constituted a severe obstacle for its activity. There were also harsh objections on the part of parents, who did not want to get used to the idea that their children would be separated from them and become farmers or just plain laborers.

Despite all these difficulties, the movement managed to expand its activities, accepted new members and developed far-reaching cultural activity. Most of the members already spoke Hebrew, and those who were not yet fluent were given the opportunity to become so.

A profound influence on the ideas and directions of the movement occurred when its members departed to a *hachshara*[9], in which the group *garin*[10] was molded. After extensive consideration, the group was organized during Pesach of 1924, and was called "hameshulash" [the triangle] (its slogans were: language, labor, country). Its members were: Yisrael Cohen, Asher Cohen, Fischel Neiberger, Herzl Margalit, Shmuel Karbas, Zipporah Judenfreund, Shoshana Narpan, Tzvi Pikholtz, S. Wisinger, Moni Landman, Arieh Kopler and Moshe Held.

This step had a profound impact on the life of the town, particularly amongst the youth. As a result, a large *hachsharah* movement arose in the town, and the Shomer Hatzair movement was also revived. Some of the members made *aliyah* to Israel, while a few others ceased believing in the Zionist idea after a short while and turned their backs on the country.

Other *hachsharah* groups were established on the model of the *"meshulash"* group at that time.

The group's first steps were in Lvov. There, the members found work in construction, and here they were first faced with all the problems which were typical of any group at the beginning of its way, such as: difficulties in adapting to physical labor and to communal life, which demands giving up various habits. They managed to overcome all these problems by means of goodwill and mutual understanding, which later accompanied the group during the entire period of its existence in Israel and abroad.

After a few months of work in Lvov, they decided to go to an agricultural *hachsharah*, in order to crystallize the group in preparation for *aliyah*. And indeed, after a period of *hachsharah* and after various trials and tribulations of *aliyah*, the group immigrated to Palestine and settled in Petach Tikva, in Emek Hasheva.

Moshe Held

Endnotes

5. Lit. "the pioneer" (Hebrew)

6. Aliyah: immigration to Israel; lit. "ascension". There were several waves of Aliyah. The Third Aliyah was between 1919 and 1923, and consisted mostly of Jewish immigrants from Eastern Europe, primarily from Russia.

7. Lit. "union" or "federation" (Hebrew).

8. Lit. the feminine form of the adjective "Hebrew" (Hebrew)

9. Lit. "training" (Hebrew). These were training camps set up in various places in Europe, intended to prepare young Jewish men and women for their impending life in Israel as agricultural workers.

10. Lit. "seed," "core" or "nucleus." This refers to groups of young people who went through various social and training activities together, and then either settled in an established kibbutz or moshav, or founded their own new settlement.

[Page 180]

Hospital and Old Age Home in Buczacz
Translated by Jessica Cohen

When you walked up the steps next to the synagogue, then passed the "*leitze stiebl*" and turned right, you were immediately faced with a serious looking white building, two stories high, with large windows with three window panes in each, a low fence on both sides, and a few steps in the middle which lead to a strong, heavy door, which was usually closed. On the front wall, between the two stories, large letters read: "Szpital Izraelicki." On each side of the entrance were plaques bearing the names of the founders, Yisrael Moshe Stern and Yisrael Moshe Preminger. This was the most popular building in town, respected and beloved by all strata of the residents and interwoven in their lives. The hospital was involved in any happy event or sad occasion, and always contributed to alleviating the pain or increasing the joy.

In the hospital yard was a large ice storehouse, almost the only one in town, which served the residents. At times of sickness, not only patients who were being treated in the hospital itself benefited from it, but also any people who needed it. There was no celebration in town, in which the celebrator would not remember the hospital and contribute a small or large sum to it. A lovely custom took roots during the last years among the residents: before every important event they would donate meals to the hospital and to the old age home. Whether it was a bar-mitzvah or a wedding, a birthday or a yarzheit, the lady of the household would take pains to appear in the hospital office to consult with the manager of the institute with regards to which items were needed and how much she should prepare, and she herself would enjoy the act of giving, more than the elderly people and the patients enjoyed the dishes she prepared.

The hospital had one more interaction with the public. Every year a *minyan* was arranged on the top floor of the building for the High Holy days. Anyone who did not wish to pray in the synagogues, whether because of their crowded conditions or for any other reason, reserved a place there. *Aliyas*[11] were purchased for small sums and were not used, and their places were taken by patients or elderly people from the institution. Of course, the number of women was significantly greater than the number of men registered at the services. This *minyan* generated a decent income for the hospital fund, particularly since all the organizers and the service leaders were volunteers. I would like to mention

Mr. Gdaliyahu Duchovny, of blessed memory, who led the *Mussaf* prayer. He was a God-fearing Jew, with a most pleasant voice.

There was also a traditional ball held during the winter months for several years, to benefit the hospital. The ball was held in the large hall in the town, in the "Sokol" building, and almost all the townspeople took part in it, both Jews and non-Jews. All the Polish aristocracy with the "*starostwa*" at the head, took part in the ball.

The hospital began to operate even before the great fire of 1866; in that fire, the hospital building was burnt along with a large part of the town. Only the walls remained, which were temporarily repaired. It was a neglected building, which the townspeople used to call "a poor-house." This poor-house served as a shelter for the poor, the sick and the maimed, who could not afford to rent their own apartments. The house was managed by an old man who lived there, who was referred to as "*der hekdesh-man*" [the poor-house man]. The residents of the poor-house survived on money they begged for, and on meals sent to them by the townspeople.

In 1891 some of the Buczacz residents established a committee for the renewal of the hospital. Among them were Yisrael Moshe Stern (whose mother, Fiegeh Waksler, donated a large sum of money for this purpose), Yisrael Moshe Preminger, Yitzhak Seidman, Isaac Nacht, Yoel and Nathan Neiman, Reuven Leib Pohorile, and others. They gave their own contributions for this purpose, and raised other donations. They renovated the building and set up a modern hospital on the first floor for the community of Buczacz and the surrounding areas. The late Y.M. Preminger was president of the hospital for many years, and the late Y. M. Stern was its director. The latter devoted most of his life to directing and maintaining the hospital and also tried to ensure a future existence for the institution. For this purpose, he built and renovated a few houses left by various estates, including the house of the Margolis family, where the community committee was later located; the stores adjacent to this house; the lot opposite the community house including its stores; the chicken slaughterhouse; the stores and mainly the butcher shops and the "folks-kich" above them. Some of the income from these buildings was devoted to maintaining the hospital, and some to the *Talmud Torah*. In addition to all this, many of the townspeople agreed to give monthly donations to the institution.

For a few years, the hospital building was rented out to the Baron Hirsch's school, and the folks-kich (public kitchen) was also located in it for a while, and in this way it was possible to furnish and arrange the top floor of the institution.

Dr. Fabian Nacht was appointed medical director of the hospital from its first day, and he served in this capacity for over thirty years.

In 1908, an old age home was set up on the first floor of the building, with room for 15 people. Among the founders of this institution were Yisrael Moshe Preminger, Yisrael Moshe Stern, Avish Stern, Yitzhak Seidman, Leibish Fried and David Neiman, who was for many years a voluntary secretary. Moshe Farb donated the first ten beds for the opening of the old age home. In order to enable the maintenance of the old age home, the community committee donated the right to collect payment for tombstones, for this purpose.

In this way, the two institutions were conducted until 1914.

When the First World War broke out, almost all the Jewish residents left the town and the building became ownerless. Between 1914 and 1920, following the various occupations of the town, the building served periodically as a hospital for the war casualties of the various sides. It should be noted that the only patient who remained there during that whole period, was Leah (Abenstein) with her sister "Baba," who was lame. They later moved to the old age home and remained there until all the residents and employees of both the institutions were killed by the Nazis in 1942.

When the war was over in 1920, a general assembly was held to elect a new board for the two institutions. The following were elected: David Neumann – Chairman; Zigmunt Cook – Assistant Chairman; Leib Roll – Vice Chairman and Administrator; Monish Frankel – Treasurer; Tzvi Nirenberg – Secretary. Other members chosen were Ms. Shnitzi Herzes, Ms. Paula Marengel, Ms. Frieda Rosen, Julius Tzeler, Fischel Skalka, David Shechner, Moshe Wolftal, Pinchas Weinstock, Yosef Knobler, Haim Frankel, Yehuda Pitzel, Fischel Kittenflon, Alter Goldberg and Itzik Wolf Yorman.

The new board found the hospital and the old age home in a terrible condition. The building was decrepit, there was no linen, the few pieces of furniture had been tossed in the corners of the rooms, and the patients used dirty rags to dry themselves instead of towels. The nutrition was very poor, and only saccharine was used to sweeten the food, and even that only a little. The patients were literally starving. It was winter, and of course there was nothing to fuel the heaters with.

The board immediately conducted a once-off fund raising campaign, to raise money, food and linen. They fixed the building and organized the rooms and the yard. All the rooms were thoroughly cleaned, linen was purchased, the kitchen was improved and dinnerware was purchased. As we have mentioned, the head physician was Dr. Nacht. At the same time, the board requested assistance from the Joint and was given a number of beds, sheets, linen, medicine, surgical and medical devices, and a large amount of soap, tooth powder, toothbrushes and more.

The institutions had five sources of income at the time:

1. The rent from the houses and stores mentioned previously;

2. The right to collect payment from erection of tombstones, which was estimated and assessed according to the individual's financial situation;

3. Annual support from the community committee (which was never given in full);

4. Monthly payments from some of the townspeople, which the new board obtained for the two institutions;

5. Pledges and donations to benefit the institutions on any occasion such as weddings, balls, etc.

The patients were taken in free of charge, as were the elderly people. A clinic was organized for poor patients outside the institution, and they were also given free medication. The condition improved from one year to the next, thanks to the dedicated work of the administration members. Ms. Adella Pines was the manager of the hospital at that time, and she was tireless in her efforts to improve the health and nutrition conditions in the institution.

In 1923, Leib Roll was elected as Chairman of the institution, and he served in this capacity until the end of 1934, at which time he made *aliyah* to *Eretz Yisrael*. From that time until the hospital ceased to exist, Monish Frankel was the Chairman, and Paula Marangel and Yosef Knobler were Assistant Chairs. At first, there were 16 beds in the hospital and 15-16 elderly residents. More improvements were introduced, including electric lighting and running water in the building. A pretty garden was arranged around the building, a hut for infectious patients, a morgue, a laundry room and an ice storehouse.

In 1925, after more than thirty years of dedicated and fruitful activity in the hospital, Dr. Nacht stepped down as head physician, due to his age, and was replaced by Dr. Mordechai Hirschorn, who remained in this capacity until the hospital was transferred to the authority of the Soviet government.

Over the course of time, the hospital's character changed, and their was a need to expand it and add more beds, and therefore the old age home was moved to a new building which was acquired from the *Talmud Torah* committee, and four additional spaces were added in it for elderly patients. Since this was the only hospital in the entire district – there was no governmental hospital – the workrooms and storage areas had to be expanded. The expanded hospital included a delivery room, two quarantine rooms, a surgery room, and a bathroom with hot water. The situation in the hospital, both medically and organizationally, improved so much that even patients from the wealthier classes of town endeavored to be accepted as patients, in return for pay of course.

In 1929, due to the economic crisis and the impoverishment of the Jewish population, the hospital's external sources of income decreased and the institution was forced to become self-supporting. Only after a number of years was there an interest in this public institution on the part of the Buczacz *Landsmannschaft* in America, and they supported it with considerable donations. At the same time, in 1936, a new physician was hired by the hospital, Dr. Tzvi Rosenman, and more nurses were also hired. That same year, a medical laboratory was also organized in the hospital, where Dr. Yoachim Gottfried (who is now in Israel) worked. The number of beds in the hospital was increased to 40.

Much of the improvement in the situation and in the internal conditions, must be credited to the managers, the first of whom was Ms. Adella Pines, who worked until 1932. After her, the management was given to Ms. Esther Besner (Eisenberg), who remained in this capacity until she moved to Israel in 1935. The final manager was Ms. Betty Medwinska, who worked until 1942, when she was transferred along with part of the townspeople to the gas chambers in Belzec.

From the beginning of the war, in September 1939, the hospital served as a military hospital, where all the war casualties during that time were treated. After a few weeks, the hospital was moved to the governmental buildings (in Podlesie), where Dr. Avraham Khalfan worked as director of the internal and X-ray department, and Dr. Blottreich and Dr. Gottfried also worked there. The abandoned hospital buildings, and the old age home buildings, became a governmental old age home for both Jews and Christians. This old age home was under the medical supervision of Dr. Hirschorn, and was managed by Ms. Medwinska. Of course, the Jewish character of the institution was completely eradicated, and the elderly residents went hungry as they could not eat the non-kosher food.

During the Nazi period, the hospital was managed by a Jewish doctor, whose name it would be best not to mention.

It should be noted that all the physicians who worked at the hospital in Buczacz during the final period, whether full-time or part-time, are all still alive, including all the nurses who worked there during that time.

Today, the building is in ruins, the doors and windows are broken, the roof and some of the internal walls are destroyed. It is a ruin, in which such beautiful Jewish life once flourished.

(compiled by Khaye Roll, of blessed memory)

Endnotes
11. This refers to the honor of being called up during the reading of the Torah to recite a blessing.

[Page 184]

The Orphanage
Translated by Adam Prager

I do not remember the exact date of the founding of the orphanage in Buczacz, however I believe it was between the years 1920-1922. I think that the first director of the orphanage was Mrs. Pohorila. As far as my feeble memory allows me to recall, she was of medium height and pleasant features, with good pedagogic skills. I do not know who the members of the orphanage committee were. Mrs. Pohorila was followed by Miss Sonia Blutreich, who was a good friend to the children. After Miss Blutreich's marriage, Miss Paulina Anderman was appointed director and educator. This was in the years 1930-1931. Besides the director-educator there were the matron and an assistant.

The orphanage, which was co-educational, had 50 children, aged 19, 18, and 5, an obviously undesirable age distribution. However, it was impossible to let the older ones leave without receiving a high school diploma of some kind. The institution, or more exactly, its managerial committee, did not fulfill its task by this alone. It also took an interest in the lives of its graduates: it found them suitable jobs in those hard times and arranged scholarships for the talented ones so that they could continue their studies. The Buczacz orphanage was known for the quality of its graduates, individuals of understanding and character who were well prepared for the struggle of life.

One of the graduates, a second-year medical student, fell while fighting for a free Spain. This was Karol Neuberger, brother of a teacher in the Stanislevov gymnasium.

The orphanage pupils were for the most part accounted to be good workers, their labor and energy serving as an example to others. I would also like to mention a boy by the name of Zelig Lampert. He was an illegitimate child who had apparently been handed over to peasants in a village either by a mother who was cruel or who in those years had been rejected by society, and who later left for America. Under a false name, claiming to be his aunt, she would send money from time to time to cover the expenses for the child's upkeep. The managerial committee heard about this boy. In order to "save" a Jewish soul, the committee arranged to transfer him to the orphanage. Of course, this called for a certain amount of monetary persuasion. The peasant family was not eager to lose a cheap source of labor; perhaps it had already become used to the child it had raised from infancy.

He was a clever and talented boy, but difficult to teach. He was full of resentment towards the world that had deprived him of a normal childhood. People's personalities can change from one extreme to the other in times of war. Fear has often changed the bad into good and the noble into the bestial. What of Zelig? This youth, who didn't look Jewish, had the opportunity to save himself; instead, he defended the lives of other Jews at the cost of his own. I heard this story from an acquaintance who lived in Buczacz during the war and who had little to tell about other orphanage pupils. He had heard that some succeeded in fleeing to Russia, a few abroad and the rest were murdered. This war claimed many victims.

I should mention the activities of the supervisory Committee for Jewish Children and Youth. The orphanage was maintained partly by contributions and partly by the Jewish public and the kehila [Jewish community]. The above Committee directed and supervised the orphanage. The Chair was the lawyer Mrs. Paula Marengel, a dear woman; unable to have children of her own, she devoted her life to the Jewish child. The vice-chair of the committee was the lawyer Mrs. Clara Gross, who was in charge of the house. The treasurer was Mr. Henrik Kriegel, a teacher; his substitute was Stanislav Neuberger. The supervisory Committee for Jewish Children and Youth had many members whose names I cannot recall. They helped mainly by collecting donations and organizing special evenings and the like. The most active were the four members of the Executive Committee whose names I have mentioned.

Worthy of special mention – in addition to the lawyer Mrs. Marengel – is Mr. Henrik Kriegel, a man of broad public awareness, who cared for the orphans. Mr. Kriegel tirelessly divided his time between his professional and social activities. Neither rain, snow, nor the burning noonday sun could prevent him from visiting the children daily, checking every corner to be sure no one was in need, the storeroom full and lunch satisfying.

Two other active friends of the Committee who devoted much of their time to the well being of the children were Samuel Neuberger and Clara Gross.

Pepe Anderman-Neuberger

The Orphanage

The Orphanage Committee

The Hospital and Old Age Home Committee (1934) Sitting from the right: Frida Rosen, Dr. F. Marengel, Aryeh Roll, Esther Bazner, Khaye Roll.
Standing: Joseph Knobler, Pinchas Weinstock, Zalman Baltuch,
Monish Frankel, Alexander Tseler, Moshe Wolftal.

Talmud Torah pupils with their teachers Haim Kopler
and Isaac Kirshner, 1936

The kheyder [elementary religious school] of Reb Mendele with the melamed ('teacher') Reb Mendele and his assistant Elye;
Tsi Heller is among the seated pupils

[Page 185]

More about the orphanage

In our town there has always been a Polish and Ukrainian boarding school for secondary school students. Jewish high school students from Buczacz and its surroundings felt that they should have a similar institution, one that could help provincial youth to an education.

It was necessary to find funding for the project. A group of young students decided to stage a theatrical play. They bought the production rights from the Tanentzap Troupe, hoping to raise funds for the project. The students sold all the tickets and gave the proceeds to the gymnasium teacher Yitskhok Falk as a start towards establishing the school. Prof. Falk, who showed a deep concern for the project, dedicated all of his energy and practical skills to increasing the initial sum, taking it upon himself to realize the plan of the Jewish boarding school. Near Fedor Hill[1] he found a small house surrounded by a garden, which was suitable for the purpose. Thus many youths from the area who couldn't afford private studies could be enrolled immediately. From the first day till 1914 it was managed by a group of Jewish teachers from the Polish secondary school in Buczacz, with the aid of important communal leaders. However, the political and financial changes caused by the First World War, especially the increase in the number of children who had lost parents during the war, made it necessary to turn the school into an orphanage.

The goals and plans of the orphanage changed and again it was Professor Falk who cared for the institution, introducing new people to assist it. Among them were Mrs. Marengel, Clara Gross, Sheyndl Herzas and other women. The orphanage's primary goal was shelter and upbringing for the full orphans. But it also tried, with the help of the families, to care for the single-parent orphans by keeping them in the orphanage during the day, tending to their education and health.

Dr. D. Pohorila

Endnotes

1. 2 kilometers from town, site of the murder of over 5000 Jews in 1941 and 1943 – ed.]

[Page 186]

WIZO
Translated by Jessica Cohen

On Shabbat afternoons, one could see women rushing from all over town to the town center, to the home of Sigman-Hirschorn, where the Hebrew school was located. The Hebrew school served as the location of the Zionist women's group, "Wizo" – "*Kolo kobiet zydowiskich*" and every *Shabbat* afternoon there was a lecture, a reading or another event held there. I believe it was the first time in the history of Buczacz that women gathered amongst themselves and lived their own lives. Not only young women, but also mothers and grandmothers gathered together and listened attentively to interesting lectures on Jewish or general topics. The debates were sometimes fierce and the atmosphere was always refreshing and lively. We did not miss any opportunity: a visitor in town, a townsman who had returned from a trip abroad, particularly from *Eretz Yisrael*, any cultural or social event – all these were echoed in the women's organization.

The founder and the first chairwoman, who continued in this capacity for several years, was Ms. Betty Medwinski, whose energy and dedication contributed to the organization's development and to its becoming a wide-reaching and influential institution. We maintained contact with the kindergarten and with the Hebrew school. We had a committee for social welfare and especially for assistance to expectant mothers without means, for whom we delivered various food items, soap and diapers both during the months before the birth and afterwards. A poor mother who was in distress, always found a listening ear and quick assistance. Apart from all these, the young members collected donations for the Jewish National Fund and participated in any other Zionist activity. Hebrew courses and craft courses were organized.

In order to attract members from all different circles and to strengthen the warm ties, tea parties ("herbatki") were held from time to time. Usually, one of the members would compose a feuilleton on current affairs, and others contributed to the success of the parties by serving good cakes. We were in touch with the Lvov center and sent delegates to all the congresses, and that was where we received our directives for activity. Among the first chairwomen were, besides Ms. Medwinski, Dr. Paula Wolftel-Asenfeld, Chaya Roll, Esther Eisenberg and others.

Some jokers would say that the only man who belonged to the women's group in our town was the headmaster of the Hebrew school in Buczacz, Mr. Yisrael Farnhof. He supported the group in every way, provided us with the school auditorium for our *Shabbat* meetings, and even gave lectures. He admired the women's organization very much, and presented it as an example for all the other Zionist organizations

Khaye Roll

[Page 187]

The Jewish Health Organization
Translated by Jessica Cohen

During 1919-1929, a severe epidemic of typhus fever spread through Buczacz and left many victims. Apart from the Jewish hospital, which was in an extremely neglected condition since the war, there was no other hospital in town, and certainly not one for contagious diseases. The Jewish hospital took in people who were convalescing from the illness. There was a military hospital for contagious diseases in the courtyard of Count Potozki, which took in also a small number of private patients, however the Jewish patients in town avoided going there. All told, there were two or three Jewish patients there.

I recall that once we went with Dr. Khalfan to visit "the Count's" hospital. I was already "immunized" after having been gravely ill. During one general assembly, Dr. Khalfan announced that only two people out of all those who had been seriously ill were still alive: Roll and Alter Goldberg (who is now in Haifa).

At the same time, a committee was established by the name of: *Tow szerzenia higeiny wsrod Zydow*. Dr. Nacht was appointed as head of the committee, however the practical management work was assigned to myself, with the help of Mordechai Rotenberg and Baruch Shechter. We were provided with a shack in the "Square of Pigs" and the committee's activities were managed from there. The Joint sent us soap, soda, tooth-powder and toothbrushes, which were distributed to the needy. Every day we purchased large amounts of milk, which we gave out to the poor people in town. We also used to visit the homes of sick people, together with Benjamin Tziring, who was also "immunized," and help in whatever way we could. The convalescents would receive wine and various nutritious items from us. Through its meager means, the committee did all it could to help the victims of that terrible epidemic.

It is worth mentioning an interesting episode from the same period. We once learned from the newspaper that Dr. Cohen would be coming to Lumberg, sent by the Joint. Of course, we immediately contacted the center in Lumberg, with which we always maintained close ties, and asked them to inform us whether Dr. Cohen would also visit Buczacz. We received an immediate reply via telegraph from Dr. Martin Seltzer, the chairman of the center, in which he informed us that Dr. Cohen would visit all of eastern Galicia. This telegram was sent to the address of Dr. Nacht, who transferred it to me, and I transferred it to Dr. Khalfan. At midnight, I heard someone pounding on my door and when I opened it, several police officers and military secret police officers stormed in and investigated me regarding the telegram and who was Dr. Cohen, and other such questions. In order to spare Dr. Khalfan from any unpleasantness, I did not want to tell them that he had the telegram, since they already knew its content from the censorship anyway. I only showed them the newspaper and the correspondence in the matter, and they soon realized who this Dr. Cohen was. The whole fuss ensued because at the same time, another Dr. Cohen – a known communist – had moved to Poland, and the police were searching the whole country for him. Since our Dr. Nacht was known as someone with "leftist" opinions, they justified all their suspicions.

After Dr. Cohen from the Joint arrived, I went to welcome him. He was on duty and wore an American military physician's uniform. On that occasion, I told him about my visit from the police during the night. It turned out that he know exactly who he was being mistaken for and he was intending to go to the police to present himself.

[Page 188]

Buczacz Jews in Vienna
Translated by Norbert Porile and Alejandro Landman

Many Jewish Buchachers abandoned their town on August 21, 1914, in face of the advancing Russian army. They fled in all directions: to Hungary, Western Galicia, Silesia, and Moravia. However, a large fraction of them made an effort to reach Vienna, with the hope of finding a safe haven in the imperial capital. While the refugees who reached Vienna were able to secure decent living conditions, the others suffered hunger, abuse, and poverty, particularly in the 1916-18 period. Even though they received a government subsidy of money and food, they had to make a real effort to get an amount that was barely adequate to live on. This was the situation in Moravia, where many younger refugees were forced to live in shacks in various refugee camps. Many Buchach Jews wrote me about their desperate situation. I visited Nikelsberg and Bagei in Moravia and saw with my own eyes how difficult their lives in the shacks were. Many men, women, and children were squeezed into a single large shack, built by the government according to standard specifications that made no provision for any sanitary facilities. Drinking water and food were contaminated by sewage, leading to the outbreak of epidemics in which many refugees died.

The government instructed us to determine the needs of the refugees with respect to food, clothing, and shelter. However, our reports fell into the hands of the local officials, who were more interested in enriching themselves at the cost of the refugees than in providing adequate services. I met with Dr. Rudolf Shvartz-Hiler, the chief of the refugee center, to discuss the situation of the refugees. He explained that he was powerless to do anything and that any change had to be initiated by the government in Vienna. At the death of the Emperor Franz Josef in 1916 the young Emperor Karl took over and was introduced to the Parliament. The Galician representatives, Braiter and Raizes, asked for his help in improving the living conditions of the refugees in the Moravian camps. After a vigorous discussion, a parliamentary commission was chosen and given the task of studying the conditions in the refugee camps and make public their recommendations. The decision of the Parliament was all that one could hope for. The Parliament resolved to close the refugee camps immediately and house the refugees in available private housing. So was this sad affair brought to an end. While many of the refugees stayed on in various Moravian towns, the majority opted to settle in Vienna.

In November, 1918, after the end of the War and the breakup of the Austro-Hungarian Empire, the new Czech government suddenly, and without any public discussion, evicted all the Jews who had settled in Moravia and sent them to the Polish border in order to return them to that country. The Austrian government, which had just been reorganized under a social democratic majority, also took action to settle the question of war refugees. The leader of the socialist government, Albert Lever, issued a decree requiring that refugees who had arrived in Vienna after July, 1914, and who wished to stay in the city, had to submit a petition requesting permission to stay on.

All the petitions were delayed, of course, and eventually turned over to the police, who summoned all the petitioners and informed them that, because of security and civil order considerations, they could not stay in Vienna for at least 10 years. They were given 2 weeks to leave the city without any possibility of appeal. This was the beginning of a difficult time. Jewish refugee families were evicted from their homes, taken to the police station, and then, by train, to the border town of Lindenburg. Since the Czech authorities didn't allow them to pass through, these unfortunates had to return to Vienna. There they were grabbed by the police and accused of entering the country without permission.

The efforts of Dr. Robert Shtraiker, a Jewish Parliament member, were to no avail, especially after Chancellor Karl Rener declared that the new Austria was not responsible for the decision of the old Austro-Hungarian Empire to admit the refugees in the first place. The Galician Jews were in a terrible situation. In order to help themselves, they formed an Organization the purpose of which was to plan for an orderly return to Poland. This Organization included Dr. J. Halraih and Yacob Feldman, my fellow Buchachers, and me. In a meeting with the police chief arranged by Robert Shtraiker we reached the following agreement: those war refugees who indicated to the Organization that they wished to leave Vienna and return to Poland received permission from the police to do so and were not bothered further.

Actually, several families, and among them some from Buchach, really did want to return to Poland. However this was not possible because they lacked the economic means to do so. The Austrian government refused their request for help arguing that this was the business of the Polish government. However, the Polish representative in Vienna told us that there were enough poor Jews in Poland and that there was no interest in increasing their number. While the majority of poor Jewish families wanted to return, Jews who were well off were interested in staying in Vienna.

Many months passed until Robert Shtraiker ended his involvement in the refugee question. Thereafter, JOINT (Jewish American Organization for Help and Settlement of Refugees) took over this problem and so ended the affair of the refugees.

Some 1500 to 1800 Buchachers stayed in Austria after the War, 95% of them in Vienna. After overcoming many difficulties, for example in obtaining citizenship, the refugees were able to establish themselves on the basis of the St. Germain accord, which benefited refugees throughout Austria. Many were able to establish successful businesses. However, a significant number of refugees were stuck in marginal business activities and could not set roots in the community. Their small shops or other businesses eventually folded and many of these Buchachers were left without adequate means of support.

The "Viennese" Jews, particularly those who established themselves in Vienna years before the Polish Jews, regarded the latter as undesirable competitors. Thus, the Polish Jews were steered into specific districts of Vienna and there was little contact between them and the more established Jews. There was also little contact between Buchachers – little sharing of either happy or sad occasions. There was even little social contact between family members and friends, to the point that few in the community heard about it when a Buchacher died or became ill. (Translator's note: this was not true for all families, in particular not so for the translator's (N.P.) family). In spite of these problems, the Jews from Eastern Europe played an important role in the politics of the Viennese Kehila, where they strongly supported the Zionist party with their votes.

In order to improve conditions, I invited some of my Buchach friends and discussed with them the possibility of forming an association of Jewish former residents of Buchach. They concurred with this idea. I began by gathering names and then went to the police to obtain the corresponding addresses. When I had put together a list of some 200 families I advertised the formation of the group and prepared for a general meeting.

The first meeting of the Association took place in 1929, following government approval. Several hundred Buchachers attended and it was a very successful meeting. A directorate was elected and began to function. The name given to the group was "Association of Buchach Jews in Vienna". Its mission was to work on community, educational, and primarily, social welfare issues. We organized meetings on various topics, as well as recitals, theatrical performances, and visits to the sick. Many of these activities were designed to attract the younger people. The income derived from these functions was used to help the needy. In time we were able to hold a Minian at "Iamim Noarim". The services were attended by Jews from Buchach and its surroundings and were very successful.

Some twenty families asked for our help, which we gave within the limits of the available funds. There were others who suffered hardships but were too ashamed to ask for help. They constituted our biggest problem because we had to give them substantial help, but both in secret and indirectly. Eventually we were able to set up a charitable fund that was used for both gifts and loans. This permitted us to help members of the community to establish or improve their businesses. We also sent funds to Buchach at Passover time to be distributed to the poor Jews remaining there. Our Association also participated in the communal life of the city, and helped mark the passage of both happy and sad occasions.

The Jewish Kehila of Vienna joined us in many social welfare projects. Our Association and its effective work were frequently mentioned in "Der Shtime" and "Olam Hadash", the Jewish newspapers of Vienna. My job was not an easy one as the Buchachers did not have much faith in our efforts and left us the most difficult tasks. However, I derived great pleasure when I could help the needy. In praise of my fellow Buchachers I do have to say that they always helped me and contributed funds when asked. I was the president of the organization from 1929 until 1938, as no one else was willing to assume this office. All the work was done in my office and the help I was able to provide was my only reward.

In March of 1938, when Hitler annexed Austria, there were several hundred Shillings in our account, and as it was just before Passover, I distributed them to the needy. I was summoned by the Gestapo and directed to turn over the records and funds of the association and, finally, to dissolve it. Thus ended our charitable association. The directorate consisted of Leon (Leibush) Frid, honorary president, Yehezkiel Adrer, Yakob Kraminer, Aprim Alpenbein, and Matitiahu Waiser, vice presidents, Egon Maiziger and A. Ginsberg, treasurers, M. Jugendorf, M. Weiser, Abrim Levi Fridman, members of the financial committee. Other members were Zelman Neiman, Aron Anderman, Ing. M. Shainberg, Dr. David Pohorille, Shaul Weiner, Paul Adelshtain, Sh. Wildman, and M. Torten. Mrs. Cila Gancer and Mrs. Ofner served as secretaries.

After the war between Germany and Poland started in September, 1939, a number of Buchachers who had remained in Vienna were arrested and sent to Dachau. Among those who perished on "Kidush Hashem" were Moshe Jugendorf, Hirsh Preminger, Moshe Hofman, Mendel Jurman, and Josef Rozenfeld. Blessed be their memory.

Yehezkiel Adrer
New York City

[Page 191]

Activity of the New York Buczacz Jewish Welfare Society
Translated by Jessica Cohen

In the annals of the *Landsmannschaften* in America, which shall be written in the future, the United Butzatzer Ladies Auxiliary will occupy one of the most respectable chapters. It is a history of hard work and tireless efforts, of self awakening for the benefit of the injured and the oppressed, who, in their moments of desperation, turned to us – their brothers and sisters overseas.

In 1934, when the fascist Polish government was increasing its economic pressure on the Jewish people, letters came from our hometown, filled with tears and sadness, describing the distress and poverty which had befallen a large part of the Jewish population. The cry of pain from our afflicted brothers did not fall on deaf ears. Upset by the terrible news, a small group of people gathered on a cold winter day in January of 1935. These were simple and innocent men and women, with hearts of gold, who gathered in order to establish a welfare organization for the benefit of our hometown and the suffering people of Buczacz. And thus, on January 20, 1935, the "United Butzatzer Ladies Auxiliary" was established.

It would be unjust if we did not mention the names of the people who founded the organization, as many of them devoted hard work and extraordinary efforts in order to help their townspeople.

Honorable mention must be given to Abush Anderman, a tireless activist and one of the founding members. His intelligence and agreeable nature affected many people and were a source of inspiration for our continued, dedicated work. He is sorely missed by us and we shall never forget him. Among the other founders who have passed away, we should mention the following: Ms. Dara Boyer, Ms. Anna Pek, Max Zilberbush, Anna Nachtigel, Anna Adler, Leon Rosenblatt, Moshe Stein, Yetti Stein and Sam (Shmuel) Schwartz, who passed away recently. The annals of the Society are a long succession of wonderful accomplishments and noble acts, of sacrifice and fraternity. The heart-breaking letters of the activists and the community representatives from that time (Mendel Reich and Pinchas Wienstock) were a decisive influence on us and the touching and intelligent words fell on fertile ground.

The initiator and primary founder is Leibaleh Farber, a man with a kind disposition and liked by all. But the other organizers are also worthy of commendation for their extensive and plentiful work. And these are their names: Moshe and Dara Boyer, Lewis and Anna Pek, Morris and Anna Adler, Bernard and Sloe Gotforcht, Sam and Fannie Kopfler, Yisrael and Hinda Shere, Max and Tzili Silberbusch, Paul and Clara Silbersein, Louis and Reda Rosenblatt, Louis Gotfried, Avraham and Reda Zomer, Abush and Jenny Anderman, Louis and Lena Duchovny, Moshe and Anna Stein, Anna Nachtigel, Izzi and Tilli Wieldman, Sam and Esther Schwartz, Millie and Bessie Wassner, Reda Sneider, Alter and Ethel Farber, Meir Klienfeld. However, not only the founders and organizers fulfilled their duties, but also all the members and many of our townspeople assisted us, out of enthusiasm, and contributed greatly during the thirties – until the Second World War broke out – in order to alleviate the distress and poverty of our brothers in Buczacz. Among the significant contributors of our organization, we should mention Philip Silbersein and Yisrael Neiman, the son of Avraham Yona Neiman.

The activity of the "Auxiliary" can be divided into three periods. The first period begins in 1935 and ends with war breaking out in 1939. The purpose of our activity during that period was twofold: in order to awaken the spirit and prevent desperation, we would support a few individuals financially, according to the instructions of the community, which was also doing as much as it could to alleviate the distress. However, we did not ignore the important Jewish institutions, which were destined to deteriorate without our assistance. We assisted the following institutions: the orphanage, managed by Paula Marngel and Yosef Kornbly; the hospital, directed by Monish Frankel and Arthur Bik; the *Talmud Torah*, directed by Haim Kofler and Mendel Reich; the *Gmilat Hessed* Society, managed by Monish Frankel, Dr. Yeshayahu Hecht, Pinchas Wienstock and Yakov Margaliyot.

The second period continues throughout the Second World War, from 1939 until 1945. During this period, our contact with Buczacz was cut off, although our activity did not cease. In a nervous condition and with beating hearts, we awaited the moment of renewal of our contact with our dear brothers. Horrifying news spread of pogroms and mass murder of the Jewish people in Poland, but we hoped that the accounts were exaggerated and that the cultural world would not allow the annihilation of an entire innocent people. How innocent was our faith!

In fact our work during the war was more intensive, we collected money and waited impatiently for the moment when the world would once again be open and we could assist our brothers and heal their wounds. At that time, our organization fulfilled its patriotic obligation in our country's war against the Nazi enemy by contributing to the "Red Cross" and other national institutions. And of course we donated significant sums to support our Jewish-National institutes (such as the Joint, United Jewish Appeal and HIAS [Hebrew Immigrant Aid Society], Jewish National Fund, Ort, etc.).

The third period begins with the end of the Second World War. This was the most intensive period of action in the history of our organization, which expresses the noble character and sensitive heart of Buczacz Jews. Unfortunately, the dreadful news of the war was confirmed, and to our horror we learned that only a small handful had been saved of our large and famous Jewish community. Some 65 survived in Buczacz itself, and almost 400 who had escaped into Russia. In 1946-7 a large portion of the survivors moved to Germany, hoping to leave soon and go to America and to *Eretz Yisrael*. And the situation in the temporary camps on the cursed German land, was unbearable. And again, the Auxiliary began to receive sorrowful letters, full of despair, and the organization gave help and awakened hope. With great energy and extraordinary efforts, the women and men of the organizations began the welfare activities. They searched for relatives, sent clothes for the unclothed and food parcels for the hungry. During the six years following the war, our organization spent more than 20,000 dollars, an amount which can be considered huge for a small organization. By means of the great assistance we also offered spiritual aid to the misfortunate people, who had been brought to the abyss of desperation by the horrors of the war. The outstretched helping hand enabled them to get through the crisis period which followed the war, with hope for a better future.

*

On April 5, 1955 we will celebrate the 20th anniversary of the "Auxiliary" – twenty years of hard work by an organization small in numbers, but large in spirit. Unfortunately, many of our good people are not with us anymore, and their parting left an empty space within us. The number of active members has decreased in recent years. There has also been a decrease of interest among American Jewry in philanthropic activity, after the large surge immediately following the war. Many of these kinds of organizations have been completely dismantled, recognizing that they have fulfilled their function. However we still exist, and despite the shrinking number of members, we continue our hard work. Our activity is now devoted, primarily, to assisting with the building of the State of Israel, the land of our dreams and the country of our national future.

The annals of our "Auxiliary" would not be complete if we did not mention the names of our members who still fulfill their human obligation loyally, despite their old age and personal difficulties. Our spiritual leader is Rabbi Yisrael Schor, who is well-known among the Jews of New York. He is always prepared to heed our call, at times of trouble and at times of happiness. His appearances at our various gatherings add honor and benefit.

I would be honored to mention the members who, after 20 years of difficult activity, have not lost their spirit and are ready and willing, to the best of their ability, to continue the noble work in support of the injured and the poor. And these are their names: Leibeleh and Zaide Farber, Alter and Ethel Farber, Louis and Jenny Esienstadt (Anderman), Louis and Lena Duchovny, Bernard and Sally Gutfrocht, Yisrael and Hinda Schor, Louis Gottfried, Meir Kleinfeld, Avraham and Reda Zomer, Reda Sneider, Lola Peler, Dora Kirschner, Esther Schwartz, Morris Potshter, Sloe Kilreik and Regina Galbreit.

And last but not least: the finest and most dedicated among the workers are Zalman Neiman and his wife Dara, who are beloved to all the former residents of Buczacz in New York. Neiman is a true Buczaczer Jew. His strong personality influences all who meet him, and we view him as the second spiritual leader of the Buczacz organizations, after Rabbi Schor. We are proud of him, and he and his wife deserve to be engraved in gilded letters in the annals of the "Auxiliary."

Here ends the short history of our welfare organization – the history of fearless and tireless work performed by a few people, for the common good. It was not for their own honor that our people gave their time, their energy, their strength and their money. The painful cry of brothers and sisters overseas was the only motive which moved them to act in such a way that might heal, if only partially, our brothers' wounds.

The history of this small society revealed the solidarity and mutual responsibility, which are the defining characteristics of our people.

Avraham Zommer

[Page 194]

From the Town's Life
(From the end of the 19th century)
Translated by Adam Prager

The Town's Representatives

Buczacz was basically a Jewish town and its center was completely Jewish; the Christian population lived in the suburbs. The Jews even inhabited the area where the churches stood. Jewish Buczacz was mainly a mitnagdim town, the mitnagdim being the most influential force in it. The municipal administration and community [kehilla] cultural-educational policies were predominantly in the hands of the mitnagdim. The hasidim were a minority though there were a number of prominent figures such as Zeidman and others among them. Thanks to the high cultural level of the Buczacz Jews, this did not lead to conflict between the two factions and the minority adapted itself to the situation. The general attitude was anti-hasidic. Nonetheless, due to the respect for renowned hasidic figures, the hasidim were allotted representation in the community council. The town's leadership – municipal and communal was in the hands of the Shtern family. This is why an opposition to this family arose. However, it was very hard to oppose them seriously, because every one of the important people concentrated on his vocation, leaving no candidates for public office – in the same sense that "the olive tree said unto them, should I leave my fatness, wherewith by me they honor God and man, and go to be promoted over the trees?" [Judges 9:9] In other cities and towns of eastern Galicia there were usually two families who contended against one another, but not so in Buczacz.

Officially the community was only founded around 1890. The reason for this late date is unknown – either the authorities objected earlier or the Jews themselves were not interested till then.

Following the death of the tsadik, Rabbi Israel Leib Wahrman, no one in Buczacz was given the title "Rabbi" and no one was found worthy of this title till the beginning of the 20thcentury when R' Meir Arak, the rabbi of Yazlovits, was appointed as Buczacz's rabbi. During this long interim the Jews made do with the title "Preceptor" [moreh hora'a]. Though a Tshortkov hasid, R' Arak was forbidden to pray in their chapel [kloyz].

The Economic Situation

of approximately 60,000 inhabitants. The material situation was usually bad, the town becoming more and more impoverished. The reason for the decline originated from the town's inability to keep up with the general advancement throughout the modern world. Many Galician towns were lagging behind, Buczacz among them. In contrast, however, there were towns that progressed. Buczacz's problem was the nearby town of Tshortkov, which was in a much better financial situation for two main reasons: a) Tshortkov had a large infantry and cavalry barracks. b) the court of a tsadik of the family of the tsadik of Ruzhin. The tsadik's court was an important economic factor. Members of his family and court lived in luxury. Hasidim from all parts of Galicia, Bukovina and even the Ukraine would frequent the "rebbe's" house, improving Tshortkov's finances considerably.

The town's leaders tried, of course, to obtain from the authorities a military installation, a district court house, railroad lines (for the Buczacz-Horodenka and Buczacz-Podheytse routes), but to no avail. Tshortkov received the district court house and the above railroads were not built. Buczacz was awarded a magnificent high-school [gymnasium] building, the most beautiful high-school building in all Galicia.

Buczacz had no industry. There was only a carpet "factory" that was actually a workshop. Buczazc and its vicinity were agrarian, characterized by large estates. Their owners employed many agricultural workers who received minimum wages that covered only their basic needs. Buczacz, whose main income was from commerce, suffered from this situation. It traded in grains, spirits, textile; in several other areas there was even a certain amount of transit trade, as in agricultural machinery. In addition, there was export of poultry, eggs and butter. Some merchants employed Christian workers, especially female (in the selecting of beans and other kinds of pulses). The young lower-class Jewish women, mainly from the area, worked as underwear seamstresses, cheap-confection makers, cooks etc. Buczacz buckwheat was of fine quality and its buckwheat groats were renowned near and far. In Bukovina, they would say: a Jew of Buczacz on his return from synagogue on Saturday morning recites the blessing over wine and has buckwheat groats for dessert.

A source of income for Buczacz's small and large merchants was the fairs, of which there were three:

a. the weekly fair, held on Thursdays. On that day peasants of the vicinity would gather in town to bring their goods to the three markets: the horse market, the pig market by the Strypa river, and the general market surrounding the town hall (Ratusz). In this market chickens, geese, ducks, eggs, vegetables, fruits etc. were sold. The peasants would buy and sell. They mostly bought salt and sugar.

b. A group of small traders known as *antloznikes* (Entlassene) "the released" (from jail) would journey to the second fair in the market of Tlusta Ves' (Tovtse). These were shrewd and crafty people, well known for their cunning and thievish ways. There were even cases when they cheated each other. Many tales of their slyness and swindling were common. In order to avoid being caught, they would adopt different nicknames and call each other by them at the fairs.

c. An important source of income was the annual fair held in the town of Lashkovits. This was a large fair that lasted 2-3 weeks. Merchants from many towns thronged to this fair, some even from abroad. Of course, it had its share of thieves. When someone appeared suspicious because of his external appearance, people would say, "He has the face of a Lashkovits thief."

The crafts also did not do well. Tailors were mostly busy before the holidays, namely at the end of winter and the end of summer. This trade was solely in Jewish hands, as was the fur trade. The furriers' season was the end of summer. In the fall they mainly worked for the peasants, who wore simple fur caps and coats during the winter. Shoemaking was mostly in Christian hands, only a small percent of the shoemakers were Jews. Before the holidays the shoemakers were busy with orders from the Jews. During the rest of the year they would make boots for the peasants and sell them to shops or directly to the customers. In time the shoemakers were pushed aside by the shoe factories that eventually took over the market. Other craftsmen, such as carpenters, locksmiths etc. were both Jewish and Christian. Craftsmen were not well off, even though there were experts in fields such as furniture-making, carpentry, building, etc. All barbers and tinsmiths were Jews, as were the carriage (fiacre) drivers.

Buczacz had three large bakeries that supplied fresh bread and rolls three times a day. The small, domestic bakeries supplied backed goods only on Fridays – all kinds of *knishes* or *kashe* pastries and, in the summer, pastries with green onions and cheese in them, etc. For the Sabbath, top-quality khales were provided, mainly by special order. This was an extra source of income during 2-3 days of the week. These domestic bakeries also prepared pastries for the fairs, especially for the annual fair that was associated with the Christian "Shkapirna" pilgrimage.

Poverty and unemployment caused many to emigrate, especially to America and Canada.

Buczacz had an excess of intellectuals. Buczacz Jews sent their children to high school (gymnasium) and later to the university. This led to unemployment in the liberal professions, and in many towns these professions were taken over by former residents of Buczacz.

Leaving Buczacz did not solve the problem of poverty or improve the situation. Many depended on the community's charity.

   a. Some would beg from door to door and on the Sabbath poor women would go from house to house and collect slices of bread.
   b. There were street beggars.
   c. On Purim, people who did not beg from door to door did so now by hiding behind their costumes, for they were ashamed to be identified. Also Jewish policemen in civilian clothes (there were such policemen) would beg for charity.
   d. Before Passover, the town would hand out holiday provisions [meot khitim] to the poor.

During the winter, the poor would receive a hot lunch at the soup kitchen for a symbolic fee and, in the morning, bread and tea for almost nothing. There were also the "hidden" poor, people who became impoverished and were ashamed to beg. These people received charity, collected in various ways and sent to their homes. One way of gathering charity was through the "matan be-seter" [anonymous giving] fund – a collection box built into one of the pillars of the Great Synagogue. Bad housing conditions resulted from the deep poverty. The poor lived in decrepit houses at the side of the hill called *baszty* [tower; dungeon?], or in basements. No wonder that epidemics, quite common in Galicia, did not spare Buczacz – despite the fame of its excellent water. Best remembered is the cholera epidemic of 1894 or 1895 that wrought havoc throughout Galicia, including Buczacz. In order to pacify the angel of death, a wedding sponsored by the community was held for a poor couple. The wedding ceremony was held at the cemetery and, after the ceremony, a procession headed by the young couple went through the streets of the town accompanied by musicians.

Education and Culture

Education was varied: there was Jewish education and general education. In the competition between the two, Jewish education had the upper hand for many years. However, as in other places, general education grew stronger in time and finally overcame Jewish education. Most people were indecisive as to which to chose. Parents saw that there was no choice but to educate their sons and prepare them for the struggle for existence. This meant acquiring a broad knowledge of languages and secular subjects. The Jews may be divided thus: a) parents who did not send their children to general schools but to the kheder, and at home the children were tutored privately in general studies. b) parents who sent only their daughters to general schools. These girls would attend kheder in the afternoon to learn to read Hebrew and the Yiddish translations of sacred texts [ivre-taytsh]. Sometimes the teacher [melamed] would come to their homes during the day for a half-hour to give them reading lessons. The boys would study all day at the kheder, morning and afternoon, and a tutor [moreh] would come to their homes for an hour a day to teach them general subjects. c) parents who sent their sons and daughters to general schools and their sons to kheder as well. These were Torah-loving Jews who were compelled to send their children to general schools only because of the "yoke of exile" [ol hagalut]; however; they did not give up Torah studies. Their sons, of course, were the talented and diligent ones who also studied in the kheder; in the evening, after studies were over, 2-3 prize pupils would stay on from 8-9 to study the Talmud. These pupils were under great pressure because they studied from morning till night. d) parents who saw general education as the top priority and sent their children to kheder for a few hours of cursory ["al ketse hamazleg"] Torah study. For this reason the kheder, too, was highly varied. There were:

One)   The kheder dardaki [yopung child's elementary school] for 3-5 year-old boys and girls together, with five levels. They would start with the first portion of Leviticus, and sometimes they would prepare the children to "interpret" [lidrosh] a portion, and would hold a feast [seuda] at the child-interpreter's home.

Two) The kheder irbuvia [jumble kheder], one level higher than the previous one. Here the children would study khumash [Pentateuch], a bit of Rashi and the Early Prophets. The name *irbuvia* did not change even though only boys studied in that kheder. Girls did not continue their studies after "graduating" the kheder dardaki. Nor did they study the Five Books of Moses [khumash]. For the girls, reading Hebrew and the stylized archaic Yiddish of sacred texts [ivre-taytsh] was sufficient. Winters in this kheder irbuvia and in the higher levels, the pupils studied until 8 PM in the evening by oil lamps or candlelight. Each child shared in the lighting expenses – 1-2 kreutzers a week. The boys would return home, torches in hand, singing songs. Evening studies would end a few days before Passover, and this event would be celebrated with a feast at the kheder. Each child participated in the expenses. Wine was bought and the rabbi's wife would prepare fritters [levivot] filled with potatoes or buckwheat groats.

Three) From the "jumble" [irbuvia] kheder, a 7-8 year old boy would proceed to the Talmud teacher. Talmud kheders were on two levels – from ages 7-8 till 12-13, and from 12-13 onwards. On the first level Talmud was mostly taught before noon. In the afternoon, for 4-5 hours, pupils were taught the Latter Prophets and Writings [Ktuvim]. In the winter after evening prayers, or in the summer just before evening, they would be taught Pentateuch with Rashi's commentary according to the portion of the week. Besides the above, they also studied (in the "jumble" kheder) seasonally appropriate texts: Sukkot they studied Ecclesiastes, before Purim the book of Esther, before Passover the Song of Songs and the Haggadah, before Shavuot the book of Ruth and Akdamut [Aramaic poem read on Shavuot], and before the Ninth of Ab the book of Lamentations.

Most of those who attended the general schools gave up Talmud studies and only the gifted few stayed on during the winter evenings between 8 and 9. In the summer they made do with a lesson at dusk after the rest of the pupils had left, but most of these talmud studies were held while the general schools were closed for holiday. A Talmud kheder [kheder gemara] of the second kind did not accept pupils from the general schools. It had two streams: the Talmudic – in which the Talmud (including the Mishnah) [Shas] and commentaries [Poskim (text has psukim 'Biblical passages' – apparently an error] were taught, and the maskilic in which maskilic "melamdim" ['progressive teachers'] taught their pupils Shas and Poskim, and in addition Bible, especially the Latter Prophets, grammar and letter-writing in Hebrew and in Yiddish. In both streams together in these kheders the number of pupils was small – usually no more than 7-8. Instruction here was indeed given individually. Most distinguished among the heads of the 1st stream was "Yaane-Melamed" (Yaakov Roykher) and among those of the 2nd stream was "Pessi-Melamed" (Pessakh Biller), a maskil knowledgeable in the Hebrew language and its grammar and translator of several poems from Yiddish to Hebrew.

In the young child's kheder [kheder dardaki] the *reysh dukna* [teacher's helper], familiarly known by the Yiddish term *belfer* [bahelfer 'helper'], held an important role. The belfers were also of two kinds: a) reysh dukna, the melamed's assistant in teaching to read the Pentateuch, who held a special title: *oyber-belfer* ['head assistant']. b) the regular assistants, who actually helped the parents. They would go from house to house in the morning and wash the children's hands and faces; they would recite with them the "modeh ani" prayer and would escort them to the kheder (during the winter months on their shoulders). Then in the summer they would set out to collect the second breakfast (*podvaremes*) or in the winter *varemes* (lunch). In the afternoon they would bring the children their late afternoon meal. These assistants would watch over the children as they played in the yard during recess. They were adored by the children and in most cases by the parents. They were practically "family members," compensated for their efforts with meals at the children's homes, each day with a different family [known in Yiddish as "esn teg"]. On Fridays they would shine the household's shoes and would receive payment for doing so. They also made toys for the children: flags for Simkhat Torah, lead tops for Khanuka, rattlers for Purim, bows and arrows for Lag BaOmer [33rd day of the Counting of the Omer], and "rifles" for the Ninth of Ab. Before sunset they would align all the children in the yard in a strict and orderly fashion, after which the rebbe or the reysh dukna would instruct them in the rules of proper behavior and good manners. The assistants would then take the children home. The assistants had an additional responsibility: when a boy was born to one of the pupils' parents they would take the pupils to the house of the woman who gave birth, read the *shma* prayer with the children, give each child a drop of wine, a small cake filled with honey and another in the shape of an 8. The children would leave the house cheerfully, happily bidding the mother and the newborn baby good night.

On the Sabbath all rested in the young child's kheder – the rebbe, his assistants and the pupils. Not so in the other kheders. On Sabbath afternoons pupils would come to those kheders for 2-3 hours. They would play outside till the rebbe would awake from his nap and call them inside in order to teach them Borkhi Nafshi ['bless God, o my soul!'; Psalms 103-4 were recited before minkha on the Sabbath] in the winter and Pirkey Avot ['Ethics of the Fathers', a tractate in the Mishna] during the summer. On Shabbat Khazon [the Sabbath before Tisha B'av] the rebbe would read the story of Kamtsa and Bar-Kamtsa [according to the Talmudic legend in Giten 55] and other legends of the Destruction of the Temple [khurban]. Pupils were also examined on the Sabbath. In the winter before noon and in the summer before sunset, the rebbe would come to the parents' homes (each Sabbath to one or two houses) or to the pupil's relatives, test the pupil and receive refreshments. Outstanding pupils did not require the presence of the rebbe and would be tested by their father or by relatives.

During Lag BaOmer the official excursion for all the kheders was held. The pupils would receive several kinds of pastries, especially cakes dipped in honey ("krafen") [fritters] and, instructors leading the way, set out for the country and its fresh air. They would visit the Pedor, the Bashtim or the fortress. There were also instructors who would prepare a big flag and the prize student was given the honor of carrying it behind the musicians who lead the procession. Some instructors would take the pupils for a dip in the river and it should be noted in their praise that not a single case of drowning occurred.

We should also mention the negative side of this educational system: the punishments. In the lower grades, the rebbe would sit at the head of the table, kantshik [cat-of-nine-tails] in hand, and at times would wield it (this depended on the teacher's nature and the pupil's character). Also known in the young child's kheder was the "kuneh" (not the genuine article). In this method of punishment, a shabby turban with feathers was put on the "sinner's" head, after which he had to stand on top of a table and be made a fool of in front of the other children.

The religious education of poor pupils was funded by the public. Householders would donate to the Talmud Torah fund that for many years was headed by Avrahamtsi Ginsburg. These poor pupils attended various kheders and their teachers would be paid from the above fund.

General Schools

Pupils whose parents wished to give their children a general and systematic education studied in two schools. a) The school named after Baron Hirsch, which most of the Jews attended. This was a primary school with four grades. For the most part it was a good school. The children studied 6 hours a day: 4 hours before noon and 2 in the afternoon. The workload of the pupils was considerable, but the teaching (in three languages: Polish, German and Ukrainian) was thorough. Torah and some grammar were also taught. Those who taught Hebrew and religious studies were maskilim "who had peeped [into secular studies?] and been stricken" [hetsitsu ve-nifge'u]. These were Moshe Khayim Tauber and Mordechai Kanfer. Following primary school the pupils proceeded either to high school (gymnasium) or to commerce and crafts. Poor pupils would also receive winter and summer clothing from the "HaKeren" fund and, in winter, a hot meal. Those who chose crafts became craftsmen's apprentices for a period of three years in order to learn the trade. A few were sent to Germany to study at the agricultural school founded by Baron Hirsch. There was a Polish general school but few Jews attended it. Many of our high school teachers admitted that the graduates of the Baron Hirsch School were better educated than those of the Catholic school.

The kheder was not the final stage in Jewish education. Many continued with their studies. A considerable number frequented the study houses [batey midrash], especially the Old Study House. But many turned to commerce and crafts, studying Talmud and Midrash in the synagogues in spare moments ["between minkha and maariv," i.e. briefly]; and, more leisurely, on Saturdays and holidays. Some studied alone while others studied under one of the instructors. There were also societies for the study of Talmud and Poskim. These were mainly in the study houses of the mitnagdim and operated voluntarily.

Characters and Customs

Buczacz had various customs, most of them like those in other Galician towns; however, a few were unique. There were general public customs connected with religious duties and practices and there were playful and amusing ones as well.

On Sabbath eve, the town's sexton [shamash] would herald the start of the Sabbath: "In shul arayn!" ['To the synagogue!'] Every morning at dawn he would walk through the streets waking up everyone with the tapping of his cane, three taps at each gate (two taps if someone had passed away during the night). During the penitential days [slikhot], the sexton would wake up the townspeople at 3 AM. He would loudly declare in a melodious fashion: "Awake, awake Israel, holy people, awake to worship the Lord." [kumu, kumu yisrael am kedoshim, kumu la-avodat habore'.]

The sexton would also announce the funerals in the town, calling out "met mitsva" [Megila 3: "talmud tora umet mitsva – met mitsva adif" 'honoring the dead at a funeral takes precedence over studying the Torah'].

The penitential days were days of prayers and pleas, but also days of fun and mischief for the youth. The boys would wake up together with or before their parents. On their way to the synagogue they would pass by the Strypa River and float wooden boards covered with lit candles – at that moment the river was a truly magnificent sight. It is no wonder that the youth sought relief in such a way. Playgrounds in Buczacz as well as in other towns were scarce. The Strypa River thus became a place for recreation: during the summer, bathing or rowing; in the winter, skating over the ice that covered the river during most of the winter. The summer supplied the town with occasional attractions such as a wandering circus, a zoo, and a panorama [primitive cinema] that would stay in Buczacz for a few weeks. Sometimes a professional athlete would arrive and run around the town hall or display his rope-walking skills. Or a gramophone player, a magician and juggler would come by. Gimpel's Jewish Theater from Lvov would also visit Buczacz for a few weeks during the summer and erect its stage in a barn by the bank of the Strypa River.

Before Passover the young male hasidim would be busy in their chapel [kloyz] baking matsa shmura [unleavened bread prepared in the strictest manner]. It was a pleasant task albeit a serious one. In contrast to them, the idle youth and pranksters would get ready for Shabat haGadol ['the great Sabbath', the Sabbath before Passover].

The ordinary young people arranged processions on the Great Sabbath. At the head walked a boy carrying a stuffed image (pants and a coat stuffed with straw), while several others beat on tin drums and everyone sang:

> Halelu, halelu min ha-shamayim
> Kol ha-parkhes le-mitsrayim!
> Praise, praise! The Heavens will drive
> All the scurfs to Egypt!

When they arrived at the house of someone with scabies [Yiddish *parkhes*], they came to a standstill and sang "their song" [see the ten plagues of the haggada].

Relationships between people were graced by lovely customs. For a circumcision people would send sugar, conserves, etc.

At the synagogue when a bridegroom read from the Torah, women from the women's section [ezrat nashim] threw raisins, almonds and candy at him. On Simkhat Torah the khatan-tora [the person honored to read the last portion of the Torah] and the khatan-bereyshit [the person honored to read the first portion of the Torah] treated the congregation to cake and brandy in the synagogues and in the homes of the elders.

Buczacz had many characters and it is impossible to write about them all. I will mention a few that were especially strange in their ways:

Yankl Grosfeld. An educated man, he was always in a good mood. He was very poor and no one knew "what this vegetable lived on." Most hours of the day he would spend with Avrahamtsi Fisher (owner of a shoe store), both of them seated playing chess, competing with each other in telling jokes day in and day out.

Among the musicians, Elazar the Cripple (Leyzer der kalike) stood out, not for his musical talent – he played the cymbals, but for his merriment and for the Yiddish songs he sang on various occasions – especially on days before army conscription when potential conscripts (plogers) ['sufferers'?] "tortured themselves" in order to be disqualified from service.

Ayzik Volf Yurman was a man of several crafts, but the saying "many crafts but few blessings" [Yiddish: a sakh melokhes un vintsik brokhes] did not apply to him. On the contrary, he was a wealthy homeowner. Throughout the year he worked with a carding machine, and at the end of summer he prepared shofars, He had two additional year-round occupations: during the day he traded in rags and junk, while during the night he was a wedding jester [Yiddish: batkhn]. At weddings he wore two guises: a serious man before the canopy, and one who would turn with his rhyming to the groom or bride, causing weeping and tears among the women (especially when one of the newlyweds was an orphan). But after the wedding meal, he would grow merry and comical and would call out the gifts from the guests on the bride's side and the groom's side respectively (droshe geshenk) ['wedding gifts']. At weddings of wealthy people he would receive extra pay for reciting in Hebrew and translating into Yiddish songs such as "ish khasid haya" [He Was a Hasid] and others.

Lastly, let us favorably remember the old vinegar-maker (esikmakher) who used to talk Hebrew to his mare on the Sabbath. He would lead her to the well to drink, urging her on with phrases like "holekh lamayim" ['going to the water']. Since many people were somewhat tipsy on the night of Purim and thus liable to forget to attend the evening prayer service [aravit], he would go through the streets on Purim night and call out: "Don't forget evening prayers!"

Dr. David Pohorile

[Page 202]

Fragments
Translated by Jessica Cohen

During the tombstone unveiling for Yisrael Moshe Stern (founder of the hospital), the entire Stern family ("Rodzina") was invited by the hospital committee. After the ceremony, the guests toured the hospital. When Yisrael Shlomo Stern, who was a very shrewd Jewish man, saw the impeccable order in the institution, he turned to the people accompanying him and said: "*ihr hat gamacht a-tel fonem hekdesh*" (The hospital was once a poorhouse).

*

Once, before Passover, the management wanted to make new pairs of trousers for the men in the old age home, for the holiday. They purchased some fabric and a few tailors were asked to sew the trousers for free. There was one elderly man in the home by the name of Sozie Alexander, a *Hassid* from Czortakow, who was an expert on everything and was particularly talented at sewing. They gave him the fabric and said: "Reb Suzie, take this fabric and sew yourself a pair of trousers." Reb Zuzie's reply was to ask: "And who will pay me for this?"

*

Once a traveling salesman came to Buczacz, and stayed there for a while. When he returned home, they asked him: what kind of a town is Buczacz? He replied: [Yiddish] (Buczacz is a strange town; in the middle of the town, stands the council house. Above the council house, stands the great synagogue. Above the synagogue, stands the bathing house. Above the bathing house, is the hospital. Above the hospital there is a church, and above it, seven mills spin round).

*

Baruch "Luli" once lay in a hospital in Vienna, and next to him lay a local Jew. The latter wanted to make fun of the bearded Galician Jew, and asked: "[Yiddish]" (How do you say louse in Yiddish?) – Lice, Baruch replied. – Yes, that is in the plural, but how do you say it in the singular? – We don't have them in the singular – Baruch "Lulu" replied.

*he town mayor, Barris Stern, liked to play cards, and Tzadok Avraham Yankels was his regular "kibitzer". One Thursday, he was engrossed in a game, and only as evening fell did he remember that he had not left his wife any money to buy things for Shabbat. He turned to Tzadok and said:

– Tzudik, take these 10 crowns and take them home to the wife, for the Shabbat groceries.

Tzudik took the ten crowns and took them home to his own wife. Later than night, B. Stern returned home and was "warmly" welcomed by his wife for not having left her the money for Shabbat.

The next day when he met Tzudik, the mayor asked: - why did you not give the money to my wife, like I asked you? – But you told me to give the money to the wife, and so I gave it to my wife. If you had asked me to give the money to the lady, I would have given it to your wife. I have a wife, and you – a lady.

*

The same Tzadok Avraham Yankels once said: — when I lie on my deathbed and you see me moving my lips, you will know that I am insulting my lord.

*

Moidel "goy" (a Jew) went to Rabbi Yudlei Shapira before Passover and said to him: Reb Yudlei, please buy some potatoes for Passover from me. Reb Yudlei became angry and answered: Potatoes, potatoes – even potatoes have their limit!

- My potatoes have a "limit" too, Moidel replied, believing that "limit" was something that potatoes must have in order to be kosher for Passover.

*

On the morning of *Tisha Be'Av*, Moidel "Goy" went to pray, carrying the tefilin bag. He came across Antashki Kastalawski (a Christian, who was knowledgeable in the customs of Judaism), who told him: Moidel, you goy – don't you know that on the morning of *Tisha Be'Av*, you don't go to pray with the tefilin bag in your hand?

*

When they asked David Wolf Shapira why he does not lay *tefilin*, his answer was: I don't want to put my head into a dispute between Rashi and Rabeinu Tam...

*

One morning, when Hersch Leibeleh Hassid stood in his home for the *shmoneh-esreh* prayer, he noticed a dog that had come into the house. He could not banish the dog, and he did not want to stop his prayer to utter the profane. He called to his wife and said to her in lashon hakodesh: "My wife, my wife – a *pas* (dog) is in the house!"

*

When Kappaleh "thief" came home from the army after the First World War, he found a baby in his home. Having no choice, he took on the responsibility. After a while, the baby became ill and died and Kappaleh sat *shiva*. When his friends came to console him, he told them: Hear this, friends – I have "sat" many times in my life, but never yet have I sat when I am so free of blame.

Compiled by Khaye Roll

[Page 204]

Gleanings
Translated by Jessica Cohen

A few rabbis from Buczacz were previously rabbis in Yazlowitz, including the author of *Neta Shaashuim* and afterwards the *tzadik* from Buczacz, the son-in-law of [the author of] *Neta Shaashuim*. One of them was stolen in the middle of the night from Yazlowitz, because the Yazlowitz community did not want to dismiss him from his position.

The *tzadik* Rabbi Avraham David Warman, of blessed memory, was born in Nadworna. One Friday, the *tzadik* passed through town and saw that someone was eating a late lunch. The *tzadik* said to him: Why are you eating now? You could have waited and eaten in the evening, with a full appetite, for Shabbat. The man replied: If I satisfy my hunger now, I will eat in the evening only to honor the Shabbat, but if I starve myself, I will eat on Shabbat only for the bodily pleasure, and not to honor the Shabbat. The *tzadik* admitted the truth of his argument.

*

A few months before the death of the *tzadik*, the leader of the town died. And a few weeks before the death of the *tzadik*, the leader came to him in his dream. The leader brought a fish in a bowl, but he took back the head of the fish with him. The *tzadik* told his dream to the members of his household next morning, and said that he was afraid this was a sign that the head would go to the leader. And this did occur. A short while later, the *tzadik* died.

*

It is said that on Shabbat, during the *seudah shlishit*, when the *tzadik* spoke from the Torah, some people fell asleep. Because they were not all worthy of hearing the secrets of the Torah.

It is told of Michal Preminger, the grandfather of Zvi Preminger, that when he was 15 years old the *tzadik* chose him as his cantor, and he served in this position his whole life. And once he said to Michal that his grandchildren would be better than his grandchildren.

*

The builder of the Great Synagogue in Buczacz was a Christian engineer. After he finished the building, namely – after he had positioned the final stone in the vaulted ceiling, he held this stone in both hands, and his legs dangled in the air. He wished to illustrate in this way, that the building was strong and complete.

*

It is said of Dr. Bloch, that in his youth he worked at a bakery, and then he rose to become a representative in the Austrian parliament and fought in the wars against the enemies of Israel. When he was elected for the second time, there was great joy in our town. The Jews wore their *streimelach* and acted as if it were Purim, with barrels of beer rolling down the streets. And the city of Buczacz was merry.

Dr. Bloch once came to a voters' gathering in winter and asked the voters what portion was being read this week. They told him: *va'yeshav* portion. And he told them that *vayeshav* [Hebrew characters: vav-yod-shin-vav] was an acronym: "*valt Josef Shmuel Bloch*" (vote for Yosef Shmuel Bloch)...

*

During one meeting in the Fobiat house, to support products made in Israel, with the presence of Count Potozki, the mayor Barris Stern quoted a verse from the Tanach. When he finished his speech, Count Potozki went up to him and said: Excuse me, Sir, the verse which you quoted from the Tanach is in fact an explicit *mishna*, and does not originate in the Tanach. All the people present were amazed at this expertise.

*

A wagon-owner from Buczacz conveyed goods to Lvov. One night, on the way, the goods were burned and there was a dispute between the owner and the wagon-driver, as to whether the latter was an unpaid keeper or a paid keeper, and who was to pay for the damages. They came to Lvov for a *din torah* before Rabbi Yosef Shaul Nathanson. And the rabbi justified the owner. But the wagon-driver contradicted the Rabbi and told him that he must look in a particular book and he would realize his mistake. Finally, the Rabbi admitted to the wagon-driver and kissed his forehead, saying that even a wagon-driver from Buczacz was an exemplary *talmid chaham*.

*

I also heard a story about the *Gaon Bechohmat Yefet*, who was esteemed and honored in Vienna, Professor Dr. Heinrich Miller, a native of Buczacz: in his youth he studied Torah with Avramtzi Ginsberg, the *talmud Torah* treasurer. Later, he had the legal right to travel at any time on a special train (saparat-tzug, in foreign language). And in the royal house, Archduke Rauner – the uncle of Kaiser Franz Josef – would boast about being a friend of Professor Miller.

*

It was said of one of the elderly people of the previous generation, Mordechai Spielberg, that he was the pride of the generation and a great scholar. He was the only one in town who spent his nights as he did his days, both during summer and during winter. In the middle of the night he would get up and leave his house to go to the old Midrash and study Torah until morning. He would always take with him a candle and matches from his home, to light up the Beit Midrash. Once he forgot to take matches, on a winter night. And when he took out the candle, he had nothing to light it with. He stood in the dark in the Beit Midrash, not knowing what to do. But suddenly the candle lit up on its own and he did not see or hear a soul in the Beit Midrash... They honored him greatly when he died. Along all the streets where they carried his coffin, they closed down the stores, and on Shabbat evening he was buried, and was eulogized by Rabbi Meir Arek, of blessed memory.

*

Near Buczacz, a Jew would transport brandy from one town to the next, without paying the excise tax on it. A *goy* policeman saw him and was going to deliver him to the court. When the Jew saw this, he took out some money and tried to bribe the policeman. But the policeman gave him over to the court anyway. This happened on a Friday afternoon. And when the day of the trial came, the judge was a Jew, a Torah scholar, and before the trial started the judge said to the accused: Jew! Did you not recite: "If darkness falls while you are travelling, you must give your money to a Gentile"? The Jew understood the hint, and then claimed before the judge that he had not intended to bribe the policeman at all, but since he was an observant man and it was dusk, he gave his money to the first Gentile he met, because it was forbidden to carry money on Shabbat. Based on this argument, the Jew was released.

*

My grandfather, Yosef Engelberg of blessed memory, was a great *talmid chaham*, and was also learned in external wisdoms, fluent in French and extremely modest and retiring. He died at a young age and was survived by a few daughters. My grandmother cried when he saw the patient's condition. Grandfather asked: why is she crying? And when they told him that she was crying because of the children, he told her not to cry, and comforted her by saying that if he left this world, the children would have a greater father then him, because *hashem* is "the father of orphans and the judge of widows."

*

My brother-in-law Moshe had a son, also a Rabbi, whose name was Yehosha. He took the place of his father. And when he was given the office of Rabbi in place of his father, they wrote to him: before the sun of Moshe set, the sun of Yehosha rose.

My brother-in-law, the Rabbi mentioned previously, had a sister named Tova, and she had a son called Haim. When he was bar-mitzvahed, they wrote him a blessing, which was: since he is a Haim [life] of Tova [goodness], may he also be Haim [life] of blessing, a life of wealth and honor and also a God-fearing sin-fearing life.

*

Before the First World War, Rabbi Meir Arek, of blessed memory, from Yazlowitz, was accepted as a rabbi in Buczacz. A few years previously, he had visited Rabbi Matzortakow, because he was one of his followers. And he said to him: Greetings, Buczaczer Rabbi! For in previous years, the rabbis from Yazlowitz had been appointed Buczacz rabbis several times. And so the rabbi thought that this time it would happen too. When Rabbi Matzortakow's followers heard what their rabbi had said, they were concerned that the rabbi's promise should come true. And indeed, the *Gaon* Rabbi Meir was accepted as the Buczacz rabbi with great pomp and circumstance.

Rabbi Gedalia Margaliyot from Saraki gave his two horses – which were the finest in all the district, and had carried princes several times – to the carriage which was going to Buczacz. And Rabbi Yisraeli Stein, the son-in-law of Mordechai Lieb Bergman from Potok, one of the wealthiest men in all the district, was the wagon-driver himself, to transport the honorable rabbi to Buczacz. And that was on a Thursday, in winter, and the town of Buczacz was merry. That Shabbat, there were many guests in Buczacz, including the students of the Rabbi, who were rabbis themselves. Among them was Rabbi Meir Shapira, of blessed memory, the founder of the *Chahmei Lublin* Yeshiva and founder of the *daf yomi*. Another student rabbi was unable to attend, and he sent a telegram saying: "Rejoice and sing, Buczacz, for in your midst sits the greatest of Israel."

I recall that on that Shabbat night, I was with Rabbi Meir Shapira, of blessed memory, and he told a joke. Once on Shabbat morning a *Hassid* was leaving the *mikveh* and he met three Ashkenazim who had finished their prayers. And since the *Hassidic* circles do not deal with the Tanach much, they decided to test him. They asked the young man: What is the difference between "diadem, crown and wreath." The young man understood that they were trying to trick him, he held up his hand and pointed at each one of them, saying: You tell me the difference between "this is my exchange, this is my substitution, and this is my sacrifice," and he left them.

*

It is said of Fischel Aberdam, the father of Zvi Aberdam, that when he was once in Karlsbad, a nobleman lost a large sum of money and Fischel Aberdam found the treasure and did not return it. He was suspected, and they searched him and found the treasure, but he claimed that all the money was his and that he was rich. He told the searchers: ask in the town I come from, and you will hear. The police asked in the town where he had come from. The townspeople thought they were talking about a healing fee which everyone who came to the bathing town paid, and because he had enemies in the town who wanted to get their revenge on him, they told the bathing town that Fischel Aberdam was truly a rich man. And so they left him alone in the bathing town and all the treasure remained with him. When the real reason for the questioning was discovered later in the town, they were angry at them, because they had thought badly of him and it had turned out good.

*

His son Zvi Aberdam was a learned man in *chohmat shem ve-yefet* and was very handsome. He had a noble appearance, he was wealthy and respected and famous. Once, someone came to his house and he was not at home. Zvi Aberdam's wife said to the guest, walk through the town and when you meet the most handsome Jew in all of town, you will know that it is my husband Zvi Aberdam. (This was no exaggeration.)

*

Our teacher, Rabbi Zvi Meir Arek, of blessed memory, had a brother called Fischel, who had a son called Zecharia. On his mother's side, Zecharia Arek was a grandson of Mordechai Lieb Bergman, owner of the Potok estate, which was previously the estate of the eminent Rabbi Yisrael from Rozin. The same Zecharia was married to the house of an important family from Krakow. The young and wealthy woman was learned and educated, as most Jewish girls were in Krakow. But her devout husband was not to her liking, and she rebelled against him, left him and went to Vienna to study secular studies. No amount of requests and imploring could bring her back to her husband. And finally she even refused to separate from her husband by means of a *get*. Time went by and she did not change her mind. She mocked him and the Jewish custom of the *get*. In such a case, there was only one solution. With the *heiter* of one hundred rabbis, the husband could marry another woman. And thus he did. Zecharia came to the Rabbi from Rodi, Rabbi Mendel Steinberg, of blessed memory, and he also gave him a *heiter*, one out of a hundred, and invited Zecharia to later take his daughter as a wife. And thus it happened. For after he had obtained a *heiter* from one hundred rabbis, Zecharia married the daughter of Rabbi Steinberg, of blessed memory. And I recall that after a son was born to him (this was before *shavuot*), the Rabbi, of blessed memory, came to Buczacz to celebrate Shavuot and the *briss*. The Rabbi's coming to town made a great impression and I had the honor of hearing the address he gave to the public. And the *Hassidic* circle was very joyful.

*

Michal Preminger was, like his father Zvi Preminger, of blessed memory, a prominent student of Rabbi Meir Arek, of blessed memory. When the Rabbi passed away, Michal recited *kadish* over the Rabbi, while his parents were still alive. Michal had no sons for a long time, and once the Rabbi came to Michal in a dream, and told him that his wife was pregnant and she would have a son, and he must name it Meir after him. And Michal asked the Rabbi in the dream for another son, and the Rabbi told him that in those days, it would be better to have just one son. But Michal asked again the Rabbi for a blessing which he could study in detail, and the Rabbi promised him this too, and it came to be. Later, he learned that his wife was pregnant, and a son was born and he named it after Rabbi Meir.

Joseph Urbach, Herzlia

TOWN WORTHIES

Rabbi Haim Weinraub
By S. M.
Translated by Jessica Cohen

He was the last in a generation of talmidei hachamim and scholars in Buczacz, who gave it the reputation of being a town of Torah experts and scholars. Born in Kalush in 5623. At the age of 17 he married Pia, nee Anderman, and moved to her hometown of Buczacz. Here, in an atmosphere soaked in knowledge and wisdom, he found satisfaction in continuing his studies, and set aside time to study Torah. He would sit in the old Beit Midrash, finding pleasure in the rare and valuable books it housed. He soon began to offer his extensive knowledge to others in that Beit Midrash. Every Shabbat, for many years, he lectured on the weekly portion, and on Shabbat evenings taught Moreh Nevukhim [Maimonides Guide to the Perplexed] and Akedat Yitzhak. His words were imbued with knowledge and skill. Being blessed with a wonderful memory, he was able to pepper his lectures with witty phrases and the everyday talk of talmidei chachamim. He drew and fascinated an audience of listeners, who became his followers. His Bible commentary, which was published in 5699, was lost in the Nazi Holocaust. He educated his sons in the national spirit. He died in Buczacz in the year 5699. His eldest son, Matityahu, an enthusiastic champion of the Hebrew language and preacher of Zionism among the youth, and his daughter Prima, both died as martyrs at the hands of the Nazis. His son Shaul, an activist in the Hitachdut, Poel Hatzair and Tzeirei Zion and a leader of the Jewish community in Vienna, and his son Michael, live in Israel.

[Page 211]

Rabbi Yakov Leib Alfenbein
By Efraim Alfenbein
Translated by Jessica Cohen

More should be said of my father, of blessed memory, Rabbi Yakov Leib Alfenbein, who was an enthusiastic Zionist in his youth, even before the Zionist movement existed and before Herzl's "The Jewish State" appeared. I will briefly mention the founder of the first Zionist association in our town of Buczacz (the "Zion" association), the establisher of the "Safa Brura" ["clear language"] society, and the founder of the Hebrew school of the same name, and I shall outline some of the features of his life.

As the president of "Safa Brura," my father, of blessed memory, often spoke with the children who learned in the Hebrew school, and encouraged them to love the Hebrew language and Eretz Yisrael. The parents of these youngsters, mostly from the Haredi circles, objected to this and complained to my father, saying that he was a negative influence on them and that they would deviate from the proper path because of him.

And some complained to him: "what use is it for you to awaken others to fulfill the mitzvah of settlement, when you yourself do not fulfill it?" To this my father, of blessed memory, would reply: "I belong to the generation that must prepare itself in the diaspora, to go to Israel and build it." Even so, he intended to make aliya, but he fell ill and passed away.

And indeed, his influence on these young schoolchildren from "Safa Brura" was evident. Despite the objection of their parents, some thirty of them made aliya after World War I, comprising the first large group of immigrants who went to Eretz Yisrael from Buczacz.

* * *

In 1921, as is known, Keren Hayesod was established. At that time, I was able to donate a respectable sum of money to the fund (25,000 korona), and I told my father, of blessed memory, about my donation from the city of Vienna, where I then resided. My father, who returned to Buczacz after World War I, responded to my letter, saying amongst other things:

"Your letter telling me that, thank God, you have donated 25,000 crowns to Keren Hayesod, breathed life into me, for I realized that you have a Jewish heart and you know the soul of our faith and that you wish to fulfill your obligation to our nation and our country. At once I said: a son of Israel – if he refuses to give a tithe for the construction of our country, he is an apostate to his people and his country. Even if he prays every day according to the law and sways forward and back as is customary, but if he opposes the construction of our land, his prayer is idolatry. For the time has come to build our land and plant our vineyards..."

My father, of blessed memory, was highly educated, a talmid chacham and a Hassid. His entire life was dedicated to Zionist and Hebrew activity, and to Jewish-national work in our town (he worked hard, and under difficult conditions, for the Jewish candidates in the elections for the Austrian Parliament).

Until his final day, he took an interest in the building of Israel and a few hours before his death he asked a friend who was visiting him: "Tell me, how many people made aliya this month?"

During his old-age too he was very active in favor of the Zionist idea, and knew how to enthuse younger people as well, for he himself remained young in spirit.

[Page 212]

About Several Figures in Our Town
Translated by Adam Prager

I would like to mention in these lines the names of noble figures of the last few decades, the last generation before the destruction of Buczacz. They excelled in that the foundation stone of their lives was the integration of Torah with worldliness ["tov tora im derekh-erets']. The daytime was devoted to business and the night to Torah. I have already referred above to Reb Osher, Reb Yanay, and Reb Ayzik, the three pillars of the Old Study House. To their names I would like to add those of householders, humble individuals, among whom were authors of books such as Reb Zeev Pohorila[1], Reb

Abraham Riblin[2], and just plain Torah scholars like Reb Mendele Hornstein, Reb Mordechai Shpilberg[3], Reb Yudl Shapiro, my older brother Reb Abraham Jonah Neuman[4], Reb Sholem Mordechai Czaczkes[5], Reb Leibush Glantser[6] and others.

End notes

1. Reb Pohorila was a banker and a writer. He wrote Khomat anakh on the Torah and Shearit yehuda

Dr. Avraham Silberstein

on the Talmud.

2. Reb Abraham Riblin wrote Peyrush al haRamnan.

3. Reb Mordechai Shpilberg was an outstanding scholar, a fierce misnaged who remained opposed to the Hasidic rabbis till his dying day. He died at the age of 85.

4. Father of Irving Israel Neuman of New York, known for his contributions to the Histadrut HaIvrit HaOlamit ('World Hebrew Federation').

5. The father of the writer Sh.Y Agnon.

6. In his old age Rabbi Leibush Glantser served as dayan in the religious court of Buczacz.

[Page 214]

Two Figures
Translated by Adam Prager

Zionism in its first days in our town (during the years 1894/95) was a youth movement. It consisted of boys from the bet-hamidrash [study house] and youth from bourgeois homes; later on it was joined by student youth. Among this youth two older prominent figures stood out.

One was the first chair of our town's Zion Society, founded in the year 1894 – the venerable and honorable Reb Hershele Shtern, (of blessed memory). He was an educated man with a deep knowledge of the Bible; he was much involved in communal life and wore a long white beard. An enthusiastic Khovev Tsiyon ['Lover of Zion'], he brought up his sons to be enlightened Zionists in a religious-national spirit. He wielded great influence on all of us.

The small branch of the Shtern family also included Reb Hershele Shtern's sons Meir Haim and Abba, and his brother Israel Solomon, who has family in Israel.

The second was a Hasid in every respect. Mr. Jacob Leib Alfenbein (the uncle of Mordechai Shenhavi from Mishmar HaEmek) was highly knowledgeable in the Torah and a respected householder. His love for Zion was as intense as a sacred flame. Following the Balfour Declaration, he wholeheartedly proclaimed that every Jew must immediately sell his property and emigrate to Eretz Yisrael. He actually carried out his belief. He intentionally sold his house and the one belonging to his relative Reb Reuben Leib Pohorila (two high-story houses) to gentiles, for Jews must leave for Israel. He received a worthless amount for them due to the inflation, but all was for the purpose of emigrating with his family to Eretz Yisrael. Unfortunately he fell ill and died at the age of seventy, his aspiration unfulfilled. When I visited him before his death he asked how many Jews were in Eretz Yisrael at the time. After telling him there were about 80 thousand Jews there, he replied in low spirits that he was convinced that in the years to come there would be a Jewish majority in the Land of Israel.

With the verse "And the sons shall return to their lands," he passed away in the year 1924.

* * *

I am fulfilling my duty by erecting a sacred memorial and a marker for the memory of a pure soul, one in thousands, my most learned teacher, Rabbi Samuel Issachar Shtark, of blessed memory, who was a dayan [rabbinical judge] in Buczacz. I studied under him for three years. He wrote several important books in a beautiful style, Minkhat Oni ('Gift of Suffering') on the Talmud, Avney Shayish ('Stones of Marble') on the Torah [Shayish 'marble' is an acronym of his name Samuel Issachar Shtark], Petakh HaTeyva ('Portal of the Ark') on Seyfer Teyvat-Guma and others. Among his pupils were the Chief Rabbi of Italy, Dr. Sh. Margoliuth of Florence, the son of Reb Jonah Margoliuth of Bresni. My teacher Rabbi Samuel Issachar, possessed a phenomenal memory. He knew the entire Talmud by heart. If a passage in a tractate was read to him, he immediately cited the page on which it was found. In his old age he was invited to fill the imposing post of Head of the rabbinical court in Vizhnits, Bukovina. May his memory be blessed.

D. N. Bet-Alfa

[Page 216]

Shlomo (Solomon) Dik[7]
Translated by Adam Prager

A.

Who was Dik and what was his history? As one of his students and friends I shall try to portray him in general terms. He was born in Buczacz. In his youth he studied horticulture in Germany where he attended a seminary, after which he became a teacher for one year at the Jewish Colonization Association [ICA] agricultural school in Slovodka. My friends and I attended the school between the years 1905-1908.

As to the question which teacher was the most memorable and influential, the answer would be unanimous: Shlomo Dik. What was the secret of his success and influence upon us? We had many teachers and some may even have been better. However, he was exceptional in his devotion to his students and their problems. We concealed nothing from him, be they the most intimate and personal matters or simply issues concerning our studies. One could always find in him a sympathetic listener, one willing to offer true help. He had one aim in life for which he strove tirelessly in all that he did: Drawing Jewish youth closer to nature, which he loved and had a great knowledge of. The surroundings, with their dense forests, streams and fields were of great help, and he knew how to take advantage of every element and opportunity with utmost efficiency in order to attain his goal. He wasn't satisfied in teaching a vocation alone; he wanted Jewish youth to regain their identity and self-esteem as human beings as well as Jews.

This was the period of the pogroms in Russia and some pogrom attempts were also made in Galicia. I shall never forget Dik's words when he demanded we be prepared to aid the Jews who lived in the Jewish town of Kolomea, which feared an onslaught. He warned us not to be provoked into attacking anyone, but to demonstrate our right and duty as Jews and human beings to defend ourselves from any assault. He would include in his words historical facts of how the Jews used to defend themselves and their land and showed his disdain for Jewish submission in the diaspora in more recent times.

Dik also knew how to show his young students that only cooperative and organized forces could achieve substantial progress in the present and in the future. He was the first to organize a student board by which students could tend to their own affairs, with special committees that dealt with cultural, professional, and legal matters. Success here led to his request that students be allowed to take an active part in their institution generally. Here, too, he was successful, even though the rest of the teachers, who believed in a different kind of educational system, tried to lay obstacles in his way.

The ideas of Dik, the teacher and educator, provoked much opposition. His fellow teachers, as was mentioned above, opposed his approach to education. Nevertheless, he remained fearless and undeterred. The conflict reached its peak when senior officials from the Jewish Colonization Association [ICA] in Paris decided that the level of studies and cultural activities for the boys must be reduced to that of the farmers in the area. "For only such men can be farmers". Contrary to their views, Dik wanted the range of education to be expanded; he wanted students to learn the latest scientific developments in the field of agriculture, to improve work methods by means of modern machinery, to deal with eradicating pests, etc.

His ambition was to prove to the Jews that it was possible to live from farming and to do so on a much higher level than that enjoyed by the neighboring farmers and the Jews with their "luft" ('air') occupations. We students felt that the dispute concerned our lives and our future, therefore we organized and supported him with all our might. He succeeded in canceling the edict from Paris.

It can be said with great satisfaction that from all the classes under Solomon Dik's tutelage over 80% stayed in the field of agriculture (unfortunately, they are scattered all over the world), an achievement that no other agricultural school can claim.

Dik, who dreamed of a wider educational purpose for the Jews of that generation, went to complete his agricultural studies at a university in Berlin. Upon completing his studies he was offered the position of principal at the Jewish agricultural school in Steinhurst, Germany. Here too he met with great difficulties. Once again the dispute concerning system and goal arose. And again he encountered narrow-minded employers, giving him no choice but to leave.

Dik started to manage private and communal farms in Germany. He succeeded in reviving and re-organizing abandoned farms, which was met with wonder and admiration among experts. He was very happy that he could give Jewish youth from east and west a chance to learn the practical features of the agricultural profession on these farms.

His connection with Jewish youth and agriculture and his aim of bringing them together led him to Oppenheimer, to the latter's method, and to Zionism. The ninth Zionist Congress decided to establish a cooperative association at Merchavia. It was to be run according to Professor Oppenheimer's system under Dik's management. Dik immediately contacted his students from Slovodka for this purpose. A few of us (including me) went to Erets-Yisrael prior to the founding of the association in order to study the special local conditions. With Dik's arrival in Erets-Yisrael, and with the aid of a number of workers from the Galillee settlements, the foundations of the cooperative at Merchavia were laid.

This is not the place to unfold the story of the founding of Merchavia. I would only like to say that of all the settlements that were founded after it, not a single one experienced such hardships as Merchavia did during its first eight years. I will mention just a few details: about 100 young men and women, most of whom infected with various types of malaria, and about 50% to 80 % bedridden and unable to work during the most important work season, in the most primitive hospital situated in shacks swarming in every corner with fleas, scorpions, snakes and rats. True, the neglected fields were plowed with the latest machinery at the time, for there were neither tractors nor combines then. There was hardly any water; at times one had to literally fight over each and every drop. We were isolated in a savage environment surrounded by bandits and enemies. As if it were not bad enough not to receive any aid from the government, the same government made life even more difficult by false accusations and arrests, confiscation of our crops and work animals, killing of cows, confiscation of houses for the use of the army, etc., etc.

Each and every one of us, especially Dik, contributed as much as he could to the project. In addition to his vast professional knowledge he continued to learn from our neighbors and from Aharonson, of blessed memory, in Atlit. He introduced new plant species, a seed cycle and insecticides. He taught and trained the members, developed relations with neighbors and government, caught malaria and suffered with the rest of us. However, the extremely difficult conditions weakened the spirits of the members. After 4 years of strenuous work Dik left Merchavia, hoping to hear good news from afar. However, the war broke out, bringing an end to his hopes and ours.

Dik believed in and instilled in us the belief in cooperation as a system and a way of life. To this belief we added enthusiasm and devotion. Unfortunately, the combination of all the obstacles nature introduced, the neighbors and the government was stronger. By the end of the war our cooperative had been eight years in the making. We were both mentally and physically broken and exhausted, weak and low spirited. Eight of our members were gone, having died or been killed. The farm was in ruins with no water, tools, animals and all the conditions necessary for any kind of development.

Dik returned to Germany and continued with settlement activity according to the Oppenheimer system as well as manage other farms. He participated in Zionist Congresses and other public Jewish projects, appreciated and honored by those around him. In 1935 Dik came to Erets-Yisrael, and at the invitation of Dr. Ruppin, of blessed memory, prepared a report on various Jewish agricultural settlements and presented suggestions for new settlements and for the expansion of existing ones. He was against leaving things to chance and insisted on accurate and organized planning in dealing with the settlements as well as having the appropriate equipment and training. He was against monoculture in agriculture, and against the extreme kibbutz system. He hoped and believed that the extreme cooperative kvutsa and the extreme individualistic moshav would meet in cooperation; all this prevented him from living in Israel and contributing his priceless experience and devotion to our endeavor.

He left the country a bitter man and took an active part in the effort to save Jews from the Nazi Hell, but he himself could not escape the crater which was to swallow up a large part of our people. Far off in a foreign land, away from his country and friends, Dik met his death. We can but praise those first steps of his which, though they failed, constituted the basis for the new agricultural settlements and their prosperity.

G. Gafner

Endnotes
7. The Encyclopaedia Judaica in one instance spells his name "Salmon Dyk."

B.

He was born in Buczacz in the year 1884. After graduating from the teachers' seminary he studied agriculture in Germany at a horticulture school in Dahelm near Hanover and at the agricultural academy in Berlin. At that time he developed a deep friendship with his teacher at the academy, Professor Franz Oppenheimer. He was appointed manager of the newly-founded cooperative farm in Merchavia, where Professor Oppenheimers' sociological ideas were to be tested. He filled this important post for a few years during the most difficult period in the early Zionist settlement of the then wild Jezreel Valley. In the summer of 1914 he left for a convalescence vacation in Europe and due to the First World War was detained in Germany, where he lived and worked for 20 years till the rise of the Nazis.

In Germany he achieved great success and recognition in his field: as manager of the agricultural estate near the well known copper factory owned by the Jewish Hirsch family, as government inspector of the estates belonging to the former German Kaiser, and as a well known assessor for the major mortgaging banks. He was a Jew with a deep national-Zionist awareness. He was proud of his Jewish first name and of his eastern Galician origin and continued to be so when the Nazis rose to power.

During all of his stay in Germany he furthered the work of the Zionist Organization, especially in the field of agricultural training. He served as an expert in the London Committee in 1920 and at the Zionist Congress in Prague. He published articles and held lecture series on agricultural and settlement subjects.

A short while after the Nazis were well established, he left Germany and in 1934 he emigrated to Israel. Here he acted on behalf of the settlement department of the Jewish Agency, preparing reports on kibbutzim, moshavot, etc.

In 1937 he visited Madagascar as a member of the delegation appointed by the Polish government to investigate the possibility of settling Jews there. For a similar purpose but on behalf of a Dutch settlement company he toured Dutch Guiana.

These two trips affected his health and forced him to stay for some time in France to recover. Thus he was stranded in France when World War Two broke out and it was there that he died of a malignant disease at the beginning of 1944.

Chairmen of the Zion Society
top left to right: Joshua (Alter) Heller, Zalman Honig, Jacob Leib Alfenbein
bottom left to right: Isaac Hirsh Weiser, Leybush Fried, Samuel Taller

Dayan
Leybush Glantser

Mordechai Heller
(grandfather of Tsvi Heller)

Pesach Biller

Haim Weinberg

Jacob Shtern

Berish Shtern
mayor of Buczacz

Matisyohu Weinberg

Dr. (Bernard) Borekh
Fernhof

Dr. F. Nacht

Shlomo (Solomon) Dik

Chaye Roll
active in book preparation committee

Dr. Koppel Blum
active in book preparation committee

Dr. Emanuel Ringelblum

Leon Wechsler

[Page 219]

Dr. Baruch (Bernard) Farnhof
By Dr. Y. Farnhof
Translated by Jessica Cohen

Born in 1869 in Buczacz; awarded the degree of Doctor of Jurisprudence from the university in Lvov; participated in the First Zionist Congress as a Buczacz representative; was an attorney for more than 40 years, a few of them in the oil town of Drohobycz, where he founded the "Beit Ha'Am" and was very active in strengthening the Zionist movement, and the rest of the time in Stanislaw. For decades, he was a very active member in the temple committee in Stanislaw, and was its leader until the Nazi Holocaust in 1939. Devoted his best efforts to the temple and left his mark on it: as a proclaimed Zionist, it was not easy for him under those conditions, but due to his pure character, his honest ways, his respectable status in the town and his personal merits, his spirit was very noticeable within the walls of the temple. Was active in the "Bnei Brith" organization in Stanislaw and filled important posts in it.

Visited Eretz Yisrael in 1932, 1934 and 1937, spending the time from Purim until after Pesach with his family (his son made aliya as a pioneer in 1930).

The Second World War put an end to his plans to make aliya and settle down in Israel, and he met his death in Stanislaw, when the Nazis began annihilating the Jews.

[Page 220]

Dr. M. Hirschhorn
By Y. F.
Translated by Jessica Cohen

One of Buczacz's fine and loyal sons was Dr. Mordechai Karniel (or as we all knew him, Dr. Motzik Hirschhorn). He interacted with others, knew everyone and was known by all. From all the young doctors of his time he was the one who began to take an interest in the hospital in Buczacz, and after Dr. Nacht left his post, he became the medical director of the hospital. Although the patients and the hospital management were sometimes under the impression that he was not particularly courteous, they always found out that he had been right and that he had acted out of a sense of truth and realism. Dr. Hirschhorn invested great efforts in developing the hospital, and introduced some arrangements and innovations which elevated its standing until even the authorities recognized it and used it in times of need. Consistently and untiringly, he dedicated himself to developing this institution, which was one of the town's finest welfare institutions.

Dr. Hirschhorn was a popular man, and loved the masses. Many told of how when he had been in Russia and other countries, before coming to Israel, he asked about Buczaczers everywhere he arrived, asked after their fate and helped them as much as he could.

After the destruction he suffered, after the wanderings, he established a new home for himself, and shone with hope.

This sturdy man, whose spirit never fell under any of life's circumstances – is no more.

[Page 220]

Outstanding Women in Our Town
By D. N.
Translated by Jessica Cohen

As long as one-hundred years ago in our town of Buczacz, even in orthodox circles and among the landlords, there were some prominent noble figures of women who were Torah scholars, philosophers and progressive thinkers. In my opinion, they had a significant influence on several of their sons, in whom the spirit of progressive education began to glow.

I shall mention the educated woman Golda Gottfried, who was born in approximately 1820, the mother of Rabbi Haim Gottfried, who shared the views of our townsman the well-known professor Dr. David Heinrich Miller, a classic linguist at Vienna University. This woman used to study Mishnah with the commentaries just like a man, and would talk enthusiastically about the "Alshich" and "Bina Le'Etim" commentaries on the Torah.

In my opinion, a great influence on the upbringing of the daughters of this generation was the talmid chacham who disseminated wisdom and knowledge among the youth, particularly among the young women of the town from wealthy families –: the teacher Rabbi Michal Baer, of blessed memory. It is said of him that he was a wise and sensible man, and influenced the youth of his time, especially the girls. I had the privilege of knowing some of his female students, namely Shindl Segal and her sister Tova Neuman, and my mother Sarah Leah Neuman. I can testify that they were well-versed in the Torat-Chesed of Rabbi Michal Baer. In their daily talk they would always intersperse verses from the Book of Proverbs and Isaiah, with sayings from classics such as Goethe, Schiller and others.

This circle of intellectual women was influential in its time during the first Austrian Parliament elections in the Buczacz-Kolomia district, in 1886. After a stormy battle, the well-known Jewish candidate Dr. Josef Shmuel Bloch was chosen, rather than the assimilated candidate Dr. Bik from Lvov, who was supported with force by the government. He was the first in the Austrian Parliament to appear on a public stage, on his own accord, against Jewish assimilators, as a defender of all Jewish issues, especially the affairs of Galician Jews. He put up a fight against the Viennese anti-Semites, such as Leuger, Schneider and others. He played a large part in the success against the blood libel court case in Tiszaeszlar, Hungary, and in his war against the dictator Prof. Rohling, a friend of the Habsburg monarchy. His German Book, Rohling Kontra Bloch, made a great impression in its time.

Among the women who were active during those elections were my mother Sarah Leah Neuman and Shindl Segal. They took action against the government authority and won – a rare case at that time. They also founded a women's society called "Ezrat Nashim," which was active for several decades in the field of mutual assistance.

Among the Buczacz women at that time, the fine personality of Shindl Segal was especially prominent. She was born in roughly 1848 and died in 1936. She was a philosopher, studied Hebrew, read and collected many books. In the weekly "Ha'Am," published in Kolomia by the writer Silberbusch, she wrote a few articles about "Women in Israel." She told me proudly of her visit with the author Peretz Smolenskin in Vienna, how she spoke with him in Hebrew, using complete sentences. She was widowed at a young age and worked hard to bring up her only son, a talented boy, until he grew older and went to study at the university in Vienna. There, he was one of the first members of the student society "Kadima," founded by Dr. Herzl. However, as fate would have it, his life ended tragically before he finished his studies. And so, as a mourning mother, she descended into her grief.

And finally we should mention the noble soul Chaya Roll, who passed away, to our great regret, before her time.

[Page 222]

Memorable Women
By D. D. P.
Translated by Jessica Cohen

Buczacz was among the less advanced towns in terms of industry and economy. The number of people requiring assistance was great, especially during the winter months. The distress was so great, that they were unable to obtain even food, and had to emigrate or become destined to require the perpetual assistance of merciful citizens. The distress would increase on Shabbat and holiday evenings. Many had to go from door to door on Shabbat asking for bread, which was given to them customarily, and served as food for the whole week. Apart from this, the poor used to go to the stores every Friday, asking for a half a penny to meet their needs, in addition to bread.

This grave economic state, which came close to real hunger, was fully understood by Regina Reiss, an attorney's wife, who founded a soup-kitchen as early as 1890, where the town's poor received a free breakfast and a nutritious lunch for 2 pennies. On Fridays, the meal included meat as well. Apart from this, the poor schoolchildren (from the Baron Hirsch school) received food for free.

In order to obtain the essential financial means to provide this welfare assistance, Mrs. Reiss founded a women's society, whose members paid an annual fee and distributed meals at the soup-kitchen, on a rotating duty. Furthermore, she managed to interest many of the landowners and lessees in the area and influence them to provide the kitchen with potatoes, cabbages and other products. A tradition was also created whereby the wealthy citizens would mark the holidays and family celebrations by donating lunches for the poor through the kitchen.

Thanks to Mrs. Reiss' organizational talent, the soup-kitchen operated until the war broke out in 1914 – under her personal management and with the great assistance of Shmuel Teller. The soup-kitchen was an act of charity for the poor, the hungry and their children, for whom the kitchen provided warm meals, and which should be viewed as Mrs. Reiss' great merit.

In addition to Mrs. Reiss, who excelled in alleviating the shame of hunger, we should remember Mrs.

Paula Marengel and Clara Gross, wives of attorneys, who were especially devoted to the orphanage which was established after the war. Only thanks to their tireless activity did the orphanage exist until the Second World War broke out, and it served as a house for orphaned and abandoned children. The few residents of the orphanage who are still alive fondly remember the righteous activists and their great dedication.

To our knowledge, these women are no longer alive: Paula Marengel was delivered to the murderers by the farmer in whose house she was hiding, while Mrs. Gross was murdered during an aktion, along with many hundreds of prisoners. It is said that this courageous woman found the strength to encourage the other women and young girls, at the verge of a tragic end, as they stood by the open grave which they themselves had dug: "Be strong, do not be afraid, for the moment is approaching when our torture and punishment will end."

One woman who excelled in the field of political activism should be remembered. This was Mrs. Elsa Peller, the doctor's wife. She began her political activity in Lvov, moved to Buczacz, where she used her wealth of talents and experience. This was in 1905. First, she set herself the goal of awakening a Jewish, national and Zionist spirit among the women of the town. Her first step was the foundation of "Rachel," a society in which she developed a network of activity, gave lectures on national topics and arranged lectures on other topics. Over the course of time she acquired a large number of members in the society, who continued the activity, and became an important factor in the Zionist life in town. After the First World War the women's club "Wizo" continued the Zionist activity under the leadership of Chaya Roll, Betty Medwinski and others.

Mrs. Peller represented a completely new type of woman in public life. While the other intellectual women were especially understanding of welfare assistance and the humanitarian needs of the day, with no understanding of the Jewish-national problems, she would reveal the courage to awaken Jewish-national life among the women in town, and bring them closer to the Zionist questions. And that was her exclusive merit.

[Page 223]

My Brother, Shmuel
By Dr. Mordechai Karnieli
Translated by Jessica Cohen

My brother Shmuel was born in 1901 in Buczacz in Eastern Galicia. Our father was a great merchant and a prominent figure, active in public affairs and involved in the life of the town. The family's wealth enabled upbringing and education for all the members of the household, beyond the borders of the town. Shmuel, who had a weak constitution, received prolonged treatments in Lvov and Vienna.

Our house was filled with a Zionist and traditional spirit. Grandfather, of blessed memory, was a learned and observant Jew, loved and respected by his peers. Our father was a man of action and business, in keeping with the spirit of the times, and was considered a progressive. As a result, there was a more liberal spirit and a keen approach to Zionism and Eretz-Yisrael in our home.

In this family atmosphere, Shmuel was raised and educated. He studied in the town high-school and then continued in the Stanislaw town district. There, he joined the "Shomer" movement, where he first accepted the Eretz-Yisrael idea as his destiny.

The world war broke out. In 1916 the family moved to Vienna, due to the Russian invasion. He continued to study there, and was enthusiastically involved in the movement, taking part in the founding committee of "Hashomer Hatzair" in Vienna in 1917.

When he returned to Buczacz he brought with him a new spirit and initiated Zionist activity among the youth. Due to this activity he was expelled from the school, together with his friends. Shmuel and his friends drew a conclusion from this event, founded a hachshara group and began agricultural work. Shmuel had an affinity with farming work. During his childhood, he would often visit the agricultural farms leased by our father, and would show an interest in the work.

Shmuel decided to make aliya, to work in Eretz-Yisrael. He trained himself in carpentry too, and this was his first job in Israel.

In July of 1920 he left the town with a group of 30, intending to make aliya. They had no passports or other papers. They had many trials and tribulations. They crossed the Poland-Czechia border as smugglers, and had to remain in the country for several weeks, anonymously. They were often in danger of being caught by the authorities, but thanks to the community they were finally transferred to Vienna, and made their way from there to Israel, with many adventures and obstacles.

In September 1920 he arrived in Israel, from here on he began a life of work and creation, society and economy.

During the 28 years of his life in Israel, he visited family overseas twice. As happy as he was to visit us, he was eager to return to his farm and his kibbutz. He had no doubts in this regard. In the same way he had started his path, he followed it with no deviations. The path he had begun became the king's way, which he followed until that bitter day, when he was hit by enemy fire and fell dead.

[Page 224]

Meir Fried
By M. H.
Translated by Jessica Cohen

The son of Zvi and Chana Fried. Killed in December 1948 in the battle of al-Faluja, his traces never found.

Born in 1929 in Buczacz. At the age of 3 he was brought to Eretz Yisrael by his parents. An alert and sensitive child was Meir from his youth. In his father's house, imbued with the spirit of Torah and love of the land, he absorbed the values of Judaism and general humanistic ideals, which left their mark on him in all his future endeavors.

At a young age he was required to assist his parents, and already showed diligence and a love of work.

At the age of 15 he joined the Hagana and was aware of all the troubles of the time.

During the agitation in the Yishuv during and following the establishment of the state, he enthusiastically took on the duties he was given, and was always first to answer any call.

After being injured in his neck in one of the battles, he was given a recovery leave, but he did not use this leave and returned to his friends at battle, where he was killed.

[Page 225]

Emanuel Ringelblum in the Warsaw Ghetto
By Dr. Nathan Eck
Translated by Jessica Cohen

A.

Ringelblum achieved his success, as is known, with the lauded enterprise which he founded in the Warsaw Ghetto – the underground archives, of which he was the initiator and creator. These archives housed thousands of certificates and documents, descriptions and studies, written by dozens of people whom Ringelblum activated, guided and presided over their labor. In the midst of the days of destruction and the confiscation, the archives were buried and after the war some of them were found and raised from beneath the ashes, and they are now preserved in Warsaw. This historical material is now considered one of the main sources for the history of the period.

But during the war, Ringelblum did not view his scientific work as the primary endeavor, at least not during the first two years of the Nazi occupation. At that time, he valued above all his public, practical work, and fully believed that his name would be recalled in history thanks to this work, for the circumstances placed him in the center of public activism from the beginning of the war. Ringelblum would recall that first period occasionally during later conversations. He would tell proudly and enthusiastically of the important activity which he and his friends carried out in the besieged and bombed Warsaw in September, 1939, when they would provide aid to the casualties and the needy, and provide shelter for the refugees and the burn victims, while being bombarded with bullets and bombs. The aid committee which was established at that time, during the great bombardment, became over the course of time the main aid institution in the Warsaw Ghetto, known as "*Yidische Sociale Aleinhilf*" (Jewish Self Assistance).

We worked together in that institution, in the public works "sector" which Ringelblum directed. The sector's duty was to be in constant touch with the Jewish population and to help it organize self-assistance. For this purpose, we divided the city of Warsaw (later, the Ghetto) into a series of areas, and established a local bureau of our institution in each area, and in each house there was a committee of residents. The public sector recruited hundreds of activists from all over the town – later, the Ghetto

– and would conduct meetings, gatherings and many consultations. The sector's headquarters – which were housed, for most of the time, in the community library building on Tlomeczka Street – quickly became a public gathering place and a sort of "stock exchange" of information and rumors. Whoever wanted to meet acquaintances, hear about the goings-on in the capital and the provincial towns, or pick up secret information about the situation on the fronts and in the world, would come to this place. Here, the mass gatherings could easily be justified to the Germans, because we could always claim that the crowds of people were there to seek assistance.

Word of this place reached the provincial towns too, and when a Jewish man from there happened to come to Warsaw (at that time only a few Jews would travel from one town to another), he would always remember to go to the "sector." And if he brought important news from his hometown, they would immediately usher him into Ringelblum's room to impart the news. On such occasions, Ringelblum would convene the head workers of the sector in his room (L. L. Bloch, Y. Torkow, Starowinski, N. Ack and others), so that they could also hear the news. Let us not forget that there were no newspapers for Jews at that time – the only newspapers we could obtain (illegally) were from the Nazi press, Jews were forbidden to have radios at home, one could not leave the house in the evenings, the contact with the world outside the Ghetto was tenuous. It is no wonder, therefore, that there was much thirst for information – not only about the occurrences in the world at large, but also of what was happening in the Polish provincial towns and even in the Warsaw Ghetto itself.

The work in the "public sector" gave Ringelblum the opportunity to meet many Jews on a daily basis, both residents of Warsaw and of the provincial towns, and to listen to their stories and their descriptions. And when they learned that this man valued the information and sometimes even recorded what they told him, they would produce their news for him even more eagerly. Sometimes they would also bring interesting objects, as proof of the veracity of their stories. For example, a document attesting to a capricious order issued by one of the local officers; a bag made of Torah scroll parchment; a photograph of an unusual act of abuse, and so forth. Ringelblum's great merit was that he knew how to appreciate the special opportunity which fate had handed him, and to use it correctly. This public work, then, is what inspired and enabled him to establish the archives. However, as we have said, the archives were at first only a secondary activity after his public work. Only over the course of time, when it transpired that in fact there was no true benefit from all the activities, since any attempt at an act, any effort, would be shattered by the evil of the sabotaging oppressor, Ringelblum began to spend the better part of his time and energy on the historical work. For himself and his "followers" – for there were now enthusiastic followers of his work – this work became a comfort in times of trouble and became the content of life. It was clear that this labor over preparing historical material for the next generations had become, for him, an escape from the tragic vanity of the present reality. Often, as we sat depressed after an unsuccessful endeavor or a new decree, he would suddenly begin telling the story of some important document which he had obtained, or some other detail of his historical work. During those moments, his voice and the expression on his face were evidence that the man was attempting to find a pillar to lean on in the midst of his failure – the failure of us all, and he found it and was strengthened and encouraged by it.

Ringelblum loved conversations and jokes. He loved to listen and to talk. And above all – he loved to write. His hand never ceased writing notes. He wrote details of news, segments of ideas and plans, names, rumors and jokes. He wrote not only when he was alone in his room, but also during conversations with a friend, a clerk, an activist, during a meeting or a conference, even when he was the chairman. He would put the notes in his pocket, but would also leave many of them on the desk in his office, sometimes unwittingly and sometimes because he considered them unimportant.

Ringelblum's historical endeavor was known, at that time, by the code-name "*Oneg Shabbat*," and indeed, the archival workers would normally convene on Shabbat and take pleasure in the progress of their work, whose details they would impart to one another as they met.

Over the two years during which we worked together in the "public sector," we would meet almost every day, and through conversations with him I learned various facts about his private life. He told me of the days of his youth in Buczacz; he told me that in the youth movement, he was under the leadership of Dr. Zvi Heller; he told of his sister in the Soviet Union. I also visited him in his apartment, where I met his wife and small son. I sometimes saw him with his party comrades – *Poalei Zion Smol* [Left Zionist Labor]. Incidentally, they respected him very much and were proud of him, but were not always pleased with him. I once learned the reason from one of them: he is not enough of a party man, he is "innocent," he is "too honest"...

Ringelblum used to sometimes mislead people who thought to judge him by the expression on his face and his manner of speaking. Those who did not know him well might have believed that this was a sedentary man, far from life's tumult, one who did not know how to manage life. But the truth was that Ringelblum was not only a quick learner, but also had practical sharpness; he knew not only how to meditate on the problems of life, but also how to suitably handle their solutions. During the two years we worked together, I saw how he grew, how his stature increased during trying times, in face of the difficult tasks he took upon himself.

His nature was such that he belonged to that group of people who are never corrupted. In the course of his work, he met with thousands of people from all walks of life and all types of characters. He saw and knew at that time perhaps more than any other man of the scum and filth of the Ghetto life, but he was made of the stuff that nothing of that filth and ugliness could stick to. In his purity of heart and his honest ways, he was one of the illuminating figures who brought light to the darkness of the Ghetto and constantly gave it honor and glory.

Dr. Nathan Eck

[Page 227]

Emanuel Ringelblum
Translated by Jessica Cohen

In the middle of 1944, a name emerged in the Jewish press around the world and rang out as a melody – Emanuel Ringelblum. The majority of the Jewish world, who had in any case been as deaf as an adder, remained steadfast in their deafness. These people could only be awakened by the sound of a blow in their ears: *Heil Hitler!* Or: during the transfer to Treblinka. In the ears of the more refined section of the Jewish people, and particularly among the educated Jews of Poland, the sounds of that name took root as they rang out and became louder until they were the norm.

In keeping with the pathos of Jewish history, two men lost their lives together during those years of the vast Jewish holocaust, although not at the same time and not in the same ghetto. They were the elder of Jewish history, Shimon Dubnov in Riga, and the youngest of Jewish historians, Dr. Emanuel Ringelblum in Warsaw. The latter was forty years younger than his teacher.

Soon after the First World War, when Galicia was united with Poland, the Jewish Galician youth flocked to Warsaw, Bialistok and even Wilna. Galicia had always had an excess of educated Jews. Before the war, they would migrate to Vienna and Berlin. Now Berlin and Vienna were cities of scarcity, while Warsaw offered great opportunities. And so the Galician doctors rushed to the "Asian" parts of Poland. With one sweep, they infiltrated the important positions. And when, in 1930, Y. M. Neiman wished to describe a series of leading figures in the Jewish institutions in Warsaw, he discovered that they had all come from Galicia. They were quiet and generous, but would conquer fortress after fortress.

Who can say what Emanuel Ringelblum thought to himself when he came to Warsaw in 1922 as a young, shy student. He was not yet even a doctor. I happened to make note of his first entrance to our authors club. It must have been in 1928. The crisis, which culminated in the year of the abyss, 1939, had already began. And here came a tall, upright young man, wearing an artists' beret, his hair curly and his face the colors of blood and milk, with dimples. He was constantly becoming embarrassed and blushing, and had a slight stammer. He wished to join the authors organization. We began talking and I recalled that I had some acquaintances in his town of Buczacz. I advised him not to stay in Warsaw. In general, I advised young people to leave Poland, especially Zionists such as Ringelblum. I almost quarreled with him. I had shaken his innocent faith, and had seen in him my own faith of a decade prior. Faith that was proven false. He defended his enthusiasm and faith in the future of Poland Jewry. He knows better than me; he is a historian. He is not a man of moods, a poet. We did not fight: Galicians do not fight. But we made some stinging remarks to each other and bid each other farewell. And from that time onwards, I sensed an eternal sadness every time I saw Ringelblum. I had already planted my vineyard and had found that only thistles could grow here. And here comes this man and once again plants his tender years. He became a member of the association. He once presented to me, victoriously, the essay "The Young Historian" – and after all, 'the young historian' and Ringelblum became synonymous until the day he died a martyr's death.

And who could have foreseen that Jewish history, of all things, would place the thorny crown of the Warsaw Ghetto historian on his young head with the innocent face and dimples – and in the ghetto itself? Not only did he himself write, he also organized writing and collection of documents. His name is signed on the last call to the declining Jewish culture in Poland and the entire Jewish cultural world. And in that final call he recalls that Oswiecim – one of the greatest sites of murder – was called in the vernacular: Oshpitsin. And thus he did not forget, even in his final words moments before his death, to call the town by its name.

December 1934. I left Poland for ever. A hasty meeting. It might have been near the "Paviak," nine steps and nine years away from that same place and time, when the halo of the youngest tormented-historian hovered above his head. He berated me for leaving Poland. I replied that I knew better than him... He answered boldly that he knew sevenfold better than me. He knew.

Melech Rawitz

[Page 228]

Dr. Avraham Khalfan
Translated by Jessica Cohen

It was at the beginning of this century, during the early days of the flourishing of Zionism in Herzl's days. At that time, there was a great awakening among the youth studying in Galicia. A national organization called "Tzeirei Zion" [Zion Youth] was established. Its center was in Lvov, and the youth leaders of the time were very active in it, university students such as Avraham Silberstein, N. Karton-Czaczkes, Kofel Schwartz, Yosef Tenenbaum and others, including the young author and teacher, the late Asher Barash.

One of the active branches of the organization was in Buczacz. That was where the *gimnasjum* youth convened in Zionist clubs under the leadership of A. Silberstein, Matityahu Weinrab and others. There was a quiet, serious, modest and shy young man who stood out in our Zionist club, and he diligently studied Jewish studies and Hebrew: Avraham Khalfan. He had been brought up in a traditional Jewish home, and we both participated in a special Bible studies lesson in Hebrew, directed by A. Silberstein. And when the Hebrew school was established and run by the Eretz Yisrael teacher B. Berkowitz, who lives here with us, we both learned from him during Hebrew lessons. Apart from Avraham Khalfan and his sister, Tova, other participants included Zvi Heller and his two sisters, Pnina and Khaya. Avraham was noted at that time for the deep interest he showed in his studies.

When he later became a medical student at the university in Vienna, Avraham joined us in founding a Jewish academic association, "HaTkhiya," which was under the influence of such prominent Jewish activists as Dr. Haim Tratkover, Dr. Avraham Baruch (then, Rosenstein), mathematician and meteorologist Yosef Ritzes, poet Avraham Ben-Yitzhak (Soneh), author Zvi Disendrock, may their memory be a blessing, and Prof. N. Tur-Sinai, Dr. Avraham Sharon (Schvadron), Dr. A.Y. Brawer and Dr. Efraim Korngrein, may they live long and prosper. "HaTkhiya" was at that time the Jewish spiritual center for the semi-assimilationist Zionists in Vienna, because it was the first student association in the world where Hebrew was the language of conversation, lectures, extra-curricular classes in Hebrew literature and Jewish history, and arguments.

In 1911, A. Khalfan was elected president of the association, due to his distinguished character and talents. Dr. Benzion Mosinzon, who was visiting Vienna at the time and lecturing on the Hebrew culture in Eretz Yisrael, was chosen as an honorary member of the association. In those days there was also much activity in our association to support the Hebrew language and culture within other Zionist academic associations, such as "Bar Kochba," "Theodore Herzl," "Kadima" and others.

In 1914 Khalfan completed his studies in medicine and was drafted into the Austrian army, where he served as a physician until the end of the First World War.

In 1920 Dr. Avraham Khalfan settled in his hometown of Buczacz, where he was the town doctor and was later appointed as director of the internal medicine department in the town hospital. When the Nazis entered Galicia, Dr. Khalfan endured all the departments of hell which the holocaust brought, he was in a ghetto and later in the underground. In 1944 he moved to Lodz, where he directed the lung and X-ray department in the government health fund until 1948.

His great desire to make *aliya* did not materialize quickly, despite his many efforts and the endeavors of his friends, particularly his nephew here in Israel. He found some consolation in his life-long study of Hebrew literature, which he would read and reread in his great library in Buczacz, which was destroyed during the holocaust. In 1949 he managed, together with his wife, to escape the diaspora and make *aliya* to the land of his dreams. With him, he brought a Torah scroll which had been saved from destruction. Here in Israel, he entered a miserable period of searching for work, despite his training in an important profession. He almost despaired, for he could not find a sympathetic ear among the authorized persons and institutions. When he was accepted after many efforts to fulfill a professional public position as a roentgenologist in the League for the Prevention of Tuberculosis, first in Haifa and later in Hadera, he found satisfaction in this job. He devoted all his energy during the day to public work, particularly to treating the new immigrants. And in the evenings he would renounce the world outside in favor of the Torah and would meditate on both religious and secular writings. He would buy books and truly devour them. He was by nature a *"matmid"* [diligent yeshiva student] and wanted to grasp and acquire all that he had not been able to acquire while in the diaspora. He was noble spirited and quiet, but when he lectured he was like a perennial spring. He had a weak and sensitive heart, and when he lectured on occasion about the holocaust, which he had experienced first-hand, he would become extremely emotional.

The hard work exhausted his strengths, he became ill with angina, which hastened his end, and he died on 13 Shvat 5714 [January 17th, 1954].

N. M.

[Page 233]

THE SHOA IN BUCZACZ

Letter from Dr. Avraham Halfan
Translated by Israel Pickholtz

Lodz, 28 January 1946
My friend!

I am happy to see that after so many years you have not forgotten us and that you are inquiring after the Buczacz survivors. It is no surprise that you do not hear from Buczacz, because Buczacz now exist only on the map. The city was destroyed. There are only two Hebrew families and there are no Jews in the entire county. There were more than ten survivors and about 65 from the county who went west to Silesia and on from there in order to get to Eretz Israel or other countries as quickly as possible. Don't send packages, they never arrive. My opinion is that everyone dreams of aliya to Eretz Israel, not of packages... The streets of Buczacz are covered with weeds and thorns and thistles are brought forth [this is a Biblical expression]. The houses are destroyed, synagogues are public lavatories. The cemetery has been plowed under and the tombstones taken to tile the pig market. The high school, the schools and other important buildings are destroyed. The people live on the banks of the Dnieper and the Volga. More than ten thousand Jews of Buczacz have been sent from this life' their bodies in mass graves on the "_____," the _____, in the forests and the fields. [These two words are not Hebrew. I do not know what they are. The first says "fedur" and the second "bashtim."]

Unfortunately, there is nothing you can do to help us make aliyah. We appreciate your sacrifices and your efforts and we suffer with you. Perhaps there will be a change and the survivors will be permitted aliyah. – In any case, we are encouraged by the knowledge that someone under the sun thinks about us and wants to help us. You write that you have no news from Buczacz. How can I describe the situation – any description would be pale and would not truly reflect reality.

The tragedy began in July 1941 – beatings, forced labor, theft and corruption were common practice. In mid-August at four in the morning, 350 young Jews were shot on the "fedur." [see above] The young women were forced to clean the shoes of the executioners when they returned from this mass execution. People died of starvation. Outside the sword did its plunder, at home there was death. There were always new decrees, supervised by the "Jewish Council" (Judenrat) and carried out by the Jewish police. If any of these reach you alive, they should receive "special treatment." The Judenrat sent those who couldn't pay ransom to the death camps and the Jewish police hunted and beat the resistors. The Judenrat knew only dollars and gold. Furs had to be given to the Germans. Hiding furs brought the death penalty, because Jews were considered "warm" even without them. The Jews didn't know which was worse, the Judenrat or the Gestapo. This relatively good situation continued until the summer of 1942. Then began the five act tragedy – the "actions." The Jews of the towns and villages were brought to larger, central locations and from time to time there were "actions," generally late at night or towards morning. Germans, Ukrainians and Jewish police would burst into homes and whoever did not hide in basements, ditches, etc. was killed. There were several thousand victims of each "action." Terrible things happened in the hiding places. Mothers smothered their crying children or drugged them, without question. And outside death reigned. Sometimes those who were caught gave away the hiding places of their neighbors. After two days it would stop and bodies were removed from the houses and the streets and fines were paid by those who remained alive. The commerce continued: through the Judenrat you could buy and sell anything – gold, watches, jewelry, _____. [another foreign word] The non-Jews behaved badly towards the Jews. They were happy to hide their jewelry for them.

This is the way we lived from "action" to "action." each one eating away at several thousand victims. After each "action" the population was pushed into a few streets until eventually everyone was at the bottom of Podhajke Street, where the last were killed.

The tragedy had some tragi-comic scenes. There were a few instances where a person buried alive succeeded in working his way out of the ground and returned naked to the ghetto at night. Eliezer Binder, a member of my family, was twelve years old when he escaped from a mass grave which included his parents, brothers and sisters. A priest in the village, where I spent a certain amount of time, said "The Jews cheat. They jump into the graves, pretend to be dead then leave at night. You can expect anything from these Jews." Another scene: after one "action" a woman heard a child near a fresh grave "Mamma are you still alive?" A German policeman murdered the boy. He was the son of the dentist Gefner. Another story. Mrs. Clara Gross (nee Kornbluh) the wife of Gross the attorney, told hundreds of women and girls near the mass grave on the fedur "Be strong and do not fear. Any moment now and G-d will punish them..." Yaakov Margolies the baker yelled "Why are you being slaughtered like sheep and not dying with weapons in your hands!" He refused to undress before the "action" at the Jewish cemetery and spat in the face of the German. He was stoned and afterwards buried with his wife and sons.

After each "action" there were fewer hands to dig the graves and fewer people to pay the tributes. The Judenrat was killed last, in May 1943. Also killed were the Hecht, Mandel and Reich families as well as the work camp. The rest were sent to Kopicienice and Taluste [spell these how you like!] and killed there. The area was pronounced Judenrein. Any Jew found afterwards was murdered on sight. The murderers received 100 Zlotys per Jewish head. Heads fell – old and young, men and women. Anyone who succeeded in paying the last of his money to a farmer in exchange for a hiding place, was killed by the farmer or by the rural gangs or by the Ukrainian gendarmes. Oscar Friedenthal and his sister, Dr. Gross, Dr. Stern's daughter, Sabina Spiegel, the Kaner, Honig, Weiss and Zilberschlag families, Dr. Fuchs, Dr. Binenwald with his wife and sons and the wife of Dr. Hirschhorn were all killed this way. In Medidbecze [spelling??] a farmer killed Mrs. Chana Frankel and twelve others with an axe. The Glatners, the Schulmans, Mrs. Merangel, Mrs. Nacht and many others too. The city became like "the valley of the shadow of death." The Jewish bandits were no better than the murderers. They fell on the Jews in hiding, on the Jews in the forests and robbed them naked. That happened to Shaul Enderman and others. These bandits warrant "special treatment" at your hands. Jews were hunted in the villages, the fields and the forests. My wife and, my sister-in-law and her son hid in the village in the house of a farmer. It cost us much money. On 28 March 1944, the Soviets invaded but after a week, they retreated. Three and a half months – a second period of Hell. Another 600 Jews were killed, among them Dr. Goliger and her family, the physician Dr. Neuman and the Zigmans.

On 21 July 1944 we were finally freed. The count in our county was sixteen thousand murdered. Sixty five survived. They wait to be allowed to make aliyah. Try to make it as easy for them as you can. Investigate and examine the behavior during the occupation of every potential immigrant.

[Page 235]

Letter from Dr. Regina Zohker
Translated by Israel Pickholtz

Cracow, 14 January 1945

My Dear Doctor! [written with respect, using a third person form of address, which I shall ignore here]

I wrote to you some time ago, as one of those closest to me outside Poland – but did not receive a reply. Since I attribute the silence to the vagaries of the mails, I am writing again. Perhaps this time I shall succeed.

What can I write? There are so many confusing and weighty thoughts in my mind that it is difficult to force organization upon them and to express them clearly. But no one should be surprised at that, after what we have been through, irons saved from the fire, what we have seen and suffered, who can comprehend us? No man can understand it, perhaps only a mother's heart could feel the immensity of our suffering and pain.

Despite that much is being written and spoken about it, I am quite certain that you there – Jews, English, Americans – cannot fully fathom the painful events which have befallen us. Anyone who has not himself encountered the Germans, in the Gestapo, in the SS, in the gangs, who has not seen the "actions" with his own eyes – the hunt not of wild animals but of Jewish people, sick and healthy, old and young (and they all so wanted to live...), anyone who has not seen brains splattered on the walls of homes, anyone who has not seen the butchered bodies and who has not seen the rivers of Jewish blood flowing in the streets – literally that – anyone who has not spent days in a death car to Belzec with no water, no food, no opportunity for basic physiological needs; anyone who has not witnessed the heart-rendering scenes as people left this life, and anyone who has not seen the beastly and sadistic crimes of Hitler's people – cannot understand us.

I see that I have written things beyond my intent, but it is hard to restrain myself.

The only survivor from my family was Mrs. Mina Salzman (nee Halperin) and her daughter. The rest are gone.

[Page 236]

Letter from Dr. Max Enderman*
Translated by Israel Pickholtz

Buczacz, 12 February 1945

Dear ["honored"] Mr. Heller,

I was given the letter which you sent to Levi Horenstein and Rosenthal, since they are no longer in Buczacz, having gone to Poland several months ago. Most of the surviving Jews from Buczacz have left the city and I assume that they have made contact with you [plural] and that you now know the names of any survivors. The only ones left in Buczacz now are me and my family, Prof. Heller (the son-in-law of Hersch Enderman) with his wife and grandson and a few people. The city appears as a wasteland, what the German murderers did not destroy, the war did. You have surely heard already of the fate of your own family. Your brother-in-law Zelig Enderman remained alive. He left for Poland some time ago, but we do not know where he is now. The Torah scrolls were taken to Tschernovicz and given to the rabbi there. Aside from those, each family who left the city took one Torah scroll.

* This letter was the last to arrive from Buczacz from the three families who remained in the city after the Holocaust. The recipient is in Poland.

[Page 237]

How It Happened:
First Witness
Translated by Dr. Rose S. Ages (Kleiner, Neufeld)

The following pages are chapters of personal memories from the Holocaust period. Several years ago I submitted these chapters to the Jewish Council (Vaad) in Lodz. They were published, in part, by the Jewish Council, in the Polish-language collection, Akcie i Wysiedlenie (Aktsias, or Murderous Roundups/Raids, and Deportation).

This is not only the story of my life, during the Holocaust, but the story of the life of the whole kehila (community), and that of my parents, sisters, and my colleagues and friends. May these pages serve as a humble monument to their memory.

a.

With the outbreak of war between Germany and Russia, on June 22, 1941, we, the children of Buczacz, were not novices in matters relating to war: We had already had some experience with bombings, with panic, with sitting in bomb shelters, etc.

The Russian conquest, in 1939, took place with almost no fighting. But the limited opposition, by the Polish nationalists in town, to the entry of the Russian soldiers, and the few bombardments and shootings, were regarded by us as 'the real thing.'

I was a young lad, age 12, when the war broke out in 1941. However, I was quite alert, and I grasped clearly the reality of the times. I followed closely as events unfolded.

The cruelty of the Germans and their attitude toward the Jews were well known. There were many Jews who tried to retreat with the Red Army into the interior of Russia. But only a few succeeded to do so.

The Russians, whose retreat was very hasty, were not interested in taking along members of the general population with them. They took only those who had fulfilled official duties during the Soviet occupation of the town. Most of the retreating Jews of Buczacz were caught by the Germans on the road, and a large number of them returned to town after a few days, or several weeks.

The period of the first German conquest was relatively easy, compared to what came afterwards. The persecution of the Jews at this time consisted mainly of the abduction of people for different kinds of work, the wearing of the Star of David on the sleeve, the marking of all the houses in which Jews lived, the confiscation of radios, and later also of fur coats.

Of course, it also meant the destruction of all the sources of income. Enormous taxes were levied - the term 'contributions' was used in their language - on the community, at whose head they placed the 'Judenrat.'

In the early days of the conquest the Germans and the Ukrainian militia used to seize Jews for work from among those who came within their reach: old people, the sick, pregnant women, etc.. The arrangement by the 'Judenrat' with the German rulers, regarding the supply of labor, appeared much more suitable.

After a specific order for man power was received, a type of 'employment office' was created, and it was to this office that the requests of the Germans for laborers were directed. The office then tried to supply the number of workers required.

The purpose of the 'Judenrat' was to mediate between the Jewish population and the German authorities, to soften the harshness of the edicts, and to attempt to divide the burden of the demands equally among the people.

I have no doubt that this was the aim of the members of the council, and that they truly believed that they would succeed in lightening the burden placed on the Jews, and that they were working for their benefit.

They did not see, at least at the beginning, that in the end they would be turned into tools in the hands of the Gestapo, and would be forced to participate and execute all the orders of the authorities.

At the beginning the 'Judenrat' was chaired by Mendel Reich, who had been head of the community council before the war. With him on the council were Baruch Kremer (he was the subsequent head of the 'Judenrat'), Dr. Seifert, Dr. Hecht (who was in the 'Judenrat' only a very short time) and others. Altogether, I believe, there were 12 people.

Many achievements and merits can be attributed to the 'Judenrat' during the period of the first occupation, especially its organizing of mutual aid. In the summer of 1941 Buczacz was inundated with thousands of Jews who had been expelled from the Carpathian foothills, which were part of Russia. Most of them were very poor, had large families, and were extremely religious, so that even in our town they appeared somewhat out of place.

For about two months these refugees lived mostly in the different study houses and synagogues of the town, while a minority of them were billeted in private homes. One must note the great assistance that the townspeople, through the good offices of the Judenrat, gave to the refugees. After some time passed these unfortunate people were sent away to an unknown destination. Some say to the TransDniester region.

The Judenrat organized a kitchen for the poor, attended to housing for the refugees, who had come to Buczacz at a somewhat later period, from the small towns of Monastyszyska, Potok Zloty, Yazlovtse and others, when the latter were declared to be 'Judenrein.'

However, despite these activities, and despite the fact that the role of the Buczacz Judenrat was much more extensive than that of many other 'Judenrate', it is better to pass over its record in silence, especially during the period when its chairman was Baruch Kramer. I also prefer not mentioning the disgraceful role of the 'Ordnungsdienst,' which, at the nadir of its decline and decay was headed by M.A..

The various regulations and decrees came out with urgency and haste. Each one was more severe and cruel than the previous one. During one fall day in 1941 an order appeared demanding that all men, aged 18-50, were to come to the town square (which was nicknamed "hogs' square") for registration. Anyone who did not respond to this order, and did not appear, was liable to be punished by death.

A rumor spread that those who showed up at the town square would be transferred to labor camps. But despite the severe warning not to miss the registration, many escaped to the forests and the villages, and did not register.

At this point the Nazis' psychological manipulation found its most brilliant expression, as a part of their total annihilation plan. Here is what followed. Those who appeared for the registration were duly signed up, and after several hours were permitted to return home. And those who had avoided the registration procedure lived for a time in the shadow of the terrible punishment that awaited them.

After several weeks passed the men, aged 18-50, were again ordered to appear at a specific time, at the same square, for an additional registration. And actually this time most of them, if not all, appeared, relying on the first such experience of presenting themselves for registration.

Over 350 men, the best and the brightest of the youth and the working intelligentsia, gathered in the square. But suddenly the square was surrounded on all sides by units of the S.S. and the German militia, and a curfew was announced in the town. No one could leave or enter.

There were those who said that they saw how the men were led, in small groups, in the direction of the 'Fedor.' And actually after several hours shots were heard from that direction. However, no one was able to find out what really happened to the men. Had they been shot on the 'Fedor,' or were they transferred to various concentration camps?

Unlike the other aktsias, which were carried out, periodically, more in public, this event remained cloaked in darkness, and I believe that to this day it is difficult to know exactly what the fate of those unfortunates was.

And so during the span of one day hundreds of parents were bereaved, hundreds of children were orphaned, hundreds of women were widowed, and there was hardly a house without someone who had lost a loved one.

It is impossible to describe the heavy sorrow that descended on the Jews. The 'Judenrat' tried to send gentile 'messengers' to bring back some news about the fate of the men, and it contacted the authorities to this end, but without results.

Rumor followed upon rumor. According to one the men had been taken out to be shot on the 'Fedor.' But this rumor did not make sense. With all the bitter experiences that we had been subjected to during the months of the first German conquest, and despite the rumors of the atrocities that reached us about the Nazi activities in other places, no one could conceive, that it would be possible in the middle of the day, in broad daylight, to take out several hundred men to be killed.

The next day I, and some other children, sneaked out of our homes. We climbed up to the 'Fedor,' where some of us looked for their father, some for their brother, and some for other relatives. This exploration almost cost us our lives.

When we approached the forest, an armed Ukrainian policeman burst forth suddenly from behind one of the trees, and he asked us why we were walking about in the forest. We answered that we were searching for members of our families who had been taken away from us the day before.

The policeman smiled and 'promised' to bring us to them. Who knows how this matter would have ended, had not the forest guard appeared suddenly and asked the policeman to let us go home. Obviously I did not tell anyone at home about this adventure in the forest.

Another rumor said that the men were transferred to the Borki Vilki camp, and to other labor camps. And actually once a gentile related that he met one of the men, named Zeidman, in the 'Yanovsky' camp in Lvov, and this news planted new hope in the hearts of the unfortunate families. But it is very doubtful whether the men had been sent to any camp.

The 'Borki' camp was more or less an open camp. It was possible to send the inmates packages and letters. Information from the 'Yanovsky' Street camp also somehow got through. The lack of certainty with regard to the fate of the 'registration' victims aroused new hope from time to time, but there was nothing substantial on which to base that hope.

b.

Decrees of all sorts, persecutions, and abductions to the labor camps, hunger and illness all plagued us in the fall and winter of 1941. In the summer of 1942 we learned of a new form of oppression, which was worse than what we had heard up to then, and which was called by the overly modest name 'aktsia.'

On the day which was set for an 'aktsia' S.S. bands, Gestapo, and Ukrainian policemen would surround the town and close all its entrances. They raided houses, searched basements, attics, sewer pipes, etc. and rounded up all the Jews.

An aktsia generally continued for 24-48 hours, and whoever succeeded in saving his/her life during those hours, being in a hiding place, in the forest, in the field, or in a nearby village, was granted the gift of life until the next 'aktsia,' and then the cycle would repeat itself.

These 'murderous operations' were carried out with typical German thoroughness. They were planned according to the best Prussian traditions. The destruction did not happen all at once, but in stages, each stage more brutal than the previous one.

I do not intend at this time to touch upon the reasons for the lack of an uprising and the lack of rebellion among Polish Jewry. However, in my opinion, one of the most important reasons for this is due to the fact that the liquidation was carried out gradually, by stages.

Those who remained alive after the announcement that the 'aktsia' had stopped were, more or less, safe for several months (in the period between July 1942 and April 1943 the aktsias occurred in 3 to 4 month cycles), and Jews, who are optimists by nature, believed that perhaps the calamity would not extend to them.

They comforted themselves with the hope that the Russian army would soon return , and the German front would collapse, and the Jews then would experience 'light and joy.' From time to time a baseless rumor would circulate, that America had warned Germany not to harm the Jews.

The rumors, the belief in an impending rescue, and the exaggerated hopes, were like a life-giving elixir for the people, and they held on to them like a drowning person holds on to a straw. Even intelligent people, experienced in the realities of life, were influenced by these false rumors and believed in them.

The Christians made a mockery of the hopes of the Jews. The city's local paper published an article with the caption: "Zydzi mowia: s'wet zajn gut" (The Jews Say That Things Will Be All Right), thus ridiculing Jewish optimism.

During the months of May, June, and July, 1942 the murderous activities were carried out in the cities and small towns of the surrounding area, while Buczacz was spared for some reason at that time. Rumors were constantly circulating that an 'aktsia' was imminent, that the 'aktsia' would be on the following day, or week, or that there would not be any more 'aktsias' at all.

Meantime people did not sleep in their homes for weeks on end. There were those who stayed with a farmer in a nearby village, or who slept in the forest, or in the open field. The nightmare of the 'aktsia' pursued us for months, and when it did not come the tension was somewhat reduced.

One September day in 1942, I believe it was a Saturday morning, a large number of units of German soldiers, along with the Ukrainian militia, surrounded the town and spread out through the houses in order to search for Jews. Most of the people succeeded somehow in hiding in bunkers which had been prepared in advance.

My parents, and sisters and I were then in a bunker on Gimnazyalna Street, in Zhaleznik's house. The search that was carried out in that house was very thorough. Several times groups of German and Ukrainian soldiers came into the house, one after the other. They ripped out the floors, broke walls, dug in the yard, but they did not find the bunker. The officer in charge of the 'aktsia' was Krieger, the commander of the Gestapo in Stanislavov.

During the day over 1600 people were caught - men, women and children, and were brought to 'Hogs' Square', and from there were transferred by vans to the train station. Many tried to escape from the vans, and almost 200 people were shot in houses and on the streets.

The train took the people to the Belzec camp, which was near Lvov. Many dozens of people were put into a closed, airless freight car. The men used to carry with them small breakout tools (a saw, pliers, etc.) in order to be prepared for any trouble that might come. With the help of these tools, many succeeded in breaking out of the freight cars and in jumping out of the train.

The transport was heavily guarded, and many of those who tried to jump out of the train were shot by the Germans. Some were killed by jumping out the wrong way; some were run over by the wheels of the train. It was said that after every 'transport', many dozens of dead and injured people were found scattered, lying all along the train tracks, and the surrounding area, that led to Belzec.

Over time various rumors began to reach us about what was going on in this camp. It was said, that those arriving at the camp were required to undress, and had to go into a shower, so to speak, that was really a disguised gas chamber.

It was also rumored that in Belzec the Nazis were making soap from Jewish bodies. Most of the Jews, even the most informed among them, refused to believe that the Nazis had sunk to such a low point in their satanic madness.

On the same day that the murderous activities were taking place in Buczacz, similar activities were taking place all over the district. Later all those Jews who remained alive throughout the area, were expelled to Buczacz. Jews came from Monasterzyska, Yazlovtse, Potok Zloty, and from other small towns in the region, and the Jewish population in the city ballooned to more than ten thousand.

Jews who were broken and dejected, widows, orphans, people without any means of support, flooded the city by the thousands. There was the occasional person who could afford to rent a room, someone who found shelter with his relatives, but the majority of the people crowded into small, dark quarters, sometimes ten or more to a room.

It is not surprising that under these circumstances a typhoid epidemic broke out, and it consumed about 15-20 people daily. There was almost no house in which there was not someone struck by typhoid. The disease would spread and infect the whole household.

As a result of the epidemic the authorities became even more strict about not allowing contact between Jews and Christians. And the economic situation kept getting worse. Among the Jewish population a severe famine broke out. A kind of vicious cycle was created.

The famine helped spread the epidemic, whereas the epidemic tightened the noose around the Jewish population even more. That lead to more famine, and thus the cycle would repeat itself. The epidemic did not spare me either. One day in December, 1942, I returned from a lesson with the 'Pinsker,' - whom I will discuss later - and I was consumed with fever. Within several days it was clear that I was indeed stricken with typhoid.

My mother went to the pharmacy to buy medicine for me. To our misfortune 'street abductions' were taking place at that hour, and she too became one of the kidnapped. No one knew what was done with those who were kidnapped or where they had been taken. However, it was clear that the chances that they would be returned to their homes were very slim.

During that period I lay with a 40-degree temperature, without much hope of overcoming the disease, and my heart trembled with longing for my mother. My mother, whose soul was so tied up with mine, and who was dearer to me than anything, had been suddenly taken away from me. My distress grew even more with the knowledge that she had endangered her life for my sake, and because of me she had fallen victim to the beasts of prey.

That day several hundred people were rounded up and transferred to Chortkov. There they were put into prison. For two weeks during their incarceration they were given a piece of bread and a little water only once every 48 hours. Many died from hunger and thirst. My mother was among the lucky ones, who, through an open hatch, were able to gather some snow to break their thirst.

On January 4, 1943 the prisoners were put on freight trucks that drove to the mountain, where they were supposed to take out the victims to be shot. But something unbelievable happened. Because of a heavy snow storm the road was in bad condition and the trucks could not go up the mountain.

The Germans spent half a day trying to move the trucks up the mountain, but in vain. In the end they freed the people and allowed them to return to their homes. Among the lucky ones who returned home was my mother.

One cannot describe the joy the night that we saw her again, after we had almost lost all hope. That night I slept with a very high fever, and I believe that my consciousness was somewhat blurred. However, as soon as my mother opened the door, my eyes lit up. For hours she sat by my side as I looked at her, and could not get enough of that vision. How much nobility, love and intelligence were reflected in her eyes. How beautiful and fresh she looked despite everything that she had endured during those weeks.

The Nazis, trying in various ways to weaken the vigilance of their victims, exploited the above-mentioned incident to prove that there would be no more 'aktsias,' and that from then on the Jews had no need to fear for their lives.

Rumors circulated in town that an order had gone out from the world's leading powers, in the wake of American intervention (for some reason the Jews believed that America was not silent and was making many efforts to save Jews), indicating that henceforth there would be no more 'aktsias', and that the living conditions of the Jewish population would be restored to their normal pattern.

It is possible, indeed, that this assumption was strengthened somewhat by the fact that certain concessions had been granted by the authorities. But little time was granted to the Jews for diverting themselves with vain illusions.

c.

Meantime the typhoid epidemic broke out in all its virulence. According to rumors the two Ukrainian doctors, Hamerski and Vanach, had turned to the Nazi authorities with the complaint that the crowding in the Jewish neighborhoods was unbearable; that the typhoid epidemic was spreading, and that if they didn't bring an end to it, the plague was bound to spread to the Christian dwellings as well.

One night, at the beginning of February 1943, after midnight, a Jewish girl (my sister's friend), knocked on our door and told us that there were rumors in town that an 'aktsia' would take place on the following day. A Ukrainian policeman reported this to Duhl, the shoemaker.

Panic erupted. It was impossible to flee to the fields and forests because it was winter and the footprints in the snow were bound to betray those who fled. Accordingly, most of the people fortified themselves in the bunkers, which had been prepared some time earlier.

It was customary to call every hiding place a bunker, but the hiding places which could be regarded as real bunkers, were few in number. Mostly they were built in basements, and attics, etc., and were disguised as well as Jewish inventiveness could make it.

In order to build an underground bunker it was necessary to overcome many difficulties. First, it was essential that no untrustworthy persons become aware of it. It happened that the Nazis would torture one of their victims so that he would reveal the hiding place of the other Jews in the house, or they would promise to free the victim if he would reveal the hiding place.

Many actually did not pass the test. Of special note is the notorious case of N.L., the owner of the kerosene warehouse on Podhayetska Street. In return for the Nazi promise, that his life would be spared, he exposed the location of a bunker with dozens of people, among them members of his own family. One of the people in that bunker, attacked Landes with an ax. The Nazis allowed the unfortunates to avenge themselves on the traitor and the man killed him on the spot.

The major difficulty with building a bunker was where to dispose of the soil that was dug up (the Ukrainian militia carefully followed activities in the Jewish houses), and how to get an adequate air supply.

Somehow they overcame these difficulties, and in many homes bunkers were built which could withstand the most exacting searches. Much inventive talent, arduous labor, and lots of money were invested in their construction.

During the second 'aktsia' we lived in a house on Koscielna Street, in the long alley, where there was a coffee house. Our family lived in that house along with the Koffler family (the Hebrew teacher), the Dretler family, the Bick family and the rabbi from Pinsk.

The hiding place in the basement was too shallow, but it was well concealed, and the moment news about the 'aktsia' reached us, all the inhabitants of the house went down to the hiding place. We spent over 24 hours in that terrible hiding place, when each minute seemed like an eternity to us.

All the time we could hear the heavy boots and footsteps of the German and Ukrainian murderers, who turned the house upside down in order to find the hiding place. We also heard the footsteps of our Christian neighbors, who came to plunder booty. To their credit it must be noted that they were very selective and did not take everything that came into their hands.

During all those hours, I recall, Chaim Koffler, who was both my Hebrew teacher and a man that I highly respected, sat and took notes. He told me that he was recording the last events of the town's Jewish population, because, even if we didn't survive, the world had to know about the Nazis' savage and murderous acts. And one day the world would take revenge for us.

How naïve that belief looks today - that those condemned to death believed the nations of the world would avenge the spilled Jewish blood, after the victory over the Nazis.

Just as the Jews were certain of a victory by the Russians and the West over Hitler, they were also certain of the revenge that the victors would take on the Nazis. I recall a conversation between my father, may he rest in peace, and our neighbor Arthur Bick.

Bick argued, whether facetiously or in earnest, that at least we were assured of one thing after the Russian return: a military band and floral wreaths on an annual basis on memorial day. My father told him that he was deluding himself, and that in his opinion the Russians would be secretly pleased with

Hitler's acts of destruction, and that, in any case, one could not assume that they would mourn these actions. To our regret, my father was right.

About 1600 people fell victim in the second 'murder action'. Most of them were driven out of their hiding places, or were caught trying to flee the city, around which a tightening noose had been placed. They had planned to stay in the nearby villages until the danger would pass.

The people were transferred in groups of 50 to the train station, loaded onto freight trains and transferred to Belzec. The elderly, the sick, and those who attempted to flee on the way to the train station were killed by the murderers on the spot.

The day after the 'aktsia' the city streets were strewn with the dead. The Nazis used dumdum bullets on the Jewish victims, and as a result the victims' faces were disfigured to the point that most were not recognizable.

The responsibility for picking up the corpses in the streets and their burial was placed upon the 'Judenrat'. In spite of this many of those who were caught succeeded in escaping. Some of them were able to bribe the Ukrainian police guard, who turned a blind eye to their escape. However, the larger part of those who returned consisted of persons who had jumped from the train that was taking them to Belzec.

d.

At present when I examine the state of mind of the Jews in those days, it seems to me that two different attitudes prevailed among them. On the one hand there was the fatalistic attitude whereby people relied on fate and on the common destiny of the Jewish people.

On the other hand a large part of the population felt that the destruction would not reach them. There were those who hoped that with the help of God, or with the help of a 'miracle', they would be granted life until the coming victory, and be able to witness revenge on the enemy.

This part of the population felt that with time they would prevail, and that the main problem was how to hang in there under all circumstances and under all conditions. These people were under the illusion that whoever succeeded in holding out during this 'aktsia', would be assured of staying alive in the coming months.

In the meantime salvation might come. There were those who hoped that the war would end, or that the Nazis would be forced to end their murderous activities, because of the pressure of world public opinion.

They heard nothing in Buczacz about Treblinka or Auschwitz, and with regard to the Belzec camp many tended to believe (at least during the first period), that it was not an extermination camp, but only a labor camp.

The Nazis, in order to make their work easier, wanted the Jews to live with such illusions, and all their planning was directed toward this goal, to the point where they themselves would spread good rumors. They divided the Jewish population into carriers of 'good' certificates (skilled workers, specialists), which made one immune to the 'aktsias', and into those who carried regular certificates.

The purpose of the interludes between one murderous period and the next was also to reinforce the illusion that all would be well. The interludes sometimes lasted several months and sometimes one month. Meanwhile life made its own demands, and between one 'aktsia' and the next the Jews of Buczacz tried to carry on the best they could.

They loved and hated, envied and competed, and searched for ways to make a living, etc... There was also much resentment on the part of the poor toward the rich, because the poor were the first candidates for extermination (mostly because of their lack of means to build good hiding places) and they were hit the worst by hunger and the epidemics.

A moral decline was felt among a large part of the youth, and the most widespread slogan was: 'This way Fedor and that way Fedor' (no matter how we conduct ourselves, our ultimate fate is on the Fedor). There was no way to make a living. The Jews followed the dictum, 'make your living one from the other.' Of course, they also traded with the Christians, but from time to time various edicts were enacted to prevent any contact between the two groups.

The most common form of trade with the Christians was 'barter,' or as they called it then 'minyalo.' In this market one did not use currency, but paid with clothes, furniture or other valuables for basic food necessities. For a fur coat, for example, one could get a certain number of potatoes, for a gold watch, a certain amount of flour, etc.. The prices in this 'barter' market were, understandably, dependent upon the season and were subject to change.

Cultural life was also not entirely neglected. Whoever was able to do so looked after their children's education. I do not remember by whom, and how, the thousands of children in the town were educated during the period of the first occupation. However, if one is to judge by my own case, I think, that even in this area not a little was accomplished.

My father, of blessed memory, made great efforts to continue my education and that of my sisters. He did it either because he felt that very little time was left for us to acquire an education, or because he wished to remove us from our environment of persecution and humiliation, to an environment of Torah and learning.

I had time to finish only five grades of public school before the Nazi invasion. There were three grades in the Polish school, until 1939; a year in a Yiddish grade (1939-1940), and a year in a Russian grade (1940-1941).

As is known, with the Russian entry into western Ukraine in 1939, the government established Yiddish schools in the Jewish centers, in accordance with the principle of the cultural and linguistic autonomy of each and every nationality within the Soviet Union. This arrangement was abolished in 1940 and, I believe, no one was sorry to see it happen.

This Yiddish school created many problems. First, there were no competent teachers (the principal of the school was a Ukrainian named Lutsiov); there were no textbooks for most of the subjects, and there was no coordinated program.

The result was a very low standard of education. But the basic problem was that the grades that followed were all in Ukrainian or Russian, and the transfer of children from a Yiddish school to continuing grades in Russian or Ukrainian, was bound to create problems both for the class and the student.

Obviously five years of such fragmented learning could not give a child what he would learn in five consecutive years at one school and in one language. My father taught me math, reading and writing. I learned Hebrew and Hebrew grammar with the teacher, Chaim Koffler, who lived in our neighborhood. I learned Bible and Talmud with the 'Pinsker.'

The 'Pinsker', or as was his full name, Rabbi Yosef Halevi of the Horowitz family, was, until the Russian Revolution, a rabbi in Pinsk. With the outbreak of the Revolution he fled to Poland, like many others of the 'Klei Kodesh' (religious ministrants). His wife and two daughters remained in Russia, and the rabbi knew nothing about what happened to them during all those years.

The 'Pinsker', as he was known among the people, was a Torah genius, learned and erudite. He established new interpretations of the Torah, and he was a fiery Zionist (a member of Mizrachi, I believe).

I don't know what the rabbi was doing in the years 1919-1940, even though he talked to me a lot about it. I believe that he used to travel from town to town, and from village to village, in Poland, as a maggid (itinerant preacher), preaching and advocating a return to the land of Israel.

His appearance bespoke dignity. A long white beard framed his face and his words were like sparks of fire, brilliant and witty, and they were flavored with a subtle but sharp humor. To this day I remember several of the Pinsker's speeches, that he used to read to me in the evenings. They made a very strong impression on me.

In 1940, for some reason, the rabbi settled permanently in Buczacz. There he gathered a group of students around him and disseminated Torah study. With the Nazi invasion, and because there was no possibility of attending a school, my father decided that I too should study with the 'Pinsker' (until then I had private lessons with Kirshner).

After a short time I did very well in these studies. I became very close to the rabbi and his influence on me was tremendous. Even though a long white beard framed his face, he was a considerably progressive man, with a broad general knowledge, and well informed about the ways of the world.

From among the group of students that he had four of us have survived: Mordechai Halpern, Menachem Kriegel, Yona Tsaler and I. Three of us became in the meantime 'apikorsim' (skeptics), while Yona Tsaler is still keeping the 'flame' alive, and is a student at the Ponevich Yeshiva in Bnei Brak.

On winter evenings the 'Pinsker' liked to reminisce about Bialik, with whom he had studied together at the Volozhin Yeshiva, and about different Zionist personalities. He especially liked to tell humorous tales about the 'rebbis' (Chasidic rabbinic leaders). He himself was, like all the Halevi Horwitz family, a strong 'mitnaged' (opponent of Chasidism).

Another person who had much influence on me at that time was, as I mentioned earlier, my Hebrew teacher, Chaim Koffler. He succeeded in bringing out in me a love of the Hebrew language, and within a short time, relatively speaking, I knew the language and grammar fairly well.

I recall at that time we went over the novel, The Love of Zion, by Mapu. The book made an enormous impression on me and planted within me a strong love of Zion. With what love and longing did my teacher read to me, and explain those chapters which describe the Judean hills, Jerusalem, and the life of joy and tranquillity in the lap of nature. Once he even expressed his feeling that he would never forgive himself for not realizing his lifelong dream of going to Israel and settling there.

All his life he preached to others to go to Israel, but he himself did not go. He had by then already lost his two sons - Hebrew teachers also - and his crippled daughter was with him. A year later he died of typhoid fever (if I recall correctly), and his wife and daughter were lost in one of the 'aktsias.' It was said that the Nazis wanted to take his wife to the Belzec transport train, but they wanted to leave the crippled daughter behind (in order to kill her in the immediate vicinity). However, the mother refused to be separated from her daughter, and both were shot by the murderers in their apartment.

e.

After the second 'aktsia' more Jews were transferred to Buczacz from the surrounding area. The town was divided into two sections. The larger section contained the main street. That street led from the train station through Koleova and the 'Third of May' Streets, to the bridge which was called by the Jews, for some reason, 'the black bridge' ('die schwartze brik').

Jews were permitted to live in the western section only. The reason is understandable - to make the work easier for the Nazis. Every Jew who was found in the second section, would be punished by death, along with the Christian, at whose place he was caught.

And again there was horrendous crowding, poverty and shortages. But the Nazis saw to it that the excessive crowding in town would not last, and a month after the second murderous aktsia, that is in March 1943, the town was suddenly surrounded by powerful Gestapo forces and Ukrainian militia units.

The third 'aktsia' had begun, and it was the most terrible of all that had taken place previously. For almost three days and nights the blood thirsty beasts of prey went mad, and the number of casualties in those three days and nights came to 2800.

My family left the apartment on Koscielna Street, which was in the Christian section, and we moved to my uncle's place in Folkenflok's house, on Podhayetska Street.

On the other side of that street, in a small house, the residents had built one of the best bunkers in town. From the basement they dug a seven meter deep tunnel, and from there they extended a trench which was several dozen meters long, and about three meters wide.

The entrance into the basement was through a well concealed stove. The entrance from the basement into the bunker was also extremely well concealed. Even if the Nazis discovered the basement, it is unlikely that they would have succeeded in discovering the hiding place.

When the rumor spread at night about the approaching 'aktsia', several of us went down into that bunker. The entrance was most complicated and was particularly difficult for the older people.

A special challenge was involved in taking my uncle down, because he was crippled in both legs (having been wounded during World War I). The bunker was closed and covered up by someone on the outside. That person had to seek shelter elsewhere, and at the end of the 'aktsia' he was supposed to come and inform us that the aktsia was over.

After a 24 hour stay in the bunker we felt a serious shortage of air. The air tube had been blocked, it seemed, and we were facing the danger of suffocation. A match could not be lit because of the absence of air. Women started to faint, and breathing became unbearably difficult.

As for me, I was a very healthy youth and during all those hours when the danger of being suffocated threatened us, I was in a deep sleep and didn't feel what was going on around me. Because of the danger to individual lives, and the risk to the bunker as a whole, several men went up at night and dug an additional opening for air to come through. This way we felt some relief.

During this 'aktsia,' unlike the earlier ones, they did not transport the people to Belzec. They transferred them, in groups of 50 people, to the 'Fedor', and killed them there with machine guns. The harvest of death was formidable, as was already pointed out: almost 2800 souls.

The streets were strewn with dozens of bodies of those who had attempted to escape during the transfer to the 'Fedor.' The Christians from the area pillaged and laid waste to the Jewish homes. As soon as the rumor spread in the villages that the 'murderous activities' were taking place in town, the farmers immediately rushed to town to plunder and to seize the spoils.

There were even those who removed gold teeth from the mouths of the victims and removed the gold rings from their fingers. Some of them cut off fingers to make it easier to remove rings. In contrast there were few cases when Christians actually did something, for humane reasons, to save Jews.

It was said that on the 'Fedor' one woman, Dr. Gross, addressed her fellow victims, before she was taken out to be shot. She denounced the murderers as 'heroes' against an unarmed population, and she prophesied for them a speedy end and vengeance for their crimes. She was taken first to be shot, and they even mutilated her body.

Had there been any illusion whatsoever, before this 'aktsia', about the fate of those who were captured in previous murderous actions, and taken to Belzec, this massacre, committed in the open and in public, proved to those who were still deluding themselves, that only one fate awaited all those whom the Nazis targeted.

f.

The fourth 'aktsia' began about a month after the third 'aktsia', at the start of April 1943, and it followed a similar pattern. About 600 people were taken to the 'Fedor', and were mowed down with machine guns. Among those who were being led out to be killed, one youth, Yanek Anderman, shot a German with a handgun.

The Germans seized the youth, beat him hard and then led him, with hands and feet in handcuffs, to the city hall. There they doused him with gasoline and burned him alive. In another group a youth of 19 attacked a German with a knife. His fate too was death by brutal torture.

After this 'aktsia' an announcement was made that the remaining Jews had to move to Tchortkov, Kopychyntsa and Tlusta. In Buczacz itself the Germans set up a camp for 'skilled workers' in a section of Podhayetska Street. For a substantial sum of money it was possible to obtain from the authorities a 'skilled worker's' certificate and thus remain in the camp.

Since we had family in Tlusta my father decided that it would be better to move to that small town. In Tlusta, up to that point there was no ghetto, and there was hope that here it would be easier to escape death than in the other small towns. For this reason most of the remaining Buczacz Jews moved to Tlusta.

In Tlusta during that period there was horrendous congestion, extreme poverty, hunger and sickness. About 8-9 thousand Jews were crowded into this small and wretched town. Several families lived in one room. Some lived on stairwells, in attics and in basements.

Because we had family in town, our situation was a little better, and we were given the small kitchen in which five people crowded together, my parents, my two sisters, and I. Right on the day of our arrival a rumor spread, that on the following day there would be an 'aktsia.'

We spent that night in a forest, about 7 kilometers from the town. On the way we met hundreds of Jews, since everyone was searching for shelter, some among the Christians in the nearby villages, some in the field, and some in the forest.

The 'aktsia' was not held the next day and we all returned to the town. However, not much of a rest was given to the persecuted. During one of the first days of May (I do not remember the exact date), on a Thursday just before sunrise, a large contingent of Gestapo, S.S. units, and Ukrainian militia, suddenly surrounded the town, and no one had a chance to escape.

Most of those who attempted to escape to the fields met their death at the hands of the guards, who were stationed at the entrances to the town. For many weeks people had slept in their clothes. However, that particular night we slept peacefully, hoping that the danger was not close.

The shootings woke us up and within minutes the Nazis began to break down the gate. Most of the inhabitants in the house, my sisters included, managed to go up to the hiding place, that had been built in the attic. I, my parents, and several others remained stuck in the kitchen, as the S.S. men, and the militia, ran through the house.

From the kitchen there was an opening to a little cellar that served as a storage area for potatoes, coal and wood. It had not occurred to anyone to convert this little cellar into a hiding place. Since we had no other hope of escape we went down to the little cellar and covered it with the bundles of straw that had served us as bedding during the night.

The murderers entered the house four times, conducted thorough searches, removed floor boards, and dislodged bricks, but they did not find our hiding place. In the attic hiding place there were about 30 people, and among them my two sisters. They were seized, together with the others in that hiding place, and taken to the yard near the church. From there they were taken to the Jewish cemetery, where they met their deaths.

My two dear beloved sisters, who were inseparable in their lives and in their deaths: Malia, the 12-year-old, blond and beautiful, with sky-blue eyes and golden locks, and Mania, the 17-year-old, with her long black braids, the serious and intelligent one!

During all this time I, my parents, and some other people sat in the little cellar, as death hovered above our heads, and our fate hung by a thread. Neither food nor water touched our lips during all those hours.

Over the 30 hours of this murderous 'aktsia' about 3600 Jews fell victim. They were forced into the square near the church, and from there they were taken in groups of 50, under heavy guard, to the Jewish cemetery. There they were machine gunned.

The Ukrainians participated in this 'aktsia' as much as the Germans. The murderers donned dark glasses and black gloves. The Ukrainian policeman, Shaf, envious of those who were engaged in the killings, asked to join them. After he was given permission to do so, he began shooting with sadistic glee, and killed dozens of people.

Hundreds of the dead were strewn about the streets and in the houses, and for about 3-4 days bodies were being collected and buried in the cemetery. After the 'aktsia' I went out to search for my two sisters. I thought perhaps they had succeeded in escaping, or perhaps were hiding somewhere.

My feet carried me to the cemetery, and a horrible sight unfolded before me: corpses, corpses, corpses. Among them I recognized the 'Pinsker', acquaintances, neighbors and friends. Fragments of currency bills, documents and photographs were strewn about the whole area. The following day the mass graves, in which hundreds of the victims had been buried, began oozing with blood, since many of the wounded had been buried alive, and only a thin layer of soil covered the graves.

Christian doctors and engineers were brought to the place. They examined the condition of the graves, and ordered that they be covered with thick layers of soil, and that lime be poured over them. After that came the order for setting up a ghetto in Tlusta, and within 24 hours all the Jews were obligated to move to the ghetto area.

g.

In the areas near Tlusta there were many estates, 'folwarks', that at one time had belonged to Count Pototsky. Near several of the estates there were permanent Jewish labor camps. At several of the other estates, when the need arose for more workers (many of the young inhabitants were sent to work in Germany), the Germans were accustomed to seizing Jews in the morning, bringing them to the work place, and then returning them in the evening.

On Sunday, June 6 - it was a very beautiful summer day - I went to the market in the morning to buy something for the house. Suddenly the Ukrainian militia started grabbing Jews to work, and I was abducted as well. They took dozens of people to the village of Kosigora and they ordered us to weed potato bushes. I worked several hours in the burning sun, while a Ukrainian policeman taunted us all the time.

I knew that my parents were very worried about me and I decided, along with my friends, to escape as soon as the noon break came. The village was about ten kilometers from Tlusta. We walked through fields and woods, and tried to avoid going through any villages. At about 2 p.m. we arrived at the train station. How very shocked we were to see transport trucks loaded with German soldiers and Ukrainian militia entering the town from several directions.

Before we could get our bearings, we heard shots from all directions and the village was surrounded by soldiers and policemen. This was the first time that an 'aktsia' was held on a Sunday, and it had started in the afternoon hours. On Sundays the murderers generally rested and the Jews used to breathe more easily. This aktsia was a deviation from the usual strategy and custom of the murderers, and its goal was, apparently, to exploit the element of surprise.

The panic was great, everyone tried to run for shelter. My friends and I began to run backwards, but one of the policemen was watching us and he began to fire in our direction. The bullets hit people who were running to my right and to my left. The screams and moaning of the wounded and of the dying filled the air.

I ran with bated breath, as long as I could hold out, while the bullets were buzzing around me. After about 150 meters of running from a shower of bullets I found myself in a corn field. I survived. My friend also succeeded in getting through the thick rain of bullets that flew around us, and together we went on our way.

About 14 km from Tlusta there is a forest named Charnohora. We turned in the direction of that forest, and we decided to stay there until the end of the 'aktsia.' On the way we met farmers who were rushing, running to town, some by wagon, and some on foot, to claim their booty.

The Christians from the area around Tlusta were mostly poor. Many had no independent means, and supported themselves by working on the estates. Every small item was of value to them. One could see them during the 'aktsia' dragging old featherbeds and pillows, broken furniture and used clothing - items which the Christians in Buczacz would not want to even look at.

This much should be known: The destruction of the Jewish population did not merely satisfy the feeling of hatred of the Christian population in the towns and villages. It also brought them great material benefits. Thousands of Christians became wealthy on account of the Jewish tragedy.

For every service, connected with saving a life, Jews were ready to pay fabulous sums, and the 'Christians' exploited this opportunity. Many bought from the Jews luxury furniture, furs, jewels, expensive clothes and more for next to nothing. During my wanderings in the villages, I would see, on more than one occasion, a costly piano in the home of a destitute peasant, who was a day laborer on one of the 'folwarks', or estates.

On the way we met a group of farmers who were heading to town for plunder. When they realized that we were Jews they demanded money from us, threatening to make us return to town with them. By chance I had 150 zlotys, and my friend had 100, a sum too small. We offered them the money. At first they weren't ready to accept it. But when they realized that we did not have any more, they took the money and left us alone.

We continued on our way to Charnohora, and before evening we entered the forest. Many Jews hid in this forest during the day and night. The peasants from the surrounding area attacked them en masse when they felt there was a chance to plunder. They would assault the people with axes and pitchforks. The echoes from the voices of those who were being robbed and murdered reached all the way to us. It was a night of heavy terror, a night that I shall never forget.

I did not know the forest paths. I ran about like a hunted animal among the thorn bushes, that were twice as tall as I. To add to my grief, I also lost my friend. After hours of wandering about in the forest, I settled down among the bushes and waited for daylight. I hoped that with sunrise I would somehow find my way back.

Worry for my parents gnawed at my heart, and I could not stop crying. Who knows if I will ever see them again. Only a miracle could have saved them. And the miracle happened. They had stayed in the little cellar, that was in the kitchen where we lived, with several other families, and the tentacles of the murderers had not reached them.

At sunrise I left the forest and decided to return to town. It was a very beautiful summer day. The Ukrainian landscape unfolded before me in all its glory: A forest, golden wheat fields, grazing stretches and gentile youths leading the cows to pasture. Streams of water. All these sights warmed my heart, and distracted me from my agony. On the way I learned from the Christians that the aktsia had ended.

I rushed to return to town, and about noontime I found myself standing in front of the house where we were living. My heart was beating hard: Had the miracle happened, or would I hear, heaven forbid, the worst.

I knew few moments of joy during all those years, but the moments of this meeting were, perhaps, the happiest of my life. My friend managed to return to town before me and he had told my parents that I was in the Charnohora forest. My father paid a large amount of money to a peasant to search for me in the forest and to bring me home. But meantime I had managed to get back by myself.

h.

This 'aktsia' had barely ended when rumors spread immediately that a new one was about to start, after which Tlusta would be proclaimed 'Judenrein.' According to the law every Jew found in a place that has been pronounced 'Judenrein' was to be punished by death within 24 hours after being caught.

As I have mentioned earlier, there were several estates in the region of Tlusta, and near them a number of Jewish work camps. In these camps, too, life was not secure. But people there hoped that they would be able to hold out at least until the end of the harvest season, and perhaps until fall. Under these conditions they did not think ahead, about what would happen in a few months. They felt that time was working in their favor, and the important thing was to simply carry on.

The remaining Jews tried to be accepted for work in the 'folwarks,' and, of course, this depended on bribing the authorities. About 40 Buczacz people, among them my parents, decided to return to Buczacz and join the 'skilled workers' camp there. We hired seven wagons and at midnight set out on the road. We had to cover 56 km. It was impossible to go on the main road, and we traveled in a roundabout way, through corn fields and forests.

Even though the peasants that we hired for this trip were our acquaintances, and considered trustworthy, they did not hesitate, every few kilometers, to threaten to force us off the wagons in the middle of the journey, if we did not give them more money, because, according to them, the danger was greater than they had reckoned.

Before morning we passed one village where, to our misfortune, that night a punishment detail of Gestapo people had arrived. The farmers said that as a punishment for the killing of two Gestapo men, whose bodies were found in the village, the Germans had taken out all the men who lived there, and killed every tenth one among them.

We had entered straight into the lion's den. However, before the Germans had time to grasp who we were and how we had gotten into that village, we escaped into the nearby forest. A heavy fire from hand- and machine-guns rained down on us and again ll people fell dead.

In the meantime the peasants had run away with the wagons and with all our possessions, and we made the rest of our way to Buczacz on foot. I had a special feeling of relief when we approached the town, a kind of feeling of security. Everything, the streets, the houses, the trees, were so familiar to me and so close to my heart!

A Jewish mechanic by the name of Haber lived near the 'black bridge', in Buczacz. Because of his expertise, and the work that he did for the Germans, he even had a permit to live outside of the camp. At 2 a.m. we reached his house.

He was amazed when he heard that we came from Tlusta, since the Jews of the Buczacz camp were fleeing to Tlusta. These people learned that the camp in Buczacz was to be liquidated within 3-4 days, and its inhabitants were to go to other places. Several additional families from the camp joined our group. We hired new carriages and that same night we left to return to Tlusta.

About 3 km from Tlusta we got out of the carriages and decided to sneak into town in secret, in order not to arouse any special attention. It was on the day of 12.6.43, before sundown. The farmers were returning home from their work in the fields. We learned from them that on that same day, at noon, Tlusta had been proclaimed 'Judenrein'.

The authorities provided carriages for the remaining Jews to take them to the Chortkov ghetto. We hesitated: Should we return to Buczacz? Whatever will be with the several hundred of her remaining Jews that will be with us. Or perhaps we should turn straight toward the forests in the area? It was decided to return to Buczacz, and so we found the people sitting on their suitcases ready to move on.

The Germans announced that the camp inhabitants were to prepare food, linen and bedding and to be ready to move to camp Svidova that is near Tlusta. A part of the youth left for the forest, a part went out to hide with the farmers, who had prepared bunkers for them.

For most of the camp inhabitants, including us, there was no choice but to join the convoy that was taking the people to Svidova. On June 15, at 9 a.m., dozens of wagons arrived in the camp, and in a long caravan we moved off, accompanied by a heavy guard of S.S. units and Ukrainian militia. In late afternoon we arrived at the camp.

Svidova was one of the many estates in the area, and perhaps the largest one. Its peasants were well known in the whole vicinity as anti-Semites. Before the war eight Jewish families had lived in the village, and one night between the time when the Russians were retreating and the Germans were entering the village, the peasants staged a pogrom and murdered every one of the Jews.

About 560 people were housed in the camp, and among them several hundred that were brought from Buczacz, a small number from Tlusta, Yagolnitza, Zalezhchiki and other places. Most of the Jews in the camp, if not all, were wealthy. The Christians were interested in doing away with them quickly, in order to plunder their possessions.

Thus, in addition to the regular guard of the Ukrainian militia, the Christians set up volunteer guards from among the peasants of the village, and they, too, guarded the entrances of the camp. This camp was fenced in with double barbed wire.

The conditions in the camp, relatively speaking, were not the worst, even though we worked from dawn till sunset. The manager of the estate, a Pole named Musial, an evil person and a scoundrel, did his best to make life difficult for the people in the camp.

Sometimes, 'when he was in a good mood,' he would order, spitefully, that the Jews should dig up the potatoes, or weed out the green fields, on their knees. Sometimes he would order that no water be given to thirsty workers. But because they had the funds, the Jews bought the essential foods, milk and fruit, from the peasants, who used to bring the best foods to the camp gates.

Since this was a 'busy season' for field work, and there was a shortage of workers in the area, there was room for hope, that the camp's security was assured at least until after the harvest season. Life in the camp began to slowly get organized. Several cultural evenings were held, readings, singing, etc.

Among the camp inhabitants there was also the Buczacz cantor, Beno Shifman. I still remember the days when the whole town was astir because of Shifman. It happened perhaps in 1937 or 1938, and I was still a little boy at that time.

From time to time the great synagogue used to have cantorial evenings, and famous cantors, with their choirs, used to appear at the concerts. On one of those evenings Shifman was the featured cantor. He was a very young, handsome man, from Lvov, and he had a beautiful, sweet voice.

His appearance made an enormous impression, and he was invited to serve as the permanent cantor of the synagogue. However, for a large part of the population (especially the ultra-orthodox sector) Shifman appeared too much the 'free-thinker' and they did not agree under any circumstances to his candidacy.

Some argued that the old cantor, though not a great one, was at least orthodox, and there was no reason at all to replace him with Shifman, whose 'fear of heaven' was regarded with skepticism. A sharp dispute raged for some time on this issue.

The city was in turmoil and the community almost split into two factions, the supporters of the old cantor, and the supporters of the new one. In the end the supporters of Shifman came out victorious. And indeed he was a great artist in his field. What he lacked in 'fear of heaven', he made up with a voice that was full of power and feeling.

He was a very young man when he died, perhaps at age 35, and I have no doubt at all that he was destined to have a place among the great cantors in the world. After the Soviets entered the city, Shifman served as a teacher of song, and choir leader, at the school that he organized. In this area too he was very successful.

The attitude of the town's people towards Shifman was demonstrated by one small incident. During the 'High Holidays' of 1941 Shifman was not considered 'kosher' enough to conduct the holiday services (as the community's representative before the Almighty), because during the Russian occupation he had worked on the Sabbath, and had walked about without covering his head.

He had also publicly desecrated the Sabbath. Despite this a large part of the townspeople did not want to cancel his services. It was suggested that he lead the services at one of the small synagogues on the outskirts of town, and Shifman accepted.

He used to delight us with his singing when we were in the camp. He did not sing only cantorial pieces but also various operatic arias. Even though I did not understand any of it at the time, I enjoyed his singing very much. At the camp there was also a dramatic reader from Chortkov, and she too did her share to maintain the cultural evenings.

i.

On the eve of June 23, one of the most horrendous days that I shall never forget, hundreds of S.S. soldiers and Ukrainian militia surrounded the camp. Machine guns had been set up on several of the houses in the area, and on the roof of the distillery (gozhelnia in Polish).

It all happened so suddenly, and by surprise, that there was no time for anyone to flee. Every attempt to escape meant certain death. The peasants of the area participated to the best of their ability in this 'aktsia.' Despite this a few people - including my father, mother and I - succeeded in making their way out of the camp.

We jumped into the standing corn that surrounded the camp. By crawling we reached the pit, which was about 30 meters from the camp fence, and which served as a storehouse for potatoes in winter. Breathing heavily, and white as plaster, we entered the pit and our first thought was: We have been saved! However, we were saved for only two hours.

Bands of the Ukrainian militia 'combed' the whole area and spread out in the fields to check if indeed anyone had escaped. Ten Ukrainian policemen made their way into the pit and removed all the people. Somehow I found myself inside a pile of straw, in the pit, that my mother had covered well so that my hiding place was concealed. It is impossible to describe these terrible moments, moments of parting from those who were most dear to me!

That same day they also brought to Svidova people from the Mukhavka and Morluvka camps, and from other estates in the area. All the Jews were concentrated in the camp's square and from here they were transferred in small groups to the field, where they were taken to be killed.

In the evening peasants were brought in and were ordered to dig two pits, in which the slain were buried. Next to a half-destroyed, unmarked, graveside wall over 550 Jews from Buczacz, Tlusta, Chortkov and other small towns were buried.

I am almost the only one who escaped this murderous action, which was the most savage even by the standards of those cannibals. After two days I met a girl named Rosa, from Tlusta. Rosa was very beautiful, about 20.

She had been hit by two bullets, had fallen unconscious, and had been thrown into the large mass grave. After being buried for several hours she woke up. Feeling that she was still alive, she managed, after many attempts, to raise herself up from the grave.

These incidents, of the 'rising from the dead', were not uncommon in the history of Polish Jewry, which suffered such oppression during the years of the Nazi conquest. Rosa found shelter with one of the peasants, who was stunned by her story. After she recovered we wandered about together for some time, seeking shelter.

After a few weeks she joined another work camp in the area. Other Jews were working there too, but I decided that it was better for me to wander among the villages and work for the farmers.

When I returned to Svidova after the 'aktsia' the manager of the estate, Musial, was shocked to see me. He had been ready to bet anything, as he said, that not a single Jew had survived in the camp.

He stared at me for some minutes, and it seems some humane spark awoke in him. He said to me: 'Since you succeeded in saving yourself from the 'aktsia' in Svidova, it appears that it has been ordained for you to live, and so I will try to help you.'

The farmers in the area also found it difficult to comprehend how I had managed to save myself, and various rumors spread among them with regard to this matter. The blacksmith, the source of all the gossip in this village, and the local 'politician,' used to relate that he had seen me escaping.

He claimed that he saw them shooting after me, and that I had dropped down, and crawled to the fish pond. From there I was supposed to have swum to the other side until I had disappeared from view.

Others told of different heroic deeds that I performed. As for me, I confirmed all these rumors about me. I added still more stories, because I understood that these legends were bound to serve as a lifeline for me. Legends spread especially about Rosa.

I worked on the estate for a short time. I learned to do different kinds of work on the job and in the garden, but mostly I served as a cow herder. Together with the other gentile peasant youths I would go out before dawn to the pasture, and spend most of the daylight hours there.

I managed to win the friendship of the youths, with whom I went out to pasture, and each one of them saw it as his duty to bring me food. In time they worked out a schedule among themselves, taking turns. Each day somebody else would bring me food and drink.

I used to tell them stories and participated in their games. Even in the clothing I wore I was like one of them. I spoke a good Ukrainian but the 'r' used to 'betray' me, and by my accent it was at once evident that I was a Jew.

Say 'kukurudza' (corn) they used to mock me. And I used to answer jokingly, that it was preferable for me to say ten times 'pashonka' than once 'kukurudza' (both of these words have almost the same meaning). Nights I slept in the barn or the cowshed.

j.

To this day I am amazed about the peasants of Svidova. They were evil anti-Semites, who had rushed, even before the Nazis arrived, to murder the Jewish families that had lived among them for generations.

These were evil people, who volunteered to set up guards around the camp, from among their population, so that no one would escape.

These were the people who participated in the destruction of the Jews of Tlusta and the surrounding area. What did these same people see in me that they showed me a more or less humane treatment?

Not only that, but this attitude toward me was expressed already during the period after the region had been proclaimed 'Judenrein.' It had been announced that every peasant who helped catch a Jew, was promised a reward: A specific sum of money, a pair of shoes and a bottle of whiskey. Whoever knows the peasants of that area, knows what the power of bribery, in the form of a bottle of whiskey and a pair of shoes, meant to them.

One day Musial returned from Yagelnitse. He called me over, and said that at the German police station he was asked if the rumors were true that a young Jew, who had escaped the 'aktsia' in Svidova, was wandering about on his estate.

M. indicated that he had heard about it, but did not know the exact place where that individual was to be found. As a result of this inquiry at the police station, he ordered me to disappear immediately, and not to show myself again in Svidova.

A period of wandering began for me, from village to village, and from estate to estate: Mukhavka, Morluvka, Koroluvka, Ruzhanuvka, Lissovtse, Lashkovitz and others. In the daytime I worked for the farmers, mainly threshing and taking the cows to pasture. And at night I slept in the open field, or in the woods.

The farmers were afraid to have me sleep in their homes, because a death sentence awaited them for hiding a Jew. At times, during the cold nights, I used to sneak into a farmer's barn or an attic, and I slept there.

Mostly these experiences did not end well, as the dogs (every farmer's house had a dog) would give me away. Because of the danger of staying in one place too long, I used to go from village to village, then go again to the first farmer and repeat the cycle.

My good memory was very helpful to me. I remembered hundreds of the farmers by name. I knew their, their wives', and their children's names. More than once I used to come to a farmer in a village and I would tell him that I worked for his brother in the other village and that he had sent me to him.

The harvest days were coming to an end. Fall was approaching and the situation became more and more difficult. What would happen in the winter? There were rumors among the farmers that the German front had been broken and that the Soviets were advancing rapidly, but who knew if they would succeed in arriving before winter?

During those days they brought the remaining Jews from Chortkov. Most of them were skilled workers, who performed specific jobs for the German army, and because of this they survived. I returned again to Svidova. Close to 100 people were housed in the camp and the living conditions were, relatively speaking, not the worst.

I was sent to work in the distillery. As I mentioned above, the Svidova peasants had a special relationship with me, and this relationship found expression during my work at this factory: I used to help the person who kindled the fire in the furnace by supplying him with coal from the warehouse.

The work was not easy, but I did it gladly. I was a strong fellow. The hard work and sleeping in the fields had strengthened me. I became accustomed to dragging the wheelbarrows with coal from sunrise to sundown. I slept in the factory, and obviously, I had to help the workers who used to come at night to steal whiskey.

They used to insert a tube into the whiskey barrel, draining it, and in this way filling up several bottles. There was almost no worker who did not participate in these nocturnal visits. The manager, a 'Folksdeutsch' named Kotz, knew what was happening, but he turned a blind eye to it.

A large part of the workers grew to like me, and they promised that they would not allow anything bad to happen to me. They arranged a small hiding place in the basement, among gigantic barrels. When the Germans were visiting the factory I was to disappear into my hiding place.

They also brought me food, and at times they even invited me to their homes for dinner on Sunday. Most of them were used to drinking like fish. More than once they used to tease me: 'They say, that Jews are not able to drink, show us if this is true or not.' And I, in order not to shame 'the tribe' attempted not to 'fall behind' them in this area too.

If my lungs were not scorched, and the act of drinking did not harm my health, it is mainly because of the good food that the farmers used to bring me every day that I survived. However, I was never drunk. I felt that even among these 'gentiles', who seemingly took an interest in my well being, I needed to be on constant alert, and a state of drunkenness was bound to lead me to disaster.

My diligent work, the stories that I used to tell them (sometimes completely fabricated) about my experiences in other villages, and my ability to 'drink' like they did endeared me to them, and on Christmas Eve I received an abundance of invitations for the festive evening meal.

I chose to dine at the table of a good hearted old woman, whose concern for me was genuine. I felt that I could rely on her.

We had barely sat down at the table when suddenly her son, who served as a sergeant in the Ukrainian militia, arrived for the festive meal. When he found out who I was he was shocked, and made a scene before his mother: How did she dare invite me, knowing what punishment awaited her.

The old woman began to plead with him that he should let me live, because my life experiences were proof that it was God's will that I should live, and whoever would kill me would be eternally cursed.

Apparently, in order not to spoil the holiday festivity the policeman left me alone, with the understanding that I was to disappear immediately from the village.

The conditions in the camp became more severe with time. It was a hard winter, the work was backbreaking, and the food was inadequate. But a congenial atmosphere existed among the people. Our common fate brought everyone closer, and the people saw themselves as one family.

I was very happy to be among Jews again, brothers, in misfortune and in fate, and at every opportunity I used to come to the camp. There were evenings when people were sitting and singing. The wife of a dentist from Chortkov, Unger, was especially gifted in singing Yiddish songs. So also was Klara Bar from Buczacz (the daughter of Mendel Bar).

How much love and longing one could feel in their singing. How much yearning for that which was and no longer existed, for a world that was destroyed, for life that was fading. I was especially fond of the song, 'Tanchum'(Consolation). The evenings of song were a source of intense emotional experiences and comfort for us.

Not much time passed before there was another 'aktsia,' in which most of the people in the camp were murdered. The few who remained moved to other camps that were still scattered in the region, or they found shelter among the farmers of the region, understandably - in return for huge sums of money.

k.

Meantime the front was moving closer. The German retreat had begun. The attitude of the farmers toward me had changed. I learned that they were plotting to kill me, because I knew too much about their participation in the murder of the Jews.

I knew who stood at the head of the pogrom that they held against the Jews of the village even before the Germans arrived. I knew which one of them had organized the brutal civilian guard around the camp. And I could point out from whom was stolen this piece of furniture, and who was robbed of that piece of clothing.

The peasants were very frightened of the Russian arrival. They were certain that the Russians would take revenge on them for the Jewish blood that had been spilled. Among themselves they even talked about who would be hanged, who would be exiled to Siberia, and who would be imprisoned.

I was not in that region after the war and I do not know which ones were punished. But if we are to judge by what happened in other places, then not a single 'gentile' was punished for murdering Jews, because there were too many of them to be punished. Or there was no punishment because the Russians did not care much about this matter.

I heard that several of the mob leaders in that village were hung, but not because of murdering Jews - this, apparently, was not a sufficient crime - but because of their association with the 'banderovtsy', and because they had murdered Russian soldiers, who had come to collect the produce quota owed by each village.

It was a hard winter night, one of those Ukrainian January nights. Outside a storm was raging. A boy my age knocked on the factory door. He told me that in the evening he had heard a conversation between his father and several other farmers that the time had come to do away with me, because if I were not disposed of I was bound to bring misfortune on the village after the Russians return.

Two days earlier another Jew, by the name of Schmeltzer, was confronted by the stoker, Semeniuk, who murdered him in cold blood, and burned his body in the giant furnace of the factory. It was clear to me that I had to flee. But where to go?

On the road between Svidova and Mukhavka there was a small forest and within it several huts. At one time the laborers of the estate used to live there, but as their lives 'improved' a little (mainly because of the plunder of the Jews), they built themselves houses in the village itself.

The huts then began to serve mainly as a midday resting place for the peasants who worked in the area. For me these huts served as a sleeping place for a period of several weeks.

Every time I came to this place, I used to meet Jews who also came to sleep here. In connection with these huts, one day something happened to me there that I find difficult to explain to this day. I was once returning before evening from my work in the field, where I had been working near a threshing machine.

Close to the huts I was overcome by a strange weakness. My head was dizzy and my feet refused to carry me. With my last strength I made my way to one of the huts. I went up to the attic and lay down on a pile of straw. A deep sleep came over me, and in my sleep I could hear my own moaning.

After some time I woke up. It was a nice morning, I felt healthy and refreshed and my heart was joyful for some special reason. When I reached the village I realized that I had slept for over 50 hours. To this day I do not know what illness hit me at that time, and in what miraculous way I was able to overcome it.

When the camp in Svidova was liquidated for the last time, several Jews arranged a hiding place in one of the huts. Often during the night I used to come into this hiding place, bringing food for the people and telling them what was happening on the outside.

That night, when I decided to flee from the factory, I made my way to that hiding place, and I stayed there over a week. Our main goal was a race with time. Time was working in our favor. We knew that every additional day that we held out, brought us closer to the day of liberation. But in those days, in particular, the situation became unbearable.

We learned that the Christians suspected that Jews were hiding in one of the huts, and it became dangerous to remain there. I was assigned the task of going out at night to search for another hiding place, and perhaps to even contact some farmer, who might keep us until the danger would pass.

When I returned after two days I found the hiding place broken into, and from the peasants I learned that the night before several members of the S.S. units, and Ukrainian policemen, had surrounded the huts and succeeded in finding the hiding place. Not a single one of the 18 people, who were in the hiding place, was able to escape.

Again I found myself wandering in the villages, from one estate to another. And those were winter days. The peasants became more and more brutal, because they were all afraid of witnesses to the atrocities they had committed. They decided to do away with the few Jews who were still roaming the area.

In a few estates: Litovtse, Mohilovtse and Shipovtse there were still camps with dozens of Jews. The conditions were dreadful and the people were living daily with the danger of dying.

The retreat of the German troops was in full force, and with them in retreat were convoys of the most prominent collaborators in Russia. They were known by the name of 'Vlasovtsy' (as is well known Vlasov was the Russian 'Quisling').

Together with their wives and children, their cattle and sheep, they traveled in the tens of thousands in wagons behind the Third Reich troops. It is impossible to describe the savagery and blood thirstiness of these people.

When a Jew fell into their hands - and that happened to dozens in that region - they used to murder him in the most savage manner, by hanging, stoning or beheading with an ax. These sadistic murderers poured out all their wrath, for being evicted from their land and homes, on the heads of their unfortunate victims.

For some time I stayed at the Soshinovtse camp. The manager of the estate was a 'Folksdeutsch' (as is well known, after the 'Reichsdeutschen' the 'Folksdeutschen' had the most rights) and he decided, apparently, to try to save us and promised us his protection.

We were 14 people on the estate, mostly 14-17 years old. A house was put at our disposal, food was provided for us and the manager even ordered that we not be made to work too hard. However, because of an unforeseen event, we were forced to flee from this estate too.

Armed and organized gangs of Ukrainians were roaming in the area. They were part of the 'banderovtsy' whose slogan was an independent Ukraine, free of Jews, Germans and Soviets. They were in the habit of visiting estates at night in order to plunder them, and during those times they also were not above murdering Jews, when the opportunity presented itself.

One night such a band came to Soshinovtse. They stole pigs and horses, and after they finished their work they turned to the other side of the cow-shed where most of us were hiding that night, as an extra precaution.

Meantime the manager of the estate was able to notify the German police by telephone about the robbery, and within a few minutes a German unit appeared. An exchange of bullets began, great panic broke out, and in this way we escaped from the farm in the dark of the night.

We headed in the direction of a nearby estate, Mohilovtse, in whose labor camp there also remained dozens of Jews. But the fate of the Jews in this camp was not different from the fate of the Jews in the other camps.

The Jews knew the threat to their lives from the farmers of the area, and so they used to spend the nights in the barns or cow-sheds on the farm. On that fateful night, March 2 or 3, an attack came from dozens of Ukrainian policemen and dozens of people from the village.

Only one Jew, named Winkler, from Chortkov, and his sick son, were sleeping in the house, between the two floors, which had been serving as a dwelling place for the camp inmates. The rest of the people had looked for a more secure hiding place, without knowing that the villagers had been following them around during the previous two weeks, and that all their hiding places were known to them.

As for me, I used to sleep each night in the large residence, but, apparently thanks to the special instinct that I developed in those years, the instinct of a hunted animal, I went out close to midnight into the barn and 'buried' myself in a huge pile of straw. Actually the attack was carried out before dawn. This time 25 young people lost their lives, among them Klara Bar from Buczacz, who was like a sister to me. These savages took her and her boyfriend out into the wood and brutalized their bodies.

One day followed another and 'salvation' was not any closer. The Russian advance was stopped for some time near Zhitomir and it seemed that all hope was lost. I was holding on with my last strength: against the cold, hunger, wanderings, fear. But help came actually from an unexpected source.

Within the framework of the Hungarian army, that was retreating with the Reich forces, there were squadrons of Jewish sappers. These were army units for all intents and purposes, under Hungarian command. However, the Jews were forbidden to bear arms and their duty consisted entirely of digging ditches and carrying out menial jobs for the Hungarian and German troops.

Because of a temporary break in their retreat one Jewish division of diggers set up its camp in the area near the village of Lisovtse. For about two weeks I stayed with that camp, and ate and slept together with the soldiers of the squadron.

Yitzchak Shikhor (Schwartz)

[Page 258]

Second Witness
Translated by Israel Pickholtz

The following is the testimony of Mr. Shemuel Rosental

In place of an introduction: "... that the civilian Rosental Shemuel ben Moshe – during the year that the Polish Army entered the Volyn District, actively participated in the elimination of groups of Germans in the forests of Volyn, as a partisan with Kolfek's partisan troops..."

Thus Lt. Polakovnik signed the certificate and sealed it with the stamp of the Grochalski unit. And there is a second certificate – from the Jewish community of Vorotzlav: "that at the end of 1945, the civilian Shemuel Rosental of Buczacz, gave eight Torah scrolls, one silver menorah from the synagogue, two silver Torah crowns. All of these items belonged to the Jewish community of Buczacz and were transferred to the Jewish community of Vorotzlav."

And in place of a third document, this same Shemuel ben Moshe Rosental, his hands trembling, brought out a book, placed it gingerly on the table and said: "This book is four hundred years old. The Jews of Buczacz guarded it as the apple of their eye. This book was their pride and glory. The fate of this book was part and parcel of their own fate. During times of troubles (and these were frequent), the book was removed from its place of honor in the synagogue and hidden like a great treasure and only when the danger passed, it resumed it's place of honor. Honored guests, Polish Jews, men of religion and secular scholars studied it with great interest. The book was shown in exhibitions and it outlasted its admirers."

The pages had yellowed. It had been published in 1523. It was a Hebrew grammar book with Latin translation. Scholars would be able to judge its scientific and historic value and to study it because it was valued by a simple man, an artisan, Shemuel ben Moshe Rosental, spared no effort to save it from destruction and guarded it lovingly as though it were holy. This Shemuel ben Moshe Rosental, a sixty year old carpenter, his voice breaking, his pain barely concealed, spoke to us – without playing the hero – as an eyewitness to destruction of the great and ancient Jewish center of Buczacz.

During the rule of the Ukrainian Fascists

There were 15,000 Jews in Buczacz, including refugees, in June 1941, when Hitler's murderous gangs fell upon the Soviet Union. The only ones to flee were those who had held political or public positions under Soviet rule. Much of the youth had been drafted into the Red Army. The unwillingness of the general population to flee was due in part to the Jewish refugees from Germany and Austria who calmed the local Jews into believing that there was no danger to their lives, despite the suffering and discrimination. They were blinded by their own unrequited love for "western culture."

The interim period

After the Soviet rulers left the city and before the establishment of Hitler's "New Order" – lasted fourteen days and they were days of anarchy. There was only the bloody rule of the Ukrainian nationalist gangs, for whom "national liberation" meant the freedom to kill and rob anyone who was not Ukrainian. The head of the "militia" was Nikolai Kiziuk. The first victims of the militia were the Jews of the neighboring villages and towns: Jaslowits, Potok-Zloty, Zbinograd, Terevohovits, Ptelikovits, Pidlasia and others. What the militia didn't take, they burned. The riots soon came to Buczacz as well. First they gathered 85 laborers who worked in cooperatives known as artels, and shot them outside the city on a slope known as the fedur, after accusing them of being Bolsheviks. Afterwards they began looting the warehouses and the shops and then the houses. Desperate cries for help were heard for nights on end from all corners of the city. On the fifth day, the Ukrainians set up the "soyuz" and commanded the Jews to give them all their goods immediately. Since there was no chance that this demand would produce results, the militia with the help of some farmers carried out searches among the Jews, ostensibly looking for weapons. While they were searching, they confiscated everything of value, suggesting to the Jews that they bring their valuables to the soyuz themselves, where they would receive "receipts" for them.

In order to ensure the proper mood, they murdered the whole family of Solomon Binder, six in all, because they did not follows orders quickly enough. The Ukrainians did not stop with just this looting. A few days later, they set up a "treasury office, headed by the "executor," formerly the rinibitch. He began his "public duties" my setting a mandatory contribution of two million rubles by the Jews. A "kehilla" was set up to "represent" the Jews before the robbers: Mendel Reich, a valuta merchant, was chairman and members were Baruch Kramer, Samuel Harzas, Dr. Hecht, Dr. Stern, Dr. Zeifer. The kehilla collected the contribution and sent two hundred workers each day to clean streets, clear rubble, empty sewers. The only wages for this work were, of course, beatings.

"The New Order"

The new German reign brought an end to the arbitrary mayhem of the Ukrainian bullies and began to execute their murderous plans with German orderliness. The kehilla became the "Jewish Council" (Judenrat). They organized the "ordenonges-dinest" (internal police) and the "arbets-emt" (labor office).

At first, people thought they would be able to manage, for the robbery nearly ceased. The Jews, who had no rights, were not able to earn anything, but at least they were able to live what was left of their lives. The Hell began just before Rosh HaShanah 1941. The Ortescommandant (local commander) ordered the Judenrat to prepare a list of all Jews from age 14 to age 50. The Gestapo arrived regularly, surrounded the Jews that gathered and began to "sort" them. They freed the artisans and the workers after some torment, and more than 350 merchants and "intelligentsia" were jailed. The next day, they were sent to the slope of the fedur and shot. That was the beginning. After several days, the decree was issued – the Judenrat was required to supply 200 young workers and 100 elderly workers each day. Shortly thereafter, the Germans chose 55 elderly workers and shot them under (*maybe "below" [translator]*) the tunnel. Afterwards came the "furs actzia" followed by the contribution of gold. At the beginning of the winter, the Jewish police were ordered by the Judenrat to snatch people. Five hundred Jews were sent to the "Vorky-Vialki" work camp. Of course, the first to go were the poor, who could not buy freedom. Shortly before Passover, 150 artisans were put on railroad cars and were never seen again. Despair paralyzed the Jews. They were surrounded by wild animals, who even though unarmed and illegal, were able to torment and kill. Jews were not permitted to walk on the sidewalks and were required to bow before whomever they met. They were permitted to shop during only two hours each morning, or more precisely, they were permitted to barter, for that is all they had.

Memorial Days – The days of terrible and humiliating death.

Thousands fell in muted shock, not fully knowing the cruel, blood-thirsty acts that took place, such as is unknown even among wild beasts. The few survivors did not even know the memorial days for their families – was it 17 October, 27 November, 2 February, 13 April or 26 June? These were the days of "actzia" in Buczacz. On the seventeenth of October 1942, the Gestapo (with the help of the Jewish militia) descended upon the houses of the Jews and brought more than 1500 Jews to the "May Third Plaza." From there they were put on railroad cars and sent to Belzec. After this actzia, four hundred bodies were found in the houses and they were buried in a mass grave in the Jewish cemetery. In Yaakov Margaliot's yard, they found eighty-five babies whose skulls has been crushed. Every day, the Hitlerite beasts stole babies from their mothers, crushed their skulls and threw them onto piles. They were brought to a mass grave in the Jewish cemetery in four wagons. At the same time, other Jews were forced to gather the belongings of the murdered and deported Jews, and bring them to the Germans' warehouses. The second "shipment" went to Belzec on the twenty-seventh of November 1942. There were 2500 deportees and another 2500 bodies in the streets – those who tried to escape or who preferred death to deportation. Of the bodies in the streets, forty-five were children.

The actzia that began on the second of February lasted two days. Three thousand six hundred Jews were dragged from their houses and hiding places and were brought to a slope near the forest, where a pit sixteen meters long and four meters deep had been prepared. The victims were forced to strip naked and stand on a flat board above the pit. The were shot in the back of the head and fell into the pit – in most cases while still alive. This mass grave was not far from the city reservoir. Within a few days, the drinking water of Buczacz became red with the blood of the Jews and the Germans were forced to choose another place for their mass murders. Five hundred bodies, eighty-five of them children, were collected from the streets after this actzia. If it is possible to use terms like "better" and "worse," the situation for the Jews became worse after this third actzia and the Germans' main concern was that no Jew should escape their clutches.

The walls of the city began to show slogans against the Jews and announcing that the death penalty would apply to anyone who hid Jews. Bounties were to be paid to those who turned in Jews who were in hiding. Jews were forbidden from being in the streets before 7:30 AM and those who violated this edict were jailed. After accumulating a group of these "criminals," they were taken from the jail to the cemetery and murdered.

Ukrainian students enthusiastically hunted Jewish children and turned them over to the Gestapo for execution. On all the roads leading to Buczacz, the Ukrainian militia and their Jewish collaborators ambushed and killed Jews who escaped from action in their own villages and had tried to reach Buczacz.

Like Moths to a flame...

The Jews were in a state of bloody siege, pursued, surrounded by professional murderers and the crude and blood-thirsty Ukrainian mob who were always ready to kill and rob the weak and defenseless. Desperation does not always produce the best ideas and decisions. At the suggestion of the chairman of the Chortkov community, Dr. Avner, the Jews of Buczacz began to petition the German rukers to set up a work camp for them in Buczacz. The hoped that being involved in "productive" work would save them from the akziot. The Gestapo agreed to their request and gave them a permit.

The camp was set up on Podhajcke Street at the edge of Buczacz. It was located in several apartment blocks and surrounded by a three meter high barbed wire fence. The work camp accepted only those who could pay a 1000 coin entrance fee plus ten coins a day for food, which consisted of hot water and ten dikos of bread in the morning and thin potato soup in the evening. The camp commander was the cursed S.Sh. and his second in command, L.K. – and special Jewish police were chosen for the camp. Altogether 1200 Jews registered for the camp and they were required to bring all their belongings with them.

Several days after the camp opened, the Gestapo took all the children in the camp under age ten. There were thirty-eight children and they were shot, after being declared "unfit for camp life."

Every morning at sunup, there was a roll call and afterwards each work group was sent to work at whatever the Germans and Ukrainians required. They worked all day, but there was neither food nor pay. Occasionally the commander of all the work camps in the district would appear. This was Etmaniuk (Moina) from the Gestapo. He gathered all the inmates, chose the best looking young women and had them sent to his headquarters where he conducted orgies. He demanded wine, tea, salami, etc. on the spot. The German gendarmes and even the Ukrainian militiamen began making the same demands.

At about the same time, the remaining Jews were put in a ghetto. The ghetto was in a long, narrow street and the impression was that the Germans did not intend it for long term use as it was neither fenced nor guarded.

On April 13th at two in the morning, Meir Budzenover drove his wagon to the home of the writer Hirsch Yonah Kwallenberg. Shemuel Rosental and Gedalya Duchovani loaded forty-five Torah scrolls and eight sacks of prayer shawls and tefillin. This strange procession moved through Stephen Batouri Street, Targovitza Street, Gimnazialna Street, the bridge over the Stripa and Kushchelna Street to the Greek-Catholic monastery of the Basilian monks. Without concern for the possible death awaiting them, for any guard could have killed them on sight, Hirsch Yonah Kwallenberg, Meir Buzdenover, Shemuel Rosental and Gedalya Duchovani had decided to save these symbols – symbols which commanded more respect than their own lives. No sooner were the monastery gates open – shots were heard from the city. The frightened monks accepted the wagon load and told the Jews to flee for their lives. The four Jews lay for two days in a family burial plot and when they came out, they learned that the Gestapo had used those same days for the fourth actzia and murdered four thousand Jews near the cemetery. And another six hundred bodies lay in the streets.

The camp remained untouched. The Jews who remained in the city concluded that only the camp could keep them alive and they flocked to register. But a few days later, the Gestapo suddenly surrounded the camp and, from the "tower" (Baszty), the 1800 Jews who remained in the camp.

At about this time, as the inevitable end approached, the writer Kwallenberg and this witness, Shemuel (Samuel) Rosental, gathered the twenty Torah scrolls that they had hidden and gave them to the priests at the Roman Catholic church for hiding. After a few days the end came for the camp. The only ones left alive were the members of the Judenrat ("Jewish Council") and of the "Ordenongesdinest" (police), a few tens of laborers ("roishtaf") and those few who succeeded in evading death at the last minute.

The last act of the tragedy (but not the epilogue) was a few weeks later. In the meantime, people arrived in Buczacz from hiding places – from neighboring villages and even from cities which had been declared clear of Jews – mere shadows of people. But the Germans had no mercy for them and they were ordered to open the camp anew and to remain in its confines. But they were there only ten days. Afterwards they were taken by wagon to Gavitov. There, on the estate, they were all murdered and their bodies thrown into a large concrete pit full of garbage. The farmers who saw the slaughter said afterwards that during the execution, the renowned Buczacz cantor Shelomo Schiffman sang songs of mourning and was the last to be killed.

At this point, Shemuel Rosental suddenly became silent, turned his head in a rapid, nervous movement, wiped tears from his eyes and continued in a soft voice: A few days before the first liquidation of the work camp, Emaniuk took me to Chortkov as a carpenter. In Chortkov, there were Jews only in the camp, five hundred of them. These were the formerly wealthy and the intelligentsia, who had managed to hide part of their possessions. Life in this camp was different from most other camps. Most ransomed their lives and did no work and no one prevented them from purchasing even expensive items. I saw well dressed men, and women who did their nails.

Three weeks after I arrived in this camp, it was liquidated. Only eight people remained alive. Our job was to collect, clean and store the clothes and shoes that we took from the victims. The second night I fled. I reached the work camp at Jagolnici. There were six hundred Jews there. They all wore the letter "W" and they all worked growing the caochuk-cokskiz plant. They had to pay fifteen coins a day to support themselves.

There was one occasion when all the Germans suddenly fled. The farmers told us that the Soviets were nearby. We cried from happiness like little children. We hugged one another and began planning how to return to our former homes. The farmers began looting the homes of the Germans, the factories and the estate. Can you imagine our disappointment when the Germans returned a few hours later and everything returned to the way it had been.

After a time, this camp too was liquidated. A large pit for storage of potatoes became a mass grave for six hundred victims. I survived as did the painter Tchaban and his family, because we were working in the palace. They put up with us awhile longer, but when the ground began to tremble beneath us we took the advice of the old grounds keeper, Michel Kuziuk, and dug a hiding place under the greenhouse. We stayed there two and a half months and the grounds keeper protected and fed us. On the twenty-second of March 1944, Buma Schwarcz of Chortkov, who also survived miraculously, appeared at our hiding place and told us that Soviet tanks were in Jagolnici. I rushed to Buczacz and found another six hundred people who had survived, all malnourished and exhausted, dreaming only of rest. At the front it suddenly got worse.

Buczacz was one of the only places in Podolia that the Germans succeeded in recapturing. The weather was bad and the snow deep. Only a few were able to escape. Most hid but the Poles gave them away to the Germans. The Germans gathered most of them and brought them to Monastzhiska where they murdered them all at the cemetery.

I reached Skalat, but on the way I lost my daughter and my wife, who had lost her mind. I left my son with some good people and I joined the partisan forces that worked behind enemy lines. We spied and found the weakest and most critical points in the enemy forces and so we were with the first of the Red Army to reach Lwow.

After this, together with W.P. (the Polish Army) we cleared the Volin forests of German army units. We took no prisoners. "And in August 1944, when I returned to Buczacz for the second time, I found a few Jews, both from nearby and from distant places. We did our duty to the thousands of martyrs who did not live to see the victory over Hitlerism and brought them to rest in sixteen mass graves. We cleaned up the study hall of R' Abish. We took the valuable book that I mentioned earlier from the ground of the old study hall and the other holy articles that had been brought there by Fischer, Shimon Hecht, Moshe Yitzhak Stampler and others of blessed memory. I returned the Torah scrolls which we had hidden – some I took to Chernovits and gave to the synagogue there and others I brought to Broclaw." The city of Buczcaz was destroyed in rivers of blood and torture. The survivors cannot take comfort in the punishment of the perpetrators.

In the summer of 1946, a heavily guarded group of about twenty criminals were brought thorough Broclaw towards Pomorska street. Suddenly a hoarse cry was heard from across the sidewalk and into the marching group charged an old man who pointed at one of the criminals and yelled "That is him, that murderer killed tens of thousands of people." Shemuel Rosental had recognized the executioner Emaniuk.

Haporochnik (*maybe THE Porochnik? [translator]*), the commander of the guard, heard the excited Rosental, made a significant sign with his hand and added smiling: This one is in any case finished. He doesn't need anything more...

Shmuel ben Moshe Rosental

[Page 264]

Third Witness
Translated by Alejandro Landman and Norbert Porile

The following is the testimony of Elyash Khalfan

Events of the Past

I write these words while I am in a refugee camp in Germany, where I arrived with the hope of leaving the Galut and begin a new life in my fatherland (Israel). Only now am I in a position to take stock of these past days, which reach back to my early childhood.

It is the terrible days of my youth that are most clear in my mind. It is four years since the day that started the tragedy of the Jews of Buchach, some 8,000 souls at that time. That is the time when the German murderers began their threats to annihilate the defenseless Jews. The initial attack took place on August 23, 1941. The Gestapo ordered the " registration" (so they called it) of all men between 18 and 50 years old. Over 1,000 men of various ages gathered on the square next to the Judenrat[1] to wait for the orders of one Koznowski, the commander of the Ukrainian militia.

The word of the Ukrainian-German command came at 19:30. The Jews on the square were ordered to arrange themselves in columns in order to march to an unknown destination under the guard of the Ukrainian police assassins. They were marched to the prison yard and there they were pushed together by blows from truncheons and rifle butts. The Gestapo chief, the tyrannical Atmaniuk, began the registration by choosing those men who met his criterion of "being able to work" and ordering them to one side. People did not know which side was good and which was bad.

Finally, nearly half the persons present were chosen, leaving some 625 men who were among the most outstanding in the community: university teachers, people with higher education, physicians, among whom were some women, young men, etc. They were left under the guard of the Ukrainian killers, who took advantage of the opportunity to rob them of all their valuables. Their families waited for their return all night. Only at 4 in the morning did they learn the terrible truth, which shook the entire town: the 625 men were taken from the prison yard to the Fedor Sosenki forest[2]. Pits had already been dug there by those of our Christian neighbors who lived nearby. All one could do was to listen to the shots and cries of the dying.

Hysteria broke out in the town. People wailed in the cemetery for entire days and walked around as if in a trance. The situation was exacerbated by troublemakers who claimed to have seen survivors of the massacre with the sole goal of extracting something of value from the families, such as cash or clothing. Meanwhile, new restrictions and demands were imposed on the Jews of Buchach. They were forbidden to use the main streets in the town and were restricted to the left side of the secondary streets. All Jews were forced to wear a 10 cm wide white armband inscribed with the *Mogen David* in blue.

Things were calm as winter approached. The only harmful activity going on was the forcible assignment of the able bodied to work camps, the men to Braki Wielkie and to Kamienik, and the women to Yagolnitza. However, word came from nearby towns of the "Aktions"[3] carried out by the Gestapo. People began to prepare hiding places a few weeks before the first Buchach *pogrom* or *aktion*: the 28th of Tishri, 5702 (corresponds to October 19, 1941, NP).

The word spread that the Gestapo would arrive on the following day. All began to gather food in order to stock their hiding places. The Gestapo arrived at dawn, armed to the teeth as if they were afraid of the defenseless Jews. All one could hear were the shouts and curses of the Gestapo, who found it difficult to enter the locked houses. With the help of the Ukrainians the Gestapo spent all day searching for the hiding places of the Jews. The searched houses remained open during this time and our Christian neighbors took advantage by stealing all that they could. The Nazis rounded up some 1500 persons and gathered them first in a square and then marched them to the railroad station where a train was already waiting. Only a few were able to save themselves by jumping from the train as it was speeding towards the Belzec concentration camp.

The following day we realized that the *Aktion* was over. Slowly, everyone began to emerge from their hideouts onto the streets, which only a day or two earlier had been full of children playing, and of Jewish men and women. It seemed strange to us that yesterday we were being rounded up and killed and today we were being left alone. People were busy trying to find out which of their relatives had managed to save themselves from the roundup. The Jewish police had to remove the bodies of murdered Jews from the Jewish hospital and take them to the cemetery. The sick were the first to perish at the hands of the "Deutsche Volk" (local population of Germanic origin. They had special privileges and were German collaborators).

In those days an *Aktion* took place in the nearby village of Monstryska. Some 1200 Jews were taken. Women and children were sent to Belzec and men to the camp in Janovska. Afterwards a decree was issued instructing all the Jews in the villages neighboring Buchach, including members of the Judenrat, to move within 7 days to Buchach, where a Ghetto was to be set up. The affected villages were Monstryska, Potok-Zloty, Uscie Zielone, Koroptza, Barish, and Yazlowitz[4]. The decree took effect and people from the six villages were squeezed into the Ghetto. Living conditions were terrible as only those with enough money to bribe the Judenrat people could get acceptable accommodations. The rest were squeezed into the synagogues, where they were hungry and miserable.

A typhoid epidemic broke out around that time. Dozens died each day. One night a rumor spread that arrests would be made the following day. Everyone went to his hiding place and spent the night there. The next day it was learned that the Ukrainian militia had detained 80 persons and sent them to Chortkov, where the Gestapo barracks was located. Everyone staid indoors during the next few days in fear of the Ukrainian killers, but food supplies quickly ran out. Persons who had the distinctive "W" (for Wehrmacht, i.e. they worked for the German army) and "Rashtaf" (?) card were free to move about without being bothered and they supplied the Jewish homes with food.

On the evening of November 24, 1942, a rumor made the rounds that an *Aktion* was about to begin. Most everyone went to his hideout while some fled to nearby villages. Everyone worried about his own safety, without regard for that of others. The sick were left without help and the first shots heard the following morning signaled their death. The *Aktion* lasted all day. Some 1200 persons were arrested, mostly the poor people whose lot it had been to dwell in synagogues or house ruins upon coming to the Ghetto. None were able to escape from the train wagons carrying them to Belzec as they were searched while still in the station and any object of potential use in an escape was confiscated.

Life in the Ghetto went on undisturbedly, but not for long. There were rumors that there would be no more *Aktions*, that the Gestapo had promised so. News of the victories of the Red Army reached us and everyone was impatiently awaiting liberation. No one had a radio but everyone was saying "Sie Zain Guit" (it will be OK), although without knowing exactly why. However the Gestapo was aware that the respite they were granting to the Jews would lull them into a false sense of security.

The third *Aktion* took place on February 2, 1943. Some 1400 persons were rounded up and taken to the Fedor forest, where pits had already been dug by the "Boi Dinst", a band of Ukrainian murderers who engaged in finding Jewish hiding places and in killing the occupants, whose chief was Bolek Flaks. Two children were able to escape from the covered pits. One of them was Leizer Bider Maizlovich, who lives in Natania, Israel, and continuously relives in his dreams the cruelty of the Germans and Ukrainians.

Neither the remaining survivors nor the dead were left alone after the third *Aktion*. The pits had been dug very close to the source of drinking water for the town and there was concern that the blood of the exterminated Jews would contaminate the water. The corpses of the victims were therefore moved elsewhere, a task carried out by groups of arrested Jewish men and women. New pits had to be dug and the bodies were moved, at times in pieces, under the supervision of the Boidinst bandits, who took advantage of the situation by removing from the corpses whatever items of value remained, including gold teeth.

The restrictions and new demands continued. Miraculously saved refugees arrived from neighboring villages, bringing with them new techniques in the construction of hideouts. People worked intensely on this task in their homes and one could hear the sounds of tools at work during the night, indicating that this work was in high gear. No one believed in anything any more, just the certainty that the final pogrom would come one of these days. This had happened in nearby villages, where liquidating *Aktions* had taken place and these villages had been declared to be "Judenfrei".

So it was that on April 1, 1943, a large group of Gestapo and "Zonderdinst" (selected troops) led by the torturers Ruksa and Atmaniuk left Chortkov by train towards Buchach. Their sealed instructions, which were to be opened on reaching the station before Buchach, stated that part of the group was to detrain prior to reaching Buchach and the others were to get off at Buchach. The latter had orders to prevent the access of any Aryans to the Jewish quarter and thereby alert the people of the coming pogrom. The Jewish homes on the outskirts were taken by surprise in this unexpected attack. When the first shots were heard everyone jumped out of bed and rushed to their hiding places, but many did not have enough time to reach them. The first group of killers left and the second group arrived in order to search for the hideouts. The search went on all day. They rounded up 1500 persons, who were taken to the prison and then, the next morning, were ordered to march in files to the killing site in Fedor where the communal pits had already been dug.

Christian youths kept up their search for Jewish hideouts and those who were found became the next victims. The machine gun fire that one could hear was the sign to those who were still alive that the *Aktion* was still in progress. The new group of murderers who came to the killing site tried to take all the valuables that the victims might have on them. The victims were ordered to take off all their clothes and those who refused were tortured. The naked were forced to lie down in the pits, where they were shot from above and thereby either killed or wounded. A new layer of naked Jews was forced to lie down on top of the first layer, like sardines in a tin, and the killing continued.

The *Aktion* was nearly over, only 400 women remaining, whom the Gestapo chief wanted to send to the work camp in Yagolnitza. However, the commander of the Ukrainian militia objected and promised the Gestapo chief that he would round up another group of women. Thus, at the last moment, they were all taken to the killing site. One of the women, Mrs. Gros, made a brief statement in front of the pit: "We are innocent and are being murdered, but you will not be able to kill everyone. We will be avenged as you will not win the war." With these words the first of the women perished and the rest followed.

At the end of this "successful" *Aktion* the Ukrainian killers gave a going away party for the Gestapo, who left the town at dawn totally drunk. The Jewish survivors slowly left their hiding places knowing that the *Aktion* was over. Everyone was spiritually broken as there wasn't a family that hadn't lost at least one member. A profligate life style developed as every one lost all hope knowing that only the "Fedor" lay in the future. People sold or exchanged their belongings for next to nothing, stopped believing in anything, did not worry about anything, and just tried to make the most of each moment.

The Nazis gave a brief respite to the Jews but on May 15, 1943, they informed them via the Judenrat that the entire remaining Jewish population was to move to the work camps located in towns some 40 to 48 km from Buchach: Lomza, Kopechince, and Tlusti. People became desperate because they knew that, while they had hideouts where they might survive in their own town, they were certain of death in the first *Aktion* in a strange town. People went out of their minds and offered large amounts of money to local peasants to hide them. Many were able to avoid a move this way. Those without means had to trust their luck and moved to two of the above towns. Their fears were well founded as they were unable to even settle into their new surroundings. The liquidating *Aktion* was in progress when they arrived and they were immediately taken from peasants' cars in which they were being moved in order to be executed. The peasants returned to Buchach in a contented state, in possession of the belongings of the Jews. The Jews who were following this first group saw the empty cars full of belongings returning and immediately understood what was happening. They either escaped into the forest or returned to Buchach. The Gestapo then decided to open a work camp in Buchach. However, it was not open to all Jews, only to those who paid substantial amounts to the Judenrat.

In the middle of June, 1943,[5] the Gestapo decided to complete the liquidation of the Buchach Jews, including those in the work camp. They went to execute this task but this time they met armed resistance. The Jewish police (Ordnungdinst), who were also due to be killed, obtained some primitive weapons and began to resist the Nazis. The strongest resistance was mounted in the suburbs, at the home of

Gerber, where several Nazi bandits were either killed or wounded. However the Nazis brought in reinforcements and attacked the house from all sides, gassing and burning the people hiding inside. From then on the Germans entered Jewish homes with caution, often first sending in their Ukrainian lackeys, who were also scared of the Jewish resistance. The confusion caused by this resistance enabled many of the survivors to hide in the forest or in the homes of those farmers who were willing to hide them.

The *Aktion* continued in the town. People who were detained, including those in the work camp, were taken to a field next to the Jewish cemetery where they were killed in front of the non-Jewish population. When the killing was over, Buchach was declared to be "Judenfrei". The Germans then put a price on the head of any remaining Jews. This action led to the discovery of many additional hideouts. The people so captured were first jailed and then exterminated.

A certain Yacob Margalit was in one of the groups taken to the killing site. He displayed a stubborn and defiant attitude until the last moment, refusing to obey the Nazi orders and to undress. He was stoned to death. His son later went and blessed the place where he died.

As was always the case after executions of this type bands of " our Christian neighbors" came by to search for anything of value. One time a group of them heard voices coming from the already covered pits. A child was asking his mother "Mother, am I still alive?" The mother answered " Sleep child, sleep" and the child responded" It is so hard". The peasants ran to the police to tell them that some of the victims were still alive. The police came to the site, uncovered the pits and killed anyone who was still alive.

Terrible things were happening in the town and its surroundings during these days. The peasants who were hiding Jews started to kill them for their belongings, or threw them out naked into the fields, or denounced them, or kicked them out during daylight hours, all of which meant certain death.

Armed Jewish groups that had been formed after the liquidation of the Ghetto reacted to these deeds. Their first action was against a Polish woman who had turned a Jewish woman and her son over to the Germans. These Jewish boys, who were already known as "Jewish partisans", decided to avenge them and thereby frighten the peasants. They promptly arrived one night at the house of the Polish woman. A group of them entered the house and another group grabbed her husband. The Polish woman woke up and started to scream, thereby attracting many of her neighbors to her front yard. The Polish woman was punished for her crime in front of all of them. The partisans advised the shocked neighbors that the same fate awaited them and then returned to the forest. The news that a group of Jewish partisans had avenged the death of one of their women and had promised to take further revenge against future deeds spread quickly among the peasants. As they also had exaggerated the Jewish response, the result was a decrease in acts against hidden Jews.

At this time there were still numerous hideouts in town, some in the ruins of Jewish houses and others in Christian homes. Many killers were bent on discovering these hideouts. One who was effective at this task was a certain Nahiobski, who along with his band spent the day roaming through town. Whenever he came across a suspicious site he informed the police, who accompanied him to the site of the hideout. The Jewish partisans then confronted Nahiobski and his group and shot them dead.

The place of Nahiobski was taken by one Kowalski and his group, who showed a special flair in finding Jewish hiding places. The partisans resolved to put an end to his activities and arrived one night at his home. They only found his father, who began to scream in order to save himself but was wounded and died the following day in the hospital. That same day, at 2 pm, while his funeral procession was passing through the streets, a young Jewish partisan armed with a gun left one of the houses and made his way through the crowd, approaching the coffin behind which the bandits were walking. He fired three shots but did not hit the mark, only wounding several persons. The young Kowalski hid under the coffin and then ran to the police, who arrived on the scene after everything was over and all that remained on the street was the coffin and some flags. The police were very alarmed by what had transpired. This event brought some respite to the Jews who remained in their hideouts.

Jews who were hidden by local farmers had to pay a lot of money for shelter. The frivolous peasants then traveled to town and spent with abandon. The peasants were very envious of each other, which aided the work of Ukrainian killers, who started to follow the spendthrift farmers to their homes, checked them out, and if they found any Jews hidden in basements or attics, killed them on the spot. So began again a wave of denunciations on the part of the peasants, who started killing or evicting their Jewish refugees. There were rumors that the Ukrainian bandits were killing both the Jews and the peasants who hid them, and then burning their houses. The peasants believed these rumors and attempted to extricate themselves from this situation, thereby facilitating the efforts of the bandits.

The Jewish partisans could do nothing to alleviate this situation. They too were having problems as other clandestine groups, such as the Ukrainian group "Bandera's band"[6] and the Polish group A. K.[7], appeared in the forests. Along with the German-Ukrainian police, these groups tried their best to annihilate the Jewish partisans. However, despite their scarce means and primitive arms, the partisans continued their attacks. Particularly noteworthy was their reckless attempt against the " Landkomissar" of the town.

Word of the Russian victories and of their fast drive towards Buchach began to arrive. The peasants realized that the Soviets were about to arrive and, in fear of revenge, started to leave the Jews alone. One began to hear the sounds of artillery and there was much traffic on the roads indicating that liberation was near. Large numbers of German troops, with their tanks and trucks full of looted articles, passed through in retreat. They were accompanied by hordes of Ukrainian militia, who were guilty of many killings, and who mixed in with the many refugees who arrived from the more Eastern regions. The peasants, seeing that the Russians were near, began to loot German property. They removed their spoils in their cars in plain daylight, without any fear.

When the Germans had nearly completed their evacuation of Buchach, they mined the various bridges before leaving. However, the Russians arrived before the Germans could blow them up. The Russians conquered the town without encountering any resistance on March 23, 1944[8]. The surviving Jews began to leave their hideouts and return to town. More than 1000 survivors arrived in the course of the week. Everyone attempted to settle down without concerning themselves with the danger which awaited them.

Like a bolt from heaven, word came that the Germans had broken the encirclement near Tarnopol and Kamieniec Podolski and were moving with all their forces towards Buchach in order to join the rest of their army, which had stayed in Podhajce. The Jews waited desperately with their belongings all day in order to decide what course of action to follow in order to avoid falling into the Nazi claws again. All their choices seemed poor. The Soviet commander of the town asked them not to exaggerate the situation as " only a small group of Germans had been able to escape the entrapment" and "their advance would only last a few hours". These announcements were transmitted to all the Jews in town, who decided to stay in town near the Soviet garrison, which was in the town center. The Jews hoped that, in the event of a German success, they could escape along with the Soviet army. However, the Germans arrived unexpectedly from the side of the train station and captured the Soviet garrison, where everyone was asleep. The Jews, who had no time to escape, were also captured[9].

As long as I am alive I will never forget April 4, 1944. All day long word came of detentions and of the arrival of new groups of Jews. All were gathered in the jail from where some 700 persons were sent to Monterzyska and there killed. Arrest continued and each moment there were new victims. The advance of "a few hours" turned into weeks. The town was abandoned by its inhabitants (there were no more Jews except for a few who stayed hidden)[10].

The Germans began to fortify the town and prepare for the fight that lay ahead. The town was deadly quiet. At night all that one could hear were shots from all sorts of weapons, showing that the front was near. At times one could see the shadow of some Jew who had left his hideout in search of food in the ruble of destroyed houses. One could also see patrols of German killers going by. There was happiness in the Jewish hideouts only when one could hear the attacks on the German army by Russian planes. This reminded everyone that freedom was near.

The day of liberation came on July 21, 1944. Once again the survivors emerged. There were only some 30 souls, weak in body but strong in spirit. Additional Jews, who had managed to escape from elsewhere along the front, arrived. Slowly, they settled down and began to look alive once again. One of the synagogues opened and it was the site of daily prayers. We showed everyone that we were united in our religion, that we would stay united, and that we would never give it up. All in town could hear the voices of the survivors: "Shma Israel adonai eloheinu adonai ehad". We recited prayers to the memory of our murdered brethren and built them "Matzeibot". No one wanted to continue to live in a town where such unspeakable horrors had taken place. Thus everyone resolved by himself to leave Buchach and with it the *Galut*, and return to the true fatherland.

Elias Halfan
D. P. Camp, October 31, 1947

Translator notes (AL)

1. Judenrat – local Jewish council selected by the Germans. At the beginning it was made up of decent people but with the passage of time it became dominated by Nazi collaborators and delinquents. (With a few exceptions this happened in nearly all towns.)
2. Fedor – Relatively low mountain range on which Buchach is built. The forests that extend south

to the river Diester begin here and are the site where Jews hid. Towards the north, in the direction of Tarnopol, there are no woods to hide in. The Fedor and the river Strypa, which runs along its base, are the defining features of Buchach. The slopes of the Fedor are built up and the houses have the characteristic mountain town features: one story on the side facing the mountain and two or three stories on the side facing the river. "Fedor Sosenki" means Fedor of pine trees, indicating that there was an evergreen forest on the Fedor.

3. Aktion – "Aktzia" in Polish. German for action, task. This is the series of acts in which the massive killing of Jews (pogrom) was carried out during the Nazi occupation.

4. The unpronounceable names of these villages have the following meanings in Polish: Potok Zloty = Golden Brook, Uscie Zelone = Green Exit, Braki Wielkie = Large Faults, Kamienik = Little Stone.

5. I don't believe that this date is correct as I am sure that the Ghetto still existed on June 13, 1943, and that there was no Aktion on that day (I was in Buchach). The events described here probably occurred at the end of June.

6. Stefan Bandera – Ukrainian general in the Soviet army who switched to the German side along with his entire army. His troops fought against the Russians on the front and were very active in the murder of Jews in the Ukraine and in Russia. Bandera and his men went underground prior to the German downfall. Well armed by the Germans, he continued his fight against the Russians and his killing of Jews and Poles for several years after the Allied victory. I could ascertain during my 1999 trip to the Ukraine that today Bandera is considered a national hero. All the towns have streets and squares named after him and there are many monuments dedicated to him. He is almost at the same level as two other Ukrainian heroes with Jewish blood on their hands: Bohdan Chmielnicki and Petlura.

7. A. K. – Armia Krajowa = National Army. An underground Polish army that reported to the Polish government in exile in London. While they did not openly collaborate with the Germans in the killing of Jews, the ingrained Polish anti-Semitism prevented them from ever helping Jews about to be murdered, as was apparent during the uprising in the Warsaw Ghetto. The A.K. remained underground after the Communist takeover in Poland and was guilty of murdering numerous Jews, accusing them of being Communists.

8. I don't believe that this date is correct either. I am personally sure that the first Russian patrol, consisting of an irregular group not in uniform arrived in the Buchach suburbs on the 21st of March around noon.

9. I personally feel that this was the most terrible of all the tragedies suffered by the Buchach Jews, not for the number of victims, but because they had "survived" all the prior killings. As I was there at that moment I can state with certainty that a large part of the responsibility for this tragedy rests on the shoulders of the Russian authorities, who either did not know of the danger faced by the Jews or did not wish to protect them, even though they were now Russian citizens. I can add the following personal anecdote: On the ominous night of April 2, 1944, I was ten years old and was hidden in the home of a Ukrainian by the name of Synenko, who was a friend of my grandfather, Shaul Anderman.

The Russian communications group was using this house for their operations and the soldiers allowed me to stay with them. They were communicating by radio and while most everything was encrypted I could tell from their comments and bearing that things were not going well. Well along into the evening the communications were suddenly interrupted and the receiver carried the following encrypted message repeatedly: "Tarif, Tarif, Yaglat". Although I only recently learned its meaning I remember the message clearly. The soldiers began to dismantle their equipment and carry it to their jeeps. I went up to the officer in charge and asked him to take me along. He told me to rest easy and go to sleep, that they were only changing location, and that I could get a ride in the morning from any one of the many trucks that were passing through. The following morning when I woke up the German tanks were going by on the road.

10. On April 16, 1944, the Germans evacuated the entire population of Buchach in the direction of Tarnopol. The town remained deserted.

[Page 272]

Fourth Witness
Translated by Alejandro Landman and Norbert Porile

Approximately 10,000 Jews, 5,000 Ukrainians, and 2000 Poles lived in Buchach prior to the War. The Jewish and non-Jewish populations had good, and even friendly, relations before the War (at least in comparison to other places in eastern Galicia). However, after the Russians abandoned Buchach, the deserters of the Soviet army as well as the local rabble began to ransack Jewish stores. Meanwhile, Jewish inhabitants had a premonition of the danger that faced them and locked themselves in their homes.

The Germans marched into Buchach on July 4, 1941, following numerous rounds of machine gun fire. The first killer in green uniform appeared at 4 am, hid in the ruins of a destroyed house, and waited for the rest of his company while keeping watch. His company followed and then the rest of the army arrived. While Jewish houses were kept under observation, no atrocious acts occurred initially. However, immediately after the German entry, the non-Jewish inhabitants of the town took off their masks and turned into monsters. Ukrainians detained Jews on the streets and dragged them off to perform forced labor, cleaning sewers, fixing roads, etc.

On the 6th of July my youngest son, age 6, disappeared. We were desperate and searched for him everywhere. We found out after a lengthy search that a Ukrainian youth, wearing the characteristic Ukrainian cap, had taken him in the direction of Guzenka. I went there and saw my son in the distance. While crying he told me that a Ukrainian from Guzenka had kidnapped him and forced him to package used nails that he had stolen in order to sell them.

The Ukrainians completely changed their relationship with the Jews and started to abuse them at every opportunity. If they happened to spot a prosperous Jewish home they broke into it at night and stole its contents. Often, the residents were taken to the Fedor and killed. Many Jews were murdered in this manner, under the eyes of the complicities Ukrainian leadership and "intelligentsia". Among others, those killed included the tailor Kruh, Israel Landman, the wife of Dr. Foks, and the shopkeeper Polak. The Ukrainians engaged in the same form of killing in nearby villages: in Pabshovka, Zaleshchiki, Midvadbach, Plalikobich, etc. They razed Jewish homes in plain daylight, robbed and murdered, all under the uncaring view of the Germans.

After several weeks, a provisional municipal government called "Ortskommandantur" was formed. The Ukrainians stopped their killing but began to hunt down Jews who were not wearing armbands displaying the Star of David. When they found such a person they dragged him to the police, harassing him on the way. The Ukrainians, acting on their own and independently of the German authorities, organized their own police under the temporary command of Taras Hatkovich of Naguzniki. Later, one Koznowski from Gaiow, who encouraged the seizure and abuse of Jews and was involved in a number of killings, took command of the Ukrainian police.

At first, the Ukrainian command issued a series of orders designed to limit the freedom of Jews and assigned them to forced labor on their own initiative. Later, these orders had to meet with German approval. They let us know that by order of the Ukrainian police all men between the ages of 18 and 50 years had to present themselves on August 10, 1941, at 5 am at the square called "Pig's Square" to go to work. This order caused panic in the Jewish population since everyone knew that this was not a real call to work but represented a grave danger. However, in order to avoid reprisals against the rest of the Jewish community, the affected men agreed to present themselves. I remember that I woke up at 4 in the morning of the above day. Looking out the window I could see small groups of Jews who were meeting at the side of the Beit Hamidrash. I could see that some put on a brave appearance while other looked sad. Some were accompanied by their wives and children but all were afraid and insecure. I was living on St. Nicholas Street, next to the Beit Hamidrash, and I could hear the noise coming from the street. After saying goodbye to my family I went out to the Square at 5 am, together with my brother Bernard. We were met on the Square by some Jewish university students, who told us that we shouldn't let insults provoke us. The head of the Jewish community at that time was Mendel Raij, a man of rectitude who gave strength to the Jews facing the Germans. The German commandant and the Ukrainian mayor were there along with some 100 Ukrainian police, who began to insult the assembled Jews, singing obscene songs. The German commandant appointed Raij as chief of the "Judenrat" (Jewish Council) and demanded a substantial contribution of money and valuables from the Jewish community. The Jews were divided into groups and assigned work while the professionals and merchants were allowed to leave. I too was allowed to leave thanks to Abin Bubik, the Ukrainian mayor. Most of the Jews were pressed into forced labor but were allowed to return home at night.

At this time the Judenrat of Buchach was fully established. As stated above, its president was Mendel Raij. The other members were Dr. Shtern, Dr Isidor Neuman Honik, David Kanar, Baruch Kramer, Yacov Ebenstein, and Dr. Zaifer. I want to emphasize that, in contrast to other towns, the Buchach Judenrat members were honest and cared about their fellow Jews. Dr. Zaifer was the only one of them to survive the War.

Groups of Jews were sent out to do forced labor for a period of time. At the same time, there were labor roundups on the streets. Then came the terrible day of August 25, 1941. All men between 18 and 50 years were ordered to congregate next to the Kehila at 5 pm. Some 800 Jews gathered. They were divided into groups and taken by the Ukrainian police to jail, where they were held till dawn. At that time they were taken to the Fedor where they were all shot to death around 9 am. People could not believe what had just happened. There were various rumors – some of the missing had been seen in Chortkov, people had received letters from others, etc. So it went until it became known that the Germans had killed the Jews in what came to be called "Aktzias" – the Germans called them "Judenaktion – Judenaussiedlung" (Jewish campaign – Jewish evacuation). That day we lost the best people in town: doctors, lawyers, merchants, young men, etc. We subsequently received word from Stanislow that on the day of Hosana Raba (October 12, 1941, AL) the Germans had killed tens of thousands of Jews.

One day in August a group of Hungarian Jews, guarded by Ukrainians, passed through Buchach on a forced march. Jews were forbidden to stay on the street while these poor souls walked by. Many ignored this restriction and they were grabbed by the Ukrainian police and forced to join the march. Among them was one of my sons. I took off my Mogen David bracelet and ran after the marchers in order to rescue him. A Ukrainian acquaintance denounced me to a German policeman but when I explained the situation he let me follow. I reached the group and found my son near the rear, where he was helping to carry a child. I joined the group and then tried as best I could to leave with my son. I knew that they were marching us to our death. We reached the train station and they left us standing next to some shacks. The Ukrainian police took advantage of this wait by taking the best-dressed persons into a shack and robbing them. This also happened to me and they took everything I had in my pockets. I had almost lost all hope when I spotted a Ukrainian client of mine passing by on horseback. He was from Kiziuk and worked for the chief of the Buchach police. I asked for his help and he ordered the police to let us go. I took advantage of this opportunity and succeeded in freeing some other Buchach Jews: Knabler and his son Izi, Moshe Rozen, Altshuler, Aronkrantz, the son in law of Hakan, and others. I also managed to secure the release of two young Hungarians, whom we took into town with us. On the way back a Ukrainian policeman who accompanied us ordered us to sing. We had no choice and Moshe Rozen, who was the only one who knew the song, sang. Several days later we learned that all the Hungarian Jews had been killed near Monterzyska.

The Jewish population was forced to turn over to the Gestapo assorted contributions on an ongoing basis. In November 1941 several new German administrative structures were formed: the German police, a "Landkommissar", and a "Landrat" (district commissioner). The police chief was a certain Maister, an older man who was not totally anti-Semitic. With this appointment the situation improved somewhat. The Ukrainian bands stopped their killing. The Germans ordered the formation of a work detail for men between 16 and 50 years of age. They were sent to Borki Wielkie, near Tarnopol. The men had to present themselves to the Judenrat with three days worth of clothing and food. Disobedience was punished. Many Jews could not stay alive under the conditions prevailing at Borki despite the fact that they were not particularly mistreated by the Germans.

Mayor Abin Bubik, a very diplomatic middle-aged man, maintained good relations with the Jews, had a friendly attitude and always defended them, and opposed the establishment of a Ghetto. He received Jews in his office and helped them often. He personally saved those that he could from the Aktzias and never failed to greet a Jew on the street. I emphasize all this because such behavior was highly unusual. Bubik was the son of a poor shoemaker but reached the top position in the town and was able to alleviate somewhat the suffering of the Jews in these terrible times. Jews living in other towns of the region tried to move to Buchach to take advantage of these better conditions and the Jewish population increased considerably. The head of the Judenrat at this time was Baruch Kramer, who had ready access to the German authorities. Both Dr. Zaifer and he could solve whatever problems the Jews might have with the German authorities. Life was calm until the autumn of 1942. Jews who arrived from other places said that Buchach was heaven and thus the number of Jews in August 1942 increased to 15,000. Since Bubik had opposed it there was, strictly speaking, no Ghetto. The local authorities did not persecute the Jews and they could move quite freely in their zone. It was like being in one country within another, with the governing power residing in the Judenrat, supported by the "Ordnungsdienst" (security police).

And so came the terrible day. It happened on Rosh Hashanah of 1942. The Jews had a premonition that danger was near. There was talk of an Aktzia called "Judenaussiedlung" and people began to build hideouts in their basements, attics, and other possible locations. As always, the Jews gathered on Rosh Hashanah to pray. The first day I prayed at the home of Erlich and everyone was afraid for his life.

The Aktzia that all were waiting for, since it had already taken place in the nearby towns, came on November 31, 1942 (sic). It was a beautiful and sunny fall day. I was looking at the street through a crack in the curtains and all appeared normal. People were walking outside but I couldn't hear a single Jewish voice and I realized that the Jews had disappeared from the streets. The Aktzia began at 7 am and lasted until 7 pm. We could hear in our hideout the screams of Jewish victims who were being removed from their homes. The Gestapo also searched our house but didn't find our hideout. Next morning we heard Jewish voices and realized that the Aktzia was over. On this day 2000 Buchach Jews were taken to the gas chambers at Belzec. A few young people were able to jump from the wagons and return to their homes.

Following this event, the Christians completely changed their behavior towards us. They seemed to be telling us that the world was not for us to live in and that even though we had managed to save ourselves this time they would get us sooner or later. Around this time the Germans forced the Jews living on several streets in the suburbs to move into our zone and this led to considerable crowding.

The second Aktzia took place on December 1, 1942. Rumors of a new Aktzia were in the air on November 30 and many Jews took to their hiding places or hid in the forest. However, some were unprepared and were captured without opportunity to hide. The Aktzia began at 6 am, when the first shots could be heard. The Viennese professor, Dr. Klein, an outstanding individual who had lived among Germans all his life, was among those killed. He had arrived in Buchach together with his wife and they lived at the home of Sommerstein on Podhaitzka street. He refused to hide when the Aktzia began despite the entreaties of his landlord. When two Gestapo men arrived he asked them in and in a beautiful German explained that he was innocent and that he had dedicated his entire life to German science and teaching. He further told them that he was "Freidenkend und innerlich überzeugter Deutscher" (a free thinking German to the core). The Gestapo listened and then stated "Sie sind doch Jude" (yes, but you are Jew). The same fate befell Dr. Klein as the other Jews since he was guilty according to the German rules. He was taken from the house and killed.
Some 1800 Jews perished in this Aktzia, which lasted until 5 pm. After it was over the Jewish living

quarter was restricted to the following streets: Grundwalska, Buznica (the synagogue street), Kolejowa, Podhajska (left side only) and St. Nicolas. A few Jews were able to remain outside this Jewish zone by permission of the Landkommissar (none of them survived).

At this time the moral degradation of the Buchach Jews began. Even though the local authorities acted in acceptable fashion, the continuing visits by the Gestapo always led to victims and provoked mortal fear. One day in December 1942, Aba Shechter, an older Jew, and two youths were taken to the Judenrat by the Ordnungsdienst. They were ordered to line up and wait. Standing next to them was a well-known Buchach killer, the German policeman Paul. He took them to the rear entrance of Shimon Abenstein's house and there he killed them. The Ordnungsdienst immediately removed the bodies. I saw it all from my window.

Around this time a typhus epidemic broke out in the Jewish population and many died. The epidemic was caused mainly by overcrowding and malnourishment. A Ukrainian physician paid us a visit on behalf of the municipal authorities and concluded that the Jews had caused the epidemic and had to be eliminated.

Near the end of December 1942, there were street arrests. The Ukrainian police grabbed the Jews and took them to their station. Mrs. Schporn (born Hirshhorn) was killed that day as she tried to escape. Most of the prisoners were moved to Chortkow and were rescued only upon the payment of a large ransom. In January 1943 the Judenrat issued an order requiring all men between age 18 and 50 years to be taken to a work camp in Borki.

The third Aktzia, which lasted two days, took place in early February 1943. A very small number of Jews were left in Buchach when it was over. Many hideouts were discovered, a task in which Ukrainian criminals participated. At the end of the Aktzia the streets were full of corpses and blood. I will never forget these two days. My family and I, as well as Mrs. Godfrid, were in our attic hideout. My parents and a few neighbors were hiding in the basement. The Aktzia began at 6 am. I saw a Gestapo agent going into the Weiss home and kill a Jewish girl who was running to hide. We could hear from our hideout how they entered neighboring homes, discovered the hideouts, and removed the victims. Those who did not want to leave were killed on the spot. Jews were assembled throughout the day and then taken to the Fedor forest and killed. We heard the shots and knew that each one represented another victim. On this occasion the Jews were not transported to Belzec but killed right in Buchach's own Fedor. The following day cars full of corpses could be seen passing through town.

Following the Aktzia, the Judenrat gathered all the belongings that were left in the homes of murdered Jews and closed off the streets on which they had lived. Their houses were given in trust to the municipality and were then sold for next to nothing to Ukrainians.

Around this time a work camp was created under the command of Z. S. H., with L. K. acting as guard commander. They acted as if they owned the young Jewish survivors and ordered their detention. One day, my 16-year-old son was stopped and taken to this camp. I resolved to rescue him, went to see the camp commander, and asked him to let my son go, even if just for a brief time. He answered that all those in the camp had to stay there all the time and, furthermore, that I should be happy because they were safe there. In March all the members of the Judenrat along with their families were also moved to the camp. Anyone wishing to visit had to pay off the commander.

The situation of the Jewish population was getting worse. They were allowed to shop only in the market on the side streets and then only for two hours a day, from 10 to 12 in the morning. The Ukrainians harassed vendors who sold to Jews despite the fact that people already knew of Hitler's defeats. In the middle of March 1943 the Ordnungsdienst of Tarnopol came to Buchach to rob the surviving Jews. They went from house to house taking any decent furniture. At this time there were few Jews left, there wasn't a family that hadn't lost someone, and all knew that they had been condemned to death. The Jews began to sell all their possessions for half price. It was actually forbidden for Jews to sell anything since all their belongings had been declared property of the state.

A very disorganized Aktzia began at the end of March. Jews were killed all day long every day, whether on the street or in their homes. Janek Hirschhorn was killed at this time right next to our home. He was first gravely wounded and begged for his life because he had two sons. He showed his work papers but the German assassins gave him the coup de grace. The stones on which his body was left remained bloodstained for weeks.

At the beginning of April 1943, there was another Aktzia, in which several hundred Jews were killed. Several Jewish families were hiding in the home of a German in Naguzniki. Their presence was discovered and among those killed were Dr. Isidor Neuman, a Buchach lawyer, Sami Angelberg, and others. The surviving Jews drew hope from the news about Allied victories in North Africa and elsewhere. People speculated that there would be Allied advances from one side and Russian advances from the other and this gave them hope. The behavior of the non-Jewish population towards the Jews also varied with the news from the front.

Bloody Spring (April, 1943)

All the Jews who remained alive were searching for hiding places, as this was the only chance of saving themselves. Farmers charged 1000 DM per person per month to hide Jews in their attics. Jews with children were even worse off in finding shelter. Word spread about some farmers who hid Jews for a few weeks, then stole everything they had and turned them over to the Gestapo. Despite this knowledge everyone still tried to find hiding places. May 12, 1943 arrived. The Judenrat put up a notice on Boznica Street from the German commandant ordering the Jews to leave Buchach by the end of May and move Kopechynce or Tluste. The order was signed by Kramer. Panic broke out among the survivors and all tried to find hiding places in order to remain in town. Some left for Tluste as the people in this town were more trustworthy. Others went to Kopechynce and the rest remained in town, making a payment to stay in the Jewish zone, which now consisted of a single street, St Nicholas Street, near the Russian church. This took place in early June 1943.

About this time the members of the Judenrat, the Ordnungsdienst, and other people with connections were moved to a camp where Zalman Schterenberg was the commandant and Leon Kanar the chief of the guard. Right from its formation this "Jewish zone", where several hundred Jews still lived, was attacked at night and its inhabitants were killed on the spot or taken to the cemetery, where they were shot. Among those killed at this time were Yona Glazer and family, Mrs. Sztern and son, Fraibrun's brother-in-law (he of the shoe store, whose name I don't remember). I could hear how this man begged the Ukrainian killers to spare him and gave them money and valuables, but he was killed just the same.

Our house, which was on St Nicholas Street near the Jewish Hospital, was occupied by my parents and my sister and her children on the ground floor and by my family upstairs. The house was well protected, with bars on the windows. Yet nobody slept in their beds but, rather, on piles of straw scattered on the floor. I was the first to hear shots and shouting at 3 am one night. I alerted my family downstairs and even before going back upstairs I could hear the Ukrainian killers banging on the front door and shouting, "open up Jews". On that particular night an old tailor, an invalid, was staying with us. Our house had two hideouts, one in the attic and another in the cellar. The kitchen window faced the synagogue street and through it I could see armed Ukrainian guards stalking their Jewish victims. It was difficult for the impaired tailor to move rapidly. My family was already hiding in the attic and I was left alone with him. I grabbed him by the hands and, with almost superhuman strength, dragged him down to the basement where my parents were already hiding. We could hear the footsteps of the killers on the stairway but they did not discover our hideout.

This Aktzia lasted from dawn to 8 or 9 pm. At 8 it became quiet and one could no longer hear Jewish voices or screams. It was the silence before the next storm. Those who were still alive fled the town in order to hide. Many killed themselves. I remember that my sister Bronia told us on returning to our hideout (these days there were no longer Jews on the street) that the Erlich, Zajdman, Kohan, and Raij had committed suicide. A Jew who did not have a farmer to hide him was as good as dead.

On Sunday, June 13, 1943 my wife and I left Buchach. We successfully crossed the town and followed our farmer across the Fedor to his house. The farmer's name was Nicolai Zaharchiuk and he was Ukrainian. He and his Polish wife, Marina, lived in Choitova, near Buchach. We arrived at the farmer's home and went to his barn where our 12 and 18-year-old sons were waiting for us. They were very happy to see us as they had heard of the last Buchach Aktzia and had had no news from us.

In the Farmer's Attic

Our hideout was in the attic of the barn. The farmer had used boards to build a false wall in the attic, which was 2 meters in from the real wall. This 2 meter wide space provided room for 5 persons. A large amount of straw was placed in front of the false wall in order to make it less noticeable. This is where we lived during the last stage of the German occupation of Buchach, often in hunger and thirst.

The last Aktzia in Buchach took place on June 25, 1943. Many hideouts were discovered at this time and the Jewish quarter and its remaining inhabitants were liquidated. Among the hideouts discovered was the one of my parents. They took my 75-year-old father, my mother, my sister with her two children, and others who were hiding there. On this day they also killed the members of the Judenrat and Ordnungsdienst as well as others who thought that they would be spared.
News reached us daily about the discovery of hideouts in the vicinity of Buchach. Our farmer went

to Buchach two or three times a week and brought us newspapers and gossip. We were afraid that he would denounce us each time that he left. The search for these Jewish hideouts was carried out by a Ukrainian killer who was the son of Nahaiobski as well as by other bandits. They turned their victims over to the German police, who took them to the Jewish cemetery and killed them.

About this time a small group of surviving Jewish youngsters, between 17 and 22 years old, assembled in the woods surrounding Buchach. The group included the two Bravar brothers, List, Friedlander, Fritz, etc., a few dozen in all. One night this group burst into the home of the Ukrainian Nahaiobski and stabbed him to avenge the murder of Jews. The news of this event spread rapidly through town. The Ukrainians became so concerned that they suspended the search for Jewish hideouts in fear that the rumor that there were Jewish partisans in the Buchach woods might be true. It is worth noting that we felt safer in our barn attic hideout since that day as the farmers stopped denouncing Jews for fear of the partisans. Additional incidents in which Jewish partisans attacked Ukrainians who turned Jews over to the Germans also occurred. Thanks to the actions of these groups some 1,000 Jews were able to survive in Buchach until the first Russian takeover. We also had the help of a few Catholics who were different in this respect from the majority.

The Jews who survived the period between June 1943 and March 23, 1944 did so in underground or attic hideouts, or in the woods. They lived in indescribable conditions, always hungry and in fear of capture. We passed the time in our attic in darkness, lying down and talking about what was going on. We ate a late breakfast, essentially consisting of potatoes, in the afternoon or evening. Our farmer improved our treatment, as the situation on the battlefront got better. We received better food and once every four weeks he allowed us to go to his house to bathe, shave, and change our clothes. These were our happiest moments. We began to get milk when the Russians captured Kiev.

The day of liberation came on March 24, 1944. We really felt elated when a woman told our farmer that the Russians had conquered Buchach. My son began to cry at the news and lost his voice. He is still presently receiving medical treatment for this condition in Vienna. The Russians abandoned Buchach after 10 days and the Germans returned so after leaving our hideout we went to Chernovitz. Some 1000 Jews remained in Buchach after the Soviet army left. They went back to their hideouts expecting the Russians to return in a few days. However, the Russians delayed their return by 4 months and the front was located in the vicinity of the town. A short time after the Russian retreat all civilians were evacuated and the Jews were forced to leave their hideouts. I estimate that no more than 50 Jews finally survived. These survivors abandoned Buchach and traveled to the West. I have no idea how many Jews returned from Russia.

Israel Gelbert
May 15, 1946

Translator's note (NP):

The various dates cited by the authors in this section of the Yizkor book don't always agree with each other. I have consulted several additional sources, including the Encyclopedia Judaica, Buczacz Origins by M. Rudner, and I Am A Witness by M. Rosner. Most of the various sources agree on the following dates:

German entry into Buchach: July 4-5, 1941
"Registration" and execution at Fedor: August 27, 1941
First Aktion: October 17, 1942
Second Aktion: November 27, 1942
Third Aktion: February 1-2, 1943
Fourth Aktion: April 1943 (semi-continuous)
Liquidation of Ghetto: June 26, 1943
First Russian entry into Buchach: March 23, 1944
Second Russian entry into Buchach: July 21, 1944

[Page 284]

The Resistance Movement in Buczacz
Translated by Melanie Rosenberg

After thirty-three months of torture and cruelty unprecedented in human annals, the defeated German forces retreated. The day after the entry of the Soviet army (March 26, 1944), more than 800 Jews emerged from their hiding places. According to the information I managed to glean, this was the highest percentage of Jews who survived among all the cities and villages in eastern Galizia. There is no doubt that we must attribute this percentage of Jewish survival to the organization of activities by the resistance movement, whose core arose in Buchach. Their concepts were circulated by the group to surrounding villages, meriting understanding and support. The fear of collective responsibility being thrust upon the Jewish population as a whole, as well as the fact that they were unarmed and lacked proper instruction for the ranks of fighters, prevented the leaders of the resistance movement from taking vigorous steps at the start of the organization.

In our judgment, the slightest discovery of a desire for uprising and war could bring about the immediate destruction of all the Jews of Buchach. This fact must be recalled by all who wonder at the frequent ease with which thousands of Jews were brought to their deaths, with no resistance whatsoever.

The Germans entered Buchach on Shabbat (Saturday), July 5, 1941, and the very next day a large force of Ukrainian police rose up and began attacking the Jewish population. In the initial period, the fate of the Jews of Buchach was determined by Ukrainian policemen, backed by a Ukrainian committee of local intelligentsia. During this period we were witness to attacks on Jews exiled from sub-Carpathian Russia, and to massacres perpetrated by Ukrainian troops. The local Jews would receive their persecuted brothers with friendship, sharing with them their last crumbs of bread, and made efforts to redeem them monetarily from the hands of the murderers. Word reached of a pogrom in Tarnopol. Immediately following the army's entry there, more than 3000 Jews were slain. After the war, the army claimed that it had no knowledge whatsoever of what had transpired in the hinterland. In Buchach, each day Jews were conscripted for labor, where they were tortured most cruelly. (All of this was perpetrated by the Ukrainian police, who claimed to be taking revenge upon Jewish communists for their part in exiling Ukrainians to Siberia.)

During this initial period, a Jewish Committee (later to become "Judenrat") arose, taking upon itself to use monetary bribes to temper the insane, criminal acts of bloodthirsty Germans.

On one of these mornings, in the second half of July 1941, the Ukrainians compiled a list of Jews comprising more than 1500 people from the ages of 16-40. Thanks to the intervention of the Austrian commander of the forces passing through Buchach, the act, which was committed three weeks later, did not occur at this time.

In the middle of the month of August 1941, the Gestapo arrived for the first time. They compiled a list, and upon the advice of the Ukrainian Committee, selected 350 people from among the intelligentsia and the youth to execute by firing squad the following day on Fedor Hill. Two members of the Judenraat were murdered, Dr. Y. Stern Vakaner, as well as Dr. Judenfreund, who were summoned by the Gestapo. Only a youth by the name of Mendel survived. What pain and suffering plagued the hearts of the mothers and women who came daily to the Judenraat seeking help in searching for their relatives, under the illusion that their loved ones were still alive and had been sent to work on the Zabroch River. Meanwhile their bodies lay buried in a mass grave on Fedor Hill, a mere two kilometers distance from the city.

The same morning of that month of August began an odyssey of suffering and pain that ended in the obliteration of the Jews of our city, and of the devastation of those Jews who had been exiled here from neighboring villages. After the above list was compiled, a period of semi-stability reached the Jews. With it came the illusion that perhaps a German diplomatic breakthrough was in the offing for the Jews, fueling the hope that the German shield would soon be broken. The tasks of the Judenraat included supplying workers and assisting the Gestapo force, who came once a week from Chortkov to plunder Jewish wealth. The systematic destruction of the Jewish People began to be carried out. The Jews were illegally evicted, an order was issued requiring them to wear a special sign, they were denied the right of free travel and change of residence. In addition to the tax on gold and silver, furs and other household possessions, (confiscation of furniture, linens, and silverware), their food rations were reduced and a special Jewish ghetto was erected. Jews were permitted to live only on the left side of the city, the border being delineated by Railroad Street, continuing to the bridge on the road to Chortkov. The Jewish population, concentrated in this manner, thus became an easy target for the actions that followed.

Operations commenced for the second instrument of destruction, the camps: "Labor Camps" (Arbeitslager) "Jewish Camps" (Judenlager, Julag)

B.

In December 1941 the Judenraat received instructions to dispatch a group of laborers to Borki-Wilki near Ternopol. On a winter night, bitterly cold, the Jewish police (Ordnungs-Dienst) brought the Judenraat orders for mobilization within two hours. Each worker was instructed to take a backpack, blanket, change of clothing and underwear, and food for a one-week duration. Among the 200 workers, we, a group of 15 Jewish laborers who worked in the "Ligenschaft" (formerly the manor of Pototsky) also received the mobilization order. We assembled in one of the barns and took the decision not to report.

That same night the German police and the Ukrainian police carried out searches in our homes, from which our families had fled, with the intent to round us up by force. We hid in various hiding places throughout the manor. Each day the police would come to capture us, but our comrades stood guard and we took cover whenever the police appeared. This pursuit continued several weeks, until we were given assurances that we would not be transferred from this place. We were granted green permits and we, in essence, were protected. In spite of this, we did not sleep in our own homes for more than half a year, as it was clear to us that we would not be forgiven for our deed. We emerged victors from our first resistance experiment and this served as the beginning of our organization, to which we enrolled the majority of the youth over time.

From the "Julagim" in the area of Tornopol came word of acts of destruction being carried out there, and meanwhile the Jews of Buchach were found in the camps of Borki-Wilki and Kamjonka. SS forces, who stood at the head of the camps along with the Ukrainians, tortured the Jews concentrated there, with no consideration for human life. Hunger rations caused dissention among people, and the slightest offence was punished by hanging or shooting. We learned details of the situation at "Julagim" from one of our comrades, M. Weitz, who was captured and taken to this camp. Nevertheless, after one week in Komjunka, he succeeded in cutting the barbed wire that surrounded the camp and evaded heavy guard to make his way back to Buchach via fields and forests. The Judenraat organized assistance, sent weekly shipments of wagons filled with food and warm clothing, and using gifts and bribery, attempted to redeem people from the camps or at least ease their fate. Moshe Berger is to be especially commended for risking his life to travel there each week.

Jews began arriving from Stanislavov, Kalush, Talomach, Horodenka, Kolomia, and they sought refuge. From them we heard accounts of the annihilation of the Jews of Stanislavov. Gister Bildner of Talomach, who was spirited out of the Janovoska camp in Lvov as a corpse, told us heinous episodes of the acts of the Gestapo and their chief executioner, the head of the Jonovosta Camp, Wilhauz.

The relative calm which pervaded Buchach was halted by one of four Operations-Groups (einzachgroupen) made up of SS men, who carried out the "actzia" in October 1942 and afterwards an additional actzia in November of the same year. During these attacks, the SS men and the Ukrainian police encircled the Jewish Quarter, pulled the Jews out into the streets and rounded them up to the square near the former District Office, called Kargovitza. Here they concentrated more than one thousand persons, and later transported them, under heavy guard, to the railway station and sent them on freight cars bound for the Death Camp of Belzitch. The only ones to be spared were those who had managed to hide, as well as several hundred youth who had been sent some days previous to the village of Osovatza, in order to clean the area following a blaze which had broken out. After the first actzia, the director of the Judenraat, Dr. Englard, escaped with the help of temporary documents, as he couldn't bring himself to have a hand in the extermination of the Jews of Buchach.

The leaders of the resistance movement were determined to put an end to the obtuse indifference of the Jews who accepted their fate and waited with arms folded for their death or for a miracle to keep them alive. Among the leaders were: S. Margolit, Tzoler, S. Evenstein – from Buchach, Bildner and Fisher from Tolomach, S. Zilber from Horodenka, and the commander, the compiler of these memoirs, A. Bazan (Worman). We resolved to take action. We added more and more youth to our ranks, yet the nature of our work made us limit our forces and carry out underground activities in keeping with the conditions at hand. We established contacts and appointed Brish Englard, Dr. Julius Marengel, and Moshe Berger to serve as our liaisons to the Judenraat. The Judenraat committed itself to subsidize our arms purchases, since we determined that the time was not yet ripe to forcefully disarm the enemy's weapons, for fear that such actions would draw notice. Young people who had been trained in Zionist youth organizations, Gordonia and Brit Trumpeldor, joined our ranks. We also received members from among the "Ordnungs-Dienst" (Jewish Police) except for several who had cooperated with the executioners in a very effective manner. We made contact with the Jews of Tarnopol, Skalat, Borshchov, Zalschiki, Tolosta, Kopichinca, and Chortkov, in order to establish resistance centers in each and every place. The idea fell upon fertile ground. We received constant updates on what was occurring in the world at large. The engineer Tzizas from Tarnopol (who was expelled from Tarnopol back in the days of the Soviets because his father-in-law was a wealthy man) as well as Weisenger, listened each day to radio dispatches and their updates kept our hearts and spirits elevated. Dr. Y. Marengel brought us reports each night from the fronts, and from him we heard of the struggle with the enemy near the borders of Eretz Yisrael.

At the start of February 1943 we were informed of a new "akzia," this time "the typhoid akzia." There were apparently numerous people who'd taken ill, and they were to be shot to death without being removed from the area. More than 1000 people were executed at that time. The radio broadcast reported the defeat of Paulus near Stalingrad and the start of a major offensive upon German troops on the African front. We hastily requested additional weapons to bolster our supply of several pistols, short-barreled rifles and a limited number of bullets. We expected to be receiving explosives from our people working in the tunnels for this purpose, for use when needed. We received word of the existence of two small groups, in addition to our group which now numbered more than 150 men. These are the Weisinger and Friedlander groups. I conferred with them and suggested that they join our group, although Weisinger had different plans. He joined the Polish group of Nidjbeiski which operated in the forests of Posznik, yet afterwards he was forced to flee from them since they too murdered Jews. D. Friedlander and Donier were of the mind to go into hiding in bunkers in Buchach. The Jews of Buchach quickly began preparing bunkers, digging passages inside the earth, sealing walls, assembling secret entrances from the cellars to the shelters. The Jewish Quarter was extremely crowded, owing to the fact that within the quarter the area had been reduced and the Germans had herded not only the local Jewish population but also those from Monsciska, Koropitz, Yazlovsta, Potok, Zloti, and the villages in the area, in order to increase the ease of their extermination.

C.

We conferred about our tactics and our plan of operation. I made contact with the Polish Underground and acquired one of the first pistols to be purchased for an appropriate sum from the forest guard. I conversed with their messenger Mastinistlebob and received his assurance that he would supply us with weapons as well as relevant contacts, yet this promise was not kept. The head of the Soviet troops who remained in Buchach following the retreat of the Soviet army, conferred with us. He suggested breaking out through White Russia, an area which in his opinion had no enemy population and which, he felt, would soon find itself on the front lines. Taking into account the distance involved, over 600 kilometers, as well as our small numbers and the attitude of the populace along the route, we rejected this plan and opted to flee to the forest. We re-examined our stand during the "akzia." At the beginning we took a passive stance, for fear of setting off the entire extermination of the Jewish population of Buchach. Yet in March 1943 we adopted the decision that in the event of an akzia, we must assemble in the forest on Fedor Hill and aim to shoot the Germans. We were convinced that this would result in the cessation of the action and allow Jews to escape.

We began carrying out military maneuvers by night, and we learned the lay of the land. We slept permanently in the fields and the surrounding forests, believing in the false promises given the Judenraat by the local German authorities. Trusting the quiet pervading the entire Tarnopol range, we spent several nights in our apartment. On one of those mornings, in the month of April 1943, we were awakened by gunfire: the fourth akzia had begun. One by one we moved to the Aryan side, and before our people had managed to get to their designated posts to open fire, one of our members, young Anderman from Strivocovtza, was arrested by a Ukrainian policeman. Anderman pulled out his pistol and shot him to death. He himself then escaped. The entire action immediately was ended. The SS, the German police, and the Ukrainian police were concentrated near the local military police building and began loading their machine guns, believing that we were about to launch an attack. Our ammunition supply was far too low to dare to take such a step. The Ukrainians gave the policeman a "show" funeral, complete with impassioned speeches. The self-confidence of the cruel invaders and their wicked comrades had disappeared. Again, they did not set out on a forceful mission to uncover shelters, knowing well that they could pay for this with their lives.

We received accounts of the uprising in the Warsaw Ghetto, and this added to our courage: again, we were not alone in our actions. Among the Aryans, the word began to spread of the existence of our group as a strong military command. Brish Engelberg brought us word from the Ukrainian police commander that not only were they taken by surprise, they also expected offensive operations from our side.

The Judenraat had promised money to purchase additional weapons, and we had the opportunity to receive machine guns. We collected information and acquired maps of the area. On the assumption that it would be possible to escape to the forest, we decided to send individual groups to the forests in order to learn the terrain. The vast area of forest, encompassing thousands of hectares of trees, gave us the space to believe that our plans to remain alive in the forest might indeed succeed. We prepared plans to divide our people into small individual groups to bivouac over an area of several kilometers. This should enable us to easily pass from place to place in the event of possible danger to one of the groups.

Three groups set out, equipped with ten days' worth of food rations, weapons, and tools to create temporary hide-outs. Heading the first group was Artrachter, who knew the forests in the Poznik region. Heading the second group was my wife, who had acquaintances among the "Sobotniks" in the Vadova region, located on the way to Koropitz. The third group was headed by Nudelman from Potok-Zaloti, who knew the forests of Sokolov near Potok. After these three look-out units set out, we tensely awaited their return. They fulfilled their missions under extremely difficult conditions: heavy rains fell almost the entire time and turned the forests into rivers of mud. They returned fatigued and weary, hardly believing that it would be possible to remain alive in the forests.

We received word that the Germans had taken a decision to completely exterminate the Jewish community of Buchach. After several days an order was received that the majority of the local Jews were to be transferred to Chortkov, Talusta and Kupichinska. Approximately 20 families received permission to remain in the Jewish Quarter, which had been reduced to a mere few houses. In addition, a labor camp was set up for several hundred Jews. The first delegations set out and we received reports that along the way Ukrainian farmers ambushed the Jews, robbing them of the remains of their possessions. There were even cases of murder.

Among our people, opinions were divided. Some felt that the time had come to head for the forests. The second half thought that it necessary to join the refugees, noting that also the Jews from Stanislavov Range, who had sought refuge from us, succeeded in holding out for several months. Opposing opinions were held among the leadership and expressed at a general meeting which I convened. At this juncture in time, I could not imagine another conspiracy regarding the Jews. We reached the following compromise: Part of the group would go into the forests, as per the original plan. The remainder would be instructed to intensify the work of organizing the groups in Chortkov, Talusta and Kupichinska, and prepare the groundwork, together with the group from the Kupichinska forest, whose numbers were growing to our proportions. Srulik Zilber from Horodenka travelled to Talusta. Upon his return he reported that he had found a satisfactory framework and understanding on the part of the head of the Judenraat who presented him with a program for organized resistance in Talusta. I traveled with a group to Kupichinska for several days to lay the groundwork for our activities. Under our protection, several hundred wagons set out, filled with families who had been evicted from Kupichinska. We trekked through fields, since the Gestapo forbade Jews to travel the main roads. During the night, we passed through a village whose citizens used to attack Jews. When they tried to hold us up, we pulled our weapons and they retreated.

After I reached Kupichinska, I consulted with the head of the Judenraat and discovered full understanding between us. I received assurances of support and aid to our people. He even gave us a house for our own use. At our final meeting I had given instructions, but suddenly we received word from Talusta that the very same day an "aktzia" had been carried out. The anguish of our people was great: They weighed the possible advantages of returning to Buchach and fleeing with us to the forests. On the other hand, it was very difficult for them to part from their families, and they decided to remain. I turned over the leadership of the group to Magister, Fisher and Bildner, and we determined that the following morning we would set out for the forests and not return, save for replenishing our food supply and getting news. On my way back, I was stopped by police from the village of Patlikovska, but my threatening them with a pistol was quite effective: they cleared the way and I returned to my group in Buchach where we began intensive efforts towards our move to the forests. Over the next few days we received accounts from Fisher. His group had already begun working in earnest and had established contact with former Soviet officers in Husiatin.

On the Friday of their presence there, we received word of a large scale "aktzia" in Kupichinska. According to a secret report, the German police were preparing a list of the members of our group. On the way to the camp, where I had shown my face to give instructions to our people, I encountered the infamous murderer, Policeman Paul, and he ordered me to enter the camp. I was forced to avoid settling accounts with him, for two other policemen arrived just at that moment.

Only a few hours prior to our exit we found five of our people in my apartment on Railroad Street. Suddenly a group of policemen appeared. We were convinced that the were coming for us, and we released the locks on our ammunition and waited. These policemen were armed with light weapons, yet they continued along their way. Had they approached us, we'd have had a chance to seize their weapons and to settle accounts with them, yet on the street they held the upper hand.

D.

During the evening hours, we gathered together and distributed the remains of our ammunition. We divided into two groups, with one set to leave the next evening for Vadova. Our group, which numbered 18 people, crossed the bridge at 10 in the evening. Near Pototsky's land, we crossed through paths between the fields in order to avoid any undesirable meetings. This was on June 10, a hot and quiet evening, and the stillness of the night was broken only by the echo of our footsteps and the barking of dogs in the distance. We had in our possession five pistols and four short-nosed rifles. In one of the villages we were stopped by police, but they quickly lost their will to get involved with us and they retreated.

Dawn was breaking. The time was 3:00 A.M., and we, loaded down with ammunition, hid amongst the harvest since the forests of Puzhnik were still separated from us by over 10 kilometers. During the day, the sun beat down upon us relentlessly, and in our thirst we looked forward to the evening so that we could resume our march. We detoured around the Puzhniki village and arrived in the forest that was our life saver. Our guide was Helzel Makoropicz who was well acquainted with the forests. We made our camp in the five-year-old forest where the bushes were thick, yet suddenly rain began to fall and the next day we were forced to dry out our clothing throughout the daylight hours.

By night we descended to the river, bathed and filled our utensils with water so as to be able to cook supper over a fire made from wet branches. This was our first hot meal after 24 hours of freedom in the forest. Several days later I selected several individuals and accompanied them beyond Vodova to search for our second group. We also wanted to determine to what extent we could hope to acquire food from the forest guard and from the Soviets with whom my wife had made contact previously. The supplying of our food had been carried out quite well during the entire time. Two or three times a week we would receive the bread which had been baked for us as well as other food products which were prepared for us, yet each time we had to surround the house and make certain that we were not about to be ambushed. Only afterwards did we enter the house to receive the food, after leaving guards posted in the surrounding area.

At the appointed place we met with our people, and joining them were the survivors of our friends who had succeeded in escaping from the pogrom in Kopichinza. They filled us in on the details of what had taken place there. The "akzia" had come upon them suddenly before dawn. Our group had tried to forge a path to the forest, but they encountered Germans and the people scattered and hid inside the forest. Most of them fell victim to the murderers. One of our people, at his post near a mass grave, managed to pull his pistol and shoot Gestapo members, yet the gunfire was met by significant resistance. Among the several thousand Jews who fell were 30 of our people, including the commanders of the Buildner and Fisher groups.

There were also incidents where the earth covered people who were stunned or injured, and witnesses reported that the ground actually moved. Command over the survivors was assumed by Tziler, a youth from T'lomatcz, who was brave yet had a black past. He brought those survivors with him to us. We prepared a plan of action for the future and returned to the forests of Poznicki. Here we proceeded to build our first underground shelter. Several days later we suddenly heard German-language cries in the forest. The forest guard led the Germans. We heard several single shotgun bursts beyond us and then they retraced their tracks. They had no intention of deepening their penetration into the thick bushes, for they understood that they might have to pay for this with their lives. We permitted them to escape for we did not know the area so well and we took into consideration their superior armaments.

My wife took upon herself the task of surveillance. More than once she would go, disguised as a village peasant, to the surrounding villages and gather extremely valuable information which enabled us to avoid many dangers. Due to our desire to avoid meeting with the forest gang of Nidjovitski, we moved to the Vadova forests, and after several weeks to the Sokolov forests. Here we divided into three groups, one of which was well-armed and changed its position from time to time and also staged attacks to increase weapons and food supplies. At one point during their activities on a farm on the Dneister, a police unit suddenly attacked. Our forces climbed onto the rooftops and began firing at the Germans. The Germans retreated, yet returned afterwards to take out their anger upon the farmer by setting fire to his premises. Over time, some of our people rebelled and began to steal, in spite of our forbidding this. In such instances, Buchach natives abandoned these groups and those that remained were natives of Horodnika, Dilatin and Stanislavov. Our people did not agree to such methods. In addition there was one group among us composed of tens of families who sought refuge in the forest, inspired by the ideal of the Jewish partisan. Here again the engineer Zisser carried out his mission: we confiscated a battery-operated radio, stolen from a Jew. Its broadcasts announced the resignation of Mussolini. At the beginning of August 1945 we heard of the conquering of Bilgrod and Oriel, yet at the same time we heard of the extermination of the Jewish survivors of Buchach.

Throughout the villages, popular legend held that exceptionally well-armed groups of Jews lurked in the forests, and farmers did not dare to enter the forest. By night we heard echoes of gun battles of the Russian partisans, who headed by Kolpokov succeeded in penetrating to the Dilatin. After they were hit there, they returned in small groups. We encountered two such groups, yet they refused to include Jewish fighters, and that put an end to our internal debate whether or not to join them.

From Buchach we heard reports of the daring campaign by the Friedlander group, of the breaking into the home of the "Land commissar" and of their revenge upon some Aryan informers who revealed information about Jews in hiding. Three of our people returned to Buchach. There Margolit, a member of our directorate, was turned in by a farmer in whose home his wife was hidden.

E.

Autumn came. Outstanding weather, yet short days which passed quickly and nights which found us by the campfires holding endless discussions over reports we heard from the battlefront. On one such lovely autumn night, a group of 25 Ukrainian policemen attacked a group of Jews who were located not far from us. The murderous bullets killed Brish Engelberg and his sister, Dr. Reitman and his wife and his six-year old son from Potok Zloti, and one of our people who was there by chance. We rushed to their aid, but we did not find a soul. The next day we searched the thick underbrush and placed the six corpses in the trench they had begun to dig, covering them with a layer of earth so that the wolves would not find them. We marked the place of their eternal rest.

Several days later I went with two other members of our group to the forests of Puszniki. Among our missions was to examine by dawn's first light the possibility of our relocating to these forests. Along the road in the forest we came upon fresh tire tracks. We cocked our weapons and advanced a total of several hundred meters to suddenly find yet another corpse of a woman. Once again we found ourselves forced to perform the bitter task of burying another victim of one of the farmers of Puszniki who had robbed and murdered this woman who had hidden with him.

During the hour that we spent carrying out this tragic task, we heard shots nearby. The police had discovered 8 Jews being hidden by one of the farmers and had taken them to the forest to shoot them to death. This was the high school teacher Henig and his wife and 16-year-old daughter, as well as a family of five from Monstajiska.

Radio broadcasts brought us the sound of festive cannon fire from Moscow, which echoed and warmed our hearts, yet the front was still before us and winter was impending. We decided to build shelters, and the Weitz brothers, Kopel, Manio and Izzio, assumed responsibility for this assignment. They also succeeded in building several bunkers which enabled us to endure the freezing winter full of snowstorms. We dug a pit around four meters deep, two and a half meters wide and quite thick. At a depth of two meters we erected walls and spread straw and thin boards across them. We then covered them with earth which we trampled well and then planted trees and shrubs similar to those in the area. We also fashioned an entrance, a sort of drawer, and ventilation through underground pipes. Inside – double beds and a narrow passageway which gave shelter to 16 people. A kerosene lamp provided light in the evenings.

On one of the winter days, 600 SS men surrounded several sections of the forests. In their possession were several tanks and artillery. At noon, the opening volley of cannon fire marked the beginning of the attack. I examined the prospects and firmly concluded that we had no possible means of defending ourselves. The only option open to us was to escape through the deep river bed. We murdered two SS men who were in our path, seized their weapons, and succeeded in removing the entire group from the attack without harming anyone.

A different fate awaited 300 Jews who had hidden in a different section of the forest. A path led to them in the snow, and more than 200 were murdered by gunfire or blown to pieces by hand grenades hurled into their shelters. We came to their camp in the evening and found people dying, their hands and feet amputated, parts of human corpses who had been doomed to perish by torturous inferno. We assisted the survivors as best we could and advised them to disperse throughout the forest since we were certain that the butchers would return the next morning. We were correct in our assumption.

Over 100 Ukrainian police murdered those who had survived, and only 30 people, barefoot and naked, survived. The police had robbed and looted all that was in the shelters. On the other hand, we succeeded in hitting several of the murderers on their return. We decided to acquire clothing for these poor unfortunate people. To do so we ventured out the next night to a village around 20 kilometers away. There we surrounded the home of the Ukrainian police chief where, according to information we'd received, the majority of the booty taken from the Jews was located. We rounded up all of those present into one room and stood guard over them. Within an hour we left the house, laden with clothes for the people. By dawn we returned to the forest. The heavy snow had erased our footsteps, and we fell exhausted into a heavy sleep.

Our enemies were joined by a gang of Ukrainian robbers, led by the notorious thief Lutchka, which preyed on attacking Jews in hiding. Among those who fell into their hands was the head of the candle factory Katz and all his family. We resolved to eradicate Lutchka, yet he always succeeded in escaping any ambush. At one point he was injured and hospitalized for several weeks.

Not one day were we able to relax from the stringent measures of caution in order during that hard, snowy winter. The essential mission at hand to supply provisions was carried out by the brothers Munio and Izio Weitz. They would set out each night to distant villages, and return carrying food on their shoulders for all of our group. Sometimes this was done at great risk to their lives.

The end of January came. On one of the winter evenings a reconnaissance group dispatched to gain information reported that the next morning the forest would be surrounded. Our people returned at midnight, and within an hour we left our warm shelter to take to the snow. The sounds of gunfire, the howling of the winds and the snowstorm accompanied us during our wanderings. Within 24 hours of Herculean efforts to dig away at the frozen earth, we had at our disposal a new shelter in the pine forests near Novosioleka-Koropitzka.

Twice a week we would "invade" the villages. From time to time we sneaked into the home of a Polish merchant to enjoy two or three hours in a heated dwelling, to eat warm food and to gather news. The front came nearer and went. By night we could hear echoes from the battlefronts, and we discerned the first signs of a retreat. From nearby camps, all those who had served the Germans began to escape. We heard the rumbling of lorries from the Buchach-Stanislavov road: the retreat of the defeated armies of the "herren-folk." On March 23, 1944, we went down to Novosioleka. The ardent rumors indicating that the front would be formed along the line of the Strippa River, and the implication that we would be situated on the German side, adjacent the front, made me firmly convinced that we must move 20 kilometers eastward. I made a foray into Sokolov and noticed that the defeated troops were continuing their escape.

F.

March 25, 1944. Silence reigned over the road throughout the day, and suddenly before nightfall the first Soviet guards appeared. We are free. We sleep in the village. The villagers of Novosioleka give us a hearty welcome. It is the first night that we spend with a roof above our heads, following a year of wandering in the forests. Our joy at having survived and of being worthy of witnessing the demise of the German monster was hampered by the terrible realization that we were very few in number and many, many of our relatives were missing.

Our living conditions had been terribly difficult from the moment the murderous army had entered. We had gone into the forest with no experience or prior knowledge, and totally unprepared for the difficult conditions. We were powered by our will to live and our sense of national pride. We organized a resistance movement among the youth of Buchach as our declaration of war against the obtuse and defeatist apathy towards our fate. We maintained our strength and overcame difficulties.

And we returned once more to Buchach. We were more than 800 people, most of whom came from the forests, for thanks to our example others had depended on us and gone into the forests. Those who had been expelled by farmers who had refused to shelter them also came to join us. Also returning to Buchach were those who had succeeded in hiding in the villages, as well as those who had survived through temporary papers. Yet there was no joy, for so many were missing. However, life has a way of making its own rules. We soon took apartments and began thinking of the present and the future,

We arrived in Buchach on March 26, 1944, yet already by April 6 at 3 A.M. we left the city in the direction of Trambobella. The Soviet army command advised us that this was the sole direction where passage was still clear, for German troops had advanced on all sides. We left a Buchach illuminated by fireworks, with an air battle being waged in the sky and in her streets the sounds of battles on Railroad Street. Our group was the last to leave, surrounded by the thunder of cannon fire and the roar of fighting. We could already hear the sound of commands being shouted in German. Before us was a group numbering around 300, most barefoot, running in escape upon roads full of mud and snow. People who had sat for one year in their places of hiding now advanced one step at a time, as if crippled on crutches.

At 7:00 AM we arrived in Darachov. Here a high-ranking Jewish officer supplied us with lorries and we were transported to Trambovlah and from there to Skalat. Along the way we encountered a large group of German prisoners. How different is the likeness today of yesterday's world conquerors. At Skalat we surrendered our weapons, and some of us were taken into the Soviet army. After three months of battle the Germans continued their retreat, and we returned to Buchach. This time, from the 300 people who had remained, we met only around twenty. Following our retreat from Buchach, the German police, led by the notorious murderer Paul, had returned to Buchach where they slaughtered several hundred people.

The city's Aryan population was also absent. They who had rejoiced in the calamities of the Jewish People, had met their own end. They too were forced to take stick in hand and begin wandering, from the knowledge and unfounded fear that they would be made to pay for their participation in the massacre of millions of innocent victims.

This short account of a group of young Hebrew youth of Buchach will be added to the annals of the history of the vast Holocaust of European Jewry. These pages are a ray of light from within those days of slaughter and annihilation. While our tale is not one of the heroic exploits of hundreds of forces, it is nevertheless the saga of a superhuman endeavor by Hebrew youth surrounded by enemies, determined to live in spite of all.

A. Bazan

Dr. Carla Gross

Ya'akov Margaliot

Resistance leaders during the genocide

Shmuel Karniel (Hirshhorn)

Meier Fried

Mass grave

Mass grave holding 3635 martyrs who perished on 27 Shvat 5703 (February 2, 1943).
This picture was taken in 1945 after the war.

[Page 295]

Birthday in a Concentration Camp
Translated by Jessica Cohen

It was April 20, 1943. The town was festively decorated. The streetcars were adorned with flags. Above the concentration camp in Lvov, the sun was shining gloriously that day. Perhaps not in honor of the 'Fuhrer,' but rather in order to provide the hungry, weary prisoners with some warmth. It was a real spring day. On beautiful days such as these, the view enclosed within a frame of barbed-wire was truly heart-breaking. The SS patrol guards had been drunk since the morning. The camp administrators took advantage of the opportunity to drown out the bad rumors coming from the eastern front, in a sea of wine. This was after Stalingrad had fallen.

The work brigades set off to work outside the camp, in the sun-drenched world, which to them seemed gloomy and dark. Tired and weakened figures, heads bent, who once were human beings. At the exit gate they were ordered to sing, so that people would see how happy they were to go off to work. The patrol guards took part in the singing.

At the mess in the guards' barracks, many preparations for the festive gathering were underway. At that time I was working as a sign-maker and painter in the camp workshops. The camp had to make an outwardly impression of being perfect and organized, so the signs were frequently repainted. The windows of the death-huts were always repainted.

At ten o'clock, second in command Diega came to the camp workshop and took myself and two other people outside. There, we saw that a few people had also been taken from the technical office. We were taken to the place called "Nad." The inner courtyard was surrounded with a double layered barbed-wire fence with a two-meter gap between the layers. This passageway was called "Nad." One of the exits from this "Nad" led to the sand pit where all acts of murder were committed. The "Nad" had taken on the meaning of a passageway to death.

A group of some twenty prisoners was already waiting at this "Nad," including a few women. We were all the remainder of the professional *intelligentsia*: doctors, engineers and lawyers, who only by chance were still alive.

Why? No one asked this question. That word had been erased from our vocabularies, along with another few words. At last there would be an end to our daily suffering.

As if to complement the gloom of our thoughts, the skies darkened. True April weather: rain, snow, sunlight...much as hope rises and falls.

And then came the SS second in command, Kautser, with an automatic pistol and eight SS men.

"Go!" he ordered curtly. No one said a word. We were each lost in our own thoughts. At that time, none of us had any family left. Some of them had walked down this very path, or through other factories of death. We were alone, and that was our strength. Our borrowed time was coming to its end.

After walking for half an hour, we came to the sand pit. I counted exactly thirty-eight men and six women. A long pit, about two meters deep, sprawled out in front of us.

It contained naked corpses and puddles of blood which had not yet dried from the previous days. They only covered the pit once it was completely full.

A truck stood in front of us. "Undress!" "Separate shoes from clothes! Underwear in one pile!" The bloodthirsty SS men screamed. "Quick! Hurry!" They beat and struck us during the last few minutes. And the clothes were piled up as ordered. The first six candidates for death load our clothes and our shoes on the truck (after all, the Nazi Reich government was eagerly awaiting our possessions).

The truck sets off on its way. And now it began. "Stand!" Kautser screams at the naked group. One behind the other by the pit! I was the twenty-second in line. Kautzer stands holding the pistol a few steps in front of the row of people.

"Turn!" he commands loudly.

And now he is read to shoot us in the back. I see the first man being shot and falling into the pit, then the second, the third...one of them does not fall straight into the pit, and an SS man has to kick him into it. Only six more before me! We are all wet from the rain, and stunned from the shots and the screams. My life passes before me like a film screened in the wrong direction. I am in shock.

Suddenly we hear a long whistle. The shots stop. Are we already dead? We stand there lifelessly. An SS man is in the distance, approaching. After a few minutes he is here, it is the work commander, Kolanko.

I hear a shout, but I cannot understand it. When it is repeated I answer.

"Step out of the line!" Kolanko growls. Kautzer turns to him: "And the others?"

"Continue!"

I walk as if drunk and my face is slapped, which brings me back to consciousness.

I look back, the final shots ring out, the entire group has been killed.

The way the prisoners in the camp look at me reminds me that I am naked and wet. Kolanko leads me to the clothes warehouse, where the SS man Blum gives me torn trousers, a coat and shoes.

Now Kolanko leads me back to the workshop, where the SS squadron-head, Schultz, waits for me with a task: to prepare announcements for the celebration.

"You were lucky we still needed you," he said with a twisted smile.

The time is one o'clock. The work divisions set off for their afternoon shifts. The sun is shining again, covering the new corpses with a glimmering veil.

The camp band plays: "Everything will pass..." An old friend says to me that night in the hut: "On April twentieth, two people were born."

"What do you mean?"

"The 'Fuhrer' and you!"

Linz, Simon Wiesenthal

[Page 297]

Shoah Echoes in Buczacz
Translated by Jessica Cohen

A fourteen-year-old girl writes

The United Committee for Assistance to Polish Jews received this letter, sent from a 14-year-old girl to her relatives in Israel. The girl escaped Buczacz, in Eastern Galicia, and reached Trembowla. She sent this letter on June 5.

"My dear Aunt Fruma and Uncles Beryl and Isaac,

I send you very sad news. I have been through terrible, difficult days. As I write this letter, tears run from my eyes. You will probably not believe me. I was left on my own, entirely alone. No one is left from the entire family; of all the relatives, only I, Rosa, remain. I have lost my mother, my dear, devoted mother, Father, Rivka, my little brother Avram, dear Grandfather and Grandmother. There were extermination acts in Buczacz, and each act sent 1500 Jews to their deaths. My Grandmother Leizi was killed on February 2, 1943. [Yiddish] Grandmother was killed during the third massacre, and she is buried on Fedor [Hill] in Buczacz. Where once people took walks, now there are 8000 murdered Jews. Together with Grandmother, we lost Devorah from Potok, and Aunt Esther with her husband and children. Not one of our relatives remains alive. After the last extermination act, my father gave me to a rural woman who hid me from May 10, 1943 until March 25, 1944. Father found a cave in the forest, and the whole family fled there. They were in the cave for 8 months. Then the Germans discovered the cave and killed them all. I do not know where there bones are.

I somehow managed to stay alive through this time with the Germans – I will tell you when I am with you in Israel.

On March 25, 1944, the Soviets occupied Buczacz. They stayed for 5 days and then the Germans came again. I barely escaped alive, and went with the Soviet army to Trembowla. I stayed with a Christian woman and shepherded her flock, because the Jews who were still alive – and there were only a few – had no food. Like myself, all they had saved was their souls. I cannot describe everything to you because I am very anxious. We are now about 22 kilometers from the front. All we hear is airplanes and sirens. I am begging you: please, take care of me; please, bring me quickly to you in Israel.

"Davar," **1946**

P. Lander, special correspondent for *"Ha'Aretz"*, reported:

The story recounted here occurred the day before yesterday in a crowded spot in Paris. A young Jewish man from Buczacz, Adek W., who is currently visiting Paris, was strolling through the Place de Republique on a Saturday. He saw a well-built figure approaching him from a distance. He immediately recognized him as his townsman and childhood friend, who during the Nazi occupation had been the head of the Jewish "Ordnung-Schutz" and served as a representative of the Nazi Gestapo leader, sending hundreds and thousands of Jews to their deaths. He shouted to him in Polish:

"Are you the murderer of the Jews of Buczacz and the murderer of my family?"

The other young man froze in his place, stunned by the sudden cry. Then he replied: "Yes, it is me. What do you want me to do?" Adek W. replied simply: "Come with me."

The two went to Adek's hotel. When the door closed behind them and they were both in the room, Adek asked the murderer: "Have you reflected about what you did? Did you know you were executing innocent people, your own people? Tell me, murderer, why did you do it?"

For apart from the general score of the murder of Jews, Adek also had a personal score. His childhood friend had come to their house during one of the *aktzias* and executed his mother and father. Only he and his brother remained. During another *aktzia*, this friend came again to take them both away. The brother was taken to the death camps and never returned, and he, Adek, managed to escape during the search. He hid out through the entire Nazi rule, and manage to stay alive. When Poland was liberated, Adek began to search for this murderer, his childhood friend. He heard that he was still alive, had left Poland and disappeared. Now when he came to Paris with a student delegation, he suddenly found the murderer walking through the Place de Republique.

"Murderer, why did you do it?" he shouted again at his friend the murderer.

And the latter replied calmly: "I admit that I have 'killed and also taken possession.' At the time, I did not contemplate the things I was doing, but now I know, and I am willing to be punished.

Adek W. knocked his friend to the ground and beat him viciously. Then he began to stomp on him. The murderer was covered with blood, but he did not utter a word. Adek W. beat the murderer with heavy objects and smashed some bottles against his head. The murderer lay in a pool of blood without moving, although he could easily have overcome his tormentor.

Finally, Adek W. said: "And now I will tattoo your forehead, so that everyone shall know who you are." And with a large needle he began to carve out the word "*ordnung-schutz*" on the murderer's forehead. He got as far as the Latin character "O", and could not continue. He was exhausted.

Finally, he said to the murderer: "Give me your papers." The latter was bleeding heavily, wounded and cut, his clothes ripped and dripping with blood. He silently took out his papers, including his passport and an entry visa to Venezuela, and gave them to Adek W.

"You must come back tomorrow at ten," Adek W. ordered him.

The murderer agreed.

Then next morning at 10, the murderer returned to Adek W.'s hotel. The latter beat him again, until he was exhausted. Then he said to the murderer: "Come with me." They went to the nearest French police station. There, Adek W. reported the case and demanded that the murderer be arrested. The police officer tried to evade the demand and said that it was not within his jurisdiction, and that he should address the higher authorities. Adek W. went to the Polish consul in Paris. After the Polish consul intervened, the French police agreed to arrest the murderer. When the next shipment of criminals to Poland leaves, the murderer of the Jews of Buczacz will also be sent, and will stand trial there and surely be punished.

Paris, early January 1947.

The story of a girl for whom gold was promised

When the Jewish population of Buczacz in Galicia found out that they would soon be deported to the death camps, Ms. Sleicher brought her only daughter, Leah, to the Polish woman Helena Poloch, and told her:

"Take the child and care for her as the apple of your eye. Her father lives in America, and after the war he will pay you in gold."

The Polish woman could not resist the promise of dollars, so she took in the girl and raised her. After the war she began to search for the girl's father in America, but was unsuccessful. She happened to hear that in Lodz there was an institution which took in Jewish children and paid for their care during the occupation. Mrs. Poloch went to Lodz with the girl, and after negotiations the committee took the girl and paid the woman 360,000 gilden. But when Mrs. Poloch went home, she found a letter from America written by the girl's father, in which he wrote that he was trying to obtain an American entry visa, not only for the girl but also for her, the Polish woman who had raised his daughter. So Mrs. Poloch hurried back to Lodz and demanded that the girl be returned to her. When the committee refused, because the girl was already settled at an orphanage, the woman went to the attorney general and invented a terrible story: that three of the committee members had broken into her apartment and kidnapped the girl. The attorney general summoned the committee representatives, and they showed him a receipt from the woman for the 360,000 gilden. The attorney general not only revoked the woman's claim, but also sued her for libel.

Of course, the girl is being sent to her father in America.

"*Haboker*", 9/12/1947.

A. Lanman

Yitzhak Bornstein, "*HaAretz*" correspondent in Warsaw, published the following description on 9-28-1949:

Anyone wishing to know if there were Jewish survivors of a Polish town that was destroyed, needs only to glance at the number of typed pages neatly classified and stacked at the archives of the Central Jewish Historical Institute in Warsaw. Each town has its own corner at the institute – namely, the history of its destruction. The material includes testimonies give by Jews who miraculously survived the hell. If a town does not have much of this literature of destruction, you can surmise that the destruction there was great, massive and terrible...

I was interested in one town, a vibrant Jewish town which had barely been mentioned until now; a town of 16,000 Jewish artisans, laborers and merchants. A town which had a strong Jewish social life. A town with any number of Jewish parties, from the *Haredim* to the extreme left. There were also people from Belza, Czortkow, Boyany, Sasowe, Zydaczow and many more. Of all these, not even a single typed page remains. With great effort, a living Jew from the town of Stry is sought, so that he can give testimony. There is one testimony there, less than two pages long, from a living Jew from Stry who escaped the terrible Janowska camp in Lvov. But from Stry itself, not a soul survived – so awful was the destruction there.

The town whose history of destruction we are describing here belonged, much like Stry, to the area where the "spirit" of the infamous SS General Katzman prevailed (according to rumors, he is now located in Lebanon). The name of the town is Buczacz, it is located on the way from Stanislaw to Czortkow. Buczacz is the birthplace of the famous Jewish historian, Dr. Emanuel Ringelblum, *may the Lord avenge his blood*, who, during the terrible Ghetto Warsaw days, led a group of people from the Jewish intelligentsia in recording and writing anything relevant to the time. And when the murderers opened fire in the streets of the Warsaw Ghetto as the Jews were being led to the deportation square, these devoted people managed to bury all this material. It was excavated two years ago, and constitutes the historical Ringelblum Archive.

An Occupied Town with no Ghetto

In contrast to Stry, the town of massacres, Buczacz has a rich collection of historical material. This town, whose Jews numbered less than half the number of the Jews in Stry, occupies a prominent place at the Jewish Historical Institute archives. Many testimonies were collected about Buczacz, detailing how the Jews of the town were killed. Some of the Buczacz survivors describe the town before its destruction, when there was vibrant Jewish life. The many testimonies complete each other and combine into a whole picture of the town.

One of the Buczacz survivors, Yosef Kornblei, says that until the awful war there were 7,500 Jews, 1,000 Poles and 3,000 Ukrainians in Buczacz. It was, therefore, a Jewish town. For 45 continuous years, the town mayor was the Jewish Bernard Stern. After his death in 1921, until 1937, the position was occupied by the attorney Dr. Emanuel Marengel.

Kornblei recalls that Dr. Emanuel Ringelblum's father died of natural causes during the occupation, while his mother was murdered by the Nazis.

There were two synagogues in Buczacz, which were counted among the town's historical sites.

There was no permanent Gestapo office in occupied Buczacz. Once in a while the Gestapo officers would come down from Czortkow or Stanislaw. Incidentally, the Gestapo did not need to be present in Buczacz because they had people they could trust there...there were Ukrainian murderers who excelled at their job no less than the Hitlerists. In any case, it is clear that the absence of Gestapo officers in the town did not alleviate the bitter fate of Buczacz Jews.

Buczacz did not have a ghetto such as the ones established in other occupied towns. This does not mean that the Jews of Buczacz were free to move around the town. For example, Jews were not permitted on the main street, Kolejowa. But the fact that the Jews of Buczacz were not fenced in and imprisoned was extremely important, particularly during the pogroms which occurred after a while: brave Jews who found out in advance that an "act" was being planned, fled to the surrounding woods, and those who had the strength to endure the travails and who were fortunate enough, survived. A witness named Ferber recounts that he hid in a bunker with 17 other Jews. This was in March of 1944. Fierce and bloody battles were raging in the Buczacz area at the time, between the Red Army and Hitler's brigades. Buczacz changed hands twice, and those Jews who were fortunate and managed to turn themselves in to the Red Army when it entered Buczacz for the first time, are still alive today. The Jews who were afraid to come out of the bunkers because of the heavy fire coming from both sides of the front, were eventually slaughtered by the Ukrainian Fascists and the Hitlerists as they withdrew.

The First Pogrom Victims

On July 1, 1941, the Soviet forces evacuated Buczacz. 500 Jews went with them to the USSR. On July 5, the Germans entered. The did not spend long in the town, but rather continued on their course. However, the Ukrainian nationalists immediately took control of all the authorities in Buczacz, and as early as the first day they shot dead 4 Poles and 2 Jews. From time to time the Ukrainians would kidnap Jews to send them to work for the German army. As they walked to work, the Jews were ordered to sing *Hatikvah* and whoever did not sing would be beaten to death. The Ukrainian fascists issued various decrees according to the German occupiers' orders, such as a 6 o'clock curfew for Jews, a prohibition against walking down the streets on the sidewalk, and so forth.

On August 27, 1941, 4 Gestapo men came from Czortkow and issued a command that all Jewish men between the ages of 18 and 50 must report in front of the courthouse. Some 800 Jews gathered. The Gestapo sent a few doctors and artisans back to their homes. The others were ordered to remain standing, and they themselves went to drink with the Ukrainian doctor named Bonoch. At 4 in the morning, they led all the Jews some 2 kilometers out of town to the Fedor Woods. There, they were told, cars would be waiting to take them to work.

There were no cars there, but there were large crates, and the Jews had to place all their belongings in them. The echoes of shots coming from the forest could be heard all morning in town. All the victims were thrown into pits that had been dug beforehand. Among the victims of this terrible massacre were some prominent Jewish townsmen: attorney Dr. Yedenfriend, two Lustgarten brothers, Elhanan and Avigdor Sterensus, Moshe Erlich, Elazar Iserlis (a descendent of Rabbi Moshe Iserlis), Getzil Schor, Leibusch Shoval, Buchwald, five members of the Hassidic family Kreitner, Anshel and Avraham Isakover, Yoseleh Worman (grandson of the *tzaddik* of Buczacz), Yisrael Fuhrman, and other martyrs. One heroic young man, Yitzhak Reich, escaped the executioners, but was murdered later.

Upheld their Honor

Establishing a Jewish council was not easy for the Hitlerists. Several times they summoned R' Mendel Reich, a Mizrachi member and former head of the community, and ordered him to establish a Jewish council with 12 members of the former community board. He managed to evade this "noble" job a few times with various excuses. Finally, he gave into a vehement order that was accompanied by a death-threat, and set up a council. Besides himself, the members were Attorney Hecht, Dr. Engelberg, Dr. Y. Stern, Munisch Frankel, Rabbi Haim Shapira, David Kaner, Kreigel, Dr. Zeiper, Zlaznik and Freund from the "Yad Harutzim" society. During the massacre on August 27, the Jewish council members were also rounded up, and Dr. Stern, Kreigel and Kaner were murdered.

It is evident from the testimonies of the Buczacz destruction that the members of the Jewish council, most of whom were *Haredi* Jews, were not "yes-men", and took a stand of honor and pride. They did not kneel down before the executioners, and not all the Hitlerists' demands were carried out. They Jews told themselves that it was better to die with dignity than to die in shame.

On one occasion, the Gestapo agents from Czortkow came and commanded that by Sabbath eve (the witness did not recall the date) the Jews prepare 4 sets of luxury furniture for their salons. The Jews were in no hurry to fulfill the order, and the Hitlerists were furious when they came to town on Sabbath eve and the furniture was not ready. As punishment, they imposed a 25,000 gilden fine on the Jews, which was to be paid within half an hour. But the Jews paid no more than 5,000 gilden.

The Last Pogrom

In 1942, Jews from the nearby villages of Tlumacz, Cucniow and others began to be deported to Buczacz. Meanwhile, a terrible typhoid epidemic broke out, wreaking havoc on the Jewish population. Some of the Jews, who knew they were destined to die in the bleak Fedor woods or the forests of Belzec, began to flee to the surrounding woods.

March 21st marked the sixth anniversary of that freezing day when, early in the morning, the German officers and the Ukrainian police seized every Jew they could find, whether in their houses or on the streets, and led them all to the bleak woods on the shores of the Strypa river. That day, 1300 Jews were shot – men and women, old and young, even small children.

Ferber completes his testimony: "I recall some names of the executioners: Koznowski, the Ukranian Chief of Police and the officer Otomanjuk, and the Germans Hunt, Feil, Patz and Koch."

But there were many, many others...

Yitzhak Bornstein

[Page 304]

The Buczacz Memorial Committee
Translated by Jessica Cohen

Ederer, Yehezkel – New York
On (Eiserson), Zeev – Tel Yosef
Alfenbein, Efraim – New York
Besner, Esther – Mishmar Ha'Emek
Blum, Dr. Kopel – Tel Aviv
Goldberg, Yehoshua – Tel Aviv
Goldberg, Alter – Haifa
Ginsburg, Gershon – Jerusalem
Hirshorn, Dr. Mekhes – Ramat Yohanan
Held, Moshe – Tel Aviv
Heller, Dr. Zvi – Tel Aviv
Weinrab, Michael – Tel Aviv
Wexler, Leon – Jerusalem
Weisser, Matityahu – Tel Aviv
Weinrab, Shaul – Haifa
Wiesenthal, Shimon-Linz – Austria
Silberstein, Dr. Avraham – Genf
Zomer, Avraham – New York
Halfan, Dr. Avraham – Hadera
Cohen, Yisrael – Tel Aviv
Menatzeach, Dr. Naftali – Hadera
Neiman, David – Beit Alpha
Neiman, Zalman – New York
Stempler, Yehiel – Tel Aviv
Fried, Yehiel – Tel Aviv
Pohorile, Dr. David – Tel Aviv
Tzoler, Dr. Rega – Tel Aviv
Roll, Khaye – Tel Aviv
Roll, Aryeh – Tel Aviv
Schechner, Dr. – New York
Shapira-Wolkowitz, Dr. – Kiriat Haim
Gilad (Smeterling), Yehudit – Degania Aleph

www.ingramcontent.com/pod-product-compliance
Lightning Source LLC
Chambersburg PA
CBHW082005150426
42814CB00005BA/230